Hypnotize This!

Secret Hypnosis Principles And Techniques

Written and Compiled

By

Zali Segal

booksryou.com

Hypnotize This!
Secret Hypnosis Principles & Techniques.

By

Zali Segal

Published by booksryou.com

ISBN, print ed. 0-9746484-0-X
ISBN, PDF ed. 0-9746484-1-8
ISBN, e-book ed. 0-9746484-2-6

First printing January 2004
Printed in the United States of America

Visit our web site:
www.booksryou.com
www.hypnotizethis.com

Dedication

I dedicate this book to my mother Ester and in memory to my father Natan.

Your endless love, forgiveness, gentleness and generosity are with me always.

Your support and approval gave me the impetus and courage to explore life to the fullest, to dare to push the envelope and go beyond perceived limitations.

Thank you, I love you.

Zali

Disclaimer

This book was written to provide information regarding the nature and practice of hypnosis. It is not designed to be a course in counseling, psychology, psychotherapy or to offer medical advice. It is not meant to represent all the information that is required to do any kind of therapeutic work.

This book is meant to help individuals wishing to help themselves. When working with individuals carrying any kind of diagnosis of mental illness, implementation of the information in this book, should only be done under the guidance of a trained professional.

This book is sold with the understanding that the publisher and author are not engaged in rendering legal, accounting or other professional services beyond the scope of offering insight and understanding regarding the nature of hypnosis.

Furthermore, this book and its author do not, in any way or fashion, encourage any layperson or professional to engage in any practice or behavior that is illegal. Anyone using any of the techniques described in this book does so entirely at his or her own risk.

Every effort has been made to make this book as complete as possible given the nature of the topic. Much of this book contains information based on the experience of the author, who does not claim that each article of information has been empirically studied or proven.

This book is for educational purposes only. The author, publisher, producer shall have neither liability nor responsibility to any person or entity with respect to any loss or damage caused, or alleged to be caused, directly or indirectly by the information contained in this book.

If you do not wish to be bound by the above, you may return this book unused to the publisher for full refund. For more information log onto: www.hypnotizethis.com

Acknowledgments

I want to extend special recognition and thanks to my teachers and mentors:

Dr. George Bien
Mary Vanderwart Ph.D.
Kevin Creedon
Doug O'Brien
Don Mottin
Gerald Kein
Anthony Robbins
Jerry Valley
Dr. Al Krasner
Dr. Richard Harte

I consider myself fortunate to have known them all. They are my role models and inspiration, each in their unique way. Each one of them expanded my horizons and enriched my life in more ways than I can count. For this, I am grateful.

My thanks also to the others, who taught me through their books and audio/video cassettes, who are too numerous to mention.

I also want to acknowledge and thank all the wonderful people who were involved in producing this book.

Editing:
Banning Lary
Valerie Vande Panne
Donna Gianell

Contents in Brief

Table of Contents

CHAPTER 1: INTRODUCTION TO HYPNOTHERAPY

What Do You Know About Hypnosis?

For your amusement and education, please take a moment to answer the following quiz:

(Circle True or False)

1. Hypnosis is a paranormal, supernatural phenomenon. T F
2. Hypnosis is sleep. T F
3. A hypnotized person has a weak willpower and surrenders to the strong will of the hypnotist. T F
4. Hypnotized people involuntarily reveal secrets. T F
5. Relaxation is not necessary for hypnosis. T F
6. People cannot get stuck in hypnosis and never emerge. T F
7. Hypnotized people do not remember what happened during the session. T F
8. People of certain personality types are more likely to be hypnotized. T F
9. Hypnosis can enable people to perform impossible feats of strength, endurance and sensory acuity. T F
10. Hypnosis is not dangerous. T F
11. Responding to hypnosis is responding to a placebo. T F
12. Only about 33% of all people are hypnotizable. T F
13. A person's ability to enter the state of hypnosis depends on the technique used and the skill of the hypnotist. T F
14. How many hypnotists does it take to change a light bulb?

Answers to the quiz on page 21.

What is Hypnosis?

Hypnosis (or Hypnotism) is the science of how the human mind functions. Hypnosis is an art, too, because, while there are a few widely accepted theories, we do not fully understand how it works. Hypnosis is not a religion, it is not a belief system, and it is not a supernatural power. Hypnotism is the study and use of the hidden powers of the mind.

In this book, you will learn much about hypnosis and hypnotizing. Yet, there is so much to the field of hypnosis that this text is far from being complete. You are encouraged to continue to expand your knowledge base.

This book is an opportunity for you to achieve personal transformation. As you gain knowledge, you will also be able to address personal issues and take yourself to the next level.

In the journey to mastery, we go through four phases:

1. Unconscious Incompetence – You do not know that you do not know.
2. Conscious Incompetence – You know that you do not know.
3. Conscious Competence – You know and act consciously.
4. Unconscious Competence – You know and act subconsciously.

Accordingly, it is suggested that you start with phase two. Briefly leaf through this book in order to become familiar with the scope of what was, so far, the unknown. Then, as you read again more thoroughly, and allow the material to sink in, you will get to phase two - Conscious Competence. Be patient and trust that with time and practice you will reach the phase four - Unconscious Competence.

The techniques you will learn in this book are not the only ones available. They are designed to be a template to provide you with a solid base from which to grow and develop. First learn the rules, and then I encourage you to break them. It is in the breaking of the rules where growth and learning occurs. I encourage you to break the mold, experiment, explore and share your findings.

Hypnosis is a natural phenomenon. All humans have an innate ability to be hypnotized. A trait that is different in each person and can be tested. It is an ability that is not related to intelligence, character, personality or imagination. Some people are easily hypnotizable and can reach deeper levels then others. We may make an analogy to a person's IQ (Intelligence Quotient). Every one has a different IQ and it can be measured. Likewise, everyone is born with a certain HQ (Hypnotizability Quotient) and it can be evaluated and measured. (Hypnosis is not connected to IQ. This is just an analogy.)

Our brain is active all the time. However, the level of activity changes in cycles. We can measure the brain's electrical activity with the electro-Encephalo-Graph (EEG), and can discern four distinct levels:

A) Beta 14-21 CPS (Cycles per second): The awake, alert and cognitive state.
B) Alpha 7-14 CPS: Awake and relaxed; daydreaming and considered a light hypnotic state.

C) Theta 4-7 CPS: Light sleep, dreaming and a deeper hypnotic state.
D) Delta 0.5-4 CPS: Deep sleep and a deep hypnotic state.

Normally, during the day, we drift naturally between the Beta and Alpha states in cycles. When you are daydreaming, you are in the Alpha state. People in deep prayer or meditation may achieve an Alpha state. The Alpha state, which we can also refer to as the "trance state," is the light hypnotic state. In the "hypnotic state," the mind temporarily suspends the process of authentication of sensory input. That means the process of criticizing, analyzing and judging is temporarily off-line to varying degrees.

In that state, when the guards are down, the mind is more open and receptive to suggestions than in the normal Beta state (the awake state). It allows a window of opportunity to enter the inner mind. In the hypnotic state, the filters and superficial defenses of our conscious mind may be bypassed, and direct communication with the subconscious mind is possible.

Thus, hypnosis can be described as the vehicle we use to bypass the critical/analytical faculties of the conscious mind and communicate with the subconscious mind.

Example of a bypass of the critical faculties of the mind:

How many times have you been emotionally moved by a movie? Have you ever laughed or even cried in a movie? Sure you did. In essence, what you are watching is light projected on a screen. The film, comprising of a sequence of still pictures, is passing in front of a projector to create the illusion of motion. The characters on the screen are not real. They are actors who play a role. The story line is a figment of someone's imagination. Everything about a movie is fictitious and you know it. Yet, in order to enjoy the experience and get involved, you allowed yourself to suspend the conscious judgment and critical faculties of the mind and accepted the imagery of the movie as real. At least for the time being you are willing to suspend disbelief.

It is important to understand that only the superficial analytical mechanism is bypassed. The natural self-preserving defense mechanism is hardwired into our mind and cannot be bypassed. Thus, a person in hypnosis can respond to danger and resist complying with harmful suggestions.

Common Applications of Hypnosis

Hypnosis has proven to be effective in a myriad of applications:

- Changing habits: Smoking, overeating, nail biting, etc.
- Insomnia.
- Stress management.
- Overcoming fears: Public speaking, animals, flying, heights, etc.
- Preparing for tests by reducing anxiety, improving retention and recall.
- Shortening psychiatric treatment time to achieve rapid change.
- Medical Applications: Pain control, anesthesia, allergies, accelerating the pre/post surgery healing process and more.

Hypnosis may be used to enhance and improve your life in:

- Sports performance.
- Sexual enhancement.
- Forensics; improving witness' memory.
- Finding lost items.
- Remembering suppressed events through regression.
- Artistic expression.
- Gaining deep rest and rejuvenation.

Some of the more controversial and esoteric applications of hypnosis include:

- Past-life regression.
- Communicating with spirits.
- Healing through divine communication and intervention.

Answers to Quiz (From Page 17)

1. False. Hypnosis is a natural phenomenon that occurs in ordinary daily life in every person. It is an innate trait. Just as your IQ (Intelligence Quotient) is an innate trait, so is your HQ (Hypnosis Quotient). No correlation has been found between Hypnosis and IQ. Every person may drift in and out of a state of hypnosis numerous times during the day. Hypnosis is not a force from the outside world and it is not subject to special powers of the hypnotist. Every person has experienced hypnosis in one form or another. They just do not call it hypnosis.

Example A: You are driving a car (or commuting on train). All of a sudden, you realize you have arrived at your destination without being aware of how you got there! This is a light form of "Highway Hypnosis." Your conscious mind was preoccupied and you naturally shifted control to the subconscious mind. The subconscious mind took safe care of you.

Example B: You are watching TV. Your significant other says something to you. Even though you know someone is talking to you, it goes right over your head. In addition, you did not comprehend a word. You were so focused on the TV that you were in a form of hypnosis.

2. False. British doctor James Braid coined the word "hypnosis" in the mid-19th century. It comes from the name of the Greek god of sleep, Hypnos. However, hypnosis is not sleep. A person's eyes may be closed but he is not unconscious. Hypnotized people are fully aware and responsive. They hear everything; they can talk and move about with open eyes. As a matter of fact, the senses become hyper-acute and one can concentrate much better and become more aware. Dr. Braid recognized his mistake in naming this phenomenon and tried to change it to "Mono-Ideaism." However, the name "hypnosis" stuck.

3. False. People cannot be hypnotized against their will and without their cooperation. Hypnotized people retain control and can terminate the hypnotic state at will. If it were true that the hypnotist has full control over a hypnotee, then some unscrupulous person could commit "theft by hypnosis". He would simply hypnotize people and command them to bring him all their money and jewelry and then to forget about it. The fact that such things do not happen is the proof it cannot happen.

4. False. One cannot be made to reveal something one does not want to disclose. To the contrary, one can lie, fabricate and confabulate when one is in hypnosis. Moreover, the confabulation is more convincing because it appears more real and believable to a person who is in hypnosis.

5. True. Hypnosis can be induced during vigorous physical activity and under emergency situations. Being hypnotized often brings about profound relaxation, but relaxation is not a prerequisite for hypnosis.

6. True. Hypnosis is a natural state of mind. We naturally drift in and out of this state of mind in cycles; it is impossible to be stuck in one state. Left alone, a hypnotized person will emerge naturally into the awake state or drift into a natural sleep.

7. False. Most people remember everything. However, a small percentage experience spontaneous amnesia. In addition, the hypnotist may choose to instruct a person to forget, temporarily what transpired in a session in order to facilitate subconscious processing. In time, most people recall the details.

8. False. There is no correlation between personality types and hypnotizability. Hypnotizability is a character trait all its own. Some people are easier to hypnotize than others. This trait can be measured and quantified. It is named Hypnotizability Quotient.

9. False. Hypnosis can help people operate very close to their natural physiological limits but not exceed them. Hypnosis can help people achieve peak performance and develop their physical and mental abilities but not to perform unnatural feats.

10. True. Since hypnosis is a natural built-in trait, it is no more dangerous than listening to a lecture.

11. False. The Placebo response means responding to suggestions in a normal awake state. Responsiveness to suggestions in the hypnotic state proves to be far more effective than Placebo alone.

12. False. Only a small percentage of the population is not hypnotizable. This includes young children until the age of 5-7. People with an IQ lower than 70 and deeply emotionally disturbed people like paranoid schizophrenics also tend to be unhypnotizable.

13. Neither. A person can go into the hypnotic state by listening to a recorded induction by someone who has absolutely no education or experience in hypnosis.

14. Only one. But the light bulb must want to change.

Definitions of "Hypnosis"

Psychologists and hypnotherapists in different camps take varying views of hypnosis. The following is a representative collection of definitions from respectable sources and professionals.

• **Webster's dictionary** (1876) defines hypnosis as:
1) A state that resembles sleep but is induced by a person whose suggestions are readily accepted by the subject.
2) Any of various conditions that resemble sleep.

• **The Skeptic's Dictionary**:
Hypnosis is a process involving a hypnotist and a subject who agrees to be hypnotized. Being hypnotized is usually characterized by:
(a) Intense concentration
(b) Extreme relaxation
(c) High suggestibility
Hypnosis is commonly used in behavior modification therapy to assist clients in overcoming phobias or bad habits. It also has other uses that are more controversial.

• **A dictionary of psychology and psychiatry** defines hypnosis as follows: *"A superficial or deep trance state resembling sleep induced by suggestions of relaxation and concentrated attention to a single object. The subject becomes highly suggestible and responsive to the hypnotist's influence, and can be induced to recall forgotten events, become insensitive to pain, control vasomotor changes and, in the hands of an experienced hypnotherapist, gain relief from tensions, anxieties and other psychological symptoms." (Goldenson, 1984, p. 358)*

• **1990 Grolier Encyclopedia***: "Hypnosis refers to a state or condition in which the subject becomes highly responsive to suggestions. The hypnotized individual seems to follow instructions in an uncritical, automatic fashion and attends closely only to those aspects of the environment made relevant by the hypnotist. If the subject is profoundly responsive, he or she hears, sees, feels, smells, and tastes in accordance with the suggestions given, even though these may be in direct contradiction to the actual stimuli that impinge upon the subject. Furthermore, memory and awareness of self can be altered by suggestions. All of these effects may be extended post hypnotically into the individual's subsequent waking activity. It is as if suggestions given during hypnosis come to define the individual's perception of the real world. In this sense, the phenomenon has been described as a Believed-in Fantasy."*

• **Weitzenhoffer, 1953**: *"An artificially induced state, usually (though not always) resembling sleep, but physiologically distinct from it, which is characterized by heightened suggestibility, and as a result of which certain sensory, motor and memory abnormalities may be induced more readily than in the normal state." (p. 3)*

- **Barber, Spanos, & Chaves,** *"Behavior resulting from positive attitudes, strong motivations, and positive enhanced expectancies toward the situation in which the subject finds himself thus willing to follow suggestions of the hypnotist." (1974, p. 23)*

- **Orne**, *"A state or condition where the subject focuses his mind on the suggestions of the hypnotist so that he is able to experience distortions of memory or perception. For the time being, the subject suspends disbelief and lowers his critical judgment." (1983, p. 67)*

- **Erickson**, *"The induction of a peculiar psychological state which permits the subject to re-associate and reorganize his inner psychological complexities in a way suitable to the unique items of his own inner psychological experiences." (1980, Vol. III, p. 188)*

- **Araoz,** *"A natural state of mind better understood in terms of two familiar functions . . . imagination and self-suggestion." (1981, p. 1)*

- **Gill & Brenman**, *"An induced psychological regression issuing in the setting of a particular regressed relationship between two people, in a relatively stable state which includes a subsystem of the ego with varying degrees of control of the ego apparatuses." (1959, p. xxiii)*

- **Marcuse**, *"An altered state of the organism originally and usually produced by a repetition of stimuli in which suggestion (no matter how defined) is more powerful than usual." (1959, P. 21)*

- **Marmer,** *"Psychological tetrad of altered consciousness" consisting of:*
  1) *Heightened suggestibility;*
  2) *Narrowed awareness;*
  3) *Selective wakefulness;*
  4) *Restricted attentiveness (1959).*

- **Herbert Spiegel,** *"Psycholophisiological state of aroused attentive receptive focal concentration with a corresponding diminution of peripheral awareness."*

- **Fromm and Shor,** *address this problem by looking to the philosophical bases of the study of science. They explore hypnosis, both as a subjective experience that can be best understood by reference to the internal workings of the subject, and as a group of objective, observable behaviors. This distinction has direct relevance for the practice of hypnotherapy in conjunction with the forensics. (1979)*

- **Dictionary of Occupational Titles (A U.S. Government publication)**:

As a direct result of the efforts of hypnotherapists Gil Boyne and Dr. John Kappas, the occupation of "Hypnotherapist" was defined and assigned an identification number (079.157.0110). It reads as follows:

"Hypnotherapist induces hypnotic state in client to increase motivation or alter behavior pattern through hypnosis. Consults with client to determine the nature of problem. Prepares client to enter hypnotic state by explaining how hypnosis works and what client will experience. Tests subjects to determine degrees of physical and emotional suggestibility. Induces techniques of hypnosis based on interpretation of test results and analysis of client's problem. May train client in self-hypnosis conditioning."

More briefly, hypnosis has been defined as follows:

1. "Altered states of mind"; (Hilgard, 1965; Orne, 1959)
2. "A trance"; (Erickson, 1967)
3. "A controlled dissociated state"; (West, 1960)
4. "Intensified concentration"; (Debetz & Sunnen, 1985; Frankel, 1976; Spiegel & Spiegel, 1978)
5. "Concentrated awareness"; (Morgan, 1983)
6. "Atavism"; (Meares, 1960)
7. "A non-state explainable by experimental and relationship characteristics"; (Barber, 1969)
8. "Role enactment"; (Sarbin & Coe, 1972)
9. "A habit of heightened susceptibility to prestige suggestion"; (Hull, 1933)
10. "Goal-directed behavior"; (White, 1941)

Many investigators have taken a "mix-and-match" technique, combining definitional elements to fit their particular clinical or experimental utilization of hypnosis. Some researchers argue that there is no such "state" of hypnosis at all (e.g., Barber, 1957, 1962).

Which of these definitions is the correct one? They all are, to some extent. In order to lay to rest the ongoing discussion of trying to define "Hypnosis," let us try a simple exercise:

Participants get together in small groups (4-6 people).

1) All the groups are given two subjects: "Learning" and "Sex".
2) Each person in the group lists ten words, which he/she associates with each of the above subjects (two lists).
3) The group elects a secretary who then lists only the words that ALL the group members have on their list (example: the secretary will enter "love" only if everyone listed "love" as one of their associations to "sex").
4) If there is more than one group, the secretaries compare their list to identify only the words common to all the groups.

Invariably, the result of this exercise is that no group gets more then 2-3 words in common! And the more people who participate, the less chance for an agreement.

The point of this exercise is to demonstrate how little agreement there is about common everyday concepts. And if people do not agree on a simple definition for everyday concepts like "learning" or "sex", why then fuss about a definition for hypnosis?

I am inclined to borrow from a higher power. As Chief Justice of the Supreme Court Marshall Thurgood said about pornography: "I cannot define it, but I know it when I see it."

Likewise, I can say: "I cannot define hypnosis but I know it when I see/experience it."

All we really need as hypnotherapists is a "working definition" One that is comprehensive enough to cover most practical aspects without having to be all-encompassing.

Dave Elman's definition is the one widely accepted:
"The bypass of the critical faculties and the establishment of selective acceptable ideas, concepts and thoughts."

To sum it up:
Hypnosis is a state of mind that we use as a vehicle to communicate with the subconscious mind. In this state, the subconscious is more open and receptive to suggestions.

By combining the power of suggestion with the power of imagination in the hypnotic state, we create a powerful environment for change and growth.

The Triad of Powers

To achieve a desired change through hypnosis, we utilize the **power of suggestion**, the **power of imagination** and the **power of the subconscious mind.**

The Power of Suggestion

Every sensory input is a suggestion. A suggestion tends to create expectation, which tends to be a self-fulfilling prophecy. We move in the direction of our most dominant thought.

The following are a few examples to demonstrate the power of suggestion:

1) Clasp your hands together with your index fingers extended and separated. Imagine that there is a vise clamped around them, and, as I tighten the vise, your fingers get closer together. As I continue to tighten this device, your fingers move in closer and closer ... tighter and tighter, until they are touching together.

Was there really a vise? Of course not. It is the power of suggestion.

2) The hypnotist demonstrates the following while saying: "Quickly! Do as I say! Hold your hand up (fingers spread)... make a fist... make a gun... make a circle (with thumb and index finger)... put the circle on your chin! (Simultaneously, with the last instruction, the hypnotist places his/her circle on his own forehead). Most people will follow the visual queue and will also place their circle on their forehead. This example shows how the visual suggestion overrides the auditory one.

3) Feel your shoes/clothes/watch/jewelry. Notice that, until the suggestion was mentioned, you were unaware of the sensation of your clothes.

4) One of the most common demonstrations of the power of suggestion is the Placebo Effect. This is a suggestion given in the awake state. It is most profoundly demonstrated repeatedly in scientific trials conducted by all pharmaceutical companies. It is proven that people respond, with physiological changes, to a sugar pill simply because they believe they received a drug that is supposed to cause these changes.

5) Negative suggestions (Negation): The subconscious mind needs to first conceptualize the affirmative in order to process the negation. Sometimes a negative suggestion will have the opposite of the intended effect.

Examples:

a) Look around you and ignore anything that is RED!

b) Do not think of a monkey with a magician's hat riding an elephant.

c) Occupational Safety & Health Administration (O.S.H.A.) requires safety posters in factories. One of their posters shows a person stumbling down a flight of stairs. The caption reads "Beware of step, do not fall". This, of course, is a conflicting suggestion because the subconscious mind processes the visual image of falling as more dominant then the wording. This poster caused more accidents than before they had the poster up.

d) A person, who is trying to change eating habits, may repeat again and again, "I don't want chocolate". This is an autosuggestion that directs the subconscious mind to focus on chocolate and consequently increases the craving for chocolate.

The Power of Imagination

"Imagination is more important than knowledge." – Albert Einstein

Suggestions are often delivered by utilizing the power of the imagination. The subconscious mind does not differentiate between that which is vividly imagined and reality.

To demonstrate the power of imagination, try the following experiments:

1) The Twist: Stand up comfortably facing forward. For the duration of this experiment, maintain this position without moving your feet.

Extend your right arm forward at shoulder level. Keeping your feet glued to the floor, move your arm to the right and turn your torso as far as you can, without straining. Make a mental note how far you were able to turn, and then return to face the front and lower your hand.

Now close your eyes. Imagine that your spine and muscles are made of rubber. They are pliable, flexible, loose and relaxed as warm rubber.

And now, in your imagination only (without actually moving your hand or body), raise your hand and repeat the exercise, only this time imagine you can twist your body to turn a full 360 degrees. Then, in your imagination, unwind to the original position.

Repeat the above again and, this time, imagine you are so flexible your upper body is twisting around three full circles and unwind.

OK, open your eyes. Now physically lift your hand up and twist around. Notice how much further you could twist. Your body became more flexible thanks to the mental exercise using your imagination only.

2) The Lemon: Close your eyes and imagine you have a yellow sour lemon in your hand. Now imagine cutting it in half. The juice is dripping. Imagine squeezing one half of the lemon into your mouth. The juice is sour, bitter and tart. As you swallow the juice, your face grimaces.

Now take the other half and squeeze the lemony sour juice into your mouth, feeling the juice drip down your lips and tongue and feeling all tangy.

If you vividly imagined the scene, you have most likely salivated, even though there is no lemon in sight.

The Power of the Subconscious Mind

To facilitate our understanding of the workings of our mind we utilize a two-part mind model. The conscious mind and the subconscious mind.

The subconscious mind is the automatic servo-mechanism that operates our body and mind, *automatically*. It is where all habits reside and where all of life's programming and imprinting takes place.

The conscious mind is the seat of the willpower, which is a function of the conscious decision-making capability.

If we attempt to create any change, it has to be done on the level of the subconscious mind where memory, programming and habits reside.

The hypnotic state is the tool that we use as a vehicle to communicate with the subconscious mind.

What are the Functions of the Conscious Mind?

Cognitive, logical decision-making. Analyzes sensory input. Reasons, criticizes, evaluates. Judges, accepts or rejects ideas and/or suggestions

What are the Functions of the Subconscious Mind?

Runs automatically all bodily functions – heartbeat, blood pressure, digestion and endocrine systems, etc. Stores all memory (Automatic behavior, i.e., habits, are also memory). Acts out, automatically – without question or hesitation – any ideas, images or thoughts that are allowed in (akin to a computer executing a program).

The following chart outlines the current understanding of functions attributed to our two-part mind model:

Conscious Mind	Subconscious Mind
1) Analyzes and evaluates sensory input Criticizes, judges, accepts or rejects.	1) Takes actions without questioning, analyzing or judging.
2) Processes information serially, one issue at a time.	2) Capable of multitasking; runs all bodily functions.
3) Short-term memory.	3) Long-term memory.
4) The seat of willpower.	4) The seat of habits.
5) Understands humor, sarcasm, innuendo and negation.	5) Literal. Does not understand humor, sarcasm, innuendo and negation.
6) Slow and imprecise.	6) Quick and accurate.
7) Eager to try and learn new things.	7) Slow to change.
8) Ego, self-importance.	8) Self-preservation mechanism
9) Past – Present – Future.	9) Singular time frame: Now
10) Logic, reasoning and rational decision-making.	10) Seat of emotions.
11) Awareness	11) Unawareness

When we do things on the subconscious level we do them automatically, quicker, more efficiently and more accurately. It is a great advantage that we can relegate many tasks to the subconscious so as to free our conscious mind.

To demonstrate the functionality of the subconscious mind, try the following exercises:

Exercise 1: the A-B-C's: First time around say the entire alphabet as fast as you can, and notice how long it took.

Next, say only one half of the letters. That should be easier and quicker, right? Well try it by saying every other letter.

The first time around you were reciting something you already knew on the subconscious level, and thus it was easy, fast and accurate. The second time around you had to think consciously about what you were saying so, of course you found that to be a much slower process, fraught with mistakes.

Exercise 2: The Hands Clasp:

Clasp your hands (interlacing the fingers) three times as fast as you can. Notice how comfortable, quick and easy this action is.

Now clasp your hands with the other thumb on top (i.e., Interlace the fingers the other way).

Do it three times as fast as you can and notice how uncomfortable and slow it is compared to the way you are used to doing it. Again, when you do it habitually and subconsciously, it is easy and fast contrasting with the slow and cumbersome conscious way.

Exercise 3: Typing:

If you know how to type properly - i.e. with all fingers and without looking at the keyboard - you know how fast you can go when you are in the flow (typing subconsciously). However, when you do stop to look at the keyboard and spell out the words (typing consciously), you find that it is much slower and you are prone to making mistakes.

Exercise 4: Driving:

Remember learning to drive? Remember how difficult it was? You had to remember to place your foot on the brakes, insert the key, start the car, use your blinkers, put it in gear, step on the gas pedal etc. Then you had to deal with the traffic! Everything was done consciously thus slower and with effort. Now you can drive in rush hour without blinking an eye, with your radio on, coffee in one hand, cell phone in the other.

Generalizing and Filtering

Generalizing and filtering are manifestations of ancient adaptive strategies, which have facilitating the survival of the human species.

When faced with any situation our subconscious mind automatically asks three questions: What is it? What does it mean for me? What should I do about it? The answers must come quickly and action taken immediately if it is a dangerous, life-threatening situation.

Thus evolved our ability to generalize and filter.

Generalizing: The ability to see the big picture, making sense, extrapolating, understanding and conceptualizing when having only scant input available. This ability to reach conclusions and decisions, construct a bigger understanding with only few details, was a necessary evolutionary trait that enabled our forbearers to flee or fight in a split second.

Filtering: Eliminating unimportant details to make that which is important stand out; reducing the clutter; focusing. This ability to concentrate without distraction was also a necessary evolutionary trait that enabled our ancestors to enter a contemplative, thoughtful mode of operation.

Generalizing: Thinking in Concepts

In order to make sense and understand the world around us, the mind uses perceptions as shortcuts to facilitate processing of data. A shorter reaction time is efficient and economical and safe.

Our mind processes information in big chunks; in concepts. It takes only a few clues to create a meaningful, understandable construction of the situation.

The following pages contain examples that demonstrate this ability:

What are these abstract blotches?

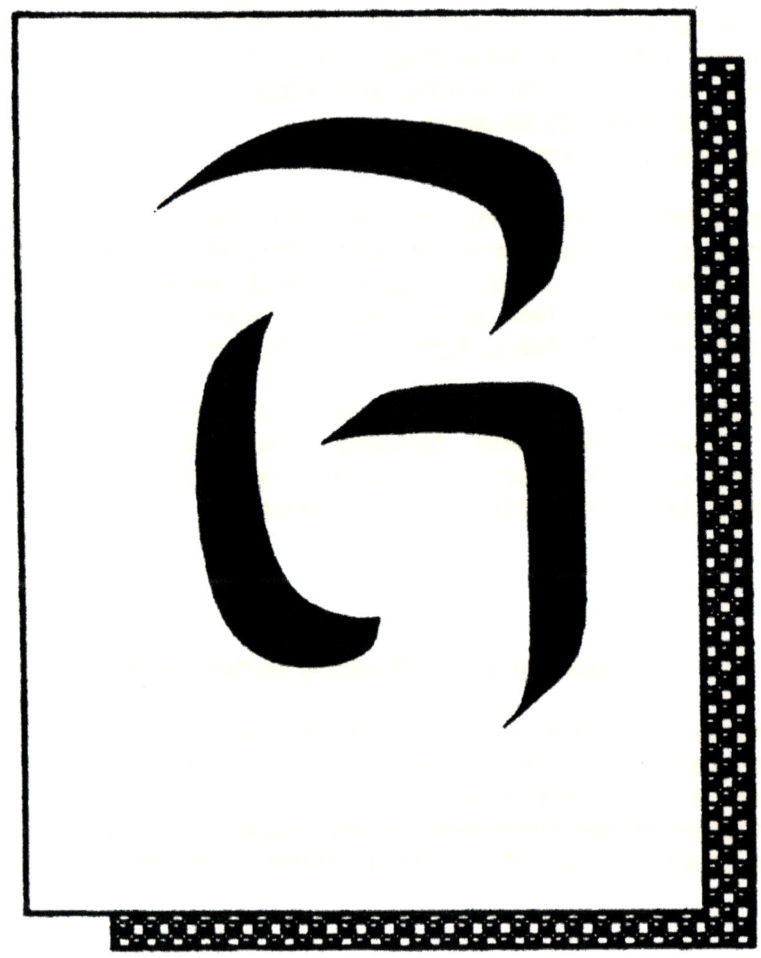

Can you figure out what this set of abstract symbols represents?

Answer on next page

Answer to previous page:

They form the letter G.

Your mind was able to decipher the quiz with little difficulty even though there was not much information provided.

Can you read the following?

Aoccdrnig to rscheearch at an Elingsh uinervtisy, it deosn't mttaer in waht oredr the ltteers in a wrod are, the olny iprmoetnt tihng is taht the frist and lsat ltteer are in the rghit pclae. The rset can be a toatl mses and you can sitll raed it wouthit a porbelm. Tihs is bcuseae we do not raed ervey lteter by it slef but the wrod as a wlohe and the biran fguiers it out aynawy.

Even though many of the above words are horribly misspelled, you most likely understood everything with little difficulty. This is because your subconscious mind instantly grasped the concept and made sense of jumbled symbols.

Mystery Numeric System

How would you like to learn a whole new numeric system? It will take only a few seconds to learn and you will be able to remember it for life with ease.

The following is the phone number for the BreakThrough Institute. Can you decipher it?

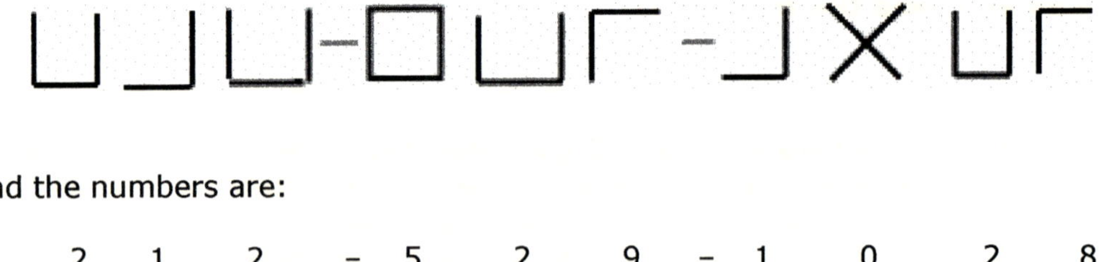

And the numbers are:

2 1 2 - 5 2 9 - 1 0 2 8

Here are the Arabic numerals and their equivalent in the new numerical system.

How long will it normally take you to memorize them?

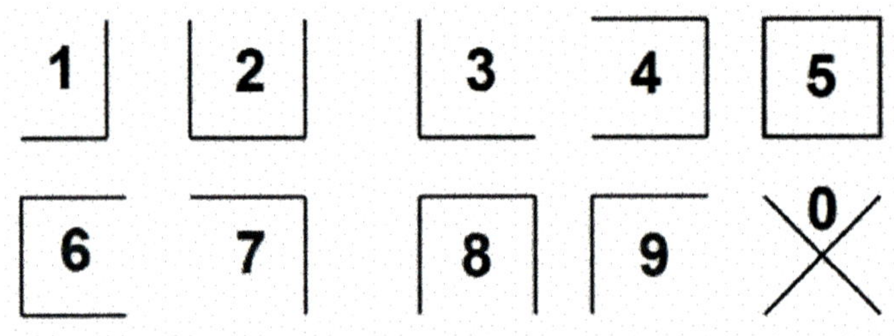

"But wait a minute," you say. "How would I remember such a complex system?"

I will let you figure this out by yourself by looking at the next chart. Then you will realize how easy it is to remember this system, once you understand the concept.

Tic-Tac-Toe and Voila a New Numeric System

1	2	3
4	5	6
7	8	9

As you can see, the number 5 is in the center of this Tick-Tack-Toe structure. And it is surrounded on all four "walls". Thus, in the new system, a box (four walls) is equivalent to 5. The numeral 3 is surrounded by two "walls" only; to the left of it and at the bottom. Thus an **L** shape is equivalent to 3. Numeral 2 will be a **U** shape and so on. The numeral 0 (Zero) is marked as an **X.** Thus the number 203 will translate to **UXL.**

Once you get the concept, all you need is to visualize the matrix and you can translate any Arabic numeral into "walls" or lines in a square.

Filtering

Filtering out and deleting is one of the most useful functions of our mind. The mind is bombarded with millions of bits of information every second. The subconscious mind has the power to filter out the unimportant stimuli. We pay attention only to what is important. Having the ability to ignore 99% of the input is a great natural gift and we could not survive and operate efficiently without it.

We are blessed with the ability to block input from all our senses. This deletion/filtering function is designed, by nature, to enable us to not waste time and energy on concepts that are deemed "understood" by our mind.

We may refer to the deletion function as "Mental Scotoma" or "Negative Hallucination." To understand mental scotoma, let's first look at physical Scotoma.

Physical Scotoma

Scotoma is the phenomenon of looking at an object, yet not seeing it. It is based on the physical structure of the human eye.

Try the following experiment:
Hold the book about five inches from your face. Close your right eye and look at the right star. Now slowly bring the page towards you. What happened to the left star?

At some point the left star disappears from view. Yes, it is still there, but you just don't see it. The explanation is simple. On our retina there is a spot without any light-sensitive cells. This is the notorious "Blind Spot".

This is due to the fact that all the nerves from the light-sensing cells lining the retina converge in one spot to form a thick "cable" of nerves that exit from the eye and into the brain.

Mental Scotoma (a.k.a. Negative Hallucination)

Like physical scotoma (Blind Spot), we also have mental scotoma – i.e., blockage of sensory input or of ideas and thoughts.
When the mind locks onto one thing it may discontinue the consideration of other options. It deletes and filters out all other input. Thus, it eliminates other possibilities and prevents us from recognizing the "other side of the coin," even when it is in plain view.

The following are a few demonstrations of the phenomenon of mental scotoma (Mental Blind Spot) or as it is known in another name "Negative Hallucination".

1) How many times does the letter "F" appear in the following sentence?

Finished files are the result of years of scientific study combined with the experience of many years.

Answer on next page.

2) The Statue of Liberty:

Answer to exercise 1:
There are Six (6) "F"s in the sentence.
If you saw less than 6, you most likely missed the "OF"s.

Answer to exercise 2:
The caption spells: "The Statue OF- OF Liberty"

The examples above illustrate how we develop a mental scotoma to what the mind perceives to be of minor importance once we understand what is presented to us. The word "of" is only a linguistic construct that acts like the "mortar" between the other building block of the sentence. Thus, not really detrimental to our understanding of the sentence.

3) What do you see in the following picture?

The picture above depicts two women. An old woman looking down to the left towards you. The other, a young woman, looking away from you. (Clue: the necklace on the young woman is the mouth of the old one).

When the mind locks on one image or idea, it automatically stops from considering other alternatives. After all, if you "know" something, there is no need to waste precious resources by occupying the mind on stuff that it deems "understood"

Read the following sentence from right to left.

."rat eht saw tac ehT"

Did you read: "The Cat Was The Rat"?

The correct answer is: "The Cat Was The Tar."

Visual Negative Hallucination (Scotoma):

When your spellchecker tells you that a word is misspelled, the computer then gives the correct spelling. But you cannot see the difference between your spelling and the one suggested by the computer. To you, it seems that your spelling is the same as the computers'. Yet, upon close scrutiny, you realize you indeed made a mistake.

Auditory Negative Hallucination:

Do you have a ticking clock, or a loud refrigerator or air conditioner? Notice how often you do not hear them. You filter out this unnecessary sensory input. Quite often, you become aware of a background noise only when it is shut off.

Kinesthetic Negative Hallucination:

You probably did not feel the following until you read this. The feel of your shirt? Pants? Shoes? Do you feel your watch/jewelry on your skin?
Now that your attention was directed, you are aware and feel these items. But normally, our mind blocks this sensory input from our awareness so the conscious mind is not overloaded.

If the above exercises made you feel stupid or inadequate, fret not. These exercises prove that your mind is working properly just as it was designed to. These exercises exemplify the affects of mental scotoma or negative hallucination, which are our mind's natural filtering mechanism.

How can this knowledge be utilized in the service of our clients? Well, if we have a natural ability to ignore sensory input, as witnessed above, then we can utilize this phenomenon to teach and train people how to ignore chronic pain, trinities (ringing in the ears) - even how to ignore temptation of food or other cravings. Also, when a client is stuck on a counterproductive idea or a negative pattern of thought we may direct him/her to alter the point of view to look at the issue from a different perspective.

Knowing that our mind plays tricks on us and prevents us from seeing everything, we need to change our point of view in order to see things (or think) differently.

The following is an exercise that demonstrates how changing your point of view opens up the opportunity to discover new possibilities.

Another Point of View

Can you discover this secret word?

Answer: What, at first glance, looks like a crossword puzzle, actually spell the word: "LAUGH."

You don't believe it? Change your point of view and you will actually see it!

Follow the instructions and find out for yourself:

Hold the book as shown and look in the direction of the arrow. Sometimes it's easier with one eye closed.

An Analogy to the Conscious/Subconscious Relationship

From what we have discussed so far, it is obvious that the subconscious mind is very powerful. It is assumed that the subconscious mind utilizes 92% to 98% of our mind's power.

In India, elephants are used in the logging industry. It is common to see a young boy (the master) directing and instructing this giant, powerful animal. In a similar manner, the conscious mind is driving the subconscious mind. However, every now and then, the elephant will refuse to obey and all the efforts from the boy/master are for naught.

In likewise manner, in a conflict between the willpower (conscious mind) and a habit (subconscious mind), the habit prevails.

Take for example a smoker. The habit of smoking (the programming) and his self- image as a smoker are firmly embedded in the subconscious mind. Then, one day the smoker wants to quit smoking (conscious mind). The conflict between the willpower on the one side and the self-image and the programming for smoking on the other, results in a struggle, which ends up, most of the time, with the willpower coming up short.

Hypnotizability and Suggestibility

Hypnotists typically treat the terms "suggestibility" and "hypnotizability" as interchangeable. This is not strictly correct, since suggestibility is a generic term that encompasses the two components, hypnotizability and suggestibility.

Hypnotizability Quotient (HQ): Akin to IQ (Intelligence Quotient), it is a natural trait that is independent of other personality traits. It is the natural ability of a person to enter a hypnotic state induced either by self or another person.

Suggestibility Quotient (SQ):
The ability of a person, to accept and respond to suggestions to a greater or lesser degree.

High Suggestibility:
Highly suggestible people tend to be highly hypnotizable. Highly suggestible people tend to be able to learn fast, be flexible and adaptive. The flip side is that they also tend to be easily influenced.

Low Suggestibility:
Highly hypnotizable people are not necessarily highly suggestible. They may be easily hypnotizable but that does not mean that they will follow suggestions. Persons with low suggestibility tend to be good troubleshooters (accountant, lawyer, mechanic). They tend to be skeptical and cynical, thus less influenced by hype. They often learn the hard way since they tend to need to discover things by themselves.

We can define suggestibility and hypnotizability by a person's response to items on a test of suggestibility and hypnotizability.

The methods to administer these tests are covered in detail in later chapters.

Hypnosis from an Evolutionary Perspective

By: Baruch Elitzur, Ph.D. Clinical Psychologist.

Fundamental Assumptions of Evolutionary Psychology

A new branch of psychology is attempting to explain the behavior of humans in light of the theory of evolution.

Evolutionary-psychology assumes that all behavior common to the entire human race has a genetic basis. In the course of the past six million years, humans' behaviors have evolved through mutations, which are embedded as instincts in our genes. The same genes that helped ensure the survival of the species over the years continue to exist in modern-day humans.

Evolutionary-psychology hypothesizes how character traits, emotions and behavioral patterns that are present in modern day humans, have evolved to contribute to the survival of our ancestors.

Since the ability to enter a hypnotic trance is common to the entire human race, regardless of gender, race or culture, it is safe to assume that it is an inherent property that played an important role in the survival of the species.

In the present article, we hypothesize that the ability to enter a hypnotic trance and to accept suggestions may constitute behavior essential to the survival of the species.

The Process of Hypnosis and its Induction

There are many definitions of the state of hypnosis. Most of them include the following four elements:

1. Focal concentration;
2. Heightened suggestibility;
3. Low analytical judgment;
4. Imagination;

Hacher (1990) refers to hypnosis as "a state or condition in which the subject becomes highly responsive to suggestions [heightened suggestibility]. The hypnotized individual seems to follow instructions in an uncritical, automatic fashion [low analytical judgment] and attends closely only to those aspects of the environment made relevant by the hypnotist [focal concentration].

Araoz (1995) has emphasized for over 20 years the importance of imagination as a generic concept towards understanding hypnosis. He claims that in a good hypnotic subject, "It is not will, i.e., left-hemispheric functioning, that produces change but *imagination*, i.e., right-hemispheric functioning," (1995 p. 4), and, "These cognitive processes used by the person in search of the hypnotic experience are imagination and fantasy." (1995 p. 17)

Barber, who coined the term "fantasy-prone personality", in 2000 said, "We found that a subgroup of `high' (in their ability to fantasize) are very responsive to hypnotic suggestion primarily because they utilize their special talent for fantasizing, vividly and realistically ... they could see, hear, smell, touch and experience what they were fantasizing." (p. 210)

Hypnotic inductions are numerous and varied. In most of them, the hypnotist leads the subject to; gradually diminish the number of stimuli perceived by the mind. The most common way is to direct the subject to concentrate on one of the senses, on one thought or on an image. Diminishing the number of stimuli leads the subject to a state of relaxation.

In the following pages, we will examine the connection between focal concentration, heightened suggestibility, low critical judgment, fantasizing and the survival of the fittest.

The Process of Concentration

We regard the ability to concentrate as being paramount during relaxation, but diminish in direct proportion to the level of tension and anxiety. For example, students tend to complain they find it difficult to concentrate during tests that invoke tension and anxiety.

The effect of stress on the level of concentration is common to all people. It is therefore reasonable to assume that the ability to concentrate is a genetic trait that contributed to the survivability of the fittest. In order to clarify this effect, we need to re-frame our point of view concerning the process of concentration and to re-label the different levels of concentration. We suggest referring to difficulties in concentration as "wide-angle concentration," and focal concentration as "narrow-angle concentration."

The following example will help clarify our new point of view regarding the levels of concentration. Let's imagine that one of our ancestors found a plant's root. In order to figure out whether this root is edible or poisonous, he would have to focus on the root (narrowing the angle of concentration). That could only be done in a state of relaxation, achieved after looking around (widening the angle of concentration) in order to verify that there was no danger lurking in the vicinity. Only when the parasympathetic system is active, is one able to narrow his angle of concentration.

If suddenly, a suspicious noise or movement should occur, the sympathetic nervous system would be activated, and the angle of concentration would be widened in order to enable heightened alertness and a quick scan of the surroundings for potential danger.

This example explains the inability of the modern day student to concentrate on a test that is perceived as a threat. Anticipation of failure activates the sympathetic nerve system, which evokes worry and anxiety and widens the angle of concentration. In such a state, any noise or movement in the exam room distracts the student from concentrating on the test.

In order to examine the connection between focal concentration and hypnosis, we shall expand our discussion to include two more Gestalt psychology terms: Figure and Ground. The object that a person focuses on is called Figure, while everything else is referred to as Ground. The Figure has a well-defined shape, whereas the Ground seems to have no shape. The Figure appears to be closer to the viewer and seems to have a definite position in space. The Ground seems farther away, at some unspecified location in the background. The Figure-Ground distinction pertains to all our senses, not just to the sense of vision. We can distinguish a violin solo against the Ground of a symphony and a roar of a lion against all other sounds of the jungle. The more concentration there is on the Figure and less on the Ground, the less aware and responsive the person is to peripheral stimuli.

Stages of Concentration

The following graph portrays four stages of concentration according to the relative ratio between Figure and Ground.

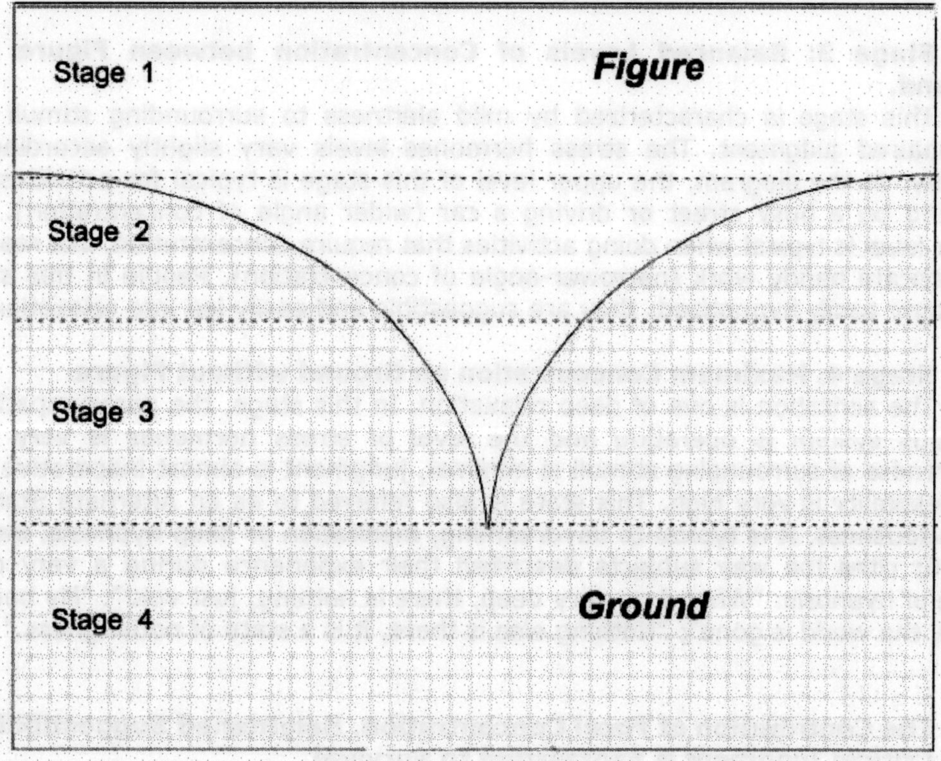

Stage 1: Maximum Concentration on Figure without Ground.

In this state, there is a sense of being overwhelmed, resulting from the flooding of stimuli, i.e., a very wide-angle of concentration. In this stage, the sympathetic nervous system is operating and the level of stress hormones is very high. The accompanying emotions include a high level of anxiety and a hyper vigilant state.

This state is common after a trauma such as a severe car accident or a brutal rape. In ancient times, it helped our ancestors stay extremely alert after a predator hurt them. The modern psychiatric diagnosis is Post Traumatic Stress Disorder. In this stage, it is very difficult to enter a state of hypnosis because it is almost impossible to concentrate on one stimulus, i.e., narrowing angle of concentration.

State 2: Wide-angle of Concentration on the Figure vs. Narrow-angle on the Ground.

This is a state of high alertness of all the senses, i.e., a wide-angle of concentration. The sympathetic nervous system is operating and the level of stress hormones is high, causing feelings of fear and anxiety. This is common during a stress situation where a person feels threatened or vulnerable. In ancient times it helped people to stay alert to face a threat. The modern psychiatric diagnosis is Generalized Anxiety Disorder. People in this state can be hypnotized and are suggestible, but it is important to proceed gradually by utilizing various relaxation techniques.

Stage 3: Balanced Levels of Concentration between Figure and Ground.

This stage is characterized by mild alertness to surrounding stimuli and unimpaired judgment. The stress hormones levels vary slightly according to activity. In the diagram, the upper level of this stage is typical for activities like walking on a busy street or driving a car (wider angle of concentration). The lower level is typical when doing activities that require concentration, like reading or intricate handy work (narrower-angle of concentration). People in this stage are fairly easily hypnotized; they are suggestible and easily led into relaxation.

Stage 4: Maximum Concentration on Ground without Figure.

The sensation is one of deep relaxation. In this stage, the parasympathetic nervous system is operating and the level of stress hormones is very low. Awareness of surrounding stimuli is minimal, judgment is almost inoperative and suggestibility is very high. This state is also referred to as an Alternate State of Consciousness. It is typical to daydreaming, meditation or deep hypnosis. Barber (2000) cites the way subjects described their experience during a very deep state of hypnosis: "When I go very deep, there is nothing, just void"; "My body is gone, the world is gone"; "Nothing else is there, it is a state of nothingness."

The Contribution of Focal Concentration, Heightened Suggestibility, Low Critical Judgment & Fantasizing to Survival

Humans belong to the group of Social Mammals. At the top of the social hierarchy in this group is a leader, designated Alpha. One of the main responsibilities of Alpha is to protect the group by being alert to the environment and warning the group to any danger. When Alpha is on duty, his level of concentration is in stage 2 of the diagram, i.e., high alertness of all the senses and a wide-angle of concentration. The level of stress hormones in his body is high. When Alpha conveys to the group that they are safe, they are free to go about their business of feeding or napping, etc. In such a case, they are at the low end of stage 3 of the diagram, i.e., low alertness of all the senses, narrow-angle of concentration, high suggestibility and low critical judgment. If they are napping lightly, they are in stage 4 of the diagram.

The moment Alpha detects a suspicious tail of an animal that could belong to a predator, like a lion or tiger, he sounds the alarm. The group may only sense the tail in the periphery, i.e., in their Ground – or perhaps they did not sense it at all. However, they do not waste time assessing the validity of Alpha's judgment. Alpha's suggestion of a danger is enough to activate the sympathetic system, causing the stress hormones to flood the body in preparation for a "Fight or Flight" response. This survival instinct, which has evolved over six million years, caused our ancestors to develop suggestibility towards the opinions of their Alpha without using their own critical judgment.

By being suggestible and lowering their analytical judgment, the group members become dependent on Alpha's judgment. When Alpha declares safety, they conserve energy by lowering their stress hormones and they relax. When Alpha declares danger, they prepare to save their lives by increasing the level of stress hormones and become ready for fight or flight.

Given that the ability to fantasize is common in most people especially children, it is safe to assume that this ability contributed to the survivability of *Homo sapiens* – the knowledgeable man and his young off spring.

The ancient human utilized the ability to imagine in many ways. When he fantasized vividly and realistically about his hunting experience, he could learn from these musings. He could project, plan and rehearse future hunting excursions. He could also learn from his past encounters with predators and plan strategies for avoiding them in the future.

The ability to fantasize vividly and realistically affects the functions of the sympathetic and parasympathetic nervous systems. Before leaving the safe confines of the cave to go to fetch water, the ancient human would imagine an earlier encounter with a predator in the same area. This image would trigger the stress response and cause his body to gear up to a higher level of alertness so he would be ready to face any threat on his way. Likewise, memorizing and visualizing the dead predator that he saw the day before, would trigger the relaxation response and cause his body to save energy on his trip to fetch water.

No doubt, children's ability to fantasize compensated for their lack of experience and contributed to their ability to survive in the ancient time.

The Effects of Suggestibility & Low Analytical Judgment on the Modern Human

Instincts, which are transferred through genes, may be compared to computer programs on a hard drive. These inherent programs, designed to contribute to the survival of the fittest, are expressed today in the process of hypnosis, i.e., focal concentration, heightened suggestibility, low analytical judgment and fantasizing. The hypnotist, who is perceived as the Alpha, takes advantage of these ancient coded programs by inducing hypnosis and delivering suggestions. The process affects not just the stress hormones, but the perception of the stimuli from all the senses. Suggestions in the hypnotic state can increase the effectiveness of the immune system to overcome viral and bacterial infections. At the same time, they can decrease the level of response of the immune system in order to overcome autoimmune ailments such as asthma and arthritis. Suggestions are also commonly utilized to affect behavioral changes, like smoking cessation, nail biting, bed-wetting, eating disorders, etc.

The Hypnotist as a Leader, the Subject as a Follower

Barber (2000) described five characteristics that are common to good hypnotists. These characteristics may also describe a good leader:

1. They are confident in their own abilities.
2. They have high levels of energy, vitality and willpower.
3. They are well-functioning individuals with exceptional wisdom.
4. They have original ideas they communicate with persuasive authority.
5. They are emphatic individuals who relate to their subjects in a close personal way.

Spanos (1986) described characteristics that are common to good hypnotizable subjects. These characteristics may also describe members of a group who follow their leader submissively: "highly sociable, trusting, cooperative and seemingly compliant individuals." (p. 493).

A mandated prerequisite to entering the hypnotic state and accepting suggestions without an analytical examination of their reality base, is that the medium trusts and respects the hypnotist. It is well-known that the better the hypnotist's reputation, the faster and deeper the subject's response. This phenomenon exemplifies the contribution of suggestibility to survival theory. When Alpha sounds the alarm, the group responds to the suggestion because they trust Alpha's judgment. There is no need for each individual to waste precious time analyzing and judging the situation while doubting Alpha's declaration.

The Effect of Post-Hypnotic Suggestions

According to the evolutionary perspective, the ability to accept a suggestion in the present and execute it in the future is another inherent characteristic that contributed to the survival of our ancestors.

let's assume a group of ancient humans is busy foraging. The Alpha leader senses the presence of a predator and sounds the flight alarm. If Alpha declares that the group must always flee at the sight of this kind of threat, the group will accept his suggestion and flee even when he is not present. They trust his judgment and they want to avoid risks.

Likewise, when the hypnotist is giving a suggestion to be executed accordingly sometime in the future (a post-hypnotic suggestion), the subject will respond. For example, the hypnotist may suggest that in the future, whenever the subject lights a cigarette, it will smell awful. Because the suggestion was accepted in the hypnotic state, the person will experience a foul odor the next time he lights up.

Concluding Remarks

Stevens and Price (2000) wrote, "Darwinian paradigm is the bedrock on which all biological sciences are now based, and no psychological explanation can hope to survive if it is incompatible with it." (p. 31)

This article explains the hypnotic process in light of Stevens and Price's

(2000) evolutionary approach. These understandings may enable professionals and the general public to accept hypnosis as a natural phenomenon. It is my hope that as hypnosis is better understood, it will be elevated to its rightful place as an effective methodology for treating medical and psychological problems.

Araoz, D. L. (1981) "Negative self-hypnosis," Journal of Contemporary Psychotherapy. 12 (1), 45-51

Araoz, D.L. (1982), *Hypnosis and Sex Therapy;* New York: Brunner/Mazel

Araoz, D.L. (1995) *The New Hypnosis: Techniques in Brief Individual and Family Psychotherapy*; NJ: Jason Aronson Northvale

Barber, T.X. (1981). "Medicine, suggestive therapy and healing," In R.J. Kastenbaum, T.X. Barber, S. C. Wilson, B.L. Hathaway. "Old, Sick and Helpless: Where Therapy Begins"; Cambridge, Mass: Ballinger Publishing Co.

Barber, T.X. (2000). "A deeper understanding of hypnosis: Its secrets, its nature, its essence," American Journal of Clinical Hypnosis, 42, 3, 4, 208-273.

Hacher, J. (Ed.) (1990). *Grolier Encyclopedia*. Ct: Scholastic Library.

Spanos, N.P. (1986). "Hypnotic Behavior: A social psychological interpretation of amnesia, analgesia and trance logic"; *Behavioral and Brain Sciences,* 9, 449-467.

Stevens, A. Price, J. (2000). *Evolutionary Psychiatry*. Pa: Taylor & Francis Inc.

CHAPTER 2:
FIRST SESSION WITH A NEW CLIENT
A blueprint to a hypnotherapy session

Keys to a Successful Hypnosis Session

In order to ensure a favorable outcome, the hypnotherapist must do the following:

- ❖ Educate the client about hypnosis.
- ❖ Eliminate fears and misconceptions.
- ❖ Develop and implement a plan of action.

Stage One: Pre-Hypnosis

- ❖ Intake interview – conducted in first session only.
- ❖ Basic Assessment – conducted in first session only.
- ❖ Goal Setting and Action Plan – revisited in subsequent sessions.
- ❖ Pre Talk - conducted in first session only.
- ❖ Suggestibility Tests – administered in first session only.

Stage Two: Hypnosis

- ❖ Formal Induction.
- ❖ Depth Tests – administered in first session only.
- ❖ Interactive insight generation.
- ❖ Programming script based on information culled from assessment, goal setting and interaction.
- ❖ Teach & Practice Self Hypnosis - optional.
- ❖ Post-Hypnotic Suggestions.

Stage Three: Post-Hypnosis

- ❖ Emerging (repeat suggestions).
- ❖ Post-Hypnosis Talk:
    - Trance ratification.
    - Client debriefing (what worked, what didn't).
    - Agreement ratification (lead with questions).

Subsequent sessions require only review of the progress. Re-evaluating the course of action and adjusting the suggestions.

Stage One: Pre-Hypnosis

The Intake Interview

It is expected of you that as a professional hypnotherapist you will implement and follow professional office procedures.

The first thing you do with a client is an Intake Interview. The intake interview affords the hypnotherapist the opportunity to gage the strength of the client's desire and motivation to make a change. It is during the intake interview that you discuss with the client the plan of action. Together you develop a detailed outline of the goals and a road map to achieving those goals. It is in this stage that you may encounter the most resistance from your clients. It is of utmost importance to enroll the client and secure his/her commitment to the program right away.

The purposes of the official interview and form are two-fold:

1) To discuss client's presenting problem. To protect the therapist by including a disclaimer and having the client consent and sign it. To impresses upon the client that you are a professional and have his/her best interest in heart.

2) To assess and enhance in the client the following keys to a successful session.

Desire- I really, really want this.
Belief- I can do it. It is possible for me.
Motivation- It is a must for me to do. If I don't change the results will be horrific.
Expectation- I will be successful in this endeavor.
Commitment- I will do anything it takes. I will stop doing what it takes to be successful.

During this initial interview you fill out a form with the client's personal information including the purpose of the visit (see appendices 1, 2, 3 & 4). You discuss the issues that brought the client to you. This form contains your explanation of what kind of service you offer. The client reads and consents to the terms presented in the form. After the session, you enter your comments on the procedures you used and the observed results.

Some of the questions on this form may seem unimportant or unnecessary What is your favorite color or vacation spot? However they are designed to give you some leverage when formulating your suggestions. In the appendix section find a sample of an "Intake Form" that you may use as your template or change it to suit your needs.

Pre-Induction Protocol

I) Explain to the client what hypnosis is.
2) Explain to the client what hypnosis is not (dispel myths about hypnosis).
3) Explain to the client what to expect while in hypnosis. Emphasize that the feelings of hypnosis are subjective and vary with the individual.
4) Explain how therapeutic hypnosis works and how it differs from stage hypnosis (Only If they had seen a stage show).
5) Demonstrate clinical hypnotic phenomena by conducting various suggestibility tests.
6) Establish rapport and trust.

Pre-Talk - Explaining Hypnosis to Client

As the hypnotist, you have the duty to educate your clients on the subject of hypnosis and the process itself. It is important that any misconceptions be cleared during the pre-induction talk. Ignorance-driven fear is the number one inhibitor to achieving the hypnotic state and to a successful session.

Note: *When working is areas of hypnotic anesthesia and pain management, direct symptom removal of pain is not advisable without the written approval of a medical doctor.*

Review the quiz earlier in this book to help dispel myths about hypnotism.

Although suggestibility tests provide an indication of the client's ability to accept ideas, their main purpose is to establish a spiral of belief that enhances his/her expectation of positive therapeutic results.

A sample of the pre-talk is provided below. It is only a template. You are encouraged to rewrite and rearrange it to fit your style and comfort.

For clients who are resistant to change:

Say something like this: "You know, certain trains of thought can take you to unpleasant places. And then there are trains of thought that can give you pleasure. You have the right to try new ways of thinking just like you have the right to try a new outfit at a clothing store before you buy it. Even after you buy it, you still have the right to return it.

So, whatever we will talk about here, I want you to take it to that special place in your mind that is your fitting room. I want you to try it, tailor it to your needs. Only then you can decide if this is way serves you better. Or you may decide that you want to keep the old ways and use the new later.

Do you ever dream? In your dreams did you ever do things that you don't ordinarily do in the awake state? Of course, your subconscious mind knows how to imagine and create different realities and try them out in dreams. You have infinite possibilities in ways of thinking and the wonderful thing is that it is all your choice."

The Pre-Talk

By: Dr. Al Krasner

For me, the Pre-Induction interview is the *most important* part of the entire hypnotic process. If you handle the pre-induction interview correctly, the rest will fall easily into place. You are the therapist. The person in front of you is your client. He wants to make a change in his life, and he has come to you for help.

After the initial introductions and brief discussion of the client's reason for wanting hypnotherapy, you (the therapist) must take and keep immediate control. Now, I do not mean "know-it-all" or arrogant control. I mean a confident, self-assured direction of the session that will give your client a feeling of positive expectancy.

This is such an important topic that I am going to first go over it section by section, explaining each step as we go. You may use the therapist's dialogue verbatim, or adapt it to your own style. Do not leave any of it out, though, because as you will see, there is a reason for every single step. Assume now that the amenities are concluded. You (the therapist) take control of the session by saying:

The Pre-Talk Dialogue and Comments

1. *"Let me tell you about hypnosis."*

This establishes you (the therapist) as the authority (Remember prestige suggestions? This is one).

2. *"You will not feel hypnotized, nor will you be out of control.*

"You've seen hypnosis shows, haven't you?" (Client answers "yes".) "It looks like the subject's mind is being controlled, doesn't it?" (Client answers "yes".)

At this point you must remove the three most common misconceptions that you are likely to encounter. Notice the wording. Frame the question to elicit the answer you want.

3. *"Have you seen a hypnosis stage show? These people volunteered, didn't they? (Client answers yes.) Weren't they volunteering to have fun? (Client answers yes.) The truth is, on stage they will accept the hypnotist's suggestions as long as they have no moral objection. However, the same people who on stage will accept the suggestions to forget their name. The same ones who will happily entertain the audience by waddling around quacking like a duck will certainly not accept a suggestion to rob a bank or hurt anyone. The critical faculties will take over immediately, say, "No way!" and they will either simply refuse to comply, or will spontaneously come out of hypnosis."*

You keep getting affirmative answers. Every time that happens, you gain new confidence from the client, and make "yes" answers more likely. Here the client may begin to realize that the person on stage who is *really* in control, not the hypnotist.

4. "You know, the funny thing is that those people on stage, when asked, "Were you hypnotized?" will invariably say "No." When asked "How do you know?" they will say every time: "I heard every word that was said." Further, if

asked, "Why, then, did you behave like that?" they will say, again, every time, "I don't know!" They obviously expected to go into a deep trance or sleep which of course simply doesn't happen. You are "setting up" for the client's own hypnotic experience expectations.

5. *"Let me demonstrate to you what hypnosis really feels like. Close your eyes, please. That's it. (Pause 5 seconds.) It just feels like that! You will remain aware of everything at all times."*
You want them to know that there will be no "weird" feeling, no loss of consciousness or hearing.

6. *"Now keep your eyes closed (Client complies). Place your hands in your lap (Client complies). Now put your feet together (Client complies)".*
Here you establish how easily they can follow your suggestions.

7. *"Now go into the corner, please, and stand on your head." (client opens eyes and objects).* This reinforces the control issue. The client will relate his own experience here to the experience of the person hypnotized on stage that was discussed earlier.

8. "You agreed to close your eyes, to put your hands in your lap and to put your feet together. However, you weren't about to stand on your head. My point is this: Hypnosis simply cannot make you do anything. It only makes it easy to achieve what you want to achieve. It cannot make you want to do it, either. That's your part."
I believe it is very important to let the client know that he/she is responsible for his own motivation and participation.

9. *"The body is only a robot, controlled by the mind. What the mind sees, the body tends to do. Think of a lemon.* Now imagine cutting it in half. The juice is dripping. Imagine squeezing one half of the lemon into your mouth. The juice is sour, bitter and tart. As you swallow the juice, your face grimaces. Now take the other half and squeeze the lemony sour juice into your mouth, feeling the juice drip down your lips and tongue and feeling all tangy.

What happened?" (The client will tell you he salivated, or had a sour taste, etc.) Now think of something frightening. (Pause) What happened this time? (Client will tell you that his heart began to beat faster, or that he felt anxious, etc.) "Of course, there is nothing frightening here, but the body didn't know that. It just believed what it was told by your mind, just like it did with the lemon. Therefore, if it is told that it doesn't want cigarettes anymore (or too much food, or to react a certain way, etc.), it won't, because it doesn't know that it ever did."

Once the misconceptions are handled, it is important to get into the "body is a robot" theory. The lemon demonstration is excellent for this.

10. *"Do you have any questions?"*
At this point the client may be confused, but the concepts are beginning to come together. The client seldom has questions. If he does, answer them patiently and completely, but succinctly.

11. "Tell me. How would your life improve if you... (lost weight, stopped smoking, relaxed more, studied harder, etc.)?
Listen very carefully to the answer to this question. Your client will give you the words to use in his therapy session. He is telling you what is important to him and what his motivation is. Write down what he says.

12. *"Now I'd like to do a few suggestibility tests to see how you'll do in hypnosis. Is that all right with you?" (Client always agrees - after all, he comes to you for hypnosis.)*

The client is still unconvinced that he can be hypnotized - even though he may have cooperated completely. Always use the word *test.* This way, he thinks that if he "succeeds" in passing the tests, he will be a good subject.

13. *"Stand up here in front of me please, feet together, heels and toes even. That's it. Very good. Now I want you to watch my ring."*

I hold my hand above their head [ring turned inside] so that they must look up to see it. A ring is not necessary. You may just as well say: "Watch my hand. *As you watch my ring you will feel your eyes begin to close and you will begin to sway back and forth, back and forth. As I tap you on the shoulder, you feel your body falling forward, and you allow it to, knowing that I will catch you."*

(Client falls forward onto your hands.)

This "test" is the beginning of the client's belief system being changed. The fact is that when human beings stand with their heels and toes together and close their eyes, they <u>must</u> sway. However, the client doesn't know this. He thinks he is responding to suggestion, and his belief in hypnosis is increased. And with that, guess what else is increased? The probability of his success!

14. *"Good. You did very well on that one! Let's try another ... Now hold both arms out in front of you about shoulder height. Now close your eyes and imagine that I have just placed a very heavy book—a dictionary—on this hand. (Just lightly touch the hand) At the same time I tie a string around this wrist, (lightly touch the underside of the wrist of the other hand) to which is tied a big red helium balloon." I proceed with the "hands rising and falling" test.*

Every time I can demonstrate to the client that his body responds to his imagination, the greater his own belief in the therapy becomes. (This exercise gives you a wonderful opportunity to use your own "voice.") Make the word "heavy" sound heavy, and likewise "lighten" your tone in describing the balloon. Give the balloon a bright color. Remember the mind loves adjectives.

15. *"Now open your eyes and look at how one arm has gone up and the other has gone down. Isn't that interesting? There was no book and no balloon, yet your arms are apart! (The client is always amazed and enjoys this.) I told your robot that there was a book and a balloon there, and it believed me. Your mind "saw" them, and your body reacted accordingly. It will do the same thing when it is told that it is a nonsmoker. Now I can show you hypnosis with your eyes wide open."*

Again, I take the opportunity to reinforce the concept that the "body is a robot," blindly following whatever instructions the mind gives it.

16. *"O.K. Now clasp your hands together with your index fingers extended and separated. Imagine that there is a vise clamped around them, and as I tighten on the vise, your fingers get closer together. Watch them as I tighten this device and they move in tighter and tighter until they are completely together." (I make a twisting motion with my hands on either side of their outstretched fingers, simulating a "tightening-up" motion. See illustration at right.) As his fingers touch each other, say "Now your fingers are stuck together, so tightly that you cannot get them apart, no matter how hard you try. The harder you try, tighter they are stuck. Very*

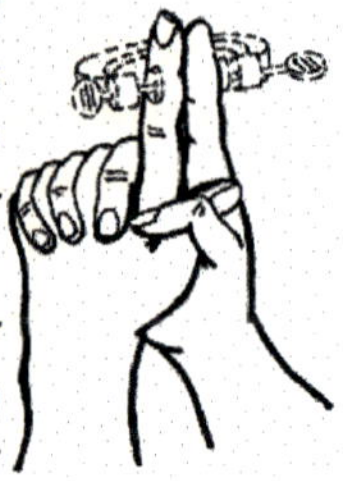

good. But when I touch them, you see how easily they get apart." (Lightly touch his fingers with your own. The fingers will come apart. Client often looks amazed and puzzled at this.) "Was there really a vise? Of course not. Again, your robot body obeyed the orders your mind gave it, just like it did with the book and balloon."

This is always a surprising demonstration for the client. As they successfully participate here, their belief in their own ability to be hypnotized is profoundly deepened.

Occasionally you will have a client who resists following these suggestions. He may look up at you and spread his fingers wide open, just the opposite of what you are telling him. Remember the discussion in the previous chapter on the resistant client. When this happens, you simply refer back to the numerous times he followed your suggestions and to your previous explanation of stage hypnosis. You say:

"See? Even though you 'saw' the book and the balloon, and you 'saw' the lemon, you chose not to accept the suggestion that your fingers were in a vise and stuck together. You just demonstrated what I've told you all along. You are always in control. The choice is always yours. I feel sure that since you've come here to stop smoking (lose weight, control stress, etc.), you will choose to accept the suggestions to stop smoking, don't you agree?" (The client will answer "yes". After all, he has come to you for help.)

NOTE: Once the client has participated in the above tests, I may or may not do further suggestibility tests. If the client is cooperative and highly suggestible, it is a good idea. He enjoys it, and it further strengthens his belief that the therapy will work. This is strictly a matter of personal choice. At this point the client is very easy to put into hypnosis. Why? Because his belief in his own ability to be hypnotized was strengthened when he "passed" the suggestibility tests; even if he did not cooperate with the vise test, his concerns about losing control are eliminated. Either way, your client will be a better subject. Immediately after the last suggestibility test, you should proceed with the induction. There are a number of inductions that you may use, but I always prefer to use the progressive relaxation method when doing therapy. Without a doubt, this type of induction is the most dependable, especially for the relatively inexperienced hypnotherapist, and it affords the least likelihood of being misunderstood by the client. In fact, if the client actually follows the steps for the relaxation of the body, the conscious mind will also be relaxed. When that happens, of course, it is easily distracted from critical assessment, and hypnosis follows easily and naturally. Additionally, I find that the client feels cheated if I do a rapid induction. They love the relaxation and the feeling they have when they leave my office. Who *doesn't* enjoy a relaxing hour of attention? Give your clients the time they are paying for and deserve.

First Session Pointers

By: Richard A. Neves, Ph.D.

As the program director for the American Institute of Hypnosis it has been my privilege to work with many degree students and beginning therapists. I have noticed that there are certain points that most beginning therapists are not clear on, which would make that first session easier and more productive.

First and foremost, keep the first session simple. Do not read anything into what the client is coming in for. Many therapists think that there has to be an underlying cause for the condition and that they must find this first before real therapy can take place. I have found that many people just need good imagery to get the results they want. Also, if you think something is there, you will have a tendency to find what you are looking for.

The second important point is to get a good concrete image to work with from the start. For instance, when you ask a person "How will your life be different when you stop smoking?" If they answer breathe easier, feel better, be healthier, you do not have a good image yet. You do not know how they would act or look if they could breathe easier, feel better, etc. So, feed this information back to them till you get a concrete image from them. That is, if you could breathe easier, feel better and were healthier, what would you do? This should lead you to a solid image, i.e., I would go running, backpack, dancing, etc. From this image you can create and add in the other ingredients.

Suggestibility Tests

In order to assess the viability of the session and the likelihood of success, the hypnotist evaluates the client's suggestibility quotient.

The Purpose of Testing Suggestibility

1) Classifying subjects: This allows the hypnotist to classify good or poor subjects.
2) Provides clues (from client's responses) for a suitable hypnotic induction. (Authoritative vs. Permissive; Literal vs. Inferential)
3) Establishes rapport (through interaction) or uncovers the lack thereof.
4) Acts as a preconditioning tool.
5) Engages the client to be a participant, not merely a passive patient.
6) Gets client used to following the hypnotherapists instructions.
7) Provides the hypnotherapist with the opportunity to uncover fears and problems.
8) By providing the client with proof that they are responsive, the hypnotherapist creates a spiral of belief and expectation for a positive outcome.
9) Makes clients feel they are assisted on in a professional manner.

How to Conduct Suggestibility Tests

The client does not need to know that you are testing and rating their suggestibility. In fact, for many people, being tested and evaluated in any way causes apprehension and stress. This is counterproductive.

Say to the client: "I would like to do a few exercises with you. They are designed to ascertain how you take in information and to help me, the therapist, tailor the treatment to your personality."

Do not tell the client exactly what you are looking for. Simply have them follow your instructions.

When conducting the tests, develop the imagery and allow time for the effect to take hold. Each test should last two to four minutes, but no longer than five minutes.

Exercise 1: Chevreul's Pendulum

This test is named after an early French hypnotist. It is a good initial test because it works with most people; it is none threatening and demonstrates the effects of thought on the body and the power of the subconscious mind. This is a test of concentration and imagination. It employs a Permissive/Inferential approach.

Equipment required: A pendulum (anything on a string will do) and the chart provided below.

Place the chart below on a flat surface. Instruct the client to hold the pendulum over the center of the chart (where the cross hair lines meet).

Say: "Just hold your hand still and allow things to happen without help or hindrance on your part. Now imagine the pendulum swinging along the line up and down (C-D). Allow your eyes to follow the line up and down while repeating in your thoughts "Up & Down".

Allow several minutes to elapse. As the pendulum starts to swing, say: "And imagine that the pendulum is swinging wider and wider". For most people the pendulum will swing with wider and wider amplitude. Now, stop the pendulum over the center and repeat the process over the A-B line. Then, over the circle in clockwise and counterclockwise motions.

If the pendulum responds as expected, it indicates the person has good imagination, concentration and willingness to follow instructions.

If pendulum is not responding, it might indicate extreme resistance. If the pendulum responds in a different way, it might indicate a "Grasshopper Mind," which may indicate that hypnosis may be counterproductive.

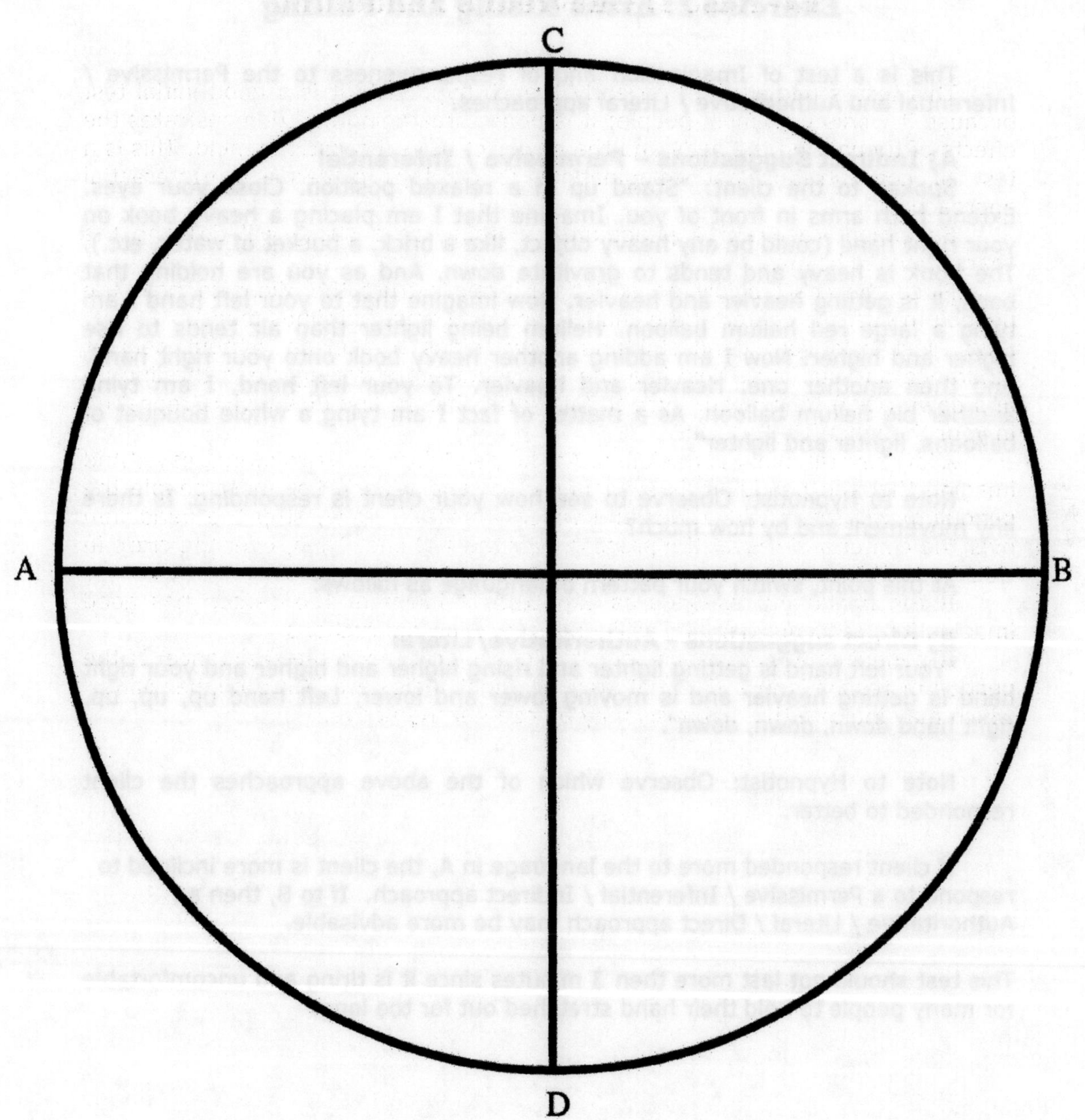

CHEVREUL'S PENDULUM EXPERIMENT

Exercise 2: Arms Rising and Falling

This is a test of Imagination and of responsiveness to the Permissive / Inferential and Authoritative / Literal approaches.

A) Indirect Suggestions – Permissive / Inferential
Spoken to the client: "Stand up in a relaxed position. Close your eyes. Extend both arms in front of you. Imagine that I am placing a heavy book on your right hand (could be any heavy object, like a brick, a bucket of water, etc.). The book is heavy and tends to gravitate down. And as you are holding that book, it is getting heavier and heavier. Now imagine that to your left hand I am tying a large red helium balloon. Helium being lighter than air tends to rise higher and higher. Now I am adding another heavy book onto your right hand. And then another one. Heavier and heavier. To your left hand, I am tying another big helium balloon. As a matter of fact I am tying a whole bouquet of balloons, lighter and lighter".

Note to Hypnotist: Observe to see how your client is responding. Is there any movement and by how much?

At this point, switch your pattern of language as follows:

B) Direct suggestions - Authoritative/Literal
"Your left hand is getting lighter and rising higher and higher and your right hand is getting heavier and is moving lower and lower. Left hand up, up, up, right hand down, down, down".

Note to Hypnotist: Observe which of the above approaches the client responded to better.

If client responded more to the language in A, the client is more inclined to respond to a Permissive / Inferential / Indirect approach. If to B, then an Authoritative / Literal / Direct approach may be more advisable.

This test should not last more then 3 minutes since it is tiring and uncomfortable for many people to hold their hand stretched out for too long.

Exercise 3: Hands Clasped

This is a test of Imagination. Authoritative/Literal

Note to Hypnotist: Before performing this test, have your client remove any rings or other objects that may interfere or cause pain.

Say to the client: "Put your hands together and interlace your fingers (clasp your hands). In a minute, I am going to count from one to five. At the count of five, you will find that your hands will be locked together, if you allow it to happen. With your imagination and your full cooperation, your hands will be actually stuck together if you allow it to happen. When I will ask you to try to pull them apart, you will find that you are unable to do so.

OK, arms stretched and locked, fix your gaze and concentrate on your knuckles. Think to yourself "My hands are locked, my hands are locked". Keep this thought in your mind and concentrate.

To the count of five: ONE, squeeze your palms tightly together, think to yourself, "My hands are locked, my hands are locked, my hands are locked." Keep that thought in your mind; fix your gaze on your hands.

TWO, imagine what it feels like when your hands are in a vise or a clamp, and the clamp is closing tighter and tighter, pushing the palms of your hands together, tighter and tighter. Just allow it to happen!

THREE, your hands are so tight you can feel the warmth in your palms. You may feel the blood pulsating through your tight fingers; you may see your knuckles getting whiter and whiter.

FOUR, you can feel the moisture between your palms; imagine your hands are glued together. Think to yourself, "My hands are locked, my hands are locked, my hands are locked." On the next count, allow it to happen.

FIVE, your hands are stuck together; if you try to pull them apart you find you are unable to. The harder you try, the tighter they become locked, try... YOU CANNOT. If your hands are locked now they will remain locked until I release you".

Observe the results. Some people will be stuck completely. To them you say: "Good, you can separate them now."

Others will be able to separate the hands with difficulty. Point out to them that they had difficulty in separating them, which indicates that they are suggestible but they also maintain their own control.

Exercise 4: Postural Sway

This is a test of Trust

This test can also be conducted to illuminate either of the following approaches.

A) Authoritative/Literal:

Have the client stand up, legs together, heels and toes together, head slightly raised. Position yourself behind the client. Extend one leg behind to brace yourself. Put your hands on the client's shoulders. Instruct the client to close eyes then say: "Imagine that your shoulders are like a bar of steel and that my hands are like powerful magnets. As soon as I move my hands back away from your shoulders, you start falling backwards. I am here to catch you". As you move, your hands backwards say: "falling... falling... falling."

Do not allow for too much falling because a person's body gains momentum and you may not be able to stop the fall.

Pay attention to these things. Did the client let go and comply easily? Did he trust that you will catch him and fell back completely? Or, did the client start to fall then quickly move his legs to break the fall? Or, was there somewhat of a bend of the upper torso without losing equilibrium?

If the client lets go and falls right into your arms, you know he trusts you and has no inhibitions of fear. If, on the other hand, the client did not let go or did so only partially, it does not necessarily mean that he does not trust you personally. It may be a fear factor that has nothing to do with you. However, it is an indication that you have to work harder on establishing that trust.

Note to Hypnotist: This test requires physical contact, so ask for permission. This test carries the risk of the client falling down. It is of paramount importance that you brace yourself and make sure that no harm comes to your client. If this test goes wrong, you have lost trust -- The most important ingredient in hypnotherapy.

B) Permissive / Inferential:

Setup is as in method A. Say to client: Imagine that you are standing on a Basketball. And the ball is starting to roll backwards. Rolling... Rolling... Rolling.

Observe the client's response. This method reveals a preference to an inferential approach.

The Eye Roll Test

Dr. Herbert Spiegel devised this test of hypnotizability. This test assumes a seven-level scale of hypnotizability.

To find your score, test the subject for eye roll-up. Rate the amount of white showing on a scale from one to four.

Then have the client squint, as if trying to look at the tip of the nose. Rate that on a scale from one to three. Now add both numbers and you have got your Hypnotizability Quotient score on a scale from one (lowest) to seven (highest). Use the diagram for guidance.

Test of Hypnotic Capacity

By: Herbert Spiegel, M.D.

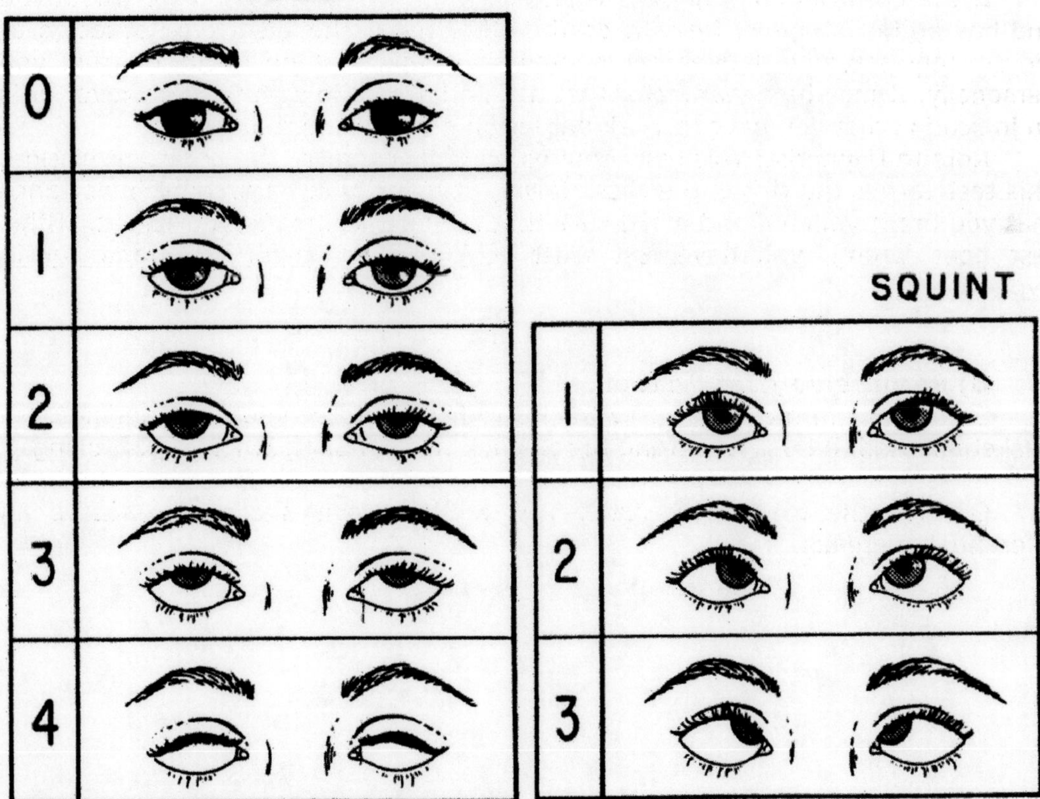

The Eye Roll Test

... Herbert Spiegel devised this test of hypnotizability. (This ...) ... scale of hypnotizability.

To find your score, test the subject for eye roll-up. Rate the amount ... showing on a scale from one to four.

Then have the client squint, as if trying to look at the top of the head ... on a scale from one to three. Now add both numbers and you have ... Hypnotizability Quotient score on a scale from one (lowest) to seven (highest). ... the diagram for guidance.

Test of Hypnotic Capacity

By Herbert Spiegel, M.D.

CHAPTER 3: INDUCING HYPNOSIS AND TESTING FOR DEPTH

Stage Two: Inducing the Hypnotic State

"The ways to induce hypnosis are countless. And while some methods take longer than others, they can all be used to produce the deep state known as somnambulism The methods of achieving the trance state are limited only by your own imagination. There is no way, in which you cannot hypnotize a person, provided you know the art of suggestion. Since eye-closure is your first goal, all you need is a device that will cause it. ***Any*** (Emphasized by Elman) device will cause it, provided you know the art of suggestion and provided the person expects to be hypnotized. This applies even to patients who have never been previously conditioned."

The reality is that people are different from each other. It stands to reason, proven in experience, that different induction techniques, produce different results with different individuals. It is also my experience that the same person may respond to the same induction in different ways at different times.

Thus, a competent hypnotist must be proficient in many induction techniques and apply them according to the situation at hand".

Dave Elman (*Findings In Hypnosis, P. 57*)

Progressive Relaxation Induction

Spoken to the client: "Close your eyes, please, and relax. Take a deep breath. That's good! Exhale now. Take another deep breath. Each time that you breathe from here on in, imagine your breath flowing out and spreading relaxation throughout your body. Feel that relaxation as I am talking to you now.

Focus your attention on your scalp. Relax your scalp. Now shift your focus to your face. Relax all the muscles around your face. Relax your forehead, your eyebrows, your eyelids and your cheeks. Even your nose. Relax your mouth, especially those muscle groups around your mouth and lips. Make sure your teeth are not clenched together. Now just relax. Relax your chin and jaw. Allow all those muscles in your face to let go. And now your neck relaxes. The front part of your neck. And the back part of your neck. Right through to your shoulders. Feel your shoulders relaxing completely. Get rid of any tension that might be in your shoulder area. It feels good to do that.

Allow your arms to relax now. Your upper arms, your elbows, your forearms. Relax your wrists. Your hands. Even your fingers relax and let go. Just imagine your arms becoming very heavy. Loose and limp. Heavy, loose, limp. Like a wet washcloth.

Now allow yourself to breathe comfortably. Notice how deep and regular your breathing has become then just a few moments ago when we started. Feel the rhythm of your breathing. Notice the contraction and expansion of your diaphragm and your chest. Allow your chest muscles to relax completely. Right down through to your stomach. Feel your stomach muscles relaxing. Get rid of any tension that might be in that area.

Now allow your back muscles to relax. Those large muscle groups in the upper part of your back. Down your spinal column and into your lower back. Just let go. Let go completely. Allow those smaller muscle groups in the lower part of your back to relax as well.

Now let your hips relax. And your buttocks relax. And especially your legs. Your thighs. Your knees. Your calves. Your ankles. Your feet. And even your toes. Just allow those muscle groups to relax completely as you begin to drift into a very deep, relaxed state. Let yourself go. Let your mind and body become one. Feeling good. Feeling so good now.

Many people sitting there as you are, report certain feelings in their body. Some report numbness in their arms or legs. Some people report a tingling feeling, such as pins and needles, usually in their hands or arms. And some report both a numbness and tingling feeling alternately...

Some people experience lightness in their body and others experience heaviness. You may experience lightness, buoyancy as though you are floating above the chair. If you experience heaviness, it may feel as though you are sinking into the chair, shoulders sagging.

When some people relax, they find they have a need to swallow because their mouth gets dry. If you have a need to swallow, it is perfectly okay to do so. Many people also find when they let go and relax totally, their eyeballs relax in their sockets and their eyelids begin to flicker or flutter ever so lightly. This is an excellent sign of letting go. Some people report experiencing some form of sensory distortion or detachment from their body. This too is a good sign of letting go and relaxing.

The important thing is that these signs represent your willingness and readiness to allow yourself to let go.

Going into hypnosis is very gradual and in a moment, I am going to count from 1 to 20. On each count, you can allow yourself to drift further into hypnosis at your own pace.

But before I do that, just imagine a custom cloud snuggling up to your body in the shape of a chair. And, imagine this chair has arms on it. It is a very warm and comfortable cloud. It is your personal cloud. Notice how it snuggles up to your body. Now, it is going to take you to a very, very beautiful place. A special place in your life. A very comfortable place. A place where you are happy. A place where you feel good. A place where you look good. So allow this custom cloud now to snuggle up to your body and to take you to your special place — where you are happy, relaxed and very calm.

Allow yourself to be there for a moment as I begin to count and you go deeper and deeper into hypnosis.

1. — deeper and deeper now. 2, — all the way down deep. 3, 4, — tired and drowsy. 5, 6, — just letting go now. 7, 8, — deeper and deeper. 9, 10,—tired, letting go now. 11, 12, — all the way down deep now. 13, 14, — deeper and

deeper. 15, 16, — just letting go now. 17, 18, — deeper and deeper. 19. And finally, 20 — deep, deep, deep hypnosis.

Your mind is now very relaxed and open to receive the helpful and beneficial suggestions I'm about to give you. You may use those suggestions that apply now and you may reject those that do not apply at this moment but which may apply at a future time".

Note to Hypnotist: At this point, the hypnotist would use suggestion to reinforce the agreements made during the session with the client, e.g., if the problem is smoking, the language in the smoking agreement would be repeated and emphasized at this time (i.e., the programming).

Deepening Techniques

To assist the client in reaching a more profound hypnotic state, following the initial induction, we utilize what is known as "Deepening Techniques". It should be noted that the concept of "Deepening" is an abstract metaphor. It's a figure of speech since it is not known what is exactly happening to the hypnotee.

Following are a few techniques that can be combined to fit a specific client.

1) Rocking: (Requires that client be standing or sitting upright.) Gently put your hand on the client's shoulder and, with small motions, rock him from side to side. Say, "The more I rock you, the deeper you go, deeper and deeper into drowsy relaxation. Deeper and deeper into a wonderful hypnotic rest, further and further into your inner self. Just rocking back and forth (or side to side), going deeper and deeper into drowsy relaxation".

2) The Countdown:
"In a moment I'm going to count from I0 to 1. On each count allow yourself to drift deeper into hypnosis.
10 - Deeper and deeper now. 9 - All the way down deep. 8 - Tired and drowsy. 7 - Just letting go now. 6 - Deeper and deeper. 5 - All the way down deep now. 4 - Deeper and deeper. 3 - Just letting go now. 2 – Feeling so good. And finally One - deep, deep, deep hypnosis".

3) The Elevator:
You say: "Imagine yourself in an elevator. The elevator is now on the 20th floor and slowly going down. Imagine yourself looking at the numbers going down from 20 to 1. With each number going down, you are going deeper into hypnosis. Here it goes, twenty... lower and lower – deeper and deeper... nineteen... etc".

4) The Escalator:
"Imagine yourself standing on top of a long escalator. As you are riding this escalator down, you are going deeper and deeper into a nice comfortable and safe hypnotic state".

5) The Staircase:
"Imagine yourself standing at the top of a beautiful staircase with a sturdy handrail and a plush carpet of your favorite color. As you start walking down the stair, each step down takes you deeper into hypnosis".

6) Silence:
"I will keep silent for a moment allowing you to drift and deepen your own state. Deeper and deeper etc."

7) Client Counts Down:
In a moment you will start counting backwards from 100. After every number you will say: "Deeper relaxed." Like this: 100 - deeper relaxed... 99 - deeper relaxed... and so on. With each count, double your mental relaxation. Soon your mind will be so relaxed; you will relax all the numbers out of your mind. You will allow your mind to relax so deeply that the numbers will just fade away. If you understand me, nod your head... good. Start counting now... That's right... Good... Let them fade... Push them out of your mind... Are they all gone? ...

Feels good doesn't it?... Good, go deeper now." (If client counts more than ten numbers say, "That's good enough; stop counting and relax deeper.")

8) The Arm Drop:

"Now, I want to see just how relaxed you are. I'm going to pick up your right hand and just let it drop down. As I take your right hand and lift it, allow it to dangle freely, just like a piece of overcooked spaghetti; totally and completely relaxed. As I drop your hand into your lap, you go deeper into relaxation and deeper into comfort. Twice as deep. Or could it be three times as deep? Perhaps it's really ten times as deep". Drop the client's arm into his/her lap and watch for signs of tension/ relaxation.

9) Fractionation: (The YO-YO effect)

Hypnotizing and alternately rousing a person a few times causes a compounding of the hypnotic state.

"Now, we are going to have an agreement. From now on when I say 'Sleep Now' and snap my fingers, you will immediately close your eyes and allow yourself to, instantly and effortlessly go into a deeper hypnotic state. Not because I say so but because you want the experience and because it is the wonderful nature of your inner creative mind to achieve a profound state of mind relaxation. Each time I say 'sleep now' (snap fingers) you will find yourself going deeper than before, easily and effortlessly. I am going to count now from one to three. Keep your eyes closed until I say 'three.' At the count of three you will open your eyes and emerge from hypnosis. One... Two... Three... open, GOOD. Sleep now!" (Snap fingers.) Repeat rhythmically until client is deep in hypnosis. Test by pausing between the count of two and three [One... Two... (pause.) Three]. If client opens eyes after the count of two, you need to deepen the hypnotic state. If he does not open eyes until the count of three, it is a good sign of being in hypnosis.

10) Association:

Tie the hypnotic state to an ongoing natural occurrence.
Example: tie breathing to hypnosis.

"Take a nice deep breath. From now on, in this session, every breath you take will cause you to go deeper and deeper."

If intruding sounds occur like a plane or fire truck passing by, you may say: "Allow any noise you may hear to lead you deeper and deeper."

Hypnotic Depth Tests

Now that you have your subject in the hypnotic state you want to assess and quantify the depth of trance. Assessment of depth of trance serves two purposes.

First and foremost, if you work with clients who want to undergo a medical procedure without chemical anesthesia, it is vital to find out if the client is indeed capable of reaching the necessary depth of hypnosis where total hypnotic anesthesia is possible.

Secondly, by performing these tests successfully, the clients get proof of the efficacy of hypnosis.

For people who are new to the experience, there is almost always the question: "Was I in hypnosis? I am not sure".

By providing proof through these tests the client is more likely to accept and follow through with the therapeutic suggestions.

The scoring system is by no means standardized. A few researchers have developed grading systems (See Appendix.)

The one that is explained in this manual is the Arons system.

Arons' 6 Level Depth Tests

Harry Arons was an active hypnotist who researched, tested and refined a systemic approach to analyzing and categorizing hypnotic states.

Following are six tests that progress from easy to difficult and provide an assessment of the corresponding hypnotic depth.

Test	Category	Application
1. Eye Catalepsy	Hypnoidal	Smoke, weight
2. Arm Catalepsy	Catalepsy	Behavior modification
3. Selective Amnesia	Full Body Catalepsy	Psychotherapy, Stage show
4. Analgesia	Total Amnesia	Dental work
5. Positive Hallucination	Somnambulism/Anesthesia	Childbirth
6. Negative Hallucination	Profound Somnambulism	Surgery

Note:
Analgesia – Sensation of pressure but no pain.
Anesthesia – Numbness with no sensation of pain.
Partial Amnesia – Remembering but not able to articulate.
Total Amnesia – No Memory at all.

The distribution of depth level in the population is roughly:
20% of population capable of reaching stages 1&2
60% of population capable of reaching stages 3&4
20% of population capable of reaching stages 5&6

Hilgard's Distribution of Hypnotizability Table

Dr. Ernest Hilgard of Stanford University conducted experiments to figure out what percent of the population is hypnotizable and to what level of depth. The following chart depicts his findings distributed on 12 levels of depth.

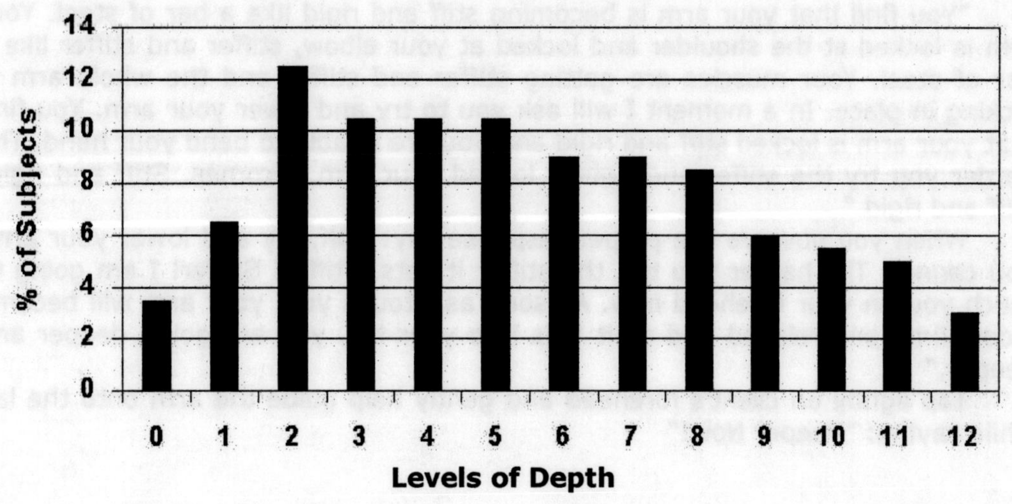

How to Conduct the Depth Tests

These tests will give the hypnotherapist an indication of the level of the hypnotic state.

We proceed from a light stage to deeper stages in progression. When client passes one stage, you can proceed to the next. However, when the client fails to pass a test, you stop administering the tests and proceed with the session. The client is classified by the last test passed. If a client fails on stage four, he is considered a level three subject.

1. Eye Catalepsy (temporary paralysis):

Say to the client: "Place you attention on your eyelids. I suggest that you relax all the muscles in and around your eyelids so much that they will simply not work.

You will find that unless you chose to remove that relaxation, your eyes remain closed shut as if they are glued together. When I ask you to, you will try to open your eyes, but you find that your eyes are closed shut tight. The harder you try to open them, the tighter they close shut. Go ahead try to open them. You find that you are unable to open them. The harder you try, the tighter they are shut. OK, stop trying and allow the kind of relaxation you experience in your eyelids, to flow like a wave down to the rest of your body and allow yourself to go deeper and deeper."

2. Arm Catalepsy:

"I am going to take your arm now and place it like so..." (Lift client's arm and extend it in front as if pointing straight forward.)

"You find that your arm is becoming stiff and rigid like a bar of steel. Your arm is locked at the shoulder and locked at your elbow, stiffer and stiffer like a bar of steel. Your muscles are getting stiffer and stiffer and the whole arm is locking in place. In a moment I will ask you to try and lower your arm. You find that your arm is locked stiff and rigid and you are unable to bend your hand. The harder you try the stiffer and tighter locked your arm becomes. Stiff and rigid, stiff and rigid."

When you observe the proper response say: "OK, try and lower your arm. You cannot! The harder you try, the stiffer it gets. Stiffer! Stiffer! I am going to touch you on your forehead now. As soon as I touch you, your arm will become loose, limp and relaxed and as it falls into your lap, you are going deeper and deeper."

Tap lightly on client's forehead and gently help guide the arm onto the lap while saying: "Deeper Now!"

3. Partial Amnesia:

In this stage we start with a deepening process that also serves as a segue to the test.

"I will show you now how you can deepen your hypnosis by yourself. In a moment I will ask you to count, SLOWLY, from 10 to 1."

In between counts say: "Deeper and deeper, more and more relaxed. With every number that you count down you are deepening your own state. Do you understand? OK, start counting slowly now. That's right. In a minute, I will ask you to count again. But this time you can manage numbers only in this way: 1,2,3,4,5,-,7,8,9,10. There is nothing between 5 and 7. 10,9,8,7,-,5,4,3,2,1. Nothing between 7 and 5. Now please count for me out loud from one to ten."

You may use an alternative way of inducing the number block as follows: "Can you imagine the number 6 written on your forehead? Of course you can. Now I want you to imagine that your index finger is an eraser and reach up and temporarily erase that number. Good. Erase it completely and until we bring it back, it is completely gone. It does not exist. Good, now count for me out loud please from 1 to 10."

If client executed this test successfully, you can move on to the next test only after suggesting that the client regains memory and returns to normalcy.

If the client counts without leaving out the number six say:
"That's right. As you can see you are in control. Now close your eyes and go deeper than before."

At this point, quit testing and proceed with your session.

4. Glove Analgesia:

"I am going to take your hand and hold it. Allow all feelings and sensations to leave your hand. From the wrist to the finger, allow all feelings of discomfort to disappear. (Rub lightly the top-side of the hand from the wrist to the finger.) Your hand is getting numb. All feelings are leaving. Now you will know that I am working here in this area but nothing is bothering you at all."

Pinch the skin on top of the hand with your nails while saying:

"Nothing, nothing at all." After you are done ask: "Did you feel anything? Yes? Pressure but no discomfort, right?" (The resulting nail marks on the skin will persuade even the skeptics.)

"Now, allow all sensation to return to your hand, back to normal and as your hand drops into your lap, allow yourself to go deeper and deeper."

5. Positive Hallucination:

In a moment I will count from one to three. At the count of three I will ask you to open your eyes but remain in hypnosis. You will open your eyes remaining in hypnosis and look at the wall in front of you. On the wall you will notice a nice picture. I will ask you to describe the picture and you will be able to describe it in detail. Now remaining in hypnosis one, two, three open your eyes, look at the picture. Please tell me what you see? (Allow for some time for the hallucination to develop.) Good close your eyes and go deeper and deeper.

6. Negative Hallucination:

In a moment I am going to count from one to three. At the count of three I will ask you to open your eyes but remain in hypnosis. I will then ask you to take some notes, but you will find that you are unable to see your pen. As a matter of fact you might even accuse me of hiding it from you. You are unable to see your pen. Remaining in hypnosis one, two, three open your eyes. Feels good, doesn't it? I would like to write some notes of your experience for your records."

If the client cannot find the pen, he is experiencing negative hallucination. Instruct the client to return to normalcy, i.e. being able to see the pen, and then proceed with the session.

Emerging From the Hypnotic State

The emerging process is fairly simple. You can simply say: "Open your eyes and emerge from hypnosis." You may empower the clients to emerge at their convenience by saying: When you are ready, emerge yourself from hypnosis and open your eyes. If time is limited you may say: In a minute you will open your eyes and emerge from hypnosis.

Even if you say nothing and simply leave the room, most people will emerge spontaneously in a short time.

Two considerations make the emerging process important and useful.

1. Emerging from hypnosis is akin to waking a person from deep sleep. We want to emerge people in a gentle and pleasant way so they feel good about the experience.
2. The emerging process is a wonderful opportunity to repeat and reinforce the suggestions and ratify the goals of the session. Thus, skilled hypnotherapists view the emerging process as an integral part of the session and utilize it to enhance the effectiveness of hypnosis.

A typical emerging script may go something like this:
"I am going to count from one to five. At the count of five you will open your eyes, and emerge from hypnosis, fully aware and feeling wonderful in every way.

One... Your subconscious mind will continue to process the experience until it is completely processed and fully integrated in wake time and sleep time. You may have some interesting dreams. Dreams of integration. I don't know what else may happen, but good things will definitely happen because you are not the same person you were when you walked in here. You will remember all that is beneficial to you now and retain the rest for future use.

Two... (Suggestion relative to client's issue)
You will hardly ever think about smoking. In the occasion that you do, you will think about how much better off you are, and how much better you feel, now that you have quit smoking.

Three... Your mind is clearing, feeling relaxed, confident and at peace. You will remember what you chose and need to remember now, and may recall in the future the things that are pertinent to you. In your future sessions with me you will enter the hypnotic state much easier, much quicker and much deeper.

Three... (Deliberately repeat **three.** Confusion facilitates the distraction of the conscious mind and enhances the communicating with the subconscious.)
You are becoming an inspiration to everyone you know. You can't wait to tell them what an amazing experience you had with hypnosis.

Four... Take a deep breath. You may feel as if you can smile on the inside and out. In the next few days, notice the changes that are taking place. (For first time clients, create time distortion by adding): It's amazing what just a few of short minutes in hypnosis can do.

Five... Eyes open and clear... Fully alert... Full awareness... feeling refreshed, relaxed and so good.

Immediately after client opens eyes make the following comment: "You did outstanding. You have an excellent mind. You kind of surprised yourself didn't you? Looks like you needed that." *(Clients need encouraging feedback)*

For first-time clients only you ask: "Off the top of your head, how long do think you were in hypnosis?" Most clients will estimate a much shorter time then in reality.

Your covert suggestion "It's amazing what just a few of short minutes in hypnosis can do" helps in inducing time distortion. It provides proof to the client that indeed they were in hypnosis and lost track of time.

CHAPTER 4: THE LANGUAGE OF THE SUBCONSCIOUS MIND & THE PSYCHOLOGY OF SUGGESTION

Following are a few definitions of suggestion:

A **suggestion** is any single thought, series of thoughts, ideas, words, beliefs or actions given in any manner. Direct, indirect, conscious, subconscious or unconscious, that changes or alters a person's normal behavior pattern.

A **suggestion** is any psychological process that produces a physiological result.

A **suggestion** is any process whereby a person accepts a command, a plea, a proposition, a thought, idea, belief or any direction, to be acted upon in the absence of any critical or reflective thoughts, which would normally occur.

A **suggestion** is any process whereby one person, or a group, may have a subtle or direct influence on another's behavior in any state, whether it is the conscious wake state or the subconscious hypnotic state.

A **suggestion** is any sensory input (External or Internal).

Suggestion-To-Outcome Chain Reaction:

A suggestion goes first through the filters of our beliefs to produce a certain feeling. Feeling affects Attitude, which is manifested in a certain Behavior.
Behavior results in a specific Outcome.

Outcome in turn serves as a Feedback of reinforcement to either Encourage or Diminish the effect of the original suggestion.

There is a tendency to view this chain as a rigid structure. However every segment in the chain can be intervened and altered in order to achieve a different outcome. The key is Flexibility.

An encouraging suggestion can be tailored to a person to produce a predictable feeling that will result in leading him/her down the chain toward the predictable desired outcome.

A person's feelings (emotional response) about a suggestion can be altered.
Attitude about feelings can be altered, changing the outcome.
And, even a certain behavior can be altered to affect a different outcome.
Achieving a desired outcome serves as positive reinforcement.
Achieving an undesired outcome serves as negative reinforcement.

Covert Hypnosis - The Language of the Subconscious Mind

In a therapeutic setting we thrive to achieve the client's goals with minimal difficulties. Alas, change is difficult and resistance, conscious or subconscious, is a natural reaction. By using the following language patterns we are able to bypass conscious resistance and communicate with the subconscious mind.

A Direct Suggestion is like a command. It tends to be evaluated by the conscious mind and may be rejected at the outset.

An Indirect Suggestion appeals more to the subconscious mind and is not evaluated as much by the conscious mind, thus it meets with less resistance.

In about 1200 BC, the army of Greece penetrated the fortified city of Troy by allowing the Trojans to capture and bring into the city a giant wooden horse. The horse contained hidden inside an elite unit of soldiers. These soldiers waited for an opportune moment to sneak out and execute their mission. This is now known as the "Trojan Horse."

In a similar manner, certain language patterns can bypass the critical/analytical defenses of the conscious mind, and deliver a payload of suggestions to the subconscious mind.

"Quotes": Is a pattern that allows the speaker to deliver a message to the listener in a way that is beautifully indirect, as the listener consciously believes that the quote is being attributed to another person, he cannot hold the speaker responsible, thus, cannot resist the suggestions.

- "Over the years my students have often told me: "*Quotes are a simple, fun and effective way to deliver a message to your listener!"*
- "I said to myself..."
- "I overheard..."
- "I was reading this article the other day and it said..."
- "I saw this interview on TV and they said..."
- "My friend always says..."

Quotes also soften and deflect a confrontational accusation.

- "He said that you lied about your whereabouts."

Shifting the responsibility and the blame.

Metaphors and Analogies: Stories or "teaching tales."

Suggesting new possible solutions metaphorically. Metaphors are powerful tools to bypass the critical faculties of the mind so as to induce subconscious learning. Metaphors were used extensively by Milton Erickson and are the hallmark of his style of therapy.

"That reminds me of a story. I recently learned that a lobster has to molt his shell in order to grow. And until his new shell is formed and hardens, the lobster is totally vulnerable. Yet it takes this risk of losing its life in order to grow."

The "What IF" Frame:

Float a trial balloon without risking rejection:

- "What if I told you …?"
- "If I were to ask you…?"
- "If you were to…?"

Playing the "What IF" game bypasses initial resistance by creating a non-threatening environment. Nothing is happening now and no action need be taken. It allows one to consider the issue without the pressure of commitment.

The "Because Frame" The word "because" has an almost magical persuasive effect on people. It lends emotional credibility to whatever goes before it. Robert Cialdini's research found that people respond to a request that uses "because" without actually analyzing it.

- "You can *use this pattern and have a tremendous effect,* because people love to hear reasons for things."
- "Because that means that…"
- "You may find that *it is easy to learn to use this pattern* because the word "because" is so powerful, it almost doesn't matter what you say afterwards."

As a strong closing, add a "because" on the end of a double bind.

- "I don't know if you'll want to *stop smoking now* or if you'll want to *stop in a day or two*, because this important development is between you and your own unconscious mind."

It further strengthens a "because" if you can successfully relate it to the person's values, i.e., have a reason that really is important to them.
As an example, if you know that the person you are dealing with places a high value on freedom, you could say something like:

- ". . . because it's your freedom that's really on the line. The freedom to live a long and healthy life, etc."

Directing attention: (We move in the direction of our most dominant thought).

A) Authoritative:

- "Stop! And feel it now!"
- "Stop and think about this".

B) Permissive:

- "Have you ever stopped to think about…?"
- "I invite you to notice..."
- "Did you ever stop to think about the difference between A & B?" (Where A & B are the same or very close and gets them to think in the desired direction.)
- "The difference between being a nonsmoker now or next month".
- "You may find yourself ..." (One finds oneself in a situation not on one's own volition. It just happens – can't resist.)
- "You may find yourself disliking chocolate".

- "You really shouldn't do it now," (Implies it will happen later.)
- "I wonder if you can imagine".
- "I wonder if you can remember a time when...and where in your body you could feel it and where was it moving".

"Embedded Commands": are commands that are interspersed within the framework of a larger sentence structure, thereby sneaking by the conscious mind.

- "Very often, people find that they *discover many useful inner resources* while in trance."
- "Maybe you'll *go into hypnosis sooner then you think."*
- "I don't know if you will *go into hypnosis before the count of five*".
- "A person may not know when exactly you *go into hypnosis".*
- "Maybe you are not *ready for hypnosis now*."

*Note: Words above in italics are to be said while creating a shift in your tonality and/or body language. This is referred to as "Analogue Marking" in NLP (Neuro-Linguistic-Programming) parlance. An "Embedded Command" can be marked out in a variety of ways. A louder voice, a softer voice, a change of vocal timbre, pausing just before the particular phrase, a hand gesture, a shift of eye focus onto the subject, adding a person's name, etc.

Adding person's name: These commands can be made more powerful if you insert their name into the sentence structure just before the embedded command.

- "One can, *Elizabeth, feel comfortable in new situations."*
- "A person could, *Phillip, notice a growing sense of distance from ones problems."*
- "People don't have to, *Bob, listen intently* to everything that I say."

"Now": used effectively can enhance an embedded command, Often the most effective way to use it is to... *pause* before you use it and then use your trance tonality when you say it. (If you run it into the sentence without this pause it can make the sentence sound too imperative and the individual feel rushed.)

- "You might want to *learn to enjoy that meaningful pause...Now."*

"Embedded Questions": Is the same thing only different. They often are really statements but are responded to as a question.

- "I'm curious as to how *you will be able to use embedded questions in your life."*

Notice the implied question in the sentence openings:

- I'm wondering if...
- I'm curious as to...

Suggestions Orienting Towards the Future:

Erickson believed that the past does not equal the future. Therefore he would orient his clients toward the future and towards solutions, believing that doing so would draw them towards those new possibilities. Get your client to indirectly visualize or otherwise imagine the future. You can do this via most of these patterns. The following openings are useful:

- "You may not know yet that you are in a trance ...
- "What happens when you...
- "How would it feel if you...
- "Can you imagine...
- "You probably already know...
- "What would happen if...

You could even join a few together, as in the following:

- "You may not know that *you'll really enjoy the feeling of control* that comes when you quit smoking, but can you *imagine* what you would do at the office tomorrow as a nonsmoker?"

The "Resistance Dodge": After an Embedded Command add the tag, "or not." This implies having the option to consider other possibilities.

- "I'm wondering if a contrarian will *accept this embedded command,* or not."

Time your delivery to when you see the resistance begin to show in their physical affect. You'll be pacing them and dispelling resistance at the same time.

The "Resistance Pace": The word "try" has failure virtually presupposed.

- "Gee Dad, I tried." Trying is Lying. Telling a person to try to resist your request implies that they may try but fail.
- "Try to resist the deepening experience of comfort and relaxation as you listen to my voice."
- "You may Try to keep your eyes open as you are drifting deeper and deeper."

"Tag Questions": are similar to the resistance dodge but different. Rather than dodging resistance, you are simply endeavoring to get agreement, are you not?

- "They can soften a statement into a question, can't they?"
- "Many people enjoy changing the time frame from present to the past, or past to future, etc., haven't they? Now?" (Notice the time shifts.)
- "They can be very useful, or they can be overdone and obnoxious, can they not?"
- "Won't you? Couldn't you? Right?"

"Negative Commands": The "**Law of Negation**" says that the brain doesn't compute negations. If you say to someone, "Don't think of the color red" what do you suppose they begin to think about? What color are you thinking about now?

A. Utilize the Law of Negation as a Trojan Horse to bypass resistance.

- "Do not *use these language patterns* too soon to empower yourself."
- "You do not have to *go into a trance* now."
- "You will not *Take action now,* until your unconscious is ready."

B. "I wouldn't tell you... because" = "*I wouldn't tell you* to *play with these patterns everyday,* because that might be dangerous to your limitations."

C. "I could tell you that... but..." = "I could tell you that *learning these patterns* will be fun and far easier than you probably imagine, but I would rather let you *enjoy that discovery* yourself."

D. Negative Tag Questions: "You cannot stop smoking, can you?" (Sure I can!)

"Pacing and Leading" Linkage:

The general concept of pacing and leading is central to Erickson's work. In this case, you comment on a true agreeable fact (pacing), then connect it with a suggestion (leading.) Salesmen might say that you are setting up a "yes" frame. People will tend to go with the flow of affirmative responses.

A. Basic form: "You can feel the chair, you can feel your feet on the floor, you can hear the sound of my voice and *you can drift off into a nice, comfortable trance*."

B. "Might notice...as..."

- "You might notice the sensations in your hands as you *continue to drift deeper."*
- "You might notice how good it feels to relax deeply as you *close your eyes and breathe comfortably."*
- (In many of these patterns it is always a good idea to suggest that they will enjoy whatever they're going to experience.)
- "You may notice your yawn even as you *start to get interested...* "
- "As you are sitting here listening (pace) and (link) you can understand in a whole new way (lead) because (link) you are naturally curious (pace) which (link) allows you to learn (lead) something of significance, all because (link) you are relaxed and open."

Some linking words:

And, as, even as, consequently, begin, start, proceed, while, so, when, if, since, you can also, like, at the same time, such as, begin to, meanwhile, continue, as you know, also, then.

"Truism Statement": that is true on the surface and contains embedded commands beneath.

A) About Time:

- "People, sooner or later, do *experience a delightful feeling of relief from their cares and woes."*
- "Sometimes, you can *enjoy a deep and meaningful trance experience."*
- "Sooner or later, *your eyes are closing."*
- "Your backache (or other symptom) can now leave as soon as your system is ready for it to leave."
- "Sooner or later, as soon as..."

B) About Sensations:

- "Most people *enjoy the feeling of a nice deep trance.*"
- "Most people *can experience one hand as being lighter than another*."
- "Most people *enjoy the refreshing coolness of a light breeze*."
- "Some people blush easily when they recognize certain feelings about themselves."

C) About Abilities:

- "You don't have to *learn how to employ these skills* to feel confident."
- "You are able to *relax your hands completely.*"
- "A person is able to *hear all kinds of meanings in one sentence.*"
- "Some People. . . You may. . One might. . You could... *learn all sorts of different possibilities for truisms.*"

D) Adding the "you know" clause implies in an ambiguous way that you knew this already.

- "People can, you know, *learn rapidly and easily,* even without knowing that they're learning."

By pretending to be linguistic filler, "you know" slips under the conscious radar.

"Binds": Tying two or more unrelated events.

- "Don't (their current behavior) unless you really want (your outcome for them)."
- "Don't open your eyes unless you are really ready to see things from a new perspective."
- It is a bind because sooner or later they have to open eyes.
- "Don't close your eyes unless you are ready to go into a deep relaxing hypnotic state." Closing eyes means they go into hypnosis.
- "Don't *listen to my voice,* unless you want to learn these patterns." One cannot "Not listen".

"Double Binds": Give the illusion of choice, while either choice is in the direction you want them to go.

- "I wonder if this relaxation will last you for the next 6 hours or for the rest of the day" (Whichever they accept is good enough.)
- "Would you like to enter trance now or would you like to try to keep your eyes open for a little longer and go into it as your body relaxes further?" (Either way they will go into hypnosis.)
- "I think your unconscious mind knows more about that than your conscious mind does, and if your unconscious mind knows more about it then your conscious mind does, then you probably know more about it than you think you do." (Either way they know something.)

"Open-Ended Suggestions":

- "We all have potentials we are unaware of, and we usually don't know how they will be expressed."
- "He doesn't know what he is learning, but he is learning. And it isn't right for me to tell him, 'You learn this or you learn that!' let him learn what he wishes, in whatever order he wishes."

Embedding suggestion by covering all possibilities of responses:

- "I really don't know if your hands will *feel heavy or light,* or if they will *feel numb or tingly,* or even if they will *stay exactly as they are.* The really important thing is to *fully explore all the feelings* that develop as they do."

(This is used in the "Progressive Relaxation" induction to cover a wide range of sensations.)

- "I do not know if your hands will stick together or if come apart. If they stick, it means you are going deeper. If they come apart, it means that you can allow yourself to go deeper."
- "Soon you will find that your breathing has changed. It can be slow or quick or perhaps just a different rhythm. The really important thing is to sense fully whatever feelings develop."

"Implied directive ("If / Then" or As/Then statements):

Tying unrelated subjects.

"**If** you can hear my voice, and listen to my words, ***then*** you can go into a trance."

"**If** you uncross your legs and you unfold your hands, ***then*** you will be ready to go into a comfortable trance state."

"**If** you sit down quietly and relax you can go into a trance."

"Now, **if** you uncross your legs and place your hands comfortably on your lap, then you will really be ready to enter a trance."

"**As** that comfort deepens, your unconscious mind can relax while your conscious reviews the nature of the problem. And **as** a relevant and interesting thought reaches your conscious mind, you may consider it."

"Cause and Effect":

The more you (X), the more you (Y)

- "The more you review these patterns, the more they make sense to you."
- "The more you breathe, the more relaxed you become and the deeper you go into hypnosis."
- "The more you practice these patterns, the more proficient you will become."

"Switching the Referential Index" (The I/You Switch):

Bypassing resistance by switching reference from me to you.

- "**I** like to take a trip on a beach. **You** can smell the salt air, **you** can hear the sound of the waves as they come in and go, and **you** can really relax completely and allow yourself to drift into a deep trance."
- "Let **me** ask **yourself** (Deliberate confusion), how soon will you discover that you already are a hypnotherapist?"

This and That:

Using the word "that" creates distance and dissociation.

- "I don't know when that hand will start floating up."
- "That problem is now in your past."

Not Knowing, Not Doing:

Absolving clients of responsibility numbs the critical faculties and overcomes resistance.

- "You don't have to talk or move or make any sort of effort".
- "You don't have to listen to me carefully".
- "You don't even have to hold your eyes open".
- "People can sleep and not know they're asleep. They can dream and not remember the dream. You don't know when the eyelids will close all by themselves. You may not know just which hand will lift first".

Deal with contrarian people by using reverse psychology:

- "It's too bad you can't..."
- "You don't need to imagine...."
- "Isn't it interesting how...?"
- "You know, I don't know if you can actually think in a different way..."
- "If you could imagine ... what would it be like?"
- "It's really interesting how some people seize the opportunity when they realize they are lucky to have one, while others manage to always miss the opportunities because of procrastination and inaction.."
- "I wonder what positive things you can notice about this situation."
- "I find it fascinating".
- "Oh, that reminds me..."

Types of suggestions

Suggestions come in a variety of ways. They have influenced us every day of our lives, and have done so since the day of our birth. Below are examples of the types of suggestions that may have had a bearing on changing or altering our normal behavior patterns.

1. Direct
2. Indirect or Inferred
3. Prestige
4. Emotional
5. Environmental
6. Conditioned Reflex
7. Unconscious
8. Social
9. Auto
10. Hetero
11. Waking
12. Specific & Blanket
13. Post-Hypnotic
14. Negative
15. Positive

1. Direct Suggestions:

A direct suggestion is any verbal statement or physical action that is direct, to the point and without camouflage. Direct suggestions are given in an "authoritarian" or "persuasive" manner.

A) Everybody stand up. (authoritarian)
B) Everybody please stand up. (permissive)
C) Pass the sugar.
D) Come here.
E) Will you please finish your food?

2. Indirect Inferred Suggestions:

Indirect or inferred suggestions may not be recognized as suggestions because they may be nonverbal motions or sounds, and the subject is not aware of its influence on his normal behavior pattern.

A) Cough... and you cause others to cough.
B) Yawn... and you cause others to yawn.
C) Smile... and you cause others to smile.
D) Look up and point at tall buildings... and you cause others to look up.
E) Light up a cigarette... and you cause others to follow suit.
F) Show fear or anger... and you cause others to respond likewise.

3. Inferred Direct Suggestions:

Nonverbal motions:

A) Pointing a finger at someone then curling it suggesting they "approach."
B) Pointing a finger at someone suggesting they "leave the room."
C) Nodding your head to indicate your "approval" or "disapproval."
D) Making a fist at someone suggesting "violent action."
E) Extending your hand out to someone to suggest a hand shake.

Verbal:

A) "I wonder what the time is" - suggesting you tell the time
B) Aren't you cold? - suggesting you wear something or get inside.

4. Prestige Suggestions:

Prestige suggestions are those you accept, and act upon, as your very own, without "second thought" or contradiction because they were given by a person of prestige and authority whom you may like, trust, respect, fear or hold in high esteem.

A) Doctor
B) Lawyer
C) Teacher
D) Clergy
E) Politician
F) Hypnotist
G) Friends, Parents, Relatives
H) Authors, Editors, News Reporters
I) Speakers, Lecturers
J) High Society, High Fashion
K) Entertainers
L) Financiers

Prestige suggestions may affect your life in some way, socially, economically, politically, academically, emotionally, intellectually, physically or psychologically.

5. Environmental Suggestions:

Are those suggestions that affect your five human senses: sight, smell, hearing, taste and touch? These are also referred to as suggestions that influence a person's conduct in the wake state.

A) Music... suggests happiness, sadness, dancing, singing, romance, etc.
B) Sight or smell of food... suggests hunger or nausea.
C) Rain... suggests freshness, cleanliness, depression, coziness, etc.
D) Street noise... suggests hyperactivity or excitement.

E) Clear, sunny days with bright blue skies and comfortable temperatures make us feel happy, content and full of vitality.

F) Dismal gray day, rain, snow or fog or heavy overcast makes us feel "down in the dumps," "blue" or "sluggish."

6. Conditioned Reflex Suggestions (Anchors):

Are suggestions that cause a person to form a habit pattern, a way of life, or a lifestyle based on a continuous, constant, repetitious learning process? This learning process is reflex conditioning. It can be a conscious or a subconscious process that will influence or alter a person's behavior pattern with or without his/her awareness. Conditioned reflex suggestions affect all five of the human senses. They can be self-induced or externally induced.

A) The "Ice-Cream Man" rings his bells. You automatically want ice cream.

B) Chain smoker. Seeing anyone else light up will invoke the urge to light up.

C) Parades, mob violence, political rallies. All may stimulate your physical/emotional responses.

D) Religious ceremonies. Accept dogmas and doctrines without question.

E) Vulgarity or obscenities. Stimulate positive or negative emotions or physical responses.

F) Police, ambulance or fire truck sirens. May invoke apprehension and fear.

7. Emotional Suggestions:

Are those that raise your emotional or sensory state, thereby setting into motion any feelings, sensations or emotional responses.

A) Shouting, making verbal threats, causing state of fear or panic.

B) Antagonizing, "needling" or making "digs" causing anger, etc.

C) Gentleness, empathy, causing happiness or crying.

8. Unconscious Suggestions:

Are those comments, statements, suggestions, stimuli received by a person. Generally, neither party is consciously aware of the consequences.

Example: When walking in a crowded street you are navigating and threading your way through the crowd easily without bumping into other people. You are not consciously evaluating all the time how to avoid collisions with people coming towards you. You are cueing into subtle body language (suggestions) other people convey unconsciously, about where they are going, thus walking without incident.

9. Social Suggestions (Social Proof):

Are those suggestions designed to "lead" or "appeal" to an individual for the purpose of "conformity." Experiments in social suggestions show that people tend to "follow the crowd." Individuals, "give in" to peer pressure.

A) In politics, people tend to vote for the person who appears to be "the people's choice."

B) In the world of fashion, people "follow the trends." To be in style is to be accepted. It is a way of belonging and being "in" with a crowd by inference. Advertisers use it often: "Most doctors recommend..." "Millions of people use..."

10. Auto-Suggestions:

Is the process of giving suggestions to one's self, either in the "awake state" or any alpha, meditative or hypnotic states. Auto-suggestions can be deliberate and conscious or unconscious. They may be positive or negative.

- "Why can **I** never do this right?"
- "**I** am such a klutz".
- "**I** can do it".

11. Hetero-Suggestions:

Are those suggestions, usually given by one person to another in any manner.

- "**You** will stop smoking, right?"
- "I think **you** should lose some weight"

12. Post-Hypnotic Suggestions:

Are those suggestions that are specifically designed to be given during the hypnotic state, and then acted upon by the subject sometime in the future.

13. Pre-Hypnotic Suggestions:

Are those suggestions used generally to prime subjects in a conscious state, prior to hypnosis induction. These may be direct suggestions: "You will become very relaxed..." or indirect: "Many people find that they become very relaxed..."

14. Negative Suggestions:

Are those intentional or unintentional suggestions that produce a state of tension, stress, anxiety, fear or confusion thereby often setting up a conditioned reflex action.

We live in a negative, aggressive, violent society. We have been exposed and programmed to accept negative suggestions as a way of life, ever since the day of our birth.

A) You can't make it in this world unless you are rich.
B) What's the use, nobody cares anyway.
C) The whole world is sick. It is going to the dogs.
D) It's not what you know. It's whom you know.
E) You will never amount to anything you dummy.
F) You just can't win no matter how hard you try.

Negative suggestions that at times produce physical manifestations:

A) I get sick to my stomach every time I think about him.
B) I can't stand my job. It gives me a pain in the neck
C) I can't sleep nights because of her. She is driving me crazy.
D) I can't stand him or her. They both drive me up a wall.

Indirect Negative Words:
These expressions produce the opposite result of what they convey on the surface.
Try, I Think, Sometimes, Maybe, Hope, Never, Wish, Can't.

Example:
"I will try to remember to..." (Most likely will not remember).
"I hope I will wake up early to go jogging... (I really prefer not to).
"I will try to call sometimes" (Don't hold your breath).

15. Positive Suggestions:
Are those suggestions that produce or/and enhance self-confidence, self-esteem, inner strength, direction, purpose, happiness, calmness, peacefulness etc.
Such as: "I can" and "I will be able to."

Rules of the Mind & the Laws of Suggestion

It is said in the *Bible*: "As a man thinketh so is he..."
We move in the direction of our most dominant thought. What your mind believes, your body will create. Physically and mentally.

Every thought has a physical affect on the body (Psychosomatic).
Every thought (Psycho) strengthens or weakens the body (Soma) directly. Thus, a persistent, emotionally induced symptom has a tendency to cause permanent change in the physical body. Stress triggers the Fight or Flight response. Prolonged stress leads to illness. Relaxation exercises trigger the body's opiates and promote healing and calmness.

Thus, one should not dwell on worry thoughts but rather cultivate a positive outlook on life.

Example: The "Placebo Effect."
The pharmaceutical industry had proven in thousands of scientific experiments that people respond with profound physical changes and healing when given a sugar pill. The implicit suggestion was that they have received a medicinal drug that includes active ingredients designed to produce those results.

The Law of Concentrated Attention:

We move in the direction of our most dominant thought. As Einstein said: "Imagination is more important than knowledge." What you expect to happen, you tend to realize. The stronger the expectancy, the better the chance of the outcome being manifested. Also known as a "self-fulfilling prophesy." Whenever attention is concentrated on an idea over and over again, it spontaneously realizes itself.

"Fake It Till You Make It". Act "as if" and your subconscious mind will accept it as real and soon will act to make it so.

The Law of Dominant Effect:

- Once the inner mind accepts an idea, it remains until it is replaced by another idea. We are creatures of habit. Once a habit is established, we tend to hold on to ways of thinking and behaving.
- A strong emotion tends to replace a weaker one.

Thus to create change, invoke the desired goal with emotional intensely.

- Once a suggestion is acted upon, it is easier for the next one to be accepted. A small commitment tends to make it easier to make a larger one. Utilize the "Yes set" to get your clients to follow through on a commitment, i.e., get them to take small, easy actions towards their desired goals first.
- Opposing thoughts cause cognitive dissonance. Thus can not be held in mind simultaneously. The conscious mind processes information serially, one at a time. Utilizing this law one can push away and replace negative thoughts by consciously focusing on positive thoughts.

The Law of Reverse Effect:

The greater the effort from the conscious, the lesser the response from the subconscious.

Examples: Trying to remember a name. Trying to fall asleep. Trying to remember a date on an exam.

To achieve your goal stop the effort to enforce your will on the subconscious mind. Tell yourself: "I will remember shortly," then relax, create a diversion and allow the subconscious to handle your needs.

Utilizing this law in hypnosis:

- "The harder you try to lower your hand, the stiffer it becomes".
- "The harder you try to open your eyes, the tighter shut they become".
- "The harder you try to sabotage yourself, the less you succeed".
- "The harder you try to bite your nails the more distasteful and repulsive it becomes."

The association (the more... the more...) is created merely by your mentioning of it.

The Law of Association (Anchoring):

Whenever a person experiences one particular stimulus in the presence of another stimulus, the person will soon begin to associate and connect the two. Then when one stimulus occurs, it tends to invoke the other.

Example A: "Pavlov's Dogs". Does that ring a bell?

Pavlov, a Russian scientist, trained dogs to salivate upon hearing the sound of a bell, by simply ringing a bell every time they received food. Soon they responded with salivation to the sound of the bell in the absence of food.

Example B: Certain music tends to trigger memories and emotions that were associated with certain events or a person in your past when the same music was played.

Likewise a certain smell tends to invoke specific memories and feelings.

A certain smell of food may invoke memories of grandma's home. A perfume may remind you of an old flame.

The Law of Delayed Action (Post-Hypnotic Suggestion):

When a suggestion is given as an inference, the person will respond to that suggestion whenever a condition or situation that has been used in the original suggestion presents itself.

Utilized in hypnosis we may suggest to a client that the next time they see a cheesecake they will feel nauseated.

Or the next time the hypnotist says the words "Power to you"; the client will immediately enter a hypnotic state.

The Law of Negation:

In order for the mind to process a negative suggestion it has to first conceptualize the affirmative (positive). Observe what happens when you hear the following examples:

1) "Look around the room and ignore everything that is Red."

   Try hard as you may, you cannot NOT see Red.

2) "Try NOT to think of a pizza with all the trimmings and some extra mozzarella."

You find that you cannot avoid what you are directed to focus on. Concentrating on something you want to avoid (the negative), is like driving a car while looking in the rearview mirror instead of forward to your destination. When one practices avoidance behavior one automatically dwells on it. Being that we move in the direction of our most dominant thought we tend to enforce and perpetuate the behavior we are trying to avoid.

In order to achieve your outcome you need to think of what you want to achieve, not what you want to get away from. Think in the affirmative not negative.

Use of Negation in Hypnosis:

When creating affirmations, avoid negation. Instead of saying:

- "I don't want to eat a lot and gain weight." Say: "I am eating healthfully, in the proper amounts and shedding unwanted weight."
- Instead of: "I will NOT eat chocolate" Say: "My desire for chocolate is diminishing."
- Instead of: "I do not want bite my nails." Say: "I keep my nails clean and healthy."
- Instead of: "Don't forget..." Say: "Remember to..."

Negation can be used to achieve positive results. Use negation to bypass resistance. To weasel your way in.

- "Try not to go into hypnosis until I count to one."
- "Do not go into hypnosis faster than..."
- "Do not think about how drowsy and heavy your eyes are getting".

On the surface, it seems you are directing them not to do something. But as you call their attention and direct their focus, you cause them to respond in opposition to your directive. Which is, of course, what you wanted all along.

The Law of Compounding (or Pyramiding):

Each time a suggestion is repeated; it compounds and reinforces the previous suggestion.

Example: Your first suggestion may be: "From now on every breath you take will lead you deeper in hypnosis".

The second suggestion: "From now on every time you go into hypnosis it will be much easier, quicker and deeper than before."

The second suggestion will enhance and drive the first one deeper.

Third suggestion: "From now on whenever you come to me for a session and I say "Power Now", you will immediately enter the hypnotic state".

The third suggestion enhances and drives the second suggestion deeper, which drives the first suggestion deeper.

Managing Suggestions

It is not what happens that matters. It's how you react to it!

The quality of your life is determined by the quality of your communication with yourself and others.

Watch Your Internal Dialogue or Self Talk.

Our words not only describe our experience, they <u>form</u> our experience. We have many different types of sensations and an almost unlimited number of emotions available to us. Yet to conduct the daily business of our lives, we develop a habitual limited vocabulary.

Certain preferred words and phrases are used repeatedly for a variety of experiences and emotions, i.e., incantations, whether they are entirely appropriate or not.

By trying to fit complex experiences into a limited habitual vocabulary, we distort, delete, or generalize and literally change our experience. This process impacts our emotional intensity, or lack thereof, in almost every moment of our waking experience. Furthermore, our daily incantations are by themselves powerful biochemical triggers or anchors to the human nervous system.

For example, if a person's habitual vocabulary for a painful experience is limited to "furious" or "angry," then he or she may not critically analyze those negative sensations and may inappropriately amplify the internal experience. Worse, people amplify very mild states into strong emotional states if they say, "I hate this" when they really only dislike it.

Other people, on the other hand, may have the exact same intensity of sensation or experience, but their habitual label for it maybe "annoyed." They have immediately transformed their sensations to a level of emotional intensity much lower than that of the person who uses the word "angry" or "hate."

Positive sensations work the same way: Using the words "passion" or "jazzed" produces a much more powerful positive experience than "okay" or "all right." Developing and enhancing the scope and quality of our Transformational Vocabulary and incantations instantly expands or limits our emotional experience of life itself.

Transformational Vocabulary

Transformational Vocabulary is the technology developed by Anthony Robbins to employ habitual vocabulary — the words we consistently use — to amplify or lower the intensity of our emotional states. We can lessen the intensity of negative states and increase positive states by intentionally choosing softeners or emotionally charged words. For example, instead of "I'm pissed," you can say, "I'm tinkled." Instead of "I'm fine," you can say, "I'm fantastic!" The objective is to make your Transformational Vocabulary so outrageous or potent that it interrupts your pattern.

Here are some examples:

Defusing Negative Words/Phrases

By changing from this	to	This
angry	to	disenchanted
depressed	to	calm before action
that stinks	to	that's a little aromatic
failed	to	learning
I hate	to	I prefer
irritated	to	stimulated
overwhelmed	to	popular
rejected	to	misunderstood
lonely	to	unoccupied

Amplifying Positive Words/Phrases

comfortable	to	smashing
determined	to	unstoppable
fast	to	ballistic
fortunate	to	unbelievably blessed
great	to	phenomenal
interested	to	enthralled
enjoy	to	relish
paying attention	to	incredibly focused
smart	to	brilliant
good	to	ecstatic

The above is utilized in hypnosis to diminish a client's negative state and amplify and enhance a desired positive state.

Know what you want

Goals vs. Ideal

Ideal is the big picture, the larger than life aspiration, your "Strategy." Goals are the steps to achieve the ideal, your "Tactics."

Ideal is like the horizon. As you approach, it extends. Goals are achievable signposts on the road to the ideal.

In order to decide what your goals are, you must first know what your purpose is. A goal without a purpose is like a leaf without a tree. In time, it will wither and die. A viable goal draws its strength from the overall purpose.

Key to your success: **You can do it, if you know why!** If your "**Why" (reason/purpose)** is strong enough, you will find the "**How"** (the means).

Crystallize your outcome. To uncover the true end goal, the ideal, ask yourself:

"What will that give me?" When you get an answer, apply the above question to that answer.

What will **that** give you? Then ask again and again until you uncover your ultimate goal. For example: your answer may be "I want money."

- "Why?"
- "So I can buy a car"
- "Why?"
- "So I can visit my girlfriend"
- "Why?"
- "Because I love her and want to spend more time with her."

So your real goal is to spend more time with her not the car.

Can you achieve this goal in another way? Maybe by marrying her?

The Driving Forces at Play in Effective Goal Achievement

The five necessary ingredients for achieving a successful outcome:

Desire/ Motivation: You have a genuine burning desire to achieve your goal, not just a wish. You must pursue it single-mindedly.

Faith/Belief: You believe it is possible to achieve.

Expectation: You know you deserve it and you expect to get it. Just like you expect to come home when you get out of work.

Imagination: You can imagine yourself having achieved your desired outcome. Whenever you hear someone say, "I can't see myself..." you know they don't stand a chance of achieving their stated goal. Imagination is used to lay a plan of action.

Commitment/Determination to Action: You are willing to do whatever it takes and you'll do it now. No excuses.

Achieving your goals can be achieved by programming yourself with a new set of suggestions/affirmations.

The most productive way is to assimilate these suggestions is to apply them in the hypnotic state.

How to Formulate Suggestions / Affirmations

Why do affirmations work?

The subconscious mind does not differentiate between a real experience and one that is vividly imagined. The subconscious mind accepts images as virtually real. When reality and virtual reality (created by your affirmations) are at odds, tension is created. In an effort to resolve that tension and regain equilibrium, the subconscious mind then seeks out ways to lead you to act in a way that will turn the virtual into reality and thus resolving the conflict.

For example, if at present you are not exercising at all, your affirmation may be: "Every day, at 7am, I ride my stationary bike for 5 minutes and it feels great." The conflict between your current reality and your installed affirmation causes an uncomfortable discontent and tension. Your mind strives to resolve this conflict by driving you to exercise. The subconscious mind executes the programming faithfully and without question like a computer loads up a program. Be careful what you affirm to yourself. The mind also executes programs that have a negative and destructive affect (like smoking), just like a computer executes a virus program even though that program may be self-destructing.

Rules for writing your affirmations

Do it with S.M.A.R.T.I.P.P.P.S.

S- Specific and Simply stated. Communicate with the subconscious on a second-grade level.
M- Measurable. Measure from where you are. Set signposts on your road to achieving your goal. You want noticeable progress.
A- Acceptable. Buying into the concept and taking responsibility.
R- Realistic and Achievable. Aim for the stars but shoot for the moon. Don't be afraid to dream big. Know your limitations. How do you know the difference? See the Serenity Prayer.
T- Time bound. Set specific time table for reaching each signpost (measurable). ***A goal without a time frame is nothing but a wish.***
I- Start with "I." Self-referenced. It must be about you and under your control, not someone else's' (Wrong="I want everyone to love me...")
P- Process. Use active verbs. Words ending with "ing." I am becoming... I am increasing/diminishing... (Passive="I want to." Active= "I am doing.")
P- Positive. State it in the positive only. What you want to achieve, not what you want to avoid.
P- Present. State it in present tense. Fake it till you make it.
S- Single-issue, one at a time. Trying to change your whole life in one session is a guarantee for failure.

Have emotional words attached. (I am **happily and proudly** giving a speech to my peers and it makes me **feel great!)**

Keep in mind that Change is Strange. It takes time to make it a comfortable habit.

Changing a way of thinking or behaving feels awkward and uncomfortable at the beginning. However with persistence and practice a new habit is formed, i.e., it becomes comfortable and easy.

Follow this demo exercise:

Clasp your hand. Notice which thumb is on top. Unclasp and re-clasp your hand quickly. You may notice that it is fairly easy to do.

Now clasp your hands with the fingers interlaced the other way (the other thumb on top.) Repeat a few times as fast as you can.

Notice that in the new position you are slower and uncomfortable. However if you persist it will become a habit and it will be as easy and comfortable as the old way.

How to Make It Stick

Now that you have set your goal you need to keep your focus on the target and keep the vision alive. Here is what to do.

1) Spaced Repetition:
Use the power of repetition. Practice Self-Hypnosis a few times a day (at least morning and evening. It is commonly accepted that repeating an action for 30 days forms a habit.

2) Usage of Imagination:
a) Disassociation: Imagine seeing yourself on a movie screen having achieved your outcome. Watch the movie with the happy ending.
b) Associated: Imagine yourself in the future having achieved your outcome. Engage all your senses. Invoke all the emotions you can master. Strong emotions are the most powerful behavior modifiers and are habit-forming. By being totally associated, you enlist the power of emotion to imprint a desired change on the subconscious mind.

3) Let Everyone Know:
Making a public commitment is your insurance policy by creating social pressure to succeed. Tell your family, friends and coworkers about your plan. Now you have your pride and ego to protect. Your need to appear congruent will ensure you take the proper actions.

4) Reward yourself:
Upon achieving each step, celebrate and treat yourself to some fun activity or a gift. Take some time off, get a massage or take yourself out to dinner and a show. When you have accomplished your goal in full, reward yourself in a big way. It is very beneficial to have in mind what kind of a treat you have for yourself so you have something to look forward to. Prepare a list of rewards.

5) Create Positive Associations (Anchors*):
Link achieving your goal with empowering feelings of pride, satisfaction, strengths, happiness, etc. You will be able to draw on these resources to help you achieve the next goal. "Anchoring" is the process of associating and fixing a specific state of mind to a specific physical sensation or action.

* *An **anchor** is an association between external stimuli (something you see, hear, feel, taste or smell) and an internal emotional/mental state. Anchors occur spontaneously, and also may be artificially induced.*

CHAPTER 5: SELF HYPNOSIS

Self-hypnosis is a simple yet very powerful technique to implement changes and achieve goals. It is a vehicle used to communicate with the subconscious mind for the purpose of delivering suggestions.

How to Do Self-Hypnosis

Self-Hypnosis in four phases:

1) Preparation.
2) Reaching the Alpha State. The hypnotic state.
3) Installing suggestions.
4) Awakening.

Phase 1) Preparation:

Define your goal in detail then formulate suggestions/affirmations in one or two sentences. Write those on a card.
(See the chapter: "How to Formulate Suggestions/Affirmation")

Phase 2) Reaching the Hypnotic State:

(Also may be referred to as: Alpha state, Altered state or Trance state.)
Sit comfortably in a quiet and private place. Make sure you are uninterrupted. (Do not lie down as you may fall asleep.)

Read the card and keep the affirmations in your mind.
Imagine yourself being in a beautiful, serene and perfect place. (Some people imagine a secluded beach. Some imagine a mountain view, a waterfall or a quiet place at home, etc.)

Take a deep breath, hold a few seconds and exhale. As you exhale count down from three to one (3, 2, 1) and think to yourself, "Relax."
To deepen your hypnotic state, take five slow deep breaths (count on your fingers as you inhale.) Each time, as you exhale, say to yourself: "Deeper and deeper, more and more relaxed."

Phase 3) Installing suggestion by repeating affirmation:

While you are in the hypnotic state repeat to yourself your prepared affirmation, for three minutes. Do it with conviction. Engage your imagination, your senses and emotions.

You may use the following affirmation during your practice sessions.

Sample affirmations:

1) Every day, in every way, I'm getting better and better.
2) I feel calm, I feel relaxed, I feel in control.
   I am calm, I am relaxed, I am in control.
3) I love myself, I think I'm great.
   I walk tall and stand straight.

When you find that you are able to enter and maintain the hypnotic state at will, replace these examples with your own affirmations.

You may find that at the beginning, your affirmations sound untrue and incongruent and uncomfortable. However in the hypnotic state the subconscious mind will accept these affirmations as truth. Soon your subconscious mind will move you to act in a way that will make it a reality.

Phase 4) Emerging from Hypnosis:

To emerge from the hypnotic state, you simply count up from one to three and open your eyes. As you count, suggest to yourself that you will emerge fully alert, refreshed and feeling wonderful.

If you practice self-hypnosis at bedtime, you may forgo the awakening step and allow yourself to drift into sleep.

This process can be very effective in overcoming insomnia.

The Danger of Using Self-Hypnosis for Pain Control

Self-hypnosis is a very effective way to control pain. However, pain is nature's way to sound the alarm when something in our body goes wrong. Eliminating the pain without exploring the cause is akin to shutting down the alarm instead of putting out the fire. It may mask a condition that may worsen and be too late to cure.

Light Switch Self-Hypnosis Technique

By: Gerald F. Kein

This is the technique I developed over many years for teaching extremely deep somnambulistic self-hypnosis in one simple session. First make sure you have the client in somnambulism. The Elman induction is my preferred way to accomplish this.

Then say: "We can go ahead and relax you mentally and physically much more, but it really is... not that necessary." Because to learn the secrets of control over your body doesn't require that we become physical or mental zombies. It just requires that our mind is open to accept suggestions of learning... and now we're going to begin to teach you how to hypnotize yourself, beautifully.

I want you to do this... I want you to use that powerful ability to imagine what (God, nature, etc.) gave you. If you are a visual person... make a picture. Some people aren't visual, but if you are... make a picture... but if you aren't visual, you can imagine. Imagine or visualize what I'm about to describe. I'm about to describe two things to you. I want you to imagine them strongly, or picture them with great clarity, whichever is easier for you. Don't question it. Success will depend on you following these instructions. I want you to imagine or visualize yourself first standing at the top of a long staircase. It extends straight down in front of you. As you look down this staircase... decorate it, carpet it any way you want to, it's yours. As you look down the staircase you notice something very unusual about it... and that is, it never seems to end... it just goes on and on. Now that's because this is the staircase of relaxation... and we have never found an end to a person's ability to relax. And I want you now to accept this suggestion, that from this moment on when you're in this beautiful state... every gentle breath you exhale... guides you deeper... and deeper. Every breath... takes you down another step on this beautiful staircase. Every breath... takes you down... more... and more. Seal that within you.

Now this is the most important thing that you're going to learn. So I want you to imagine and seal this next suggestion within you more than anything else you've ever done in your life... because it will give you the ability... to improve your life in so many ways. I want you to first imagine or visualize your brain.

I'm going to use the word "imagine" from now on. That will mean either imagine something or visualize it if you are one of those people that can create a picture. But, rather than say imagine or visualize I'll just say imagine, it'll mean either one for you.

You imagine that coming down from the base of your brain is a fairly thick electrical cable, maybe about as thick as the pinky finger on your hand. After it comes down about an inch, I want you to imagine it goes into the top of a light switch... you know, like the light switch that operates the ceiling lamps in your bathroom or your kitchen at home. Imagine that cable coming out the bottom of that switch. The jacket, the cover of the cable opens up... and from it, flows hundreds of little bitsy tiny wires... that flow through every muscle and cell of your body from the top of your head to the tip of your toes.

In a moment I'm going to ask you to move that switch from the "on."... down... to the "off" position.

Now here's the suggestion that I need you to accept... and you must accept it...if you want be able to program yourself, powerfully, quickly and easily. When you move that light switch to the down position, you'll accept the suggestion voluntarily, without any question... block all electrical current from your brain to every muscle in your body that's not needed for continued survival. Instantly every muscle will go totally dormant... unable to move... no matter how hard you may try. Should I ask you to try to lift a hand, a finger, to open an eye or even speak... when that switch is "off", nothing works. Make that your reality... with this understanding that it is your switch. You can turn it on or you can turn it off, anytime you want to. But you must accept the suggestion that when it's "off", all the muscles of your body grow completely dormant, unable to move.

When you do that, you're going to notice something else... another benefit comes in. If there's the slightest stress or tension in you anyplace, when you move that switch "off", instantly they can no longer exist... and you'll feel yourself go many times deeper relaxed.

All right. In your mind... reach up... grab hold of that switch that you have created... and now firmly move it... down to the "off" position...shutting down every muscle, every nerve, every fiber... blocking the electric current in that switch just as if you turned a light switch "off", the lights go off... and feel your body relax much deeper. If you've accepted that suggestion, right now every muscle in your body is totally shut down unable to move, no matter how hard you may try. Because this is the most important part of your training... that you must accept this... I'm now going to find out if that is your reality.

With your light switch in the "off" position, blocking all the electrical current to every muscle in your body, try to lift your right hand. (PAUSE) Wonderful. Stop trying...and go much deeper. With that light switch completely "off". Try to lift your left hand (PAUSE). That's great. Stop trying and go deeper.

So we know the right brain and the left brain have accepted that. For the ultimate test. Know that light switch blocks that electrical current. Believe it with all your heart. Seal it within you. With that light switch in the "off" position blocking that electrical current, try to open your eyes (PAUSE).
Great, stop trying. Go much deeper relaxed. You're doing beautifully.

The secret to the technique you're going to learn, is when you move that switch to the "off" position... that you know, it's not a matter of believing, it's a matter of knowing... that you know you shut down every muscle in your body. This is a beautiful state that you're in. Right now, you have a natural anesthesia that comes in, in this beautiful level. I'm going to show you what I mean. Without any suggestions of any kind of an anesthesia whatsoever, I'm just going to be doing some general testing on you. As I work with you, just feel yourself relaxing even more. It just feels good to do it (pinch arm or jaw etc.).

I'm going to lift your right hand and drop it and when I do... this beautiful anesthesia... and the physical part of you deep inside... relaxes much more (Drop hand). That's good. (Repeat practice as necessary until client is confident in the results).

Now, I'm going to teach you how to enter this state by yourself. But before I do, between now and the next time I see you, you're going to be practicing self

-hypnosis a lot. Until now and the next time I see you, this is going to be very important. When you move your switch "off", under no circumstances... are you ever to override the suggestion that every muscle in your body is turned off.

When you're practicing you'll discover that maybe some days you get an itchy nose, or you want to move your body... you're not in total comfort for some reason... fine. But first move your light switch back "on", then scratch or move your body... then move your light switch "off". Your light switch is a tool. You are never to override, the light switch. When it's "off", you are "off". No exceptions. You must believe this, You must accept this is your switch... and your switch can be turned "on" or "off" depending on what you want it to do.

All right. Now here's how you're going to enter this state:

First I'm going to give you two safety suggestions, because each time you enter this state you're going to find you go tremendously deeper than the time before. So you're only going to practice this when you are in a safe and comfortable position... like in a chair that supports your body or lying at home in a bed or something like that. Don't do it in a straight backed chair for example. As you grow more relaxed and learn this technique, you'll just fall out of that chair, there's no support. You should be in a safe and comfortable position.

Second, you'll give yourself a time limit. You're going to tell yourself, "I'm entering self-hypnosis for..." and you're going to say a time. For practice now we're going to use 30 seconds. At home (this week, etc.) I want you to vary it, from 30 seconds to about two minutes. Mix it up a little bit. You can do it longer if you want to, but I don't want to take a lot of your day up. You'll say to yourself, "I'm going into deep self-hypnosis, right now, for 30 seconds."

Then here's how you'll enter the state. After you've told yourself the time, you'll raise and lower your right index finger. When it touches whatever it might be resting on at that time... the arm of the chair, your leg, the bed, whatever... when it touches whatever it's resting on... and this is important... not before, after it touches... you'll close your eyes... you'll go right back down into this beautiful state. You'll instantly move your light switch at the same time you close your eyes... from the "on" to the "off" position... shutting down every muscle, nerve and fiber... and go right back into this beautiful state.

Then you'll do nothing. Do not think of the time... that will foul you up all the time... just enjoy the beautiful state. Your subconscious mind keeps better time than your conscious mind ever possibly could. It'll give you a feeling, a hunch that your time is up. When you feel your time is up... you'll flip your switch "on", your eyes will open... you'll grow fully alert... feeling fantastic.

So let me review that because we're going to practice it now.

First you'll be in a safe and comfortable position... as you are here.

Second, you'll give yourself a time limit. You'll say to yourself, "I'm now going into self-hypnosis for 30 seconds."

Third, you'll raise your index finger and drop it. When it touches and not before... you'll close your eyes... move your light switch to the "off" position, shutting your body down completely... and go back to this state, each time deeper. Don't think of anything, on purpose... and your subconscious mind will tell you when the time is up. You'll always have thoughts... don't worry about that, as long as you're not creating them. Then when you have a hunch your time is up, you'll simply flip your light switch "on", your eyes will open, fully alert... and when you do, notice how good you feel.

All right, at the count of three and not before, move your switch to the "on" position... and open your eyes and we'll practice this technique. One... two... three, move the switch "on," let your eyes open, notice how good you feel. A nice feeling isn't it? Remember, the most important thing now is to get that switch "off".

Have your client practice the technique with a 30-second time limit three to five times. After the client emerges, ask: "Do you feel like you really got your switch off?"

If no, have client practice more. If yes, tell client to enter self-hypnosis without a time limit and that you will emerge him. After he is in the state, say the following: "Now, I want to talk to your subconscious mind... you can listen with your consciousness if you want to... but I want to talk to your subconscious mind."

Then say: "When (client's name) tells you a time... you're to do that time exactly. If he tells you 30 seconds, that does not mean 29... it does not mean 31. If he tells you one minute... that does not mean 61 seconds or 59 seconds. You will follow his instructions instantly. Now listen very carefully to me. You are doing beautiful. You're going to do fantastic. You are now going to put your mind to school. Between now and the next time that I see you... you're going to practice using this time limit technique... and you're going to practice it ten times a day... minimum. Now that may sound like a lot of time. But say, if you gave yourself a time limit of one minute... well that's only ten minutes a day. If you gave yourself 30 seconds that's only five minutes a day... and I know you're willing to invest that amount of time... for achieving your goal. So you'll do that, ten times a day... once a day without fail. You're going to listen to a very powerful... self-hypnosis deepening tape program... that I'm going to give you. (Give them a progressive relaxation induction with a 15-second blank leader in the beginning.)

Here's how this works. You'll put the tape in a tape player, you'll get yourself in a nice comfortable position, you'll push the play button on the tape recorder... nothing happens for about 20 seconds. There's just 20 seconds of blank tape. During those twenty seconds you'll enter self-hypnosis without a time limit as you've just done. You'll go into hypnosis; you'll get your switch "off".

After that, my voice will come on... and guide you tremendously deep into this state. Each time you use this very special tape, you'll feel yourself go very... very deep... much deeper than the time before. You'll use this tape once a day... without fail. You'll find that if you follow these two instructions, when I see you next week, you'll instantly be able to go into such a beautiful deep state of hypnosis... you'll probably think you're living on the planet Mongo instead of here. But it will be wonderful... and a loving experience. I'll give you the written instructions on this... so you'll have it all. Just know there is no basement to your ability to relax. Any limitations on your ability to relax merely are your limitations... and those aren't real. You can relax much more deeply than you've ever thought possible".

CHAPTER 6:
RAPPORT

Rapport facilitates Responsiveness.

Rapport is a relationship marked by harmony or affinity; it is the foundation of all successful communication. Rapport creates the space where influence and change becomes possible. It is not necessarily about liking someone, being nice or being in agreement. It's about respect. When you respect another's model-of-the-world enough to step into it and experience it with appreciation, you'll gain and deepen rapport.

It's not about agreeing but rather about demonstrating open-mindedness and understanding the other's point of view.

The most successful communicators have developed a diverse range of matching skills because there isn't a single rapport technique that works with absolutely everyone.

Can there ever be too much rapport?

When you don't have a well-defined outcome and appropriate boundaries, you can become "lost'" in another person's model-of-the world and lose touch with your *own* resources.

Creating Rapport

Rapport relies on *matching* the other person behaviorally. You can literally match any observable behavior for rapport purposes. Matching is not mimicry. It doesn't have to be an exact mirroring of the other person.

In fact, precise mirroring can make some people uncomfortable, thus damaging rapport.

Matching begins by recognizing that people are always communicating and do so in systematic ways. You can pace anything that you can identify by adjusting your own behavior (verbal and nonverbal) to move with that of the other person. Pacing emphasizes the importance of acknowledging aspects of the other person's behavior and expressions, thereby meeting the other person at their model of the world. You simply utilize the other person's own behavior and language to establish and maintain effective rapport.

Non-Verbal Rapport-Building Techniques

Whole Body Matching

Adjust your body posture to match the other person's stance appropriately.

Half Body Matching

Match the upper or lower portion of the other person's body.

Part Body Matching

Pacing any consistent or stylistic use of body, e.g., eye blinks.

Head/Shoulders Angle

Match (without being obvious) characteristic poses that the person offers with their head and/or shoulders.

Facial Expressions

Note the ways the person uses his/her face, e.g., wrinkles their nose, puckers their lips, raises their eyebrows, etc.

Vocal Qualities

Use subtle ways to match the other person's vocal qualities including:
Voice Tempo - tempo overall, as well as the tempo changes that happen when someone emphasizes a word or phrase.
Voice Pitch - approximating the rise and fall of pitch is more useful than hitting the notes exactly - especially with very different voices.
Volume - volume in general, as well as the volume changes that happen when someone emphasizes a word.

Gestures

With minute and graceful movements of your own, match the gestures of the other person.

Breathing

Adjust your breathing to be in sync with the other person's breathing.

Representational Systems: Auditory, Visual Kinesthetic

Detect and utilize (by matching) in your own language, the primary predicates of the other person.

Repetitive Phrasing

Note and match in your own language the repeated phrases of the other person.

Mirroring

Mimicking a mirror image. Use right hand when your subject is using left hand.

Crossover Mirroring

Using one aspect of your behavior to match a different aspect of the other person's behavior, e.g., adjusting your voice tempo to match the rhythm of a person's breathing; pacing eye blinks with your finger or head nods, etc.

Criteria Words
Key words or phrases that refer to important values.

Exercise:
Get together with a partner. Match and mirror each other's bodily postures. Match five postures then, in turn, mirror five postures.
Invariably you will discover that there are not that many different postures that are natural and which you can follow without being obvious.

Representation Systems

Verbal, contextual rapport-building techniques.

We perceive our world through our five senses: Visual, Auditory, Kinesthetic, Olfactory and Gustatory. To make sense of the world around us, we interpret all the sensory input by representing the data internally.

The kinds of words we use are not random or accidental. They are a direct reflection of our internal processes.

People experience the world through their senses: sight, hearing, touch, taste, and smell. Our inner thoughts are composed of the same elements, primarily pictures, sounds and bodily sensations. (Though in some contexts, smells and tastes are actually important.) They are called representation systems because we use them to represent our external experience internally.

When people describe experiences, they express them with words that reveal the portion of experience of which they are most consciously aware.

A person in visual mode will use mostly visual words, while a person in auditory mode will use more auditory words and a person in kinesthetic mode will use more touchy-feely words.

People usually rely on one rep system more than the others (unless they have special training), even when that particular system is not the most effective or appropriate for the task at hand

You can tell what rep system a person is using by listening for sensory predicates. Sensory predicates are words that refer to a specific rep system.

Visual

I see what you mean.
Looks good.
See you later.

Auditory

I hear what you're saying.
Sounds good.
Call me.

Kinesthetic/Tactile

I grasp what you mean.
Feels good.
Keep in touch.

Unspecified (these words mask representation system preferences)

I understand what you mean.
I believe that's right.
Remember me.

Representation Predicates

Visual Predicates (Seeing Words)

Appear	focus	bright	foreground	background	foresee	clear
glance	color	glow	dark	hindsight	witness	watch
vista	dim	horizon	dream	illustrate	fade	image
look	observe	obvious	outlook	perspective	picture	reflect
reveal	see	scene	shine	show	sight	view

It was crystal clear.
She was distant.
He was brilliant.
They saw eye to eye.
I see what you mean.
OK, this is clear now.

Auditory Predicates (Hearing)

Articulate	gossip	audible	bitch	hear	brag	loud
hush	hum	inquire	cry	listen	whisper	earshot
lyrical	mutter	loud	noise	purr	harmony	rumor
shrill	say	dissonant	sing	mention	silence	speak
squeal	tell	speechless	tune	in tune	utter	Tune in.

I hear what you say. Listen to the possibilities. Out of tune.
It is clear as a bell. They were in tune.

Kinesthetic Predicates (Touchy Words)

Balanced	bearable	burden	callous	concrete	cold	crushed
dizzy	off-kilter	firm	feel	gut	grasp	rough
grip	shaky	heavy	sharp	hot	slick	pressure
Slippery	push	smooth	pull	soft	solid	stretch
Support	tense	warm	touch	sway	I get it.	

Thick-skinned. Hold on now. Weigh the consequences.
She was hot. He was callous. They were hand in hand.
He is a smooth operator. This proposition is shaky.

Olfactory Predicates (Smelly Words)

Stench	sniff	stink	scent	fresh	pungent	aroma
fragrance	reeks	bouquet	musty	smell	dank	odor

Gustatory Predicates (Tasty Words)

Bite	delicious	spicy	bitter	digest	sour
burnt	salty	sweet	creamy	savory	tasty
Tart	regurgitate	yummy			

Unspecified Predicates

These words indicate internal processing, while masking the specific rep system the speaker is using.

Consider	discover	motivate	create	deliberate
Know	remember	decide	manage	organize
relate	think	understand	wonder	divulge
experience				

Notice his actions. I understand this better.
Discover your strength. It was well thought out.
They were in agreement. This is somewhat vague.
Focus on your strengths.

Most Developed Rep System

Since most people rely on one rep system more than the others, it can be useful to identify the rep system they use most. If you know what it is, you can match it for rapport.

Exercise: Discover Your Preferred Systems

Answer the following questions and notice the predicates used.

What is your home like? (Circle one)

- More Visual - More kinesthetic - More Auditory

What do you like to do most at work?

- More Visual - More kinesthetic - More Auditory

What do you like to do most for fun?

- More Visual - More kinesthetic - More Auditory

Visual people tend to be fast-talking, high-pitched, loud, fast-walking, animated. Looks.

Auditory people are controlled volume, paused speech, medium pitch. Listens.

Kinesthetic people slower, subdued, contemplative, touchy-feely.

Exercise: Write a short story in a visual mode, using visual predicates. Repeat the same story in auditory and kinesthetic modes.

Sample subject: A New York Parade. A day in nature.

Example: My morning routines

Visual:

The alarm woke me up with a flashing "7 a.m.". I zipped to the bathroom. The reflection in the mirror looked disheveled. As I was taking a shower, I imagined my yoga exercise, which usually makes me look better. A quick glance into the kitchen revealed the blinking light on the automatic coffee maker indicating the strong black coffee is ready. The sun was shining through the window. A beautiful bird was perched on the fire escape stairs. Oh what a beautiful morning!

Auditory:

The alarm screamed "Wake up". I silenced it with a thump. I marched on the squeaking floor to the bathroom. The sound of the shower helped to wake me up. I put on my yoga music. By the time I was done, the coffee pot was percolating. A bird was singing good morning on the fire escape stairs.

I like the rhythm and harmony of this morning.

Kinesthetic: (Including Olfactory and Gustatory)

The alarm went off. I could feel the vibrations through the mattress.

With a swift motion, I hit the snooze button. I did not feel like getting up but the warmth of the suns rays invited me out. I dragged my feet to the bathroom. The strong shower massaged the tiredness away. As I was stretching in my usual yoga exercises, I could smell the coffee getting ready. I was salivating at the thought of breakfast.

A bird was hopping around on the fire escape stairs. Oh what a comfortable morning!

The Agreement Mind Set

To facilitate rapport and avoid conflict **be a "But" Buster!**
"But" builds walls, "And" builds bridges

I am a BUT Buster!!

Note: The term "However" is the same as "But"

Use the following expressions instead:

I appreciate... and...
I respect... and...
I understand... and...
I see / hear / feel what you are saying and...
And by the way...

Linguistic Feedback

As a therapist, you want to be perceived as an understanding person who gives your client a true feeling of being heard.

Carl Rogers was a very successful therapist and a master of linguistic feedback (Backtracking). He rarely added anything to what his clients said and got amazing results. Other therapists took backtracking further by rephrasing what was said. Bandler and Grinder were initially surprised to find that this was not as effective as backtracking without changing the words.

Backtracking is listening so well to what someone says that you can repeat a brief summary for the speaker to clarify. Backtracking is not parroting another's words, but gently asking a person to hear what he or she has said. Recent experiments have verified the value of this. Using MRI scans, scientists have confirmed that the part of your brain used for speech production is different than the part of the brain used for listening.

In effect, by repeating someone's words back, he or she may be hearing them for the first time.

When Backtracking:

- Start each backtrack with gentle eye contract.
- Use the speaker's key words or phrases.
- Use the tonality of questions (which rises at the end of questions in English).

Begin backtracks with a brief preface, such as"

So, what you're saying is...
Let we see if I understand you...
Let me see if I have got the gist of...

Backtracking Exercise

Groups of 3 people:
First person is the Guide/Backtracker
Second person - Explorer
Third person - Observer/Coach

Round 1: (Change the content- Key words)

1. Review the variable briefly. For round one, work with vocabulary.
2. Guide to Explorer:
   "Tell me about one of your most powerful learning resources".
   A- Backtrack for Explorer and change his/her key words or phrases.
   B- Again backtrack for Explorer, but this time do NOT change key words or phrases.
3. Coach (The observer):
   A- Share anything you noticed about how rapport was affected and then ask the Guide and Explorer what they noticed.
   B- Coach backtracks their responses.

Round 2: Switch Roles (This time change rate of speech)

Explorer tells a story: One of the most exciting adventures you had. The variable for round two is rate-of-speech: match the speaker's tempo, then Mismatch speed it up or slow it down, and then match it again.

A- Share anything you noticed about how rapport was affected and then ask them what they noticed.

B- Coach backtracks their responses.

Round 3: (Change pacing-eye contact)

Explorer tells a story: Where were you on 9/11/2001.
This round has a twist to it. As the explorer tells his/her story, the Guide pretends to be listening by keeping eye contact and nodding. The Coach pretends not to be interested, by avoiding eye contact but actually listens, very carefully to the story. Midway of the story Guide breaks eye contact and shifts body away from Explorer, while at the same time, Coach makes eye contact and shifts towards Explorer.

Everybody shares the learning experience about rapport.

Invariably you will find that rapport was established when the Guide or the Coach maintained eye contact and the Explorer thought that he/she was listened to. Rapport evaporated as soon as they broke off eye contact.

CHAPTER 7: HYPNOTIC INDUCTION TECHNIQUES

Universal Hypnotic Protocol

By: Dennis K. Chong & Jennifer S. Chong MD, CH, RN, PHN, MPNLP

In the old days (pre-1975), one of the great mysteries for clinicians, was the wonder of how a classical formal hypnotic induction protocol could get a trance with a high degree of certainty. Then of even greater mystery was, when it failed to do so after it was offered to a different person; and even yet a greater mystery it was when it failed after it was offered to the same person at another time!

This paper is not about the structural basis for these anomalies. However, what the Chongs became curious about was whether there would ever be an induction protocol that would be free of aberrations and deviancies that would work for everyone every time.

In exploring this, one thing that came out of the clinical experience of the Chongs was clear. Whatever you verbalize, if it speaks to the experience of the person or what you utter speaks to the truth within him or her, a trance would invariably happen and it would be a very deep trance. The Chongs concluded that if your verbalizations matched the semantics of the subject's ontology, a trance would be inevitable. The converse would, therefore, also be true and the evidence supported it. It is that if your verbalization were a mismatch to your subject's ontological semantics, there will be no trance.

In the context of this exploration, there were certain linguistic phrases that seemed to enjoy the property of universality. This is to say that they exist in other cultural and linguistic systems of this world.

Each of these phrases also had their converse variations. These converse variations also seemed to have the property of universality. Thus, they seemed to exist in other cultural and linguistic systems of this world.

An examination of these phrases clearly speaks to their origins that are now lost in time. We shall never know who first coined them. We shall never know how this person or persons knew to create them. We will never know what were the wellsprings from which these phrases originated.

However, it is also clear that they speak to the deep instincts and intuitions of all of us. In that they do, there is a natural assent that they speak of powerful deep truths about us. So, what are these phrases? They are:

The Phrase	Its Inversion
She is a well-centered person.	She is off her center.
	He is way off beam.
He is a well-integrated man.	He is cracking up.
	He is breaking up.
	He is going to pieces.
She is such a well-balanced person.	She is off her balance.
He is such a well-formed person.	He is kinked. He is bent.
	He is warped. He is twisted.
She is clean in her heart.	She has a dirty heart.
	She has a dark heart.
	She is black-hearted.

It was not difficult to construct a hypnotic induction protocol from and around these phrases.

In doing so, it was immediately apparent to us that the most critical thing was to guide a person to his center. It is a natural and better thing to do than to take him down to a basement room of a flight of stairs or a Hawaiian beach or an Alpine meadow. Our intuitions left us to conclude that the center would be a place of silence, peace, calm, tranquility, cleanness and purity.

It seemed to us that it is only at the center that it is possible for one to be one with One-Self. It was in this oneness with One-Self that one sees the powerful consequences of this protocol. It is in this unity of one with One-Self is the ESSENCE of us and this is what we truly are. This is the transcendent Self.
We, therefore, derived that in this unity of one with One-Self lies the power to become well-balanced, well-formed and clean of heart.

In passing, this induction protocol opens the door to dealing with the kind of baggage that we all bring with us from the days of our innocence and those facets of the Dark Side that we acquired in the course of our lives. At a formal level these things, as a category, are known as the analogical semantic ill-formedness within a person. In both current models to reverse a cancer (Hamblett/Bolstad and Chong/Chong) there is concurrence that this ill-formedness must be undone so that the conditions can come into place for a cancer to be reversed. This places this induction protocol in a uniquely powerful place in the field of Hypnotherapy.

In our application of this induction protocol, we have yet to come across a case in which the person did not go into a trance.

The structure of this induction protocol was taught at the 2000 Annual of the National Guild of Hypnotists in Nashua, New Hampshire. As part of the lecture, we verbalized it to everyone present. The feedback was that everyone present went into a trance. There was no one that did not go into his or her trance.

References:

Dennis & Jennifer Chong: *The Knife Without Pain* Communication and Hypnosis and The Blueprint of Language Structures for Surgery by Hypnosis C-Jade Publications Inc. 1994

Dennis & Jennifer Chong: *A Glimpse at Forever, a Chance for Eternity* I, The Ultimate Nominalization or TO BE C-Jade Publications Inc. 1995

The Dave Elman Induction

The Outline:

- **Relax eyelids** to the point they don't work. Unless you choose to remove the relaxation, they will not work. When you know you accomplished it, give it a good try.
- **Relax body**. Move relaxation of eyelids to the rest of body.
- **Open eyes.** Close your eyes and double relaxation.
- **Drop arm**. Lift and drop arm. Relax. (If client cannot relax say: "Make a fist so tight you cannot make it any stronger. Throw down hand and open/relax the fist.")
- **Relax mind**. Count from 300 down. Deeper Relaxed. Push numbers out of mind.
- **Fractionation**. 1-2-3, Open eyes, Sleep Now (snap finger). Test (1-2-pause- 3).
- **Deepening**. Count down from 10 to 1.

The Induction:

A) Close your eyes. Concentrate your attention on your eyelids and the muscles around your eyes. I wonder if you can relax all the muscles around your eyes and especially the eyelids to the point they will not work... that's right. Just relax them completely and unless you chose to remove that relaxation, they will not work. When you know you have accomplished this, give them a good test... (If client opens eyes say: "Good now you proved that you can control your eyes and open them. Now let's try it the other way. Use your strong willpower and prove to yourself that you can do it.") That's good... stop trying and go deeper...

B) Now spread that relaxation to your entire body...Let go of all tension in your whole body.

C) In a minute I will ask you to open your eyes and then close them. Each time you close your eyes double your relaxation. "OK now open your eyes (hold hand in front of eyes), close and double your relaxation." (Repeat a few times.)

D) I am going to lift your arm now. I want you to let me do all the work. Just let your arm be loose, limp and relaxed. (Lift arm by the wrist). As I let your arm drop into your lap you will let yourself go deeper. (Repeat and verify relaxation.) Great. Now that your body is so relaxed, I wonder how fast you can relax your mind just as well as you relaxed your body.

E) In a moment you will start counting backwards from 300 by threes. After every count you will say: "deeper relaxed." Like this: "300, deeper relaxed, 297, deeper relaxed." With each count, double your mental relaxation. Soon your mind will be so relaxed that you will relax all the numbers out of your mind. You will allow your mind to relax so deeply that the numbers will just fade away. If you understand me nod your head...good. Start counting now... That's right... Good... Let them fade...Push them out of your mind... Are they all gone? Feels good doesn't it? Good, go deeper now. (If client counts more than ten numbers say "That's good enough stop counting and relax deeper.")

F) Now we are going to have an agreement. From now on when I say Sleep Now (snap your fingers for an auditory anchor), you will immediately close your eyes and allow yourself to instantly and effortlessly go into a deeper hypnotic state. Not because I say so but because you want the experience and because it is the wonderful nature of your inner creative mind to achieve a profound state of mind relaxation. Each time I say Sleep Now (snap finger) you will find yourself going deeper than before, easily and effortlessly. I am going to count now from one to three. Keep your eyes closed until I say Three. At the count of three you will open your eyes and emerge from hypnosis. One... Two... Three... open, GOOD. Sleep Now! (Snap fingers). Repeat rhythmically until client is deep in hypnosis. Test by pausing between the count of two and three [One... Two... (pause)...Three. Client is in hypnosis if he does not open eyes until the count of three].

G) I will help you now to go even deeper. I will count from ten to one. With every count, allow yourself to go deeper. 10-Deeper now, 9-Deeper yet, 8-drift deeper than ever before...

Following are transcripts of three inductions performed **by Dave Elman** in a teaching session.

The Cigarette Induction

Excerpt for Dave Elman's "Hypnotherapy"

"... I am going to take three puffs on this cigarette. With the first puff your eyes are going to get tired, the second puff you're going to want to close your eyes, but wait until the third puff, at which time close them. They will lock and you won't be able to open them. Want that to happen - expect it to happen - and watch it happen... Here's the first puff (taking a puff) - notice how tired your eyes are getting and let them get tired. (Taking second puff.) Now they'll get so tired you'll want to close them but don't let them close yet. Now when I take the third puff they'll close and lock - let them. (Taking third puff) Now close them. You'll find they are locked... The harder you test them, the less they'll work. Test them and you'll find you can't make them work. They just won't work at all. That's right. Now when I snap my fingers you'll be able to open them very readily. (Snapping fingers.) All right, you can open them..."

The Water Drinking Induction

Excerpt for Dave Elman's "Hypnotherapy"

"... All right, want this to happen, expect it to happen and watch it happen. I'm going to take a drink of water – just one swallow -- and when I do, your eyes will close, they will lock and your won't be able to open them. Want this to happen and watch it happen. (Taking a sip.) Close your eyes and you'll find now they're locked. They won't work at all. Test them, you'll find that you can't make them work. The harder you try, the less they'll work. When I snap my fingers they'll open very readily. (Snap.) Now you can open them..."

The Head Tap Induction

Excerpt for Dave Elman's "Hypnotherapy"

"… I'm going to tap my head – and when I tap my head your eyes will close and lock and you won't be able to open them. Want it to happen and watch it happen... (Dave tapes his own head) Now close your eyes - You'll find they're locked already and when you test them they won't work at all. Test them and you'll see they won't… All right you can open your eyes now…"

Relaxation Inductions

Progressive Relaxation

By: Henry Leo Bolduc CH

Now that you are ready, just look forward or upward; you may focus your eyes on a spot or you may choose not to focus your eyes. I am going to count down slowly from ten to one. With every descending number, just slowly blink your eyes, as if in slow motion, with every number.

Ten, that's good, do it nice and slowly.
Nine, that's good,
Eight (2 second pause)
Seven (2 second pause)
Six (2 second pause)
Five (2 second pause)
Four (2 second pause
Three (2 second pause)
Two (2 second pause)
One.

Now just close your eyes, and I'll tell you why we did that exercise. We are going to do an exercise called progressive relaxation, where we simply relax the different parts of your body sequentially. That was just to relax your eyelids. Right now, isn't there a feeling of relaxation, or a comfortable tired feeling in your eyelids? Whatever the feeling is, just allow that to multiply, to magnify and to become greater. This is something that you do; nobody else can do it for you. So just take your time, and don't be concerned if there is any little movement in your eyelids. That is called REM, or rapid eye movement, and it is a perfectly natural part of this experience.

Now, just allow that feeling of relaxation to move outward, as in imaginary waves or ripples, to the entire facial area. Just think about relaxing the face. Feel the relaxation going on outward to the entire head area, relaxing the head. Now let the relaxation flow down to your neck, to your shoulders, down the arms and into the hands, relaxing that entire area.

Take a deep breath and fill your lungs with relaxation, and allow that relaxation to flow to the solar plexus, to your spine, slowly down your spine to your hips, to your legs, your feet, and all the way out to your toes, filling your entire body with relaxation. Now, just slow down a little bit and mentally examine your entire body. If there is any area that is not completely relaxed, then just allow that part to catch up and to become as relaxed as the rest. (Pause a few seconds.)

Now allow yourself to slow down just a little bit more, then a bit more, and I am going to count downward once again from ten to one. This time, with every descending number, allow yourself to slow down, becoming more still, more centered, with every number, and at the count of one, enter your own natural level of relaxation. I'll count more rapidly now — ten, nine, eight, seven, six, five, four, three, two, one.

You are now at your own natural level of relaxation, and from this level you may move to any other level with complete awareness and may function at will, because you are in complete control at every level of your mind. This is something that you want. It is here and it is now.

(Pause a few seconds.)

Now let us begin by comparing your mind to the surface of a quiet pond. On the surface everything looks peaceful and still, but below the surface there is great depth and much is happening. Think of my voice as a breeze whispering in the trees along the shore. (Pause briefly)

Not everyone realizes his or her full capacities, and you have to discover those capacities in whatever way you wish. Your subconscious mind can listen to me and, at the same time it can also deal with something else. Perhaps you can remember as a child in school, gazing out the window while the teacher was talking. (Pause) Maybe you recall walking with a friend and talking to that friend at the same time. Two separate things, yet happening at the same time. Your subconscious mind is here and can hear every word. You are in a place where you can let go safely. Just relax.

You may take a deep breath now, and you will notice that a drifting might occur. You may feel light, you may feel heavy or you may feel that your body is asleep, although your mind is alert. There is less and less importance to be attached to my voice, and more and more significance to be given to your own inner reality, to your own inner experience. Stored deep in your subconscious mind are wonderful memories of other times and other places. Your subconscious mind can call upon and access those memories, memories you only thought you had misplaced. Experiences that you only thought you had mislaid. In due time, in your own time, your subconscious mind will reveal those memories to you in a dream, or a daydream, or sometime when you are not especially thinking about it. You may experience those memories of other times and other places.

By looking deeply into the recesses of your mind, you can see your vision and hear the voice of your heart. With this insight, comes new growth and new understanding. Later, you can apply this knowledge to understand yourself and the world better. In a moment now, we can begin a series of exercises that will lead into memory recall and future possibilities.

Permissive Induction

By: Henry Leo Bolduc CH

(Start this induction with a few minutes of relaxation.) Then say to client:

"Now, with your eyes closed, it becomes easier and easier for you to become more and more aware of a number of things that could often go overlooked or even unnoticed. Thoughts, feelings, sensations, impressions - just remember now to breathe deeply and smoothly, for deep breathing is one of the most ancient and also one of the most effective forms of relaxation there is. So remember to breathe deeply and smoothly throughout the entire exercise. Just allow yourself to drift pleasantly and easily. You don't have to think, or to move about, or to make any sort of effort. You don't even have to try to listen to me, because your subconscious is here and can hear every word. You are about to enter a magical realm - please leave all doubts safely behind - then proceed.

As you take another deep breath, just experience the *feeling of* letting go, just letting go. Becoming more in perfect harmony more centered with every breath you take. Can you remember being a child and going to school? (Pause) If you recall a pleasant, happy memory, your mouth automatically forms a little smile. A smile comes easily and naturally with the memory.

As a child, did you dream? Can you dream here again, as when you were a child? Perhaps in the dream, you may be walking along the shore by the water's edge with your bare feet in the sand. Feels cool, but good. Feel the warm sun shining on your skin; there is a cool breeze that balances the warmth of the sun. And there go the seagulls. Are they laughing? Spontaneous joy and laughter. And as the dream continues, you also continue to go deeper and deeper, softly into the season of gentle dreams. Perhaps you may remember a special song or a tune from your childhood and that song or tune echoes deep, deep within. Don't analyze your responses; just allow the tune or music to return pleasantly. (Pause one minute)

If you don't recall a favorite song or tune from your youth or childhood, perhaps you can recall the tune and words of "Row, row, row your boat, gently down the stream." (Pause one minute)

The melody takes you even deeper within, deeper into your dream. And there is another dream within the dream. The dream of your eternal self, your eternal child. That carefree, innocent part of you, the part of you that is eager to learn, eager to experience, eager to grow, eager to love, to be loved. Connect now with your inner child, that joyful, wonderful, innocent part of you, and I'll be quiet while you enjoy this experience..."

A Relaxation Induction

By: Joann Abrahamsen

This induction uses language that is not grammatically correct. Because the confused, conscious mind is trying to figure out what is being said, the suggestions slip past the critical, conscious mind while it is distracted and goes directly into the subconscious mind. The induction uses many of the language patterns and techniques discussed earlier such as: dissociation, anticipation, confusion, exploration, double binds, universal experiences, the separation of the conscious and unconscious minds and metaphors.

"I would like for you to take a few minutes to get yourself comfortable. Possibly you may want to take off your shoes, and you can do that too. And... I really DON'T KNOW... just what your eyes want to do at this moment. You MIGHT want to find a spot on the wall to look at, comfortably. Not really staring at anything, but just allowing it to occupy the center of your visual field... and WONDERING what is going to happen next... You MIGHT feel more comfortable just... closing... your eyes, in a peaceful sort of way. And either way you do it, I would just like for you... to let yourself... zero in on the idea of just ... being comfortable. And there have been many TIMES, many PLACES, many SITUATIONS where you have felt so COMFORTABLE that nothing else mattered except that comfort. And you might think of them, now - and let your SUBCONSCIOUS mind... present to you... ONE SUCH SITUATION... where you really experienced the sense of physical and mental comfort.

And you CAN... recall... and RE-EXPERIENCE all the sensations, the sights, the sounds and the feelings. . which go with being extremely comfortable. And you CAN RECALL where you FIRST EXPERIENCED... feeling profound relaxation... covering your body. The feeling of every muscle in that part of your body just loosening up - and just letting go - and lying flat like a limp rubber band - very deeply relaxed - and very LIKELY that part of your body that needed the relaxation most will re-experience it first - and the feeling of every nerve in that part of your body becoming... very quiet - peaceful - not doing any more than is absolutely necessary. And, you can WONDER... what direction that relaxation is going to move through your body - whether you experience it all at once... Like a flow of comfort peacefully moving through you. And soon you get the feeling that... you don't even have to be aware of it anymore. You can simply allow... yourself to become part of that relaxation... as it... becomes part of you.

And it will be very interesting for you to DISCOVER for yourself that you... don't even need to listen to me... Because what your CONSCIOUS mind does now is not at all important. Maybe, your CONSCIOUS mind just wants... to curl up in a corner and go to sleep for a while - or go as far away as it likes - the way you did as a kid in SCHOOL when you sat in the CLASSROOM and looked out the window... and allowed your mind to drift as far away from the CLASSROOM as it could get - someplace you'd rather be - and you lost track of what was being said - and it didn't matter because your SUBCONSCIOUS mind was picking up everything which was being said... as it is doing now - and your SUBCONSCIOUS mind is HERE WITH ME - AND IT CAN HEAR ME - and RESPOND in ITS OWN TIME - IN ITS OWN... COMFORTABLE WAY.

You CAN ENJOY whatever it is you are experiencing and - right now... you can enjoy whatever sensations - heaviness or lightness - warmth or coolness - and let them become part of your relaxation and comfort. You can... go as deeply as YOU need to - at this time - for WHATEVER it is your SUBCONSCIOUS mind wants to do to help you... ENJOY this experience. And you MIGHT ENJOY that experience of going so deeply into trance that it seems to you that you are just... ALL MIND without a body - a mind floating in space and time - completely free - able to move whenever and wherever it wants to go - THAT'S RIGHT."

Final Comments

Once you understand the principles of Ericksonian language patterns you can use them to induce hypnosis, offer suggestions, propose benefits for making a change, offer post hypnotic suggestions and much more. I hope you find the study of Erickson's work to be just as fascinating as we have and that you will continue to explore "Ericksonian Language Patterns." Our selected reading list contains a small sample of written material about Erickson and his techniques.

Velvety Breathing

By: Wendi Friesen

Take a nice deep breath and as you exhale make yourself a little bit more comfortable...

Perhaps you would like to close your eyes now... or maybe you would like to close your eyes in a few moments... when it just feels right for you.

You can just listen now... to the sound of my voice... and you may be aware of those other sounds around you as well... perhaps the sounds outside of the room... the sound of the music...

Just allow all of these sounds to begin to relax you deeper and deeper. All of these sounds will help to relax you because the only sound you care to think about now becomes the sound of my voice.

As you allow my words to float in and out of your awareness, let the music gently float in and out of your awareness.

Let the tension begin to melt from your body... your body becoming just as relaxed as you can possibly imagine it could ever be.

As you are noticing how relaxed your body has already become... are relaxing even more...be aware of your body for a moment... aware of the way your hands feel as they rest on the chair.

Notice the weight of your head on the back of the chair... and you may notice that your neck and your shoulders have already begun to melt... and release all tension and tightness.

Now notice your breathing... And let your breathing become velvety soft. So soft, that every breath you breathe is natural and easily floats in and then out of your lungs... and every time you exhale... you relax into my voice... breathing so evenly and so steadily... that you wouldn't even disturb a feather. You notice yourself breathing so easily and so slowly and gently, that your breath is effortless... and soft as velvet.

And as you breathe you may notice that this velvety soft breath begins to surround you like a velvety blanket. Every time you exhale you feel the wonderful sensation of the velvet softness of your breath floating out around your body.

There may be a color, or a feeling to it... as it surrounds you it wraps you in the most comfortable feeling... so soft and so perfect... that you simply sink... surrender... and relax into that warm, soft blanket... and every time you breathe... every time you exhale... you breath out more of that velvety softness... that surrounds your body gently and peacefully.

Your heartbeat begins to slow down just a little bit to a nice relaxed resting heartbeat. Now feel your entire body slowing down... because you know that there's absolutely nothing for you to do except relax.

Nobody wants anything from you... nobody expects anything of you... and you know that now you can allow your whole body to continue to relax... and become soft, loose and limp... and gently wrapped in that velvety blanket.

Anytime that you would like to relax deeper and allow your body and your mind to go into a deeper state of trance, you take a nice, easy breath ... (inhale) and as you exhale ... (exhale)... You go even deeper inside... to that perfect place... just as deeply and comfortably into that perfect place... where you are relaxed... receptive... ready to learn... ready to explore and discover more of who you are.

(PAUSE)

There is a part of your mind that hears my voice... a part of your mind that has all the wisdom, the knowledge and the resources to make these changes you desire. This part of your mind already knows how to help you... you don't even have to try, you don't have to figure it out... since this part of your mind hears my voice now and knows exactly what to do.

There is something that you'll notice as you listen to my voice and allow my voice to guide you. Notice the curiosity about what's possible and what you can create and wonder what it would be like if you truly had the freedom to create whatever you want and then just take another breathe (INHALE) ... (EXHALE) ...exhale and sink even deeper. Good.

Let your eyelids become twice as heavy and twice as relaxed... and let that velvety blanket wrap you up gently and softly.

Circular Breathing

By: Wendi Friesen

Notice a spot on the ceiling or wall and let all of your awareness be on that single spot for a moment. As you breathe and begin to relax you may notice that your awareness of the spot changes… The way it looks, the texture, the way the light touches it, the shadows, and many interesting things about the littlest details of that spot. Now you may have noticed that as you are focusing on that spot your body is relaxing a little bit more, and you may already be aware of how heavy your arms and legs have become.

Maybe you noticed most of all that your breathing has slowed down, becoming very slow, easy, and comfortable. As your breathing becomes even more relaxed, your body will begin to feel more relaxed and the next thing you may notice is how heavy your arms are right now.

It might just seem that the more you focus on your arms the more relaxed they become, and the heavier they feel. Now, continue to notice the spot, and continue to notice how heavy your arms are and now also notice how relaxed your breathing has become.

So soft and gentle and so easy, that it almost begins to feel as if each breath in… naturally leads to the next breathe out, and that breathe out easily leads to the next breath in.

Each breath in… naturally leads to the next breath out, and that breath out… easily leads to the next breath in. It may begin to feel as if your breath is becoming more of a circle of breath… as each breath in… leads gently to the next breath out… and that breath out… easily leads to the next breath in.

Now notice how naturally that happens for you, beginning to feel as if your breath is a continuous, relaxing circle…

The more you breathe, the more relaxed your body becomes and your eyes may become so heavy and tired that you will find it harder and harder to keep them open. When your eyes get too heavy to keep open, you can just let them close… relaxing your eyelids even more… and letting that heaviness travel into all the muscles of your face.

You may already be thinking about how good that will feel… when that wave of relaxation and heaviness floats down through your face like a warm wave. So you can decide for yourself just how relaxed and tired your eyes are becoming… and how good it will feel when they really are too heavy to keep open. Now notice that circle of breath even more… like it has a flow of energy all its own.

Easy, gentle, peaceful, continuous, absolutely no effort from you. Just a beautiful… easy… circle of breath.

Begin to notice yourself inside of this energy, inside of this circle of breath, feeling the gentle movement… the color…the sensations… the deeply relaxing sensation… and let your mind be totally immersed in the freely moving circle of your breath.

Floating… freely… flowing with the soft, serene, space of your breath. Now you can really let yourself go deeper inside… to your place of wisdom… where you have all the knowledge and wisdom to find the answers you need, and to understand what your inner mind would like you to know. Perhaps you noticed that you are already in this place of wisdom... already at this place within your inner mind, where your awareness is heightened, and your inner resources so alive and so ready to discover what you are looking for.

As you hear my voice... allow my voice to find its way into your inner mind, to that place where you already know how to create what you desire. Let my voice relax you deeper with each word, each word finding its way into your inner mind to that place where you are ready to make these changes now. (Continue by deepening, or if client is in a good state of trance, with direct suggestion or imagery or future self work.)

Eye Fixation & Fatiguing Inductions

Dr. Flower's Induction

"I would like you to look at the wall in front of you. Look at it with a defused defocused gaze, as if daydreaming a pleasant scene.

Soon you'll find that all the muscles in your body will relax.

Your facial muscles will relax... Your arms will relax... Your legs will relax and your whole body will let go and be completely relaxed. And soon you will close your eyes and drift into a peaceful hypnotic rest. I want you to try and not close your eyes yet.

In a moment I will start counting. With each count you will close your eyes and then open them again (*Demonstrate*). You will find that your eyelids become heavier and heavier. It becomes more and more difficult to open your eyes after you have closed them. And the more you try to open them, the heavier they become. The more you try to open them, the more difficult it becomes. You'll find that it feels just so comfortable for you to keep your eyelids closed.

And soon maybe when I reach a count of 20 or maybe 10 or maybe even 5 you will keep your eyes closed and allow yourself to go into a deep, pleasant hypnotic rest.

Not because I say so but because it is the wonderful, natural ability of your powerful mind to respond in a way that is beneficial to you.

So, look at the wall in front of you with a dreamy defocused gaze.

Allow all the muscles in your body to relax now."

*(**Note to Hypnotist**: Talk slowly, in fragmented sentences and on the client's exhale.)*

"Your facial muscles are relaxing... your arms are relaxing... your legs are relaxing and all your body is letting go and relaxed completely. As I start counting now you close and open your eyes.

One... that's right. Two... eyelids are relaxing. Three... heavier and heavier. Four... heavier and heavier. Five... your breathing is deep and rhythmic. Six... eyelids heavier with each easy breath... Seven... eyelids heavier and heavier with each count. Eight... feeling so comfortable with each count... feeling so relaxed. Nine... eyelids so relaxed and heavy with each count. Ten... it just feels so good having those eyelids closed. Eleven... it feels so good having those eyelids closed that it's becoming a chore to open them. Twelve... so relaxed... heavy and relaxed... so drowsy... so sleepy. Thirteen... the more you think about opening those eyelids, the more they want to stay closed... feeling so heavy and so relaxed... so very heavy and so very relaxed. Fourteen... you may want to open those eyelids, but they feel so much better to keep them closed. Fifteen... the harder you try to open them, the tighter they close...

NOTE: Keep up this patter only until client is reluctant to open eyes. Then touch client's forehead and with a loud authoritative voice say: "Keep them closed and go deeper and deeper."

Eye Fixation Induction

By: Zali Segal

Have the subject seated comfortably, feet flat on the floor and hands on his/her laps with the palms down.

"Now I would like you to focus your attention on a spot on the ceiling overhead... Keep looking at that spot without moving a muscle. You don't have to use any effort. It's just something for you to focus on to eliminate any distractions that might cause you to shift your eyes. Just keep focusing on that spot and listen to my voice. You'll hear what I say. Even if you don't hear what I say it doesn't matter... You'll go in anyway. I'm not interested in your conscious mind... I'm interested in your inner-conscious mind and the less you concentrate on what I'm saying, the easier it will be for my suggestions to reach your inner-conscious mind... After all, I'm not speaking to you, I'm talking to your ears... and soon you will find just how easy it is to let go... Soon you will find just how wonderful it feels when you just relax and let go.

As you continue to gaze at that spot, you will notice that you begin to relax more and more with each and every easy breath that you inhale. Your eyelids may have a tendency to blink... and you know, as well as I do, just how good it would feel to just relax and let go... eyelids... so heavy... so drowsy. They're becoming so heavy and drowsy... so heavy, drowsy, droopy and sleepy. As a matter of fact, the more you think about keeping those eyelids open, the more they just want to close because you know just how good it would feel to just let those eyelids close right down.

It's almost like watching a late-night TV show... try hard to keep those eyes open... try hard to keep them open... they just want to close right down... try hard to keep them open... they just want to close... it would feel so good just to let them close down... and when you're ready, just let them close right down. Eyelids so very tired... so very heavy... so very drowsy... so very droopy... so... very... sleepy. They're closing... closing... closing... closing... closing... closing. Try hard to keep them open... they just want to close... try hard to keep them open but they want to close right down. They're closing... closing... closing... closing. Closing... closing... and deep sleep!"

(Timing is of utmost importance in this induction. Watch your subject very carefully and speed up or slow down the dialogue as necessary. If the subject responds very quickly, you may have to skip certain sections. If not, don't be afraid of being repetitive. N.B. If the subject appears to be staring aimlessly into space, pass your hand in front of his/her eyes. If there is no response, the subject is probably a somnambulist and is in deep hypnosis.)

The Light Bulb Technique

By: Alfred A. Barrios, Ph.D.

Step 1: You will be using a 40-watt soft-white light bulb. You should be sitting up in your chair, with your head free to move and about three feet from the bulb. The bulb should be situated so that you will be looking at the top of the bulb. And the room should be completely dark except for this one bare bulb. Now gaze right at the top of the bulb. At first, you will find it bright and fuzzy. But as the light naturally and automatically begins concentrating your mind, you'll find that the bulb will gradually become clearer, sharper and more distinct. Soon you'll be able to make out the print on the top of the bulb. It will begin to stand out more sharply and clearly.

Step 2: A feeling of peace and tranquility is beginning to come over you. As you continuing gazing at the bulb, imagine yourself outside on a warm beautiful summer day looking up at the pale blue sky. It's a beautiful day; the sun is bright and warm. Feel the warmth of the sun. A soothing warm, pleasant feeling is coming over you, all over you, especially your hands. And as the sun begins to set, you might notice that the sky is taking on a reddish hue. The feeling of peace and tranquility continues to deepen. Feel that warm pleasant feeling spread through your body - to your arms and hands, through your legs to your feet.

Step 3: Now turn off the light and close your eyes. Become aware of a yellow-colored balloon. As your mind becomes more concentrated, the color will stand out more and more brightly. See it now as a bright, almost fluorescent yellow-green with red fringes. The colors are so bright and clear because your mind is so concentrated; the concentration is intensifying the colors.

Step 4: Program in now that the balloon is going to begin to float upward, and as it does, your head also begins to float. Tell yourself that with each breath you take in, your head will seem to get lighter, as if you were filling it with air. A wonderful feeling of detachment is coming over you as you begin to feel lighter and looser with each breath.

Step 5: Now program in that the balloon is going to sink, with your head again following it, as it turns more and more into a beautiful red-magenta, with a blue fringe, deep, rich and vivid. As the colors deepen more and more, you're going into a progressively deeper and deeper state of relaxation. You are feeling very much at peace now, and your mind is most receptive to your positive thoughts.

Step 6: Do the 20 to 10 countdown.

Step 7: You are ready for self-programming.

The Concentration Spiral

By: Alfred A. Barrios, Ph.D.

Probably the most dramatic of the techniques, the Concentration Spiral shows most clearly how concentrated and responsive the mind can become after one of the SPC techniques (Self-Programmed Control). For this technique, you will need the concentration spiral device. While going through the technique you should keep your eyes on the spinning spiral at all times. There is only one point when you are to look away from the spiral, as is indicated below. At this point you are to look at some particular object. It could be the base of a lamp, a fern, a painting on the wall, etc. In classrooms the large clock usually found on the wall is ideal.

Also, keep in mind that everything you are about to see is naturally there; it's just that most people's minds are normally not focused enough to see all this. However, as you proceed through the spiral technique your mind becomes increasingly focused and you will eventually see most, if not all, of the things suggested.

Scripting of the Spiral Technique

Step 1: "Start by looking at the center of the spiral. One of the first positive signs that your mind is becoming more concentrated is a fuzziness or waviness in the lines of the spiral. After a while you should also begin to notice a yellowish fluorescent-like fringe to the black. You should also notice that every now and then the spiral seems to grow, especially if you look toward the edges. It almost seems to come out at you.

Step 2: Program in a three-dimensional effect. Tell yourself the spiral is a funnel or whirlpool. Every now and then the spiral will appear to unwind like the spring of a giant clock. You'll also become aware of dark rays seeming to spin off the edge of the spiral. All of these are positive signs that your mind is progressively becoming more concentrated and your imagination and mind are coming more under your control.

Step 3: Program in that you are in a spiral tunnel that is speeding away from you, as if you were in a train traveling through the tunnel and looking out the rear window.

Step 4: Now imagine yourself looking up at the top of a deep well. Feel yourself sinking into the deep spiral well as you continue to look up at the top. Now you can reverse this; see yourself looking down at the bottom of the well and feel yourself rising.

Step 5: All the while you have been gazing at the spiral; your mind has automatically become more and more concentrated. In this highly concentrated state, your mind comes to act like a powerful magnifying glass, intensifying whatever you focus on, especially your positive thoughts. Now, to show you how concentrated it has become, look away from the spiral momentarily at some particular object and watch how the object becomes magnified and actually appears to grow.

Step 6: As you continue looking at the spiral, a feeling of peace will begin coming over you. Program in that as you sink into a deep state of relaxation your eyes will be closing and your body will become nice and warm, especially your hands, as if you are taking a nice warm bath.

Step 7: Count backward from 20 to 10 with each breath exhaled, as in the Pendulum technique.

Step 8: You are now ready for self-programming."

What makes these techniques so effective is the fact that there is built-in immediate reinforcement for many of the suggestions. For example:

(1) In the Pendulum Technique the actual swinging of the pendulum is produced via naturally occurring ideomotor responses to the thought or expectation of swinging in a particular direction. The suggestion that the fingers will start to creak open with the pendulum eventually dropping is helped by the fact that there will be a natural creaking open of the fingers as the suggestions of the hand relaxing take hold. The suggestion of the arm eventually being pulled down is helped by the natural feelings of heaviness that eventually come over the arm.

(2) In the Light bulb Technique for reinforcing the suggestion of seeing a colored balloon after closing the eyes. Use is made of natural occurring after images from staring at the light bulb. Since such after images go through a natural sequence of color changes, suggestions of these very color changes will be automatically reinforced.

(3) In the Concentration Spiral Technique use is made of several natural occurring visual phenomena: the fuzziness in the lines of the spiral; the yellowish-fluorescent-like fringe to the lines; the dark rays seeming to spin off the spiral, etc. The most dramatic visual effect of the spiral technique - the expansion or magnification effect upon looking away from the spiral at an object - is also a natural occurring phenomenon.

Now the question arises: What do you say in the very unlikely but still possible case that the client says or suspects that all these reinforcing effects would have occurred anyway? The answer is simple and true: Yes, all of these effects are naturally occurring but all of these effects have been magnified greatly as a result of the focused attention on them. It is left to the imagination of the reader to create other hypnotic induction techniques using the same approach of focusing the clients' attention on subtle, below threshold, stimuli that are present.

Along the same lines, one can introduce stimuli below conscious awareness that will then reinforce suggestions being made. For example, if you were to suggest that the client was in a beautiful garden and was surrounded by innumerable delicious smelling roses, you could subtly introduce the fragrance of roses into the room. Or if you were to suggest that the client was out in the snow and would soon start shivering, you could slowly lower the temperature of the room. Or if you were to suggest that the client was at a concert, you could subtly introduce the musical sounds of such a concert, etc.

Double Bind Induction

By: Joann Abrahamsen

Begin by allowing the client to choose a fixation point or you suggest a fixation point such a ring, pendulum or other bright object that you hold in your hand. You say to the client that you are going to count from one to five. At the count of five the client will close the eyes and go into hypnosis. You are linking the behavior (closure of the eyes) with the response that you want (entering the hypnotic state). **At the same time** you suggest that the client may want to close the eyes **before** you reach the number five, but the client is to resist the urge to close the eyes.

You are setting the client up for the double bind because whether the client follows your instructions and closed the eyes when you reach the number five or resists your instructions and closes the eyes before you say the number five -- THE CLIENT GOES INTO HYPNOSIS!

"Pick a spot on the wall or any object that you would like to focus your attention on slightly above eye level. (Or, "just focus your attention on this object" as you hold it slightly above eye level.) "Once you pick your spot, don't change it. In a moment I am going to count from one to five. As I do, you may find that your eyes begin to blink more rapidly, your breathing becomes even slower and more regular and you feel as though you would like to just close your eyes and go deep into hypnosis. In fact, it may seem as though you cannot help but close your eyes, as though someone was gently tugging at your eyelids trying to pull down your lids over your eyes. But I want you to resist that feeling as long as you can. I want you to try very hard to keep your eyes open and not go into hypnosis until after I reach the count of five. When you do close your eyes, you will go deep into hypnosis."

"One... your eyelids are beginning to close. Two... resist that feeling, even though it would feel so good to close them. Three... eyes watery now, try hard to keep them open. Four... eyelids almost closed now... it would feel so wonderful to close them... Five... Good... Keep them closed now and go deep into hypnosis."

If your client does close the eyes before five, continue to count to five anyway and as soon as the eyes close say: "Good! Keep them closed now and go deep into hypnosis." If the client does not close the eyes at five, say: "Good! Now you may close your eyes." Sometimes the client is in hypnosis with the eyes open or is waiting for permission to close the eyes. The key is to utilize whatever behavior the client presents. Whether or not the client follows your instructions, the client is in hypnosis once the eyes close.

The Abrahamsen Induction

By: Joann Abrahamsen

Over the years, I have developed an easy, almost fail-safe induction that I use with 90% of my clients. This induction combines the double bind with some subtle tests and deepening. The advantage to this induction and deepening is that if a client **is** in hypnosis, the process will deepen the hypnosis and if the client is not in hypnosis, the tests and deepening **will put the client in hypnosis**. And, the client does not know he is being tested. You can do the induction and tests in about three minutes. Following the induction, I sometimes use a short progressive relaxation as a deepening technique. The entire induction with the progressive relaxation deepening takes about ten minutes.

Tell your client: *"Pick a spot on the wall, slightly above eye level. Once you pick your spot, don't change it."* Or, you could use a ring, pendulum or other bright object as a fixation point. Continue:

"In a moment I am going to count from one to five. As I do, you may find that your eyes begin to blink more rapidly, your breathing becomes slower and more regular and you feel as though you would like to just close your eyes and go deep into hypnosis. In fact, it may seem as though you cannot help but close your eyes, as though someone was gently tugging at your eyelids trying to pull down your lids over your eyes. But I want you to resist that feeling as long as you can. I want you to try very hard to keep your eyes open and not go into hypnosis until after I reach the count of five. When you do close your eyes you will go deep into hypnosis. ***One*** *... your eyelids are beginning to close.* ***Two*** *... resist that feeling, even though it would feel so good to close them.* ***Three*** *... eyes watery now, try hard to keep them open.* ***Four*** *... eyelids almost closed now ... it would feel so wonderful to close them ...* ***Five*** *... Good ... Keep them closed now and go deep into hypnosis."*

This induction technique connects the closing of the eyes with hypnosis. Whether or not the client follows your instructions, once the eyes close, he is in hypnosis. If the client's eyes do not close at the number five, just suggest that he close his eyes.

After the client's eyes have closed and it appears that he is in hypnosis, you should test the subject. Say to him:

"Good, keep your eyes closed and go deeper into hypnosis. Deeper and deeper with each and every gentle breath that you take. Good. Just let that wonderful relaxation that you feel in your eyes spread throughout your body. Good. In a moment, I'm going to pick up your arm by the wrist and drop it. It will drop right down like a wet cloth because it is so relaxed." Take one of the client's hands by the wrist, lift it and drop it in his lap. *"No, don't help me* (if he does); *let me do all the work."*

Lift and drop the hand in his lap for the second time. Then lift and drop it to his side, safely supporting the hand and arm with your own hand, if necessary. When the client allows you to lift and drop his arm without exerting any effort, he is in a deep state of hypnosis. The first two times you lift and drop the arm, you do so above his lap. The third time you extend the arm out to the client's side and drop it.

If the client is resisting you or making a conscious effort to help you, he would return the arm to his lap instead of allowing you to drop it and support it by his side.

This next test can deepen the state even further ***as you test*** and you can see the effects of deepening by watching the whites of the eyes in some clients turn pink.

Say to your client: *"In a moment I will count from one to three -- when I say the number three, I want you to open your eyes and then close them again. Each time I say the number three - I want you to open your eyes and then close them again. Each and every time you open and close your eyes, you go deeper into hypnosis. Is this OK with you?"* Wait for a response. *"Good, -- one -- two-- three--"*

Wait for them to open and then close their eyes - the opening and closing should be a slow blink. Encourage them to open and then close their eyes. Count to three at least three times and allow them to open and close their eyes while establishing a rhythm. Then, when they are following your instructions... count one... two... and **pause for at least three seconds** and then say the number three. If they open their eyes before you reach three, they are not deep in hypnosis. Repeat your instructions and establish a rhythm again. If they do not open eyes until you say the number three - you have established a good rapport with the client and he is deep in hypnosis.

Confusion & Misdirection Inductions

Physical confusion:

Visual - Eye Closure Confusion Induction

By: Zali Segal

Hold a blinking light in front of client above eye level (you may use any flashlight or a blinking LED toy found in a novelty store).

Instruct the client: "Fix your gaze on the blinking light. When I count "one" I want you to close your eyes. When I count "two" reopen them. Pay close attention and follow my count immediately. Soon you will feel your eyes are getting heavier and heavier and you are drifting into a pleasant trance. Very soon your eyes will feel so comfortably heavy that you want to keep them closed. I want you not to close them and to keep them closed only as fast as you are going into a deep hypnotic state."

Start counting in a rhythm at first: "One"... "Two"..."One"..."Two"

Now start changing the rhythm. After a few more counts, start deliberately confusing the client: "One... One... Two-One... Two... One-Two... Two-One, etc.

As soon as client stops opening eyes, touch the forehead and say, in a firm commanding voice, "Keep them closed and go deeper, deeper and deeper".

At this point you can put away the flashing light.

This confusion induction can be also performed with auditory or kinesthetic signals.

Auditory: Stand behind the client. Instruct him to concentrate on a focal point ahead. When you snap your fingers next to his right ear (or ring a bell) he should close eyes. When snapping on the left, reopen eyes.

Kinesthetic: Same as above. Tap client lightly on the shoulders alternately.
The key is to create a rhythm at the beginning then scramble everything.
Also remember to emphasize: "Do not close your eyes and keep them closed any faster than you are going into a deep trance!"

Auditory - Confussional Induction

By: Zali Segal

(Props: two bells or clickers or any noise producing instruments)

Have the client seated while you are positioned behind him.

Instruct the client as follows: "When I will sound the bell on your right side (not too far from the right ear) I want you to raise your left hand, then, put it down. When I sound the bell on your left, raise your right hand".

Now proceed to sound the bell alternately: right... left... right... left... left... left... right... right... both together... (Now increase the pace) left... right... etc.

When you notice that the client is confused and having difficulty following your instructions, abruptly pat him on both shoulders while authoritatively firing the command "Sleep!"

Kinesthetic - Rotating Hands Confussional Induction

By: Zali Segal

(Instruct client to place hand in front him and start rotating them, as if spooling a ball of yarn.)

Say: "Listen intently to my instructions and follow them as closely as you can. Now rotate your hands faster... faster... slower... reverse... faster... reverse... slower... faster... reverse... reverse... faster... slower... faster... faster... faster... reverse... faster... reverse..."

Continue a barrage of instructions with the intent of confusing the client.

When you notice the client hesitant and having difficulty following your instruction, it is time to induce hypnosis.

In a swift motion reach out and stop his hands from moving while at the same time fire a stern command "Sleep!"

Then drop his hand gently in his lap while saying: "Relax and go deeper and deeper".

The Vertigo Induction

By: Robert F. Otto C.Ht.

This induction is based on our natural ability to sense motion and exploits the natural trance state that occurs when we experience Vertigo.

Vertigo; as defined by *Merriam-Webster Dictionary:*

a: disordered state in which the individual or the individual's surroundings seem to whirl dizzily

b: a dizzy confused state of mind"

The Biology

A cut away view of the ear shows the semicircular canal. The semicircular canal detects angular acceleration and yaw. This canal is filled with a gel-type fluid and microscopic hairs called cupula. The cupula is imbedded within the canal and senses the movement of fluid.

Due to inertia, when the subject is rotated, the fluid in the canal lags behind the rotation, thus bending the cupula. The vestibular nerve located at the bottom of the cupula transmits a clockwise indication to the brain. As the rotation continues at about 15 RPM, the fluid begins to catch up with the rotation of the canal, while giving the subject a *false* sensation of slowing down.

Another *false* sensation is that of *no motion* at all, if both fluid and canal rotate at the *same speed.* Had the subject been kept at a constant speed of 15 RPM for several moments, the cupula would return to the vertical position.

Deceleration causes the subject to sense a counter-clockwise rotation, due to the tilt of the cupula in the opposite direction. When stopped suddenly to 0 RPM, the fluid continues to rush onward bending the cupula all the way over, indicating an extreme turn to the left. Hence, within 10-13 seconds we have induced a physiological state of vertigo that ***MUST*** occur.

The Set-Up

Equipment needed: a comfortable chair with leg support that can rotate freely and smoothly.

"OK __________ *(client's name)*, what I am going to do now is to simply ask you to seat yourself (*suggestion of compliance*) comfortably in the chair and place your hands in your lap. *(Make sure client's feet do not interfere with any obstructions, or touching the floor. Make the gesture, unconscious command, of handing them a pen/pencil, or any other appropriate modality).* After you are comfortably seated I am going to rotate the chair in a clockwise direction a few times. You will feel a few intermittent interruptions in the rotation as I do this. However, at some point, you will feel yourself moving in the opposite direction. When this occurs, you will also begin to feel a total and complete sense of total physical relaxation. When you feel yourself moving in that opposite direction, along with physical relaxation, I would like you to simply drop the pen/pencil. The rotation in the opposite direction will become as smooth as silk. No interruptions at all. What I would like you to do with the pen/pencil now is to ask that you direct the pen/pencil to the way you are rotating. When you feel yourself moving to the left, point the pen/pencil to the left. And likewise, when you feel yourself moving to the right, point the pencil to the right. When the rotation becomes as smooth as silk in the opposite direction, drop the pen. Are you certain that you understand my instructions? Good!"

The Induction

Stand behind the client that is safely seated in the chair and place your hands upon their shoulders with slight down pressure. As you do this, speak softly and begin the induction. "Just close your eyes now and listen to the sound of my voice. Any and all outside interference will be of little importance to you at this time. You are enjoying the feeling of relaxation sweeping over your entire body from the tips of your toes to the top of your head. Feeling very relaxed and comfortable. Take a deep breath in and now out. Feeling very loose, limp and relaxed in every way. Begin the rotation."

Additional Instruction for the Therapist

Rotate the client eight to ten times. No more than 13. After the rotation, allow them to come to a slow and complete stop. Help the stop along if necessary. As the client comes to a complete stop and the pencil is dropped, begin your favorite deepening techniques. Do an arm drop test and begin the session.

The beginning of the session as the client is seated in the chair to a workable state of hypnosis should range from no more than 25 to 30 seconds before you begin therapy.

Reaffirm the induction immediately after your up count; simply by asking your client how much he enjoyed the "smooth as silk" opposite rotation. "No bumps at all were there?"

Using a post-hypnotic suggestion is beneficial when using the Vertigo Induction for demonstration purposes. It gives a clear and concise demonstration that the client was indeed hypnotized!

Mental Confusion:

The purpose of this type of induction is to distract the conscious mind by keeping it occupied with a meaningless task.

Start by stating to the client that when the client completes the task *or before*, the client will enter the hypnotic state.

As the client is trying to follow the instructions and compete the task the hypnotist is giving suggestions that lead to hypnosis.

An Induction for the Analytical Resister

By: C. Roy Hunter , M.S., CH

How often do you have an analytical resister in your office? Many experienced hypnotists have often heard an analytical person emerging from hypnosis with words such as, "I didn't feel hypnotized," or "I heard every word you said."

What often happens is that the analytical person will invariably try to analyze hypnotic wording as well as the entire experience, even if he/she has a strong desire to be hypnotized. When I studied hypnosis under the late Charles Tebbetts back in 1983, I was one of the analytical ones who suffered from analysis paralysis - which prevented me from attaining even a medium depth of trance until some time after my training was complete. At Charlie's, the students that practiced with me could only get themselves comfortable with progressive relaxation or eye fixation inductions...and an occasional rapid induction which was mostly ineffective with me.

Some weeks after becoming certified, I traded sessions with someone who finally used a mental confusion induction on me - and it was the first time I really felt hypnotized! During my years of practicing clinical hypnotherapy, I've often used mental confusion inductions with others who are analytical. While some hypnotists give up on the analytical resister without understanding what he/she is feeling, I understand from experience what the thought processes are during the initial induction...and I'm willing to take the extra time when necessary to help someone achieve and believe the hypnotic experience. Perhaps that was my gift for having been slow to experience hypnosis.

There is no induction that is so effective that it will work with all the people all the time, but if you master your favorite induction with confidence and competence, it will probably work with most of the people most of the time. That being said, I cannot overstate the importance of knowing a number of inductions. Furthermore, there are some people who will resist almost any induction you use, while they may respond quite well to a mental confusion technique.

Here is an induction taken from Chapter 5 of my book, *The Art of Hypnosis: Mastering Basic Techniques* (3rd Edition, Kendall/Hunt Publishing, 2000)

The technique begins by asking the client or participant(s) to stare at the object of their choice (wall, etc.). I ask the client to then take three deep breaths, following my simple instructions, and closing the eyes upon the third breath. Then, the instructions are: open your eyes on odd numbers, and close your eyes on even numbers.

100, just close your eyes, take a deep breath, and relax...

99 open them; take another deep breath, and 98... eyes closed. Very good. Just imagine you're releasing all the cares of the day as easily as you release the air from your lungs... 97... find it's getting more difficult to even try to open your eyes. 96, eyes closed. Good. Just find yourself wanting to go deeper and deeper as you forget whether your eyes should be open or closed.... 95... easy to forget. 94... difficult to remember, whether they should be closed... and as soon as you forget, they stay closed and you can just relax even deeper. 93... good. 92.... deeper and deeper relaxed... It's so easy to respond to my voice as I say 91... 90... and your eyes just want to stay closed now.

(Start speaking somewhat quicker and with more authority now).

88... 86... Deeper and deeper. Easy to forget, difficult to remember. 84-82... whether they should be open or closed. 79... 75... 74... The numbers are skipping away so quickly now that you just find yourself wanting to go deeper as your eyes want to stay closed. And every time you forget to remember, or remember to forget, open or closed, odd or even, you just go deeper and deeper, or deeper and deeper. 60... 50... Eyes closed and going deeper. Forgetting to remember. Remembering to forget. 40... 30... Feeling good. Responding to my voice. Relaxing deeper and deeper.

Once your client leaves his/her eyes totally closed during an odd number, the moment of passivity has usually occurred. You may stop the counting if you wish and follow immediately with deepening suggestions (explained in Chapter 6), or continue on as part of the deepening.

In the above technique, Charles Tebbetts taught that you may enhance the mental confusion with incomplete sentences, or by bringing unrelated sentences and meaningless statements into the sleep and relaxation suggestions. He gave Dr. Milton Erickson credit for this idea both in his class at Edmonds as well as in his book, *Miracles on Demand*.

Note that the above script is intended as a guide only. In my opinion, scripts are like training wheels; they are to serve you until you can master the art without needing the training wheels! Add your own personality and style, adapting to each individual client. However, in a group setting, you may wish to use a script. Note that I often use a few added trance-enhancers, such as double-binds and challenge suggestions. Normally I'll include a suggestion such as: *"It's so easy to imagine your peaceful place, that you can also imagine getting sleepy, with your eyelids heavy, droopy and drowsy... in fact, your eyelids may feel so heavy that even if you try to open them, you find they just want to stay shut, and you go MUCH deeper... double the hypnosis or triple the trance. Very good... deeper and deeper... into the realm of hypnotic sleep or into profound hypnosis".*

In addition, I frequently give a time-distortion suggestion at the end of the journey, just prior to awakening. This often adds to the impact of the experience, leaving only the most ardent analytical resister with traces of skepticism.

Be aware that some clients may experience a partial hypnotic amnesia because of the suggestions. "Forget to remember, or remembering to forget..." You may need to give specific suggestions for the client to remember those portions of the session where recall is desired. Also, the use of a time distortion suggestion just prior to awakening can add to the effect of the session, providing further trance validation to an analytical person.

If you've not yet employed a mental confusion induction, learn it and use it. Also, if you've never experienced being hypnotized with a mental confusion induction, you owe it to yourself and your clients to experience it for yourself! Find a hypnotist in your area and trade sessions.

Circle in the Sand

By: Zali Segal

The following induction is designed for the analytical client who has difficulty letting go and entering the hypnotic state. The purpose of this method is to temporarily eliminate conscious interference. By keeping the conscious mind occupied with a meaningless task (the alphabet), we are able to bypass the critical faculty and access the subconscious more easily.

Say to the client: "Soon I will ask you to close your eyes and imagine yourself on a beach. Then I will direct you to draw in the sand a circle with the letter "A" inside, just like in this picture (show client the picture on the right). Then I will direct you to, very carefully, erase the corners of the "A" that are touching the circle, making absolute certain that you do not disturb the circle because we have to reuse it. When you disconnected the "A" from the circle go ahead and erase the entire letter "A." Then you will draw the letter "B" inside the circle with the corners of the "B" touching the circle, again very carefully making sure you do not disturb the circle.

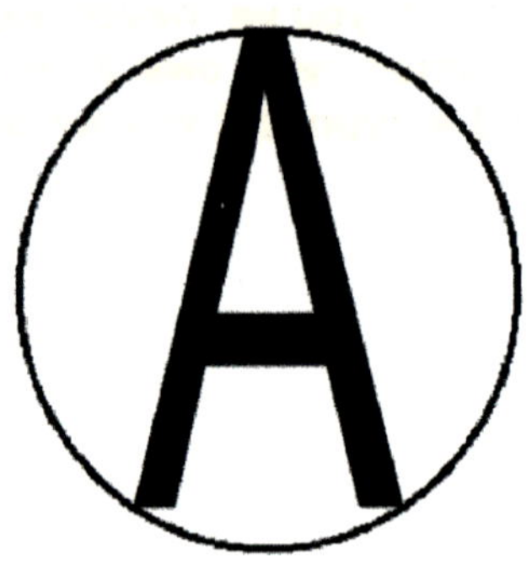

Is that clear? Yes. Good.

Now, with your eyes closed, imagine you are walking on a beautiful deserted beach. It is peaceful and quiet. The weather is mild and comfortable. The sun is gentle and the waves are lapping at the shore with a pleasant sound. You are barefoot and the warm sand feels wonderful.

With a long stick, draw a large circle in the sand. Inside the circle draw the letter "A" with the three corners of the "A" touching the circle. Now I would like you to imagine you are reaching over and very carefully erasing the three corners of the "A" that are touching the circle, very carefully, making absolute certain that you do not disturb the circle, because we have to reuse it. You have to concentrate and do it slowly and deliberately.

When you have finished and the inside of the circle is nice and smooth, go ahead and draw the letter "B" inside the circle, so it touches the circle lightly in four points.

Now hold it a moment and wait for my further instructions. When I tell you to go ahead, you will continue with the alphabet, making a "C" and erasing it, making a "D" and so forth the entire alphabet. But once you start to do that, from that point forward, don't listen to me anymore. By that I mean don't make any effort to listen to me. I will be talking, of course, and you will be hearing me, but don't try to follow my instructions. Don't try to follow what I am saying, because I will be talking to your subconscious mind, which always hears, which always pays attention. Your job is to keep going right through the alphabet, making and erasing each letter in succession, paying no attention to me at all — that is, until you have finished the whole job. When you have made and erased the letter "Z," you will then erase the entire circle and you will raise your right index finger as a signal to me that you are done. Once you have done that, you can listen to me again. By that time, you will be in a deep state of hypnosis and in a deeper level than you have been before. Remember to focus on the task at hand slowly and deliberately.

Now go ahead and carefully erase the letter "B" that you drew in the circle. Then keep on going with the entire alphabet, but pay no further attention to me. Every letter that you draw causes you to relax more and more. Each letter you erase causes you to drift more easily and more readily into hypnosis. The closer you come to the letter Z, the deeper into hypnosis you go. With each letter you make and each letter you erase, you drift down and down, deeper and deeper into the hypnotic state - feeling more pleasant, more peaceful and serene, as you keep on going down, deeper and deeper, with each letter you draw in that circle and each you erase in that circle. When you finish your job, with the entire alphabet, your right index finger will rise all by itself to signal that you are finished and then you can listen to me again. In the meantime, keep right on making your letters and erasing your letters. With each letter you make and each letter you erase, you drop further and further into hypnosis. I am talking directly into your subconscious mind and all you have to do is to keep on doing what you are doing until you have finished. And as you raise your finger to show me that you have finished, you will be in a deeper level of hypnosis than you have ever been before. Keep right on going, making your letters and erasing your letters. The closer you come to the letter Z, the deeper you go. With every letter you are going deeper and deeper into a pleasant relaxed hypnotic state.

(Keep this patter until your receive the signal that the process is finished. If it takes too long it is OK to instruct the client to speed it up.)

Now that you have finished, you can listen to me once again, because now you are in a deeper level than you have ever been before".

Hypnotist: enter our suggestions here…

Imagination Inductions

Wicker Basket Induction

By: Richard A. Neves, Ph.D.

As you relax even deeper now... use your minds eye... and bring into focus... a green pathway. It looks very peaceful... very tranquil... with all the shades of green vibrant and alive... your favorite flowers are growing along this path... and you have a strong desire to walk over to those flowers... so that you can smell their soft, delicate fragrance. Your nostrils begin to warm now... as their fragrance alerts your senses even more.

Begin to walk down this path now... ever so slowly... ever so calmly, taking into view all the beauty of this wonderful, peaceful, quiet... pathway... and in walking down this path... allow yourself to go even deeper into this state of relaxation. You come upon a flat rock... that resembles a small table... and on that rock... you notice that there is a wicker basket just sitting there... and in that wicker basket are a few small smooth stones.

There is no one in sight... so surely someone has left this beautiful basket behind... and as you examine the area even closer... you note that there are several of the smooth stones lying about on the ground... all around the beautiful foliage... there are many of these stones... each and every one of them... a different color... shape... and size.

You decide to carry the basket along with you... and in making that decision... you see yourself picking the basket up... and placing it over your arm... as you begin to walk down that pathway... enjoying the tranquility... the peace... the deep relaxation... that the clear... fresh air brings... and allowing the beauty of the path to bring into your mind and body a great sense of well being. Going further now down this path... you notice that there are more of the smooth, small rocks... at the side of the path... and each one still very different and very unique.

You begin to feel a deep attraction to some of the stones... so you begin to pick certain ones up... as you continue to walk down this path... and with each and every one that you pick up... you gently place it in your newfound wicker basket.

Feel the smoothness of each and every stone that you place in your basket now, as you continue down this path... going deeper and deeper into this garden of relaxation.

Hear the faint... click... as each and every stone gently taps the others that are nestled in the basket... look down at your basket and see the collection of smooth rocks that your basket is accumulating... as you continue to walk down this beautiful path.

As you continue to walk deeper and deeper into this garden, you gather more and more of the small smooth stones... each one unique... each and every one different.

Look there... just in front of you... is a clearing... with a small, clear, blue pond. At the water's edge... smooth, white, fine grains of sand... warmed by the sunlight that is filtering in through the tree tops. The foliage displays drops of dew on the green... green leaves... as the sun's rays bring fresh light into this wonderful, beautiful... garden setting.

You notice that there are small patches of grass all round... so that you can sit down on the soft, green, tufts of grass, if you so desire... walk over to the water's edge... and sit down in the smooth warmness of the clean, white sand or on a patch of green grass... and as you sit down... you allow yourself to go deeper... and deeper and deeper... into this state of relaxation.

Take your shoes off... and put them down to the side... so that you can wriggle your toes down into the softness of the sand... and as you do so your foot goes deeper... and deeper into the sand until you can feel the moisture beneath the surface layer of sand. It is so moist... so cool... and so soft.

As you look into the pond you can see your own reflection on the surface of the water... and you intently study your own image. Looking so very closely now... and you see yourself just as you are... and you note every detail... about yourself.

A soft breeze begins to blow gently through your hair... and causes the pond... to ripple... until your concentration is now broken away from yourself... and with each and every ripple you allow yourself to become more and more relaxed... and you find your concentration now focuses on the wicker basket... that is full of small smooth stones.

Reach down and pick up the wicker basket... and as you pick up that basket... you notice how heavy it is... and you begin to wonder why you had not noticed how heavy it was as you were carrying it.

It is so very heavy that you must set it down on the bank of this pond next to you... and in setting it down... you become attracted to the small, smooth stones that are piled up in the lovely basket... pick that first stone up... and examine it very carefully now... and in examining it... feel it... look at it... and as you turn it over, you see that there is something written on the bottom of that small stone... it says... FEAR... in big bold letters... you begin to examine each and every stone now...

And you realize that there is something written on each and every stone that you picked up along the way... and in realizing this, you decide to read them all... and to rid yourself of all the undesirable ones... so that they no longer weigh you or your basket down.

First you slowly and ever so deliberately cast the stone that says FEAR on it, right into the middle of the pond... and you watch it quickly sink to the very bottom... actually hear it plop as it hits the surface of the water... and when the rippling stops... you know that Fear is at the bottom of that pond... and you begin to feel lighter.

The next stone is spelling out... GUILT... and because you have no desire to feel that emotion... you cast that stone right into the middle of the pond... knowing that it, too, is sinking to the very bottom, and as it sinks to the bottom... and the last ripple ripples... you free yourself... by releasing and letting go of all the guilt that you have felt through accumulation over the years and times gone past. You begin to feel even lighter.

And in feeling lighter you know and realize that there is absolutely nothing to feel guilty about. The next stone is spelling out... ANXIETY... so you quickly... toss it into the pond so that it may sink to the bottom... forever... never allowing it to be a part of you from this moment on... The next stone's clearly labeled... ANGER... the next... ENVY... the next... GREED... the... next... CONFUSION... then... FRUSTRATION... JEALOUSY... FALSE EGO... JUDGEMENT... DEPRESSION...

CONTROL... OF... OTHERS... RESENTMENT... and with each and every one of these stones representing an undesirable emotion, thought or action... that has been relative to you... you throw all of these stones... into the middle of the pond... and is so doing, cast out of your life all negative emotion... and all undesirable characteristics, actions and attitudes, allowing them to disappear into the depths of this cleansing pond... for it is cleansing you of all the negativity that you have held on to in your lifetime.

As you are and as you remain cleansed... you feel lighter and lighter just as though a huge weight... has been lifted directly off of your shoulders... allow that light feeling to flow through your body now and as it flows through your body... you find you are emotionally elevated and totally at peace with your world and yourself.

Again you gaze into your basket... you see several stones are left... so you examine all of them... and in so doing you see why it felt so heavy... for they were all those negative emotions that were weighing you down... bringing the weight of the world onto your shoulders... so release and let go of all those emotions, now as you toss the entire basket into the water, now... and watch it sink to the very bottom of the pond.

And as the water stops rippling you look into the depth of the pond... stand up and look at the very center of the pond... and in looking into the depths of that pond... you see that there is not a trace of the basket or any of the small stones... for you have cast those stones and their meanings out of your life forever... never to see them again.

Now the water forms its glassy surface... you gaze at the reflection... and you see again the reflection of yourself... only... this time... void of the heaviness of emotion... and you notice that you look so self-confident... so self assured... and so very... very... poised... able... and so ready to get on with the joys of your life."

The Staircase Induction

By: Henry Leo Bolduc CH

As soon as you are ready, ask yourself to close your eyes. If you take a deep breath, you can feel your body relaxing. As you slow your breathing, you let your mind relax.

Begin by comparing your mind to the surface of a quiet pond. My voice can be as a breeze whispering in the trees along the shore. The pond remains smooth and calm, even though things go on beneath the surface. There may be much happening beneath a still surface. The gentle surface conceals an extraordinary depth. Reflect upon nature, its beauty and elegance. (Pause, one minute)

Now it is easy to dissolve this image and to form another... perhaps a stairway leading down... you can see yourself leisurely descending. The stairs are covered with a thick, plush carpet, a carpet that is like a cloud beneath your feet. Perhaps there is a brass handrail or a walnut banister. The stairs lead you to a ballroom with sparkling crystal chandeliers, or to a comfortable room with books and crackling logs in a fireplace. And, while you are here, the outside world will *stay* outside. You can take a few minutes and notice just how good you feel here. (Pause, one minute)

You can do anything you want to do. You don't even have to listen to my voice, because your subconscious hears with new awareness and responds all by itself. You are now learning to recognize the feelings that accompany inner relaxation. You may experience a light, medium or deep level of relaxation; you choose what is best for you. Your body may feel heavy or it may feel light, or it may seem to be asleep so that it doesn't feel anything at all. It may float up, or it may sink down, or it may very pleasantly drift. It may do whatever you wish. Perhaps your body feels as if it has gone to sleep even though your mind seems to be awake. Of course, you don't have to concern yourself with that.

This experience is for learning and growing. Of course, you may go very deep and safely. Your inner mind is aware; it knows when it needs to respond and it can do so in just the right way. It already has gained more awareness. If I count from ten to one, then you may go deeper... more in perfect harmony... by picturing yourself descending a flight of stairs, or going down in an elevator or on an escalator... any pleasant image that you wish... ten... nine... eight... seven... six... five... four... three... two... one....

And if I count from ten to one again, you may go twice as deep, enjoying a pleasant, comfortable feeling — any sort of feeling that you wish... Ten, Nine, Eight, Seven, Six, Five, Four, Three, Two, One.

As you relax, take a deep breath, and slow down, you may go even deeper. As you enjoy the comfort, you will note that there is less and less importance to my voice. You may find yourself drifting in your own ideal, joyful place of relaxation. Pause.

Now we can begin a series of exercises using Creative Imagination and Positive Affirmation.

The Great Brain Exercise - Induction

By: Jillian LaVelle CH.

This is an induction that I learned a number of years ago from my mentor, Jean Houston, Ph.D. It is also featured in her book, *The Hero and the Goddess*. I think that when it is done correctly it feels like you have just massaged your brain. The images you give after the induction are extremely vivid.

Script for the guide:

"Close your eyes and direct your attention to your breathing. Allow the rhythm of your breath to become regular... Focus on the breath of air, inhaling and expanding your lungs... Exhale and allow them to contract... Take a couple of deep breaths noticing the expansion and contraction... Allow your conscious to shift into your left eye. Keeping both eyes closed, look down with your left eye. Then up. Roll it to the right, then left. Allow them to flow easily up, down, right, then left. Do this at your own pace. Up, down, right, then left. Do this several times... Good. Now allow the left eye to circle clockwise. Making the circles as large or small as feels good to you...

Excellent. Now reverse the circle to flow counterclockwise. Again, take this at your own pace. Make a few circles... That's right. Now allow your eyes to become still and centered. Take a deep breath into the left eye. Allow it to relax as you exhale...Good. Now focus your attention on your right eye. Simply shift your consciousness to your right eye. Allow it to move up and down. Up and down, at your own pace. Up and down. Do this several times... Good. Now right and left. Right and left, with your right eye, at your own pace. Shifting right and left... Good. Now, clockwise circles, as small or large as is comfortable to you. Continue to make circles with your right eye... Good. Now reverse the circle. Go counterclockwise, several times with your eye. Allow it to roll freely...

Excellent. Allow that eye to rest and relax. Take a deep breath into your right eye. Allow the muscles to feel soft. Exhale and let go. Rest for a moment... Now keeping your eyes close direct your attention to your breathing and take a deep breath into the right side of your brain... Exhale and take a second deep breath into the left side of your brain... Exhale. Shift back and forth a few times, breathing into each hemisphere. Notice how it feels as you do so. Simply shifting your conscious attention from one side to another.

Now place your consciousness on your left eye and have it journey through your left brain by moving your left eye... It can randomly explore one section to another, or you can have it circle the left hemisphere, whatever feels more comfortable to you... Now take a deep breath and allow your left eye to relax. Shift your attention to your right eye and begin to allow it to explore the right hemisphere of your brain... You can make circles or allow it to dart from one part to another... Breathe deeply into your right brain while you do this. Good, now allow your right eye to rest and relax. Take a deep breath into your left brain... Exhale. Now take another breath into your right brain and exhale...

In a moment I would like for you to explore all areas of your brain with both eyes together. Simply begin by having them circle throughout the brain. Explore your whole brain from the back of the skull to the forebrain. Circling and circling. At your own pace, in your own comfort. Continue to breathe deeply into the whole brain while doing this exercise. Breathe into the parts of your brain that controls your habits. Take another breath and explore the parts of your brain that stores memories. Circle, with your eyes, the areas of the brain that control your moods, emotions, feelings, and sense of reality.

Now allow your circles to start becoming smaller and smaller around the center point of your brain. Becoming more centered with every breath that you take, with every beat of your heart. Focus your attention on the center of your brain and allow your eyes to rest there. Continue to breathe deeply into the center of your consciousness. Allow the images to begin to come forth that will help you with your goal for healing today".

Note to guide: Continue with your imagery/therapy in achieving the goal for the client. Add in a lot of textures, colors and vivid images. Their brain is very activated, use the energy.

Ericksonian Style Inductions

Storytelling Hypnosis

By: Bill O'Connell CH

My favorite way to hypnotize is through the use of stories. What makes Story telling Hypnosis so wonderful is two-fold: 1) The experience of being hypnotized by listening to stories is most enjoyable for clients, and 2) You, the hypnotist, have the added benefit of bypassing the resistance that comes with more traditional inductions.

Before I explain the process of Storytelling Hypnosis, let me first give you a very brief explanation of how hypnotizing through story telling began.

If you have studied the history of hypnosis during this century, you have undoubtedly learned of Milton H. Erickson, MD. Erickson, a psychiatrist by training, invented the indirect approach to hypnotizing others. Erickson was a brilliant and innovative pioneer who was not afraid to experiment with new ideas.

After studying the traditional direct or authoritarian approach of inducing hypnosis, and utilizing these methods for some time, Erickson tried out the idea of using indirect suggestion, permissive language, stories and metaphorical communication. While his contemporaries were going about inducing hypnosis using direct commands, e.g., "Your eyes are getting heavy; you are beginning to feel sleepy, v-e-r-y sleepy..." Erickson tried suggesting these experiences indirectly, very often by telling stories about <u>other people</u>, doing <u>other things.</u> This way he avoided making direct suggestions to his clients. Rather, he *suggested ideas through stories.*

Frequently, after gathering the appropriate background information and history on a client, Erickson would begin his hypnotic induction by saying, "I had a patient once..." and then he would tell a series of long, rambling stories that seemed to have no purpose whatsoever. At least not to the client's *conscious mind*. But within these stories were *indirect* suggestions, not only for inducing hypnosis, but for solutions to the client's presenting problem as well.

Erickson would tell story after story, about previous clients, about his childhood experiences, about people he had encountered in life, and their unique challenges and creative solutions. And while Erickson was telling these stories...

He Was Hypnotizing Them!

You see, Milton Erickson utilized a framework of story telling, which was non-threatening for the client, as a foundation for the hypnotic induction. Most people love to hear stories. Stories are interesting. Stories are enjoyable. *Stories are easy to become absorbed in.* And sitting back, listening to someone tell a story, can be a very relaxing experience. Especially if the person telling the story uses a very soft, soothing tone of voice. So the experience of *becoming relaxed* occurs naturally when telling stories. And of course, relaxing the client is one of the first outcomes a hypnotist typically strives for when using a traditional progressive relaxation hypnotic induction. But rather than give direct suggestions for relaxation, and try to "tell" the subject what they "should" experience, the same response can be evoked simply by telling stories, using a soft and soothing tone of voice. With this approach, the result *occurs naturally*.

In addition, suggestions for relaxation can be offered indirectly by talking about other people (past clients, friends, yourself, etc.) having the experience of *enjoying a relaxing experience*. The key is to simply describe the experience in rich, vivid detail. For example:

"I had a client once who used to tell me about his most enjoyable experiences of taking wonderful, long bike rides on a trail through a forest near his home. In the beginning, he was very much aware of having to make an effort to push each pedal to move forward. But before long, he completely lost awareness of pedaling at all, and he would become deeply absorbed in the delight of all God's creations. The fresh aroma of clean fall air. The chirps and peeps of the crickets, grasshoppers and birds around. The refreshing and invigorating coolness. All of the beauty of nature, such a welcome newness from his normal routine. And the further he rode the more and more r-e-l-a-x-e-d he began to feel. And as he road down the long, winding path...going deeper and deeper...into the beautiful woods, sometimes he would really begin to notice that the leaves were just beginning to change into their fall colors. You can really see the beautiful bright yellows, the deep oranges and glowing reds. And sometimes the delightful colors were so transfixing that a person could really...gaze at that one spot...and just fix your eyes there...N-O-W...as it is so nice to find oneself enjoying—really enjoying the experience completely..."

Read the paragraph above out loud, to yourself, using a very *soft, soothing tone of voice...as if you were trying to put a baby to sleep...*and perhaps you may *begin to discover* that the response of relaxation occurs quite naturally when you listen to a detailed description of a person having the experience of relaxation.

We will return to the example above, in a longer version later. For now, I want to make the point that:

All of the Direct Suggestions Used in Any Traditional Hypnotic Induction Can Be Given Indirectly Through the Use of Stories.

It doesn't matter what the suggestion is. If it can be given directly, as a command, it can also be delivered indirectly through the use of stories.
It's actually quite simple when you think about it. Instead of telling your client to "focus on any spot," and as you do, "your eyes are beginning to get heavier and heavier" you can suggest these experiences/responses *indirectly* by telling a story about someone else having the experience. As Richard Bandler and John Grinder pointed out years ago, the only way any person can make sense of an experience described in detail is to go inside their own mind and imagine the experience themselves.

The concept that all "hypnotic" suggestions, including a complete induction, can be given through the use of a story, is powerful. The possibilities are great. You can literally give a full-blown hypnotic induction to anyone, at anytime, simply by telling them a story, and including a detailed description of another person having the experience of going into a deeply relaxed state.

Additionally, every conceivable suggestion for any intervention, which can be given directly utilizing traditional approaches, can also be given indirectly by including detailed descriptions of another person experiencing those suggestions in the form of a story.

Here is my simple, three step approach to hypnotizing others through the use of stories:

1. **Have a word-for-word Storytelling Hypnosis script at your disposal.** You can use mine, included here for your convenience, or you can create your own, based upon your own unique experiences.
2. **Within this script, include suggestions that you normally use in your induction.** I have included suggestions for inward focus of attention, relaxation, visual fixation and deepening in the script that follows. Feel free to modify this script in any way that makes it more comfortable and natural for you. Remember, just as there are no "right" or "wrong" hypnotic inductions, there are no right or wrong Storytelling Hypnosis Scripts.
3. **Create different intervention scripts for the different applications of hypnosis.** This will allow you to have one interventional story script for clients who desire weight loss. A second story script for those who want to stop smoking, etc. To create these scripts, develop a story based on the outcome desired by your subject. Include detailed descriptions of both the problem and the solution within the text of your script.

What follows is the induction script I use. When delivering this story, I speak in a soft, soothing tone of voice. Before giving the story, I may ask my subject to close their eyes and explain that I am going to help them relax by telling them a nice story.

Storytelling Hypnosis Induction Ericksonian Style

By: Bill O'Connell CH

"I had a client once who used to tell me about his most enjoyable experiences of taking wonderful, long bike rides on a trail through a forest near his home. In the beginning, he was very much aware of having to make an effort to push each pedal to move forward. But before long, he completely lost awareness of pedaling at all, and he would become deeply absorbed in the delight of all God's creations. The fresh aroma of clean fall air. The chirps and peeps of the crickets, grasshoppers and birds around. The refreshing and invigorating coolness. All of the beauty of nature, such a welcome newness from his normal routine.

And the further he rode the more and more r-e-l-a-x-e-d he began to feel. And as he road down the long, winding path… going deeper and deeper… into the beautiful woods, sometimes he would really begin to notice that the leaves were just beginning to change into their fall colors. You can really see the beautiful bright yellows, the deep oranges and glowing reds. And sometimes the delightful colors were so transfixing that a person could really… gaze at that one spot… and just fix your eyes there… N-O-W… as it is so nice to find oneself enjoying—really enjoying the experience completely… beginning to feel more and more relaxed, as all of the stress and tension just f-l-o-w-s out of your body. And he would continue going deeper and deeper into the forest, just becoming lost in your own world of pleasant thoughts.

And there's really no need to pay attention to anything at all, other than the sound of my voice, as you continue to enjoy, really enjoy, this delightful story, allowing yourself to enjoy the soothing images, sounds and feelings in your own mind, in your own way. And this client of mine would continue to tell me how a person could become totally relaxed and allow all of the stress and tension to just flow out of your body now as one becomes deeply absorbed in the experience, enjoying the wonderful, deep absorption in thought, and the wonderful deep relaxation. And as you are listening to this story of this client of mine, and as you are enjoying the soft, soothing tone of my voice, and as you are allowing yourself to relax even more and more, perhaps you may begin to allow your head to gently drop down so that your chin touches your chest. That's right... your head going down... down... down... just let it go… all the way down… touching your chest… N-O-W…

And it really does not matter if your head begins to drift down slowly… or if it drifts down quickly… so long as it just happens at its own pace, in its own time… that's right… comfortably drifting down… and going deeper and deeper and deeper… and even still deeper yet… my client would continue on his most delightful ride through the wonderful, deeply relaxing experience… a person can, you know, allow themselves to just let go completely now and become so very relaxed that they become lost in the experience of feeling soooo good, feeling soooo relaxed, feeling soooo wonderfully calm… and peaceful… and safe… and secure… that's right… all of the stress and tension just flowing.. o-u-t… n-o-w…

and perhaps you may begin to notice now a wonderful... comforting warmth in the muscles in your neck and shoulders... perhaps you are becoming aware of the soothing warmth now... or perhaps it will take a few minutes to really begin to feel this wonderful, comforting warmth... and it's easy to imagine yourself... now... sitting comfortably and safely in a private tub of warm water... perhaps your own bathtub... or maybe a soothing whirlpool... wherever you are now beginning to imagine yourself, make sure it is a place where you feel very comfortable... very safe... very secure... very pleasant... becoming more and more relaxed... feeling the delightful, comforting warmth of the soothing water... and you may begin to notice that your legs are starting to relax completely... feeling so warm... so comfortable... so very, very relaxed... all of the stress and tension just melting away... such a wonderful, comforting, delightful experience... and you may begin to notice that soothing warmth spreading... now... all throughout your body...up your legs...through your abdomen...up into your chest... across your shoulders... down your arms... all the way out your fingertips... and I really do not know if you can let this happen completely now... or if you already have... or if it may take a few minutes to feel the relaxation so completely... that's right... and this client of mine would enjoy these delightful rides frequently... and times he wanted to feel good... and times he wanted to feel completely relaxed... and he would go to this special place as often as he liked... whenever he needed to go there... sometimes just for a short trip, lasting only a few minutes... and other times for hours... and a person can, you know, have those same experiences, and enjoy those same wonderful feelings anytime they choose... by revisiting the experience in the quietness of their own mind... and it doesn't really matter if it's a real bike ride, or an imagined one... because a person can, any time they wish, go to a quiet place, close their eyes, and become fully absorbed in the experience and feeling completely relaxed and comfortable... n-o-w..."

Notice how this script starts with a story, indirect suggestions are woven into the story (including classic hypnotic suggestions for relaxation and deepening) then kinesthetic sensory suggestions for warm, soothing water are given... then back to the original story. There's no magic to the form of this particular script, it's just one way that a story can be used to hypnotize indirectly.

While no special knowledge of indirect hypnotic techniques is needed at all to use the script given, those who have studied indirect hypnosis (particularly Erickson's work) will notice the script above includes a variety of methods, including:

- Permissive Language
- Embedded Commands
- Double binds
- Linking
- Confusion

I would like to draw your attention to the underlined portions of the script I have given you. If you will use a different voice inflection when reading the underlined parts of the script you are "marking out," or "embedding" these suggestions. The idea here is that by changing your voice quality slightly, by lowering, raising, speaking slower, or adding extra emphasis, the client's conscious mind does not notice the slight change, but their subconscious mind does. Here is an example:

"And this client of mine would continue to tell me how a person could become totally relaxed."

Notice the underlined part of the sentence: "become totally relaxed." It's actually a direct command to "become totally relaxed", but because it is embedded within a story, where we are talking about someone else, the client's conscious mind does not pick up on it. And by altering the tone, tempo or volume of your voice, only when you read the underlined part of the sentence, that part becomes "marked out" or an "embedded command..".

Practice this and you will find that giving embedded commands is very easy to do.

What About The Ethics of Hypnotizing Others Through Stories, Intentionally Doing So Without Their Awareness?

The ethical considerations of utilizing a disguised method of hypnosis through storytelling, or any other manner, are obvious. Rather than launch into a debate about the pros and cons of disguised hypnosis, I will leave the application of this approach up to each individual practitioner. Let your own good judgment guide your use. Those who seek only to help others will use all means at their disposal to achieve their aims. But the rogue hypnotist, who seeks only personal gain in the manipulation of others, will not be deterred by even the lengthiest admonishment or discourse on the ethical use of disguised methods.

Want to Learn More About Indirect Methods of Hypnotizing?

You might be intrigued to know that in addition to **Milton H. Erickson, MD**, **Dave Elman** was a frequent practitioner of disguised methods of hypnosis. Carefully read through Elman's book *Hypnotherapy* paying particular attention to the section on hypnotizing children, and you will enjoy a quite detailed explanation of Elman's approach to disguised hypnosis.

Harry Arrons, another major contributor to the field of hypnosis, also wrote about methods of hypnotizing others without their awareness. At this writing, a publication by Arrons, describing several different methods of "disguised" hypnosis is available through www.tranceworks.com, a web site that offers a variety of used and hard to locate hypnosis books, audio and videotapes.

Carol Sommer wrote the book *Conversational Hypnosis*, which is well worth your investment of time and money. And there is a disguised hypnosis induction script in *Hypnosis: Medicine of the Mind* by Dr. **Michael D. Preston**. (See page 114). Perhaps my favorite book on disguised hypnosis is, regrettably, no longer published. *Trance-Formations* by **Bandler and Grinder,** is outstanding, both in content and in form. If you come across this title at a used bookstore or library sale, snatch it up. It used to be readily available for about $10.00, but now sells for eight to ten times that on Internet auction sites, such as E-Bay.

Monsters and Magical Sticks - There's No Such Thing as Hypnosis? By **Steven Heller**, Ph.D. This is one of my favorite titles on the subject, and well worth picking up.

Most of the titles above are readily available, reasonably priced and highly recommended as resources for continuing your education on indirect hypnosis. Each book will expand your thinking as you learn each author's unique approach from his or her individual perspective.

Conclusion

Storytelling Hypnosis provides a wonderful approach to hypnotizing others, utilizing indirect suggestion, encased within tales of other people doing other things. As you being to practice your own application of hypnotizing through the use of stories, you may begin to discover how much you can enjoy helping others, by telling delightful tales that capture their imagination, guide their thoughts, feelings, and ultimately, their behaviors to help them achieve the outcomes they desire.

Shock to the System, Loss of Equilibrium And Other Rapid Induction Techniques

The Hand Drop Induction

By: Zali Segal

Extend your hand palm facing up. Ask your client to place his hand on top of yours and instruct him to push down (hold your hand close to your body for leverage while the client extends his hand far, so it is more difficult for him to push you down).

Say to client: "Keep pushing down throughout this process. Fix your gaze on my eye. In a moment, I will start counting from ten to one. On or before the count of "one" your hand will drop down and you will instantly close your eyes and enter a deep state of hypnosis (make sure the client will not get hurt by the arm of the chair of any other obstacle)".

Start counting slowly: "Ten- you may find that your eyes are getting tired and tend to blink and want to close but try and keep them open until you go into a deep hypnosis.

Nine - Eight - keep your pressure on my hand,
Seven – take a deep breath,
Six – keep your eyes fixed on me,
Five – keep the pressure,
Four – eyes getting tired want to close,
Three – take a deep breath keep the pressure,
Two – Take a deep breath"

At this point, before the client completes the inhale, slide your hand away in one swift motion, and at the same time, in a firm voice, command "SLEEP!"

Your client's hand will swing down with some force and a loss of equilibrium may occur, so make sure you are prepared and have your client's safety at heart.

Rapid Induction

By: Don Mottin

This induction is conducted while client is standing up. Feet together, arms comfortably by the side. Place your hand on client's shoulder and deliver the following suggestions.

"I am going to count from five down to one. On the count of one allow your eyes to close. The moment that your eyes close, your entire body will feel loose, and limp. You will feel yourself falling forward. I will catch you. You will not fall. If you understand, and agree, nod your head yes. **NOTE: WAIT FOR RESPONSE.** Five, hold the eyes open until I reach the count of one. Four, the eyes may be blinking, and feeling heavy, but hold them open until the count of one. Three, at the count of one allow the eyes to close, and the body to feel loose and limp. Two, almost there. Hold the eyes open a moment longer. Get ready. One, **SLEEP.**

NOTE: AT THE COUNT OF ONE THE HYPNOTHERAPIST DELIVERS A COMMAND OF "SLEEP!" AT THE SAME TIME THE THERAPIST IS PULLING THE CLIENT FORWARD, TOWARDS HIMSELF USING HIS RIGHT HAND THAT HAS BEEN RESTING ON THE CLIENT'S SHOULDER. THE CLIENT MAY NOW EITHER BE LOWERED TO THE FLOOR, OR ALLOWED TO LEAN AGAINST THE THERAPIST.
REQUIREMENTS FOR SUCCESS

- *The key word is TIMING. The suggestions and pulling motion must be executed at exactly the second that the eyes close. Too early, or too late will frighten the client.*
- *It is of paramount importance that the hypnotist stands with one leg back in a wide spread so to be able to prevent falling backwards.*

Blast Into Hyper Space

By: Zali Segal

This induction is based on the surprise factor. Thus timing is of the utmost importance.

Say to client: "Imagine yourself in a spaceship. You are the captain and you control the ship. You are sitting in front of the control panel full of instruments, buttons, dials etc.

In the center is a red lever. When you pull this lever down the spaceship, instantly blasts into hyperspace and you go, instantly into a deep, deep hypnosis. So reach out, and grab the lever and start aloud the count down from ten to zero. On or before you reach the count of zero you will find yourself instantly going into hypnosis".

Make sure client is extending his arm as if grabbing a real lever. Have the client start to count aloud. The client is expecting to complete the count but you will surprise him by abruptly pushing down his arm and in a loud authoritative voice command "SLEEP"!

Note: You must deliver your command when the client reaches the count of three or two. Definitely do not wait for the client count all the way to one to deliver your command. You need to create the startle affect to bypass the critical faculties to induce instant hypnosis.

Miscellaneous Inductions

Conversion Techniques

Suggestibility tests like the hand clasp test and the postural sway can be converted into inductions if it is observed that the client is susceptible.

Towards the end of the test, when you observed that the client is responding well, you suddenly and unexpectedly, command the client in a very authoritative voice "SLEEP!"

With the hands clasp test when you instruct the client to separate the hands and the client is unable to, you suddenly push down his hands while forcefully issuing the command "SLEEP"!

When using this technique with the postural sway test, you let the client fall back pretty far. You then catch the client but continue the motion all the way down to the floor while issuing the command "SLEEP!" and you lay him on the floor.

Caution: Make sure you are strong enough and braced to handle the fall.

In a similar manner, you can apply this surprise and shock technique to a wide variety of situations limited only by your imagination.

Hypnotic Induction with NLP

By: Don Mottin

NOTE TO THERAPIST: An NLP induction works best with a subject who has been hypnotized before, but will also be successful on a first induction. When using this technique with a first induction, the client must imagine the feeling that they will experience while being hypnotized. While standing behind the client, proceed in the following manner.

As I touch your right shoulder, I want you to recall the way that you felt just prior to being hypnotized. Now, as I touch your left shoulder, I want you to recall the way that you felt when you were hypnotized. Notice the difference in these feelings. As I touch your right shoulder, you are feeling the same way that you felt just prior to being hypnotized the first time. (TOUCH RIGHT SHOULDER)

As I touch your left shoulder, you are beginning to feel the way that you felt once you were hypnotized. (TOUCH LEFT SHOULDER)

As I continue touching your left shoulder, allow that feeling to grow stronger. Allow yourself to now enter a hypnotic state.

The Aromatic Induction

By: Susan Fox, CH

In my opinion, I think hypnotic inductions are the beginning steps of a trip, a mind trip. In *The American Heritage Dictionary of the English Language* the word "induce" is defined: "To lead or move by influence or persuasion..."

So, in clinical hypnotherapy practice when a person induces oneself into the trance state, it is the first step of going "on a trip." Only this "trip" is a mind destination and to get where the person wants to go, he or she begins with an induction.

Here is one of my favorite inductions:

"Relax your body and think of your very favorite fragrance. Another name for fragrance is the word aroma... Just go ahead and think of your very favorite aroma as you relax your body. You may choose to close your eyes so you can more easily concentrate on relaxing your body.

Notice as you remember your very favorite aroma or fragrance that you may also be seeing a favorite picture that seems to naturally be a part of your very favorite fragrance. Maybe your favorite fragrance is the aroma of vanilla. Perhaps when you smell the vanilla fragrance you remember a time when you were with someone whom you trusted, loved and enjoyed hugging. Remember seeing that person now... only see this person in your mind if you feel comfortable seeing this mind picture.

Whatever your very favorite fragrance is, just allow yourself to enjoy this time as you relax your body and feel happy. Each time you remember your very favorite fragrance you also remember that you are the type of person who can easily work with and usefully resolve any confusion during your life. Additionally, each time you remember your very favorite fragrance or remember the pleasant mind picture that seems to be a part of your very favorite aroma, you also relax your body one hundred times more than when you only remembered your very favorite fragrance.

Feel a relaxed feeling in your body... so relaxed and calm as you remember your very favorite fragrance. Also, as you're remembering your very favorite fragrance or aroma, you may taste a certain pleasant taste that seems to be a part of your very favorite fragrance. As you remember your very favorite fragrance and it's matching picture or taste, notice how relaxed and confident you feel about yourself. You definitely know you are the type of person who can beneficially resolve any misunderstandings in your life as you recall your very favorite fragrance and its accompanying picture or taste. And you're feeling deeper and deeper relaxed.

Notice that there may also be a very pleasant sound you hear as you remember your very favorite fragrance. Whenever your remember this pleasant sound or the pleasant picture or taste with your very favorite fragrance you remember that you are open to new ideas as you easily demonstrate the ability to harmlessly resolve any misunderstandings in your life. You're feeling so deeply relaxed, confident and pleased with your ability to feel in control as you relax yourself when you remember your very favorite fragrance and its accompanying pleasant sound, picture or taste. You remember how comfortable you feel using your personal power as you relax now... you use your inner wisdom to comfortably restore, refresh and repair any part of your body calling for this type of assistance.

Now as you are relaxing while remembering your very favorite fragrance, you know you prefer easily learning ideas so you can help yourself more easily do what you are already doing. You accept new ideas that seem beneficial to you as long as you actually experience no harm to yourself or others".

All right, this is the end of the induction. Writing out the suggestions is the next part of your journey. Enjoy the adventure!

From Sleep to Trance

By: Don Mottin

NOTE TO THERAPIST: The following induction will transform a natural state of sleep into a very deep, hypnotic state. Normally, the individual will experience total amnesia for everything that took place during the induction, as well as the suggestions given during hypnosis. While the individual is in a normal sleep state, proceed in the following manner using a soft, monotone voice.

You are now beginning to hear my voice. You are hearing my voice as simply a meaningful sound. My voice is very soothing to you. You enjoy hearing my voice because it is soothing to you. As you continue hearing my voice, you will be able to do what my voice suggests.

The index finger of your right hand is now beginning to rise up into the air. Index finger of the right hand beginning to rise up into the air. Index finger of the right hand is rising up. Index finger of the right hand is lifting up. Feel the index finger of the right hand floating up into the air.

(Continue with suggestions of "the index finger raising up." It may take three or four minutes of constant suggestions to achieve success. Once the finger has responded, you have transferred sleep into hypnosis.)

Sleep! Hypnotic Induction

By: Don Mottin

NOTE TO THERAPIST: The following induction is using the word "sleep" throughout the induction. It is important to explain to the client prior to the session that although you may be using the term "sleep," that they will not be "asleep" in the same way they are at night. Stress that they will still be aware of everything that is happening around them.

With your eyes closed, I would like you to take in a deep breath, hold it for a moment, and exhale slowly. As you continue breathing in deeply and exhaling slowly, you are starting to notice a very heavy feeling covering your entire body. Everything is becoming heavier and heavier.

It is beginning to feel as though you were moving into a state of "sleep". Now this "sleep" is quite different then the sleep you experience at night. In this "sleep", you can hear my voice and do as my voice suggests. Each time I say the word "sleep... sleep... sleep"! Let yourself go deeper into this wonderful "sleep"! As you sit there in this pleasant darkness, it is easy for you to go deeper into this perfect "sleep... sleep... sleep"!

The Pendulum Technique

By: Alfred A. Barrios, Ph.D.

Probably the best SPC technique to try first is the pendulum technique. It is especially effective because it gives you immediate concrete proof of SPC's basic premise -- that focusing on a particular thought will automatically produce the response associated with it.

First, one makes a pendulum with a piece of thread and any weighted object such as a ring or paper clip. It should be approximately two-thirds the length of your forearm. Now, sitting up, holding the pendulum gently between your forefinger and thumb and resting your elbow on the arm of a chair or on a table, keep your eye on the ring or clip, which should be reasonably motionless to start.

Step One: Program in the thought that the pendulum will begin to swing from left to right. That is, expect it to move in this direction and watch for it to gradually do just that, automatically. Once it starts moving, program in that it will move even more.

Step Two: Change the thought to one of a circular motion and look for pendulum almost immediately to start swinging in the new direction. How much you can get the pendulum to swing can be used as an indication of how concentrated your mind is becoming. The pendulum is moving because focusing on the thought that it will move produces an automatic, imperceptible, movement of your hand. This, in turn, is amplified by the pendulum.

Step Three: Now, still in the same position with your eyes closed, concentrate on the feelings in your hand. Perhaps you might notice a slight tingling sensation or perhaps you might begin to notice the pulse beating in your hand. Whatever the feeling, become more aware of it. Now program in that your hand will begin to relax and that a force will take hold of the fingers and start to gradually open them. To help this along, you can imagine a small balloon in the palm of your hand slowly being inflated and pushing the fingers open. You should soon begin to feel the hand bending at the wrist, the fingers creaking open and find the pendulum eventually dropping.

Step Four: Next, program in that your arm will begin to be pulled toward your body. Notice the muscles in the forearm beginning to tighten. Feel the arm being jerked toward you automatically. To help this along, you can imagine a rope tied around the wrist jerking your arm toward you. Continue until your arm touches you.

Step Five: Program in that your hand and arm will now begin to relax and that a force will begin pulling your arm away from you and down. As it comes down, your entire body will be relaxing, so that when your arm comes to rest you will be in a deep state of relaxation.

Step Six: Now go through the 20 to 10 countdown. Start counting backwards from 20 to 10, timing each number with the letting out of a breath; i.e., one number per breath. (There is a purpose for the timing of the countdown with the exhaling of a breath. If you will notice, you are most relaxed at this point in the breathing cycle. Also, counting backwards creates a descending effect.) Let each breath out all at once and let go completely as you let out each breath. With each number feel yourself letting go more and more, sinking into a progressively deeper state of relaxation. Notice your hands getting warmer. Imagine that with each exhalation you are breathing hot air onto the back of your hand. When you reach 10 you will be in the best state for programming in suggestions and goals -- self-programming.

After a while all you will need to do in preparation for programming is to go through this 20 to 10 countdown, known as the 20-10 shortcut technique. Most people will be able to get results with this 20-10 shortcut even after only one such exposure to it. Naturally, you should get better at it with practice.

There is another variation of the 20-10 countdown that you might want to try. It involves imagining going down an elevator from the 20th to the 10th floor as you count, with the elevator controlled by your breathing. Feel yourself sinking one floor with each breath. And of course if you wish to deepen the state still further, you can always repeat the countdown and/or continue it all the way to zero.

Step Seven: You are now ready for self-programming. Picture yourself in a typical situation dealing with your goal and see yourself responding positively.

Pencil Induction

By: Don Mottin

NOTE TO THERAPIST: The following induction can be used on either a group or an individual. Begin by having the client(s) lightly hold the tip of a pencil between their thumb and index finger. The pencil should be able to swing slightly between the thumb and index finger. Have the client(s) close their eyes and begin the following set of suggestions.

Each time you take in a breath, hold it for a moment and exhale slowly. As you exhale, feel all of the tension slipping out of your body. Let every single muscle relax. In a moment, you will feel that pencil slipping from between your fingers. Do not try to make it fall, but do not try to prevent it from falling. As the pencil slips and falls, your entire body is relaxing into a wonderful hypnotic state.

The pencil is slipping, beginning to fall. Feel it slipping from your fingers. With each breath, the pencil is slipping, falling, letting go. The moment that the pencil slips, you will slip into an even deeper hypnotic state of relaxation.

(As the pencil falls, begin with basic suggestions for deepening the state.)

Eye Blink Induction

By: Don Mottin

NOTE TO THERAPIST: The following hypnotic induction is based on the premise of using pacing and leading techniques. A client will follow verbal and nonverbal suggestions throughout the session. This procedure can begin during the preliminary session.

Say to client: "Are you ready to go into a hypnotic state? (WAIT FOR RESPONSE) I would like you to look in my direction. There is no need to stare into my eyes like they do in the movies, just look this way. In a moment, you will begin to notice changes. As the changes begin, allow them to take place".

(At this point, wait for the client to blink their eyes. You will also blink at the same time that the client blinks. If the client blinks twice, the therapist should also blink twice. Within a minute or two of pacing the client, the therapist may now blink first and watch that the client will follow and blink. As the therapist blinks slowly, the client will follow. As the therapist allows the eyes to begin to close, the client will follow. Once the eyes close, deliver suggestions to deepen the state.)

The Pendulum Induction

By: Don Mottin

NOTE TO THERAPIST: Begin with any type of a pendulum, having client hold the string or chain between their thumb and index finger. You will begin with a suggestibility test and allow the suggestibility test to change into hypnosis.

As you hold the pendulum between your thumb and index finger, I would like you to concentrate on the ball at the end of the chain. Do not try to make anything take place, but do not try to prevent things from happening. Listen to my voice and allow things to take place. As you watch the pendulum, it is beginning to sway back and forth. The pendulum is moving towards you and away from you. You are doing very well. Now, the pendulum is moving across your body from right to left. Swinging back and forth. You have just learned the two ways in which the pendulum moves.

I am now going to ask you a couple of questions. If the answer is "yes," the pendulum will begin moving towards you and away from you. If the answer is "no," the pendulum will move across, from right to left. (AT THIS TIME, ASK THE CLIENT SEVERAL SIMPLE QUESTIONS)

Is your first name ___________? (USE CLIENT'S NAME)

Is your first name ___________? (USE ANOTHER NAME)

As you watch this pendulum move back and forth in various directions, will your eyes begin to close shortly and allow you to enter hypnosis? (WAIT FOR A "YES" RESPONSE) Just before entering hypnosis, will the pendulum begin moving in a circular motion? (WAIT FOR A "YES" RESPONSE)

The pendulum is beginning to turn in a circular motion. It is going 'round and 'round, 'round and 'round. With each revolution of the pendulum, your eyes are closing tighter and tighter. Once the eyes close all the way, they will remain closed and I will take the pendulum from your hand.

Arm Levitation

By: Zali Segal

Have the subject seated in a recliner with his/her right (or left) elbow on the arm of the recliner (if the subject is seated in an armless straight chair, have him/her rest the elbow on a table or desk next to the chair). Have the subject stare at the first knuckle of the right (or left) hand.

Say to client: "As you keep your attention on your knuckle, just allow yourself to relax deeper and deeper... Deeper and deeper, just allow that relaxation to set in. Now, just close your eyelids down and concentrate on the weight of your elbow pushing down on the arm of the recliner (or *table/desk)*... and when you become aware of your elbow pushing down, shake your head 'yes' for me... (wait for response). I want you to imagine that I'm tying a string around the wrist of your right (or left) hand... and this string is attached to a large helium balloon... When you can imagine that balloon just shake your head 'yes' for me...

Now just keep focusing on that balloon and imagine that the balloon is lifting higher and higher... higher and higher with each and every easy breath that you inhale... And, as you continue to breathe, you may begin to sense a lightness coming over your hand and arm... It is as though all the weight seems to be leaving your hand... It is as though all the weight seems to be leaving your arm. Imagine that balloon lifting higher and higher and your arm getting lighter and lighter... Now I can't say whether one or more of your fingers will move, twitch or jerk... but when and if this happens, just nod your head 'yes' for me... Lighter and lighter... Just light as a feather... and the hand and arm have a tendency to lift... Lifting higher and higher with each easy breath that you inhale... Lighter and lighter, as light as a feather, lifting upward higher and higher and higher... lighter and lighter... just as light as a feather...

Now your hand begins to turn towards your body and soon it will touch and come to rest on your head (or face, chest or some other part of your body - notice what part of the subject's body his/her hand is approaching)... Hand turning and turning towards your head (or face, chest, etc.)... And, as soon as it touches your head (face, chest, etc.), it comes to rest and you go into a very pleasant state of total relaxation... Moving in and almost touching... moving in and almost touching... moving in.... almost touching... "

As the hand is touching, lightly touch the subject on the forehead and release his/her hand as you say the words "deep sleep!"

Hand Shake Induction #1

By: Don Mottin

NOTE TO THERAPIST: The following hypnotic induction may be used on either a client who has experienced hypnosis before or a client who is new to hypnosis.

I am now going to show you how easily you can enter a hypnotic state of relaxation. In just a moment, I am going to lift up your right hand as though we were shaking hands. Each time I lower your hand and arm downward, allow your eyes to close. As I raise your hand and arm upward, allow the eyes to open.
Now it may seem to become more difficult to open your eyes each time, but I want you to at least make an effort until the eyes no longer want to open.

(Begin a very slow movement of the hand and arm. Allow the client to close their eyes as the hand and arm are lowered, and then open the eyes as the hand and arm are raised.

You will notice that if you begin to slow down the arm raising and allow a shorter time period for the eyes to be open and increase the time that the eyes are closed, the client will quickly enter hypnosis and will not be able to open their eyes.)

Handshake Induction #2

By: Don Mottin

NOTE TO THERAPIST: The following hypnotic induction utilizes all three of the learning modes. The client will be responding through hearing, seeing and feelings. Begin with the client sitting in a comfortable chair, and proceed in the following manner.

Say to client: Would you like to experience the state of hypnosis? (After a "yes" response, have the client extend his or her arm to you as though you were going to be shaking hands. Take the client's hand with your right hand while making sure the client's arm is straight.) I would like you to look at me for just a moment. As you focus your eyes on me and listen to my voice, I would like you to allow things to take place. (Slowly begin raising and lowering the client's arm. The up and down movement of the arm should be about three inches each way.)

As I raise and lower your arm, I wonder if you have noticed yet that there is a drowsy, heavy feeling beginning to occur in and around your eyes. Each time I raise your arm upward, that heavy feeling in those eyes will keep becoming stronger. As the eyes begin to close down, it becomes increasingly more desirable to allow them to remain closed. They are closing down all the way now. Let it happen. Want it to happen. Feel it happening now. (Make special note to when the eyes begin to blink or start to close. This will be a signal to the therapist to reinforce that feeling by raising the arm higher into the air. The client will quickly associate the raising of the arm with closing of the eyes.)

Hand to Face Induction

By: Don Mottin

NOTE TO THERAPIST: Tell client to get as comfortable as possible with their arms resting on the arms of the chair. Show client how you would like them to hold their hand in front of their face. Palm of their hand facing in towards them with fingers pointing upward, pressed lightly together. Hand should be about eye level. Begin with progressive relaxation and then proceed with the "Hand to Face Induction."

In just a moment, when I ask you to, I am going to have you bring one of your hands up in front of your face, fingers extended upwards and pressed together. I am then going to have you try to open your eyes and pick a spot on your hand. It may seem difficult to open your eyes, or to keep them open, which is only natural since you have been relaxing so far. I am going to want you to try to open your eyes and, with a little effort, you will at least be able to get them open.

Now, the one thing that you must accomplish is that I want you to remain totally relaxed and at ease, even with your eyes open and your hand in this position. Remaining relaxed and at ease, move your hand up in front of your face with the fingers pointed upward and pressed lightly together. Now, attempt to open your eyes and pick one spot on your hand and begin to concentrate on it.

As you concentrate on that one spot and one spot only, your fingers are going to begin to spread apart. You do not have to make them spread, but do not try to stop them. Concentrate and allow things to take place. Feel them spreading apart now. Automatically separating now. It is beginning to feel as though there was a string tied to each finger pulling them apart, separating further and further.

(Once the fingers have separated, proceed in the following way.)

Now, please do not let it disturb you that the drowsy, heavy feeling in your eyes is becoming stronger now that your fingers have spread apart. It is a very normal, natural sensation. As I begin to count from 5 down to 1, that heavy, drowsy feeling will continue growing stronger.

(At this time, begin counting slowly from 5 to 1 while giving suggestions for eye closure. Deliver suggestions as the client responds.)

Indirect Hypnotic Induction

By: Don Mottin

NOTE TO THERAPIST: Begin with having the client close their eyes and listen to relaxing background music.

I wonder at what point you will become consciously aware of the fact that you are entering a hypnotic state. Many people begin to realize that they are being hypnotized as they become aware of a need to swallow more often. Other people make a mental note that their eyes are fluttering more than normal.

I really do not know if you will be entering a hypnotic state very slowly or, perhaps, you will find yourself already there. The ability to go into hypnosis is such a natural ability that some people find themselves surprised at how easy it is to let go and enjoy the benefits of hypnosis. There are so many different responses to entering hypnosis that it would be impossible to list them all. The one change that almost everyone notices is the change in feeling within the right hand. The change may be a warm or cool feeling. The change may be a numbing sensation. The change in the feeling of the right hand is surely a signal that a person is moving into a deeper, hypnotic state.

Indirect Hypnotic Induction #2

By: Don Mottin

NOTE TO THERAPIST: Start with the client having their eyes open and hands on the arms of the chair.

"I would like you to close your eyes and listen to the sound of my voice and allow things to take place. There is no need for you to consciously or verbally answer me, just allow things to take place. You really do not know where you are going. You only know that you are going to accomplish things that can and will help you. You may not even know when you slip into a hypnotic state. It could happen quickly, or it could be a slow, progressive feeling. I would like you to concentrate on the feelings in your right and left hands. You are now noticing some changes between the right and left hands. The changes may seem more evident in the right hand. The changes may seem more evident in the left hand. Once you know which hand is experiencing the greatest amount of changes, I would like you now to look down at that hand. Begin to concentrate on that hand.

Good, I see that you are experiencing more changes in your _______ hand. As you continue to concentrate on these feelings in your _______ hand, notice how that hand is beginning to feel light and airy. That hand is beginning to feel lighter than air. The hand is now beginning to float upwards from the arm of the chair, becoming lighter and lighter. Watch as that hand leaves the arm of the chair and floats up, feeling light and comfortable. As the hand floats upwards, the eyelids tend to go downward. The hand floats up and the eyelids float down".

The Power of Simply Being

By: Chuck Mignosa

Too often, we are using self-hypnosis, hypnotherapy, guided meditation and other technologies to force change in behavior and our environment. It is strange that we think that we know better than nature, what is best for us. Although it is true that we can modify behavior, the question remains as to what the behavior was creating for, and more importantly, what created the need for the behavior in the beginning.

In hypnosis, we direct and focus the mind on specific areas of behavior and thought. In Meditation, we defocus the mind and allow our awareness to expand to look at possibilities.

When Western man first heard stories about how astern holy men could control their autonomic nervous systems, these stories were considered to be in error. With the advent of biofeedback we discovered that we actually could control such responses like blood pressure, etc.

In biofeedback, we measure the desired physiological reaction and as the client/patient's body responds in the desired way, we give them positive feedback. At the same time, we ask the clients to focus their consciousness on their body. By becoming aware of what the body feels like and what we are experiencing within our body when the desired physiological response is achieved, the client/patient can learn to recreate the physiological response by recreating the sensations they experienced within their bodies.

With this in mind, we should be able to use hypnosis to enhance the meditative experience and improve our lives.

The difference between the two is similar to right and left brain function. Left-brain function is deductive and analytical. It responds to sequences of cause and effects to go from beginning to end. Hypnosis focuses on this left-brain function of cause and effect to change behavior.

Right brain function, on the other hand, is holistic in nature. It functions by seeing the end results without regard to how to get there. With right brain concepts nothing is impossible.

We are not trained to develop our right brain functions as much as our left brain functions. Creativity is reserved for the fringe members of our society, the artists, musicians, actors, etc. And yet, every great discovery and breakthrough has come from a right brain vision that was translated to cause and effects and resulted in bringing into reality that which could not be done.

The process is designed to let go of cause and effect thinking. It is designed to open the connections between the right- and left-brain functions. Rather than seeking some change in behavior or functions, it seeks nothing.

This is the power of this process; it seeks no result, only the experience. The idea is to simply become aware of what you are experiencing within your body at this moment without making any decisions about whether it is good or bad, right or wrong. It is the exact opposite of suggestions that require such judgments.

The source for such processes is lost in antiquity. They are simply processes of being with yourself with "nothing going on." In this day and age, we need to rediscover this experience. We are moving so fast that, as Joseph Campbell said, we have lost our sense of tradition, the source of who we are and why we are.

As we become more aware of our synthetic world and more aware of the interrelationship between ourselves and all of nature we are rediscovering what our ancestors knew, we are all interrelated with nature and if we do not support all of nature, we are dooming ourselves to extinction.

Within this concept is also the concept of consciousness. Consciousness is at the center of what man strives to understand. We search for many things that we put names to, but we never seem to find those things. Perhaps that is because we are coming from false cause. If this is true, then by simply relaxing and being with yourself, you just might find what you are looking for. In Eastern terms "that what you search for is causing you to search."

With this in mind I offer this process. It is a simple process just like progressive relaxation with this difference, the only purpose in doing this process is to do this process.

I have been using and presenting this process since 1974 and have found that it produces phenomenal results, far beyond what the process is.

The Being Process.

Beginning:

Sit or lay in a relaxed position. Uncross your arms and legs. Now take a deep breath in and hold it. Let the breath out slowly and as you let it out, feel your body RELAX. Now take another deep breath in and hold it. Let the breath out slowly and as you let it out, feel your body RELAX. Now take another deep breath in and hold it. Let the breath out slowly and as you let it out feel your body RELAX

Close your eyes and put your consciousness in your lungs. Become aware of your lungs as you breathe in and out. With every breath, keep your consciousness on your lungs.

The Journey

1. Now move your consciousness to the toes of your right foot
Become aware of your right foot
Notice how your right foot feels
Notice if there are any sensations
Don't do anything with your experience, just become aware of it.

2. Now move your consciousness to the toes of your left foot and repeat the process as in 1 above.
Now move your consciousness to your right foot and repeat process 1 above.
Now move your consciousness to your left foot and repeat 1 above.
Now move your consciousness to your right ankle and repeat 1 above.
Now move your consciousness to your left ankle and repeat 1 above.
Now move your consciousness to your right calf and repeat 1 above.
Now move your consciousness to your left calf foot and repeat 1 above.
Now move your consciousness to your right knee and repeat 1 above.
Now move your consciousness to your left knee and repeat 1 above.
Now move your consciousness to your right thigh and repeat 1 above.

Now move your consciousness to your left thigh and repeat 1 above.
Now move your consciousness to your right hip socket and repeat 1 above.
Now move your consciousness to your left hip socket and repeat 1 above.
Now move your consciousness to your base of your spine and repeat 1 above.
Now move your consciousness to your lower intestines and repeat 1 above.
Now move your consciousness to your kidneys and repeat 1 above.
Now move your consciousness to your bladder and repeat 1 above.
Now move your consciousness to your spleen and repeat 1 above.
Now move your consciousness to your stomach and repeat 1 above.
Now move your consciousness to your diaphragm and repeat 1 above.
Now move your consciousness to the center of your back and repeat 1 above.
Now move your consciousness to your lungs and repeat 1 above.
Now move your consciousness to your right hand and repeat 1 above.
Now move your consciousness to your left hand and repeat 1 above.
Now move your consciousness to your right wrist and repeat 1 above.
Now move your consciousness to your left wrist and repeat 1 above.
Now move your consciousness to your right forearm and repeat 1 above.
Now move your consciousness to your left forearm and repeat 1 above.
Now move your consciousness to your right elbow and repeat 1 above.
Now move your consciousness to your left elbow and repeat 1 above.
Now move your consciousness to your right upper arm and repeat 1 above.
Now move your consciousness to your left upper arm and repeat 1 above.
Now move your consciousness to your right shoulder socket and repeat 1 above.
Now move your consciousness to your left shoulder socket and repeat 1 above.
Now move your consciousness to your bottom of your neck and repeat 1 above.
Now move your consciousness to your to the base of your head, repeat 1 above.
Now move your consciousness to the top of your head and repeat 1 above.
Now move your consciousness to your forehead and repeat 1 above.
Now move your consciousness to your right ear and repeat 1 above.
Now move your consciousness to your left ear and repeat 1 above.
Now move your consciousness to your right eye and repeat 1 above.
Now move your consciousness to your left eye and repeat 1 above.
Now move your consciousness to your nose and repeat 1 above.
Now move your consciousness to your lips and repeat 1 above.
Now move your consciousness to your jaw and repeat 1 above.
With your next breath, allow your jaw to relax and drop
Now move your consciousness to your tongue and repeat 1 above.

3. Now become aware of your whole body; don't do anything with your experience, just be there with your experience.

Now start to become aware of how your body feels sitting or laying.
Become aware of the room
Recreate in your minds eye the colors of the room, the furniture etc.
Become aware of the sounds in the room.
With each breath, become aware of the whole room.
When you feel comfortable, open your eyes and be here.

Biofeedback as a Way of Facilitating Hypnotic Induction

By: Alfred A. Barrios, Ph.D.

Remember, the purpose of a hypnotic induction is to increase the belief factor. Anything you can use to reinforce or confirm a given suggestion will help to increase the belief factor. Biofeedback involves the use of special devices to magnify the response suggested - usually a relaxation response. For instance, in the case of GSR biofeedback devices, subtle changes in hand sweat response (tension or anxiety causes a hand sweat response) are magnified either auditorilly (e.g., the sound becomes more and more low-pitched as the relaxation increases) or visually (e.g., a dial moves steadily more to the right as relaxation increases).

In the SPC program use is made of a special thermal biofeedback device - The Stress Control Biofeedback Card. The shape of a credit card, there is a black rectangle of liquid crystal in the center that upon touch will change color depending on stress level. The liquid crystal is responding to fingertip temperature that is directly correlated to stress level. When a person is in a stressful or threatening situation the blood flows inward to the muscles and the extremities (e.g. the hands) grow cold. The liquid crystal tab on the Stress Card is set to turn blue at 95 degrees F, which as a result of numerous biofeedback studies has been determined to be the criterion temperature indicative of a person being relaxed. The studies found that if a person, through relaxation exercises, could consistently raise his fingertip temperature to 95 degrees/F, he could get rid of most stress-related problems (headaches, high blood pressure, etc).

The card is used as follows: the individual first determines his/her stress level before going through an SPC technique, and then checks it again after the technique. A change in the color from black to red to green to blue acts as a strong reinforcement of the technique, especially when focusing on the goal of stress control.

CHAPTER 8: HYPNOSIS THEORIES AND PRACTICAL APPLICATIONS

Making Sense Out of Hypnosis Theories and Definitions

By: Bill O'Connell CH

Ask ten practitioners of hypnosis to define the term hypnosis and you will get ten different responses - quite probably ten completely different responses.

What is this?

The answer is simple: There is no universally agreed-upon definition of hypnosis. Most hypnotists and researchers have differing opinions of what constitutes hypnosis or "the hypnotic state." Take a trip to your local library and pull ten books off the shelf on hypnosis by different authors and look up the definition. The disparity of definitions will amaze you. Definitions I've seen include: "Hypnosis is... an altered state of consciousness", "A special case of deep absorption", "A unique psychological state which affects a break between a person's habitual and unconscious associations so that new learning may take place", "The alpha state", "The theta state", "The non-critical acceptance of ideas by the subconscious mind", "By-passing the critical faculty combined with selective thinking", "Fulfillment of role expectation", "The persuasion to accept a suggestion", "Social compliance", "The response to simple suggestion", and on and on...

No Clear Answer

While a clear definition of the term "hypnosis" remains elusive, equally elusive is a clear understanding of how hypnosis works. Theories abound. In the early years of research into hypnosis it was widely believed that hypnotized subjects were in an "altered state of consciousness" and that this "special state" was responsible for the phenomena hypnotized subjects demonstrated. Early researchers believed that once the hypnotic state was "induced" the subject would literally accept every suggestion given to them, and that the acceptance of these suggestions was "non-critical" meaning that the conscious mind's ability to assess, and thus accept or reject the suggestion, was bypassed completely.

Over the years this "special state of consciousness" explanation evolved into various forms including Earnest Hilgard, Ph.D.'s "Neo-dissociation theory." Hilgard, founder of the Stanford University Hypnosis Research Laboratory, and its Executive Director for over 20 years, maintains that when hypnotized, a person experiences multiple levels of consciousness, one of which they are consciously aware of, and others which they are consciously unaware of. Hilgard suggests that it is one of the unconscious levels of awareness that is responsible for the phenomena that hypnotized subjects demonstrate.

While Hilgard has credible credentials, his "neo-dissociation theory" has not gone unchallenged. Psychologist Robert Baker, Ph.D., author of *They Call it Hypnosis* maintains that the "socio-cognitive theory" better explains why hypnotized subjects respond the way they do. The socio-cognitive theory suggests that hypnotic subjects are demonstrating learned behavior and that they are behaving the way they believe good hypnotic subjects are supposed to behave. Positive expectation, a willingness to participate, a desire to please the hypnotist and compliance with an authority figure are all aspects of this theory. The socio-cognitive theory is also referred to as the "social compliance theory."

Baker is not alone in his belief that hypnosis is nothing more than social compliance by willing participants. Nicholas Spanos, Ph.D. has amassed considerable evidence through social scientific research to support his claim that hypnotic subjects are merely behaving the way they believe a good hypnotic subject is expected to behave.

Baker, Spanos as well as other psychologists and researchers who support the social compliance theory of hypnosis essentially believe that both the hypnotist and the subject are "role playing" with the hypnotist playing role of the hypnotist, as they have learned through their training or through exposure to demonstrations of hypnosis in television and movies and live performances, and the subject playing the role of the hypnotized person, as they have learned through their exposure to demonstrations or portrayals of the behavior of a person who has been hypnotized.

Much like the dissention in politics and religion, the "neo-dissociation" theorists and the "socio-cognitive" theorists are very much at odds. Both believe their explanation is correct. Both maintain that they have sufficient evidence to support their belief. And both believe the opposing theory is wrong.

Of course the debate does not end here. There are other theories as well. Some researchers believe that perhaps all theories of hypnosis have a place, depending on the subject and the context. It has been suggested that a "unified theory of hypnosis" might include all theories. This unified explanation would account for some hypnotic subjects experiencing "multiple levels of consciousness" and others responding due to "social compliance."

The bottom line is that despite extensive research and scientific investigation, there are many theories, yet no clear definition exists today of what hypnosis is, or how hypnosis works.

What Is Agreed Is That Hypnosis Works!

It's interesting to note that two practicing hypnotists may disagree passionately about what really constitutes hypnosis, yet agree emphatically that hypnosis is effective in treating many aliments. Two hypnotists, practicing in the same city, may have diametrically opposed definitions and theories of hypnosis, yet both produce effective results and have happy clients.

And there is mounting evidence to support the efficacy of hypnosis in the treatment of many conditions. Perhaps the most cogent scientific research on the efficacy of hypnosis in the treatment of pain comes from the University of Montreal in Canada where researchers have used P.E.T. (Positron Emission Tomography) images to show physiological changes in the brain when a hypnotized subject reports the absence of pain. This is one example of the increasing momentum for the acceptance of hypnosis in the mainstream medical community.

There Is No Such Thing As Hypnosis.

While hypnosis is practiced by thousands of physicians, psychologists, social workers and hypnotherapists throughout the world each and every day, some people maintain that hypnosis does not exist.

In his book, *Secrets of the Amazing Kreskin*, entertainer Kreskin makes the assertion that there is no such thing as hypnosis. He even has a chapter entitled, "The Myth of the Hypnotic Trance." While Kreskin practiced hypnosis as part of his "concert of the mind," which to this day features feats of mentalism, magic and ESP, for over 20 years, he stopped using the term hypnosis when he discovered that he could elicit all of the same responses from subjects without using hypnosis at all. He coined the term, "suggestology" and now refers to himself as a "suggestologist." Kreskin maintains that what people refer to as hypnosis is nothing more than "the persuasion to accept a suggestion".

World-famous hypnotist Peter Reveen had a similar revelation years into his very successful career. After much investigation and introspection, Reveen determined that the term "hypnosis" did not accurately imply what he was doing. Reveen coined the term "super consciousness" and used this term to explain the experiences participants in his show were having. Super consciousness, according to Reveen, is a heightened state of conscious awareness. Reveen abandoned the use of the term hypnosis altogether and referred to himself as an "impossiblist" leading his subjects into the "super conscious" state.

Tom Deluca, a top name in college circuit stage-hypnosis, also abandoned the use of the terms "hypnosis" and "hypnotist," and now calls his show "Theatre of the Imagination."

Many books on hypnosis will tell you that "waking hypnosis" is just as effective as "genuine hypnosis" in producing most hypnotic responses. What is waking hypnosis, you ask? It's everything you would expect hypnosis to be, <u>without the induction</u>.

DeWaldoza, a famous Danish hypnotist of yesteryear, performed a complete show in "waking hypnosis." How did he do it? Very simply: he invited subjects to join him on stage, performed a round of suggestibility tests, dismissed the none responsive, and went right to the experiments, skipping the induction altogether. In other words, he performed all of the same steps that a traditional stage hypnotist usually performs, without the induction.

A contemporary British hypnotist named Martin Taylor performs a show that he calls, "Hypnosis without Hypnosis." Martin's performance includes a lecture, where he explains his belief in the social compliance theory of hypnosis…followed by a call for volunteers who then exhibit all of the phenomena of hypnotized subjects in a traditional stage show, <u>but without the induction</u>.

Joseph Barber, Ph.D. wrote an article entitled, "The Reality of Hypnosis" in which he references Ormond McGill's *Encyclopedia of Stage Hypnosis*. Barber states that McGill actually recommends against using hypnosis in a stage show because it is "time consuming and unnecessary."

Richard Bandler and John Grinder, co developers of Neuro-Linguistic Programming extensively studied the verbal and nonverbal patterns of medical

hypnotherapist Milton H. Erickson, M.D. During their research, Bandler and Grinder experimented with which hypnotic phenomena they could elicit in the various "levels" of depth in hypnosis. Up until this time it was assumed by many hypnotists that certain hypnotic phenomena could only be elicited if the subject was hypnotized to a certain "depth," specifically either a "medium state" or a "deep state." Bandler and Grinder's experimentation proved differently. They were able to elicit all hypnotic phenomena, regardless of whether the subject was "deeply" hypnotized, "moderately" hypnotized, or only "lightly" hypnotized.
They then took the experiments further and determined that all responses that they could elicit with hypnosis could also be elicited without hypnosis.
These example raise the question, is the induction really necessary?

"Pretending", May Be Just As Effective.

Research indicates that subjects "pretending" to be hypnotized are able to achieve all of the same results, including anesthesia, which hypnotized subjects are able to achieve. It's no surprise that if a person repeatedly imagines their desired outcome in rich, vivid detail, the tremendous power of the human imagination becomes engaged--whether hypnosis is used or not.

The Evidence Based Approach.

With all of the conflicting theories and definitions of hypnosis, and even the well-established perspective that hypnosis either does not exist or is unnecessary, how do we make sense of it all?

My recommendation is to focus on what can be observed and verified. We cannot observe and verify what is going on inside a subject's mind. Thus, we cannot determine with any certainty what "state of mind" the subject is in. We do not know if the "critical faculty" is being bypassed, or if the suggestions are going directly to the "subconscious mind." We cannot observe measure or validate what occurs inside the subject's mind.

What we can observe, measure and validate is the behavior of the hypnotist and the behavior of the subject. The primary behavior of the hypnotist is suggestion. The primary behaviors of the subject are the verbal and behavioral responses they demonstrate. We know that the hypnotist's behavior is effective when the subject's behavior demonstrates a positive response to the hypnotist's suggestions. This is the Evidence-Based Approach. Focus on evidence that can be observed, measured and validated through our own senses.

What we cannot answer is "why" a subject responds. Since we cannot answer that question, I believe we should not concern ourselves with it. Focus on what we can verify. Focus on the evidence. Hypnosis works, and has been repeatedly demonstrated to be effective. If our suggestions result in the achievement of the desired response, regardless of the explanation, that is what matters.

Hypnosis and Effective Communication

By: Craig Eubanks

Hypnosis is a word that can almost be guaranteed to get a strong reaction from people. But ask a hundred people what it is and you will likely get a hundred different answers.

Many times the perception is that hypnosis is what you see when you watch a stage show and you see people in a deep trance slumped in their chairs. People see this and they say "that's hypnosis!"

Yet in the same show you see people with eyes wide opening following what the hypnotist has suggested as the entertainment, and they appear quite wide awake. Does the crowd say "that's hypnosis..."? Not unless they have seen these same people in the deep trance sleep position first.

The fact is that neither of these are hypnosis. Hypnosis is not a thing. When you see a person on stage clucking like a chicken that is not hypnosis, it is the result of hypnosis. More correctly it is a result of the process of hypnosis.

Hypnosis is a Process, not a Thing

Hypnosis a process that allows one person (the hypnotist) using language to get a person into that particular state of mind. If the state of mind happens to be one where the hypnotist is taking them into a deep theta trance... that is just one use of the hypnotic process. If the hypnotist has them forget their name, that is a result of the hypnotic process.

The hypnotic process is the process whereby using language we are able to take a person from one state of mind to another state of mind. This is referred to as inducing a change of state, and thus why the process is referred to as a hypnotic induction.

State of Mind

Now that state of mind that you are inducing can be any state of mind.

- Moving them from sadness to happiness.
- From bored to excite.
- It could be a state of curiosity.
- It could be a deep trance state.

These are all normal states we experience as humans. The deep trance state is the same state of mind that each person goes through at least twice a day. Once when they wake up, and once when they go to sleep. So the destination state itself is not hypnosis, it is the process utilized to get the person into that very state that is hypnosis. If you take a person and move them from fear to confidence... the process used is the hypnotic process.

Hypnosis as a Model of Communication

As you begin to think of hypnosis using that definition, the growing realization that hypnosis is occurring all the time all around you may begin to become clear. This can be a very useful model of communications at all levels, to look for the understanding of how a communication will change the receiver's state.

In the therapeutic situation, this is common sense. When an induction is used, it is specifically designed to change a person's state. But it is done using language. And that is the same language used in everyday interactions with the world around us. So with a little thought, we can realize that we can design all our communications to create desired states in those around us.

This simple concept may already be giving you ideas about how you can better structure the way you greet clients and answer the phone. What you say during the time you are with the client. The wording on your advertisements and emails.

Pay attention when a commercial on TV sends you into an altered state, or a story in the newspaper creates a feeling of empathy for the victim being written about.

A Fun Paradox

Richard Bandler and John Grinder were known to have often had an exchange during their hypnosis seminars, where one would say "All communication is hypnosis" and the other would say "I disagree, nothing is hypnosis; hypnosis doesn't exist." With the understanding you already have, you may find it easy to accept the paradox they suggest.

Power In Understanding The Model

This is an extremely powerful concept. The concept that simply by using your ability to communicate you can induce a desired state of mind in other people! By using language and body language you are able to influence the thoughts and emotions of those around you.

With just a phrase or even a single word, we can move the listener into an alteration of their state. The idea of an altered state itself will cause most of you reading this to pull up a representation of what that means to you, and it may not be pleasant as "altered state" often has a pejorative attached to it.

When I worked in corporate America, I quickly found a great way to make my officemates change from hunched over and frowning at their computer screens to shoulders back and smiling. This was to say the word "lunch."

I understand now that this result was likely due to them having the word "lunch" generally represent leaving the building and the grounds, and getting somewhere pleasant enough to distract them from the worries of the work day. I was a hypnotist and I didn't even realize it.

This concept can be expanded beyond just a single person. Movies are a great example of a state induction. All it takes is something as simple as the words "A long time ago in a galaxy far, far away" and a whole theater full of people go into an altered state in which they suspend their beliefs and allow the story to take them to that fictional galaxy. It is also likely that now, just by having read those words you thought of a time you watched *Star Wars*. It works even in print. Powerful isn't it?

Bring It to Life with Descriptive Language

So with this new understanding, let us begin to develop the communication skills you already have.

Since you already understand that hypnosis is a process, you can easily understand that effective communication will be based on process language and not content. Sensory-based language is rich with words to enhance the experience for the listener. It is used to draw attention to what they will see, what sounds are involved, how they will feel, and can even include smell and taste. As humans we experience and describe our world by our five senses, so it only makes sense to use sensory language in our communications.

As an example, If I tell you about my recent trip to Florida and describe to you the perfect tropical climate with the slight breezes that lightly danced through the palm trees, and provided just enough cooling to balance the bright warm sunshine. How the fine grains of pure white sands felt between my toes as I walked down the beach each evening. How I would enjoy spectacular sunsets filled with bright red and orange colors, as the glowing disk of the sun slipped beneath the clear blue waters of the ocean, to the rhythmic sounds of the waves splashing on the beach.

Perhaps you found that you experienced some of the representation of what I experienced as you read this. Thus your state was altered. Perhaps you felt more relaxed, or maybe even you felt excited about going Florida yourself. Perhaps you were able to stop for a moment, and see, hear, and feel those things for yourself.

This is the process used by hypnotists. This is also the process used by great novelists, storytellers, movie makers, sales people and marketers.

Sensory Rich Language

Sensory rich language is descriptive wording that appeals to one or more of our five senses. The way we humans interact with the world is through our senses of vision, hearing, touch, smell and taste. So, at the minimum, a description would appeal to at least two of those five to give it more appeal.

Example: I was watching a band play at a festival, and they sounded great. Two of the senses are covered, but there is much more that can be added here. This can be enhanced even more by using detailed and descriptive language of the experience.

Example: I was at this festival and I saw this amazing band. They were dressed in bright blue and yellow colored silky shirts and were wearing pirate hats with big white feathers sticking out that shook as they danced. They played this delightfully energetic Latin style of music; you know the kind that just says "happy" when you hear it. The stage was filled with people playing all kinds of percussion instruments. It was just perfect, not too loud but I could notice the rumbling bass from the drums in my body. It was impossible to not feel really great and want to dance along with them.

The story begins to come to life and includes visual, auditory and kinesthetic. These are the primary systems most people use for describing and cataloging experience.

More Than Just Words

Most individuals are completely unaware that they are in effect using the hypnotic process to communicate. This process of communication has many levels, the actual words, the tonality use and the body language they use just to name a few. They cause through their actions and through their words, states of mind to be induced in other people.

The words you speak are only a portion of the total communication that occurs. How much of the message is verbal and nonverbal varies depending on what source you read, but is considered to be as much as 95% nonverbal. Even if it were only 15% or 20% it would still have an effect, so it is important to be aware of the sub communication part of any communication.

Here we will consider two parts of the sub communication, voice tonality and body language. There are more, including some would say the mental images and psychic messages we send out, but that is for another article.

Sub Communicating With Tonality

There are entire seminars devoted to tonality, but here I just want to make you aware of it. The simplest way to understand how tonality can be used to alter a person's state is to think about when you were a child, and just by the way your parent said your name you knew you were in trouble. Instant state change.

During my travels to other countries, I have been able to determine this from parents when I didn't even speak the language. And I am able to confirm that I got the message correctly by observing the body language of the child. Body language being the next type of nonverbal communication we will talk about.

The interesting thing is how I still have a similar reaction, first to the parent "uh oh, someone is in trouble" then to the child "poor guy, man I feel bad for you." They both changed my state with nonverbal modes of communication.

Sub-Communication with Body Language

There is a part of our brain, which picks up on body language whether we are actively conscious of it or not. Whether you call it the subconscious mind or the lizard brain, there is this sub-communication going on at all times. It was once described to me that as humans we are like a 100,000 watt transmitter with the power switch frozen in the on position. We can't not send signals to everyone around us.

When you pay attention, you will realize you are receiving these signals and if you think about it, you will likely understand what they mean. For instance, you can tell when someone is nervous or uncomfortable just by how they are standing, and by the movements they make. This can make you uncomfortable talking with them.

Employees in a workplace can tell if the boss is in a bad mood by the way he walks in the office in the morning. These changes their state to one best described as "walking on eggshells" so as not to be the focus of his anger.

Emotions Are Contagious

If a person is sitting in a room, and another person enters who is in a great mood, the first person in the room will shift towards that "great mood" state. Likewise, if the person going into the room is in a bad mood, it is likely this will have a similar affect on the original person in the room.

You may be able to recall a time, when you saw a presentation where the person giving the presentation was in a subdued state. Perhaps you can remember the affect it had on you. Maybe even you had trouble paying attention or staying awake.

You can use this knowledge to your advantage in business and beyond, be it for Therapeutic Hypnosis, Coaching, Consulting, Marketing or any situation where you interact with others as part of your day. When you meet with a client, communicate a positive and confident state at all levels. Lead them where you want them to be emotionally to ensure that your interaction will be the most effective.

Conclusion:

Hypnosis is an extremely useful model for understanding human communications. All of what we understand about the world is codified by language and nonverbal cues; this is after all how we communicate. Therefore, if you accept the idea that communication is hypnosis, then it follows that if you want to be really effective with communication, even a basic understanding of hypnosis principles can give you a powerful skill set to be a highly effective communicator.

What is Hypnosis?

By: Mike De Bruyn

It has been observed that if you ask ten hypnotists what hypnosis is, you will get more than ten answers. It is easy to propose theories, and there are many, but I believe that the best theory is one that gives the most useful results. Therefore, I propose a "theory" of hypnosis that will dispel some of the confusion that surrounds it and help us achieve results more quickly and easily.

To understand hypnosis, it is necessary to start with what we are, as human beings. A human being is a "system" that strives to continue existing and, in order to do that; we must achieve a state of dynamic equilibrium with our surroundings and ourselves. We often refer to this system as the "mind-body" system, to remind ourselves that mind and body are not entirely separate, but are "part" (actually more like a focus attention to facilitate understanding) of an interconnected system.

It is clear that the complexity of the system is such that in order for us to operate as well as we do, it is necessary for us to carry out our functions largely "automatically." George Miller, in 1956, concluded that we are able to be "consciously" aware of only 7+/-2 things at any moment. Obviously, since there are an enormous number of things continually impinging on our senses, it would be quite impossible for us to operate completely "consciously," "deliberately" or "intentionally." The traditional view has been to see ourselves as "conscious mental beings" and speculate about the unimportant things that might be going on "unconsciously." In fact, I believe it is more useful to take the opposite approach and see our functions to be almost completely "subconscious" and that we "delude" ourselves into thinking that we operate primarily consciously, intentionally and rationally.

For our purposes here, I define "conscious" to mean that state wherein we are fully aware of the direct sensory stimulus that we are receiving. I think it can be easily seen that such a state may not even be actually possible. As anyone who has practiced meditation can attest, to "quiet the mind" and "be aware" of only one's breathing is something that is so difficult that some strive to achieve it all their lives - without attaining it for more than a few minutes (or seconds) before the mind turns inward to comment on the experience. So, assuming for the moment that we can actually be completely aware, our experience shows us that it is only a transitory thing, at best. In this context (hypnosis) I am calling any state in which we are not fully aware, a "trance" state, and rather than understand "trance" as one single state, I see it as collection of states that have different attributes.

We enter trance states spontaneously and move from one to another throughout our waking hours. In fact, I propose that we largely live in a state of trance. You are probably aware of the more extensive trance states such as reading a book or watching a movie, and what is often called "highway hypnosis" - the phenomenon in which we arrive at our destination and have no memory of driving there. You may even have identified "daydreaming" as a trance state. But consider that in order to read these words, you must subconsciously perform a complex analysis to understand the meanings of the words in your own experience. In order to do this you must "go inside" and therefore cannot be fully aware of your sensory experience so, by definition, you are in a trance state. A good example of this is our tendency to "go blind" when we are trying to listen to a conversation as we drive. How many times have you turned down the car radio as you searched for an address or highway exit so that you could keep your full attention on your driving? (Milton Erickson may have been the first person to understand and comment on how language has the ability to induce trance and so the technique of conversational hypnotic induction is now known as "Ericksonian hypnosis.")

We know that when we are most fully aware, we have the ability to analyze and weigh the information we are receiving through our senses and make decisions about it. Some have called this the "critical faculty" of our conscious mind. Conversely, whenever we are less than fully aware, that ability to be critical is somewhat "bypassed." Whenever we are "distracted" from complete awareness of our full sensory awareness we are susceptible to "suggestion." Advertisers use this approach to good effect. We are given pictures of fast cars and sexy people while being flooded with sounds and music - all to overload our senses to induce and enhance a state of trance and bypass our ability to critically evaluate the more subtle suggestions that we buy the product. It works so well that billions are spent in advertising each year. In hypnosis, this effect is useful both in "deepening" the trance state and giving suggestions for change in therapy or entertainment in stage shows.

That is basically all there is to it! Hypnosis is nothing more than the purposeful induction of a state of trance. In other words, using our knowledge of how the mind works to enhance the normal state of trance. We may do this using any number of techniques involving language, suggestions, physical tasks, etc., but it all comes down to pulling the attention "inward" or "away" from full sensory awareness of the world around us.

So why is this way of looking at hypnosis more useful than any other? Consider how much interest there is in various methods of hypnotic induction - how many pleas for "scripts" for one thing or another. If you understand that all you need do is "tie up" the senses so that your suggestions will be more readily accepted, then all of the unnecessary "magic" will be out of it and you'll have the principles you need to be maximally flexible in any situation you may encounter. Or, as Dave Elman observed when demonstrating his "sip of water induction," anything can induce hypnosis!

Working in Trance

By: Marilyn Gordon CH.

Trance is not just for your clients. It's for you too as a practitioner. The ability to work with clients while you too are in a trance state makes it possible for you to do wondrous things. As you relax more deeply, along with your client, you become more attuned to your client and the forces at work in your session; you become more creative and intuitive. You quadruple your ability to do great work. You can pay attention to your client's well-being, to what you need to say, to the time on the clock - while at the same time going into your own deep state.

What is this trance state like? It's a deeply meditative state of focused consciousness in which you feel profoundly relaxed and connected with your inner being. We all know this state. It is not difficult to come to this state once you know the techniques. You come here in order to access greater parts of yourself so that you can do your work with more sensitivity and awareness.

When you're very relaxed as a practitioner, you send that relaxation state non-verbally to your client. Your vibration communicates itself to your client, just as it would if you were angry or elated. When you are supremely relaxed, your client can be relaxed as well. There is a special feeling that you transmit when you work in trance. Your client automatically goes more deeply, and you are in touch with the most profound parts of yourself: your intuition, your wisdom and your love.

Being in trance in your sessions gives you decided advantages over working in ordinary waking consciousness. First of all, not only does your client get to relax, but you do as well. Then there are the other advantages of being open to receiving guidance from forces that transcend the ordinary mind. You establish within yourself these internal guidance systems, and you make certain that they are coming from a place of purity, and then you can rely on them as you work. They give you knowledge about your client and about what to do next. They open the qualities of compassion and love in you as you work.

It helps if you, yourself, have a practice of self-hypnosis or meditation that is separate from your work with clients. Regularly dipping into deep states of your own makes you more adept at experiencing these states when you work with others.

How to Do It

It is possible to work in a trance state while simultaneously taking care of business. Of course, you need to make sure that your client is comfortable, to pay attention to his or her reactions, to make certain that the session is running on schedule, to know what to say next, to remain present and grounded, and to take care not to take on your clients' issues. You can do all this at once and still go into trance. It's a delicate dance, and you learn to do the choreography.

One way of achieving this trance state while working with others is to be fully conscious that this is what you're planning to do. Some practitioners naturally go into trance states as they work. Others need to create this more consciously. I, for one, like counting during inductions. I find that counting numbers (in this case from 25 to one) is a powerful induction method when combined with other inductions. The great ultra-depth hypnotist, Walter Sichort, consistently used numbers in his inductions. I spoke with him once and he said to me that he liked to do non-cognitive inductions. He liked counting and doing progressive relaxations more than visualizations. He said that he found that going beyond the intellect into the more primitive parts of the brain worked well for him in inducing trance. This is not to say that visualizations are not good to do. On the contrary, they are powerful. Nevertheless, you may want to be open to the possibility that working with less mental processing can more quickly and effectively access the reptilian brain, the no cognitive primal and basic centers of the human being.

Ormond McGill is another "national treasure" who, himself, works in trance states. When you observe him at work, you see that he is so connected with a transcendent state that he is able to simply gaze at his client, and the client will become deeply relaxed. He has so much power in his intention that his suggestions have energy behind them. When he says, "Sleep!" - it is not simply a word. It carries with it the energy of trance. He is there, too.

Going Very Deeply

So, let us say that you are using a counting down process in your trance inductions. Here is the time when you can take the cue to deepen your own trance connection. As you count down, you can close your eyes and allow yourself to relax very deeply. You can train your own inner mind to go more deeply into trance along with your client whenever you count those numbers down. You also train yourself to be aware of what is going on with your client. From time to time, you may open your eyes. You listen to the sound of your client's breathing. You pay attention, and yet you go more deeply. You may want to even consciously suggest to yourself that you are relaxing very deeply now and remaining fully aware of everything that is taking place.

You may want to call in a presence that is very loving - a guide, a helper who will be a vehicle through which you can do your work more effectively. This you can establish within yourself and you take the opportunity to call upon this healing force as you count the numbers down. When you've completed this and you're ready to begin, you find that you're in a highly receptive and responsive state for doing the work. You can now also include other processes in your induction. You can play gentle chimes and do healing touch. You can also include progressive relaxation and even visualization.

As you go into trance, you may notice that your voice will change. It will become softer. You may notice that something opens up in your heart, which translates into the ability to give more love to your client. You may notice that you know what questions to ask. You may find that you have insight into what is going on with your client, and you can preside over the session with greater sensitivity. If you make tapes for your client, these can come right through you instead of being from your mind only or from a script. They can be inspired messages that come forth from a place that is beyond your ordinary awareness.

In the same way that you work in trance with clients, you can also extend that practice to times when you're writing or creating some work of art or even organizing your office. You are able to access a state of being that allows the words to flow through you or helps you to know what colors to paint or which papers to file in which folder. It's about leaping into a state of being that brings you into an experience of *flow*. Here there are possibilities that extend beyond the ordinary. This is a remedy for creative blockages. It is also a way of doing highly creative hypnotherapeutic work.

Just imagine that you are going deeply into trance with your client. Imagine that as you count the numbers down or go through each muscle group relaxing it, you are also speaking to yourself, telling yourself, "I'm relaxing more deeply now. I'm experiencing my breathing and paying attention to my client now. There's a loving presence surrounding both of us. Let us both feel an arm of love around us as we work." At the same time, you're keeping your eye on the clock when you need to and keeping another watchful eye on your client. You stride both worlds as you skillfully facilitate your session.

We are fortunate to have been given inner gifts. These came with us at birth. It is both our challenge and opportunity to take these gifts off the closet shelves of our consciousness and put them to good use. These gifts of love and brilliant wisdom not only serve others, but they help us to become the enlightened beings that we came to this earth to be. How lucky we are to have work that reminds us of our ultimate purpose here.

New Theory of Hypnosis Opens the Way to More Effective Hypnotic Induction

By: Alfred A. Barrios, Ph.D.

A new and comprehensive theory of hypnosis based on principles of conditioning and reciprocal inhibition was recently published (fall, 2001) in *Contemporary Hypnosis* - the journal of the British Society of Experimental and Clinical Hypnosis.

The main goal of the theory is to provide a clearer understanding of how and why hypnosis can be such a powerful therapeutic tool. And, how it can lead to new ways of:

(a) Facilitating hypnotic induction, in terms of achieving greater hypnotic depths as well as reaching a higher percentage of people.

(b) Producing more in-depth hypnotic phenomena including: age regression, uncovering, pain management, control of physiological responses, control of emotions, etc.

(c) Making post-hypnotic suggestions more effective for the purpose of reprogramming negative behavior.

The main goal of this article is to point out how the theory leads to developing more effective methods of hypnotic induction, such that close to 100% of the population can be induced into a deep state of hypnosis.

One of the key factors deduced from the theory is that you can facilitate hypnotic induction by insuring as much immediate positive feedback (outcomes) as possible following each suggestion. And one way to do this is to have present subtle stimuli that evoke the responses suggested. In this sense it will be shown that the hypnotic induction techniques deduced from the theory are akin to biofeedback and in fact it will be shown how biofeedback methods can be used to further add to the heightened state of belief created by the hypnotic induction. (Hypnosis is defined in the theory as a heightened state of belief.)

The theory also suggests certain ways of insuring a heightened state of belief to begin with, even before the client is put through the first hypnotic induction procedure. This includes: (a) eliminating any fears or negative attitudes often associated with hypnosis; (b) creating a high state of prestige for the hypnotist; (c) leading the client through a number of warm-up exercises - positive responses to a set of initial high-probability-of-response suggestions.

In order to eliminate many of the fears and negative expectations often associated with hypnosis, the author decided that it might be best to not use the term hypnosis at all. Instead of having to explain to the client what hypnosis was not (e.g. not a state of sleep; not a state of unconsciousness; not a state where you have to give up control to another individual; etc.) it was decided to call the process something else - Self-Programmed Control (SPC) - and then proceed to tell the client what SPC was: SPC is described as a program for giving individuals greater control over their subconscious or automatic behavior and which allows them to more easily program in new positive behaviors to replace any negative ones causing their current problems. This approach is highly effective at getting rid of the fear of being controlled. The client is also told that he will be introduced to a number of different SPC techniques, each of which involves going through a series of suggestions aimed at placing him in a more focused and receptive state of mind. And that he is to find the one that best suits him. He is told that he will not necessarily have to respond to all the techniques. This procedure lessens the negative effects of any failures in response to the induction techniques.

With regards to building the prestige factor, use can be made of testimonials of previous successes; presentation of impressive credentials of the hypnotist; videotaped hypnotic inductions of previous clients; etc.

Warm-up exercises can include: (1) producing an automatic salivation response to the thought of biting into a tart and tangy lemon; and (2) the arms demonstration where the client is asked to hold both arms out slightly elevated above eye level, then to imaging a huge helium balloon pulling up on one arm and a heavy bucket of water pulling down on the other. In both instances there is a high probability of response (salivation to the lemon; and the two arms becoming considerably separated). These warm-up exercises are especially effective when done in a class or group setting as a group contagion effect can be quickly created when the individuals become aware of a number of high positive responses all around them. Please note that in the warm up exercises use is made of techniques that produce immediate feedback, immediate visible effects. The same will be true of the SPC (hypnotic induction) techniques.

5-PATH™ - A Systematic Approach to Hypnotherapy

By: Calvin Banyan M.A.

The field of hypnosis and hypnotherapy is maturing. The hypnosis professional, the hypnotherapist has become a stand-alone profession. These professionals along with others such as counsellors and psychologists who are now embracing these powerful hypnotic tools to help their clients are interested in one thing: results. Because of this, many hypnotherapists are moving away from working exclusively with direct suggestion and guided visualization techniques. They are beginning to incorporate more powerful tools such as age regression and parts therapy. 5-PATH™ was designed for these helping professionals so that they will have an underlying structure that is reliable and effective, while incorporating some of the most powerful techniques available to them.

History

After conducting research into hypnotherapeutic techniques, I was struck by the need to develop a systematic and virtually universal approach. I wanted to train the therapists at the Banyan Hypnosis Center for Training & Services, Inc., in a system that was relatively easy to learn, easy to supervise and foremost, it had to be a system that provided consistent results.

I was most impressed with the techniques that I learned from Gerald Kein at The Omni Hypnosis Training Center, in Deland, Florida, especially a technique that he called Universal Therapy.

Among the most important ideas and techniques that I learned were:

1. The need to properly prepare the client by sending a positive message, implying success from the very first contact.
2. The need to do a good pre-talk, where you focus on educating the client, and removing fears and misconceptions about hypnosis.
3. Using an appropriate hypnotic induction, usually a rapid or instant induction that was designed to take your client to a deep level of hypnosis called somnambulism.
4. The use of hidden tests for somnambulism.
5. Using hypnotic suggestion for the issues that brought the client in to see you only after you have tested for hypnosis and established that your client has reached somnambulism.
6. Using age regression to find the event that started the problem, using the Affect Bridge Technique.
7. Using the Informed Child Technique to neutralize the effect that the first event and subsequent events had upon your client. Generally, this involves removing fear and erroneous beliefs placed in the subconscious mind of the client because of those events.
8. Using the principle of forgiveness in therapy for removing anger toward others and feelings of guilt that the client has toward herself.
9. Using Parts Therapy, which I later modified to work with secondary gain issues.

These techniques and ideas were then organized into a systematic procedure that enhances each of the procedures as a whole, thus improving the outcome. The name of this highly systematized approach is Five-Phase Abreactive Therapeutic Hypnosis™, and is usually identified by the acronym, 5-PATH™.

Basic Understanding of 5-PATH™

This article will cover the basic structure of 5-PATH and the essential steps involved in conducting each of the five phases. Some details will be omitted because to provide all the details would require a book in itself. But the reader will have a good understanding of the process by reading this chapter and be able to decide whether she would like to pursue further study.

The 5-PATH™ hypnotherapist takes her client through the following phases, each improving the effectiveness of the subsequent phase. It should be noted here that this is not a five-session, but rather a five-phase approach. Each phase can take less than one session or more than one session depending on a number of factors, such as length of the sessions, skill of the hypnotherapist and complexity of the issue that the hypnotherapist is working on.

Here is a brief outline of the five phases:

1. Phase I: Preparation and Initial Hypnosis Phase
2. Phase II: Age Regression and Informed Child Technique
3. Phase III: Forgiveness of Others Therapy
4. Phase IV: Forgiveness of Self Therapy
5. Phase V: Parts Mediation Therapy

The Process:
Before the Hypnosis Session

The therapist needs to be aware of the principles of waking suggestion, and how the client's degree of success is in part determined by events that occur before the "hypnosis session" begins. The client's success is greatly increased if you are mindful of how the client is handled prior to the session. All of the following have an effect on the work you will be doing with the client.

- Everything she has ever heard about hypnosis and you.
- Your appearance and your office's appearance.
- Any statements that you make about hypnosis or expected outcome.

Because of this the 5-PATH™ hypnotherapist is mindful and strives to make statements suggesting an expectation of a positive outcome. She understands that you and your office must be consistent with the message you intend to send (i.e., professional). You must do a good pre-hypnosis presentation, including a pre-talk and intake. Let me now go into more detail and discuss the individual steps.

Phase I - Direct Suggestion

The main goal of this first phase is to prepare your client for successful hypnotic induction and deepening to somnambulism. Secondly, you will want to demonstrate to your client that she is hypnotized. When you have demonstrated to your client that she has become hypnotized she is more suggestible and is in a hopeful state of mind. When this has been accomplished you have created the ideal client, which greatly increases her probability of success.

To accomplish this, Phase I contains the following steps:

1. Proper induction, usually an instant or rapid induction (i.e., the Elman-Banyan Rapid Induction). Rarely does the 5-PATH™ hypnotherapist use anything but instant or rapid inductions, all of which are designed to take the client into a state of somnambulism.
2. Use of a hidden test for somnambulism. Hidden tests are used so that if the client has not yet reached the level of somnambulism, the test does not allow your client to become aware of the failure. The 5-PATH™ hypnotherapist carefully guards the client to prevent the experience of failure. If a client knows that she has failed a test, then it will have a negative affect on the session. It will decrease her confidence. This lack of confidence can inhibit reaching deep levels of hypnosis. An example of a covert test can be found in the Elman-Banyan Rapid induction, and in the original Elman induction in which the client is asked to count and go deeper with each number until the numbers have disappeared. This is a very elegant test for the threshold of somnambulism. It is a hidden test for amnesia by suggestion.

Deepening must be done to ensure that your client is well below the threshold of somnambulism, preferably as deep as the level commonly called profound somnambulism. Remember that Phase II consists of hypnotically age-regressing the client, which requires that the client hallucinate. A true age regression is a hallucination, in which she perceives that she is reliving the earlier event from her life.

3. Use of convincers, so that the client knows that she was hypnotized (i.e., eye lock). Convincers are tests for a level of hypnosis that is much lighter than the one that you have verified through covert testing. You know that she is going to pass this test. So, it is not really a test but rather a procedure that you guide your client through so that she can experience a hypnotic phenomenon so that she realizes that she is hypnotized. This both deepens the hypnosis and builds confidence.
4. Suggest to the client that each time that she uses hypnosis she will go deeper into hypnosis. Once she is hypnotized it is good form to suggest that from that point on she will go into hypnosis readily than the time before.
5. Give your client a post-hypnotic suggestion for re-induction of hypnosis in subsequent sessions. This can be done as easily as suggesting to your hypnotized client that, "The next time we do hypnosis together, all I will have to do is drop your hand and say the word 'sleep' and you will instantly return to this state of hypnosis or deeper." This is a form of instant induction that will save the hypnotherapist a great deal of time in the subsequent sessions.
6. Use of Direct Suggestion techniques, including giving some suggestions that were agreed to by the client ahead of time (during the pre-hypnosis interview). This may consist of a hypnosis script of a set of suggestions developed for an individual case.

7. Making additional suggestions during the emerging process for post-hypnotic suggestion (i.e., more convincers), such as time distortion and sensitivity to a color such as red. When your client experiences these post-hypnotic suggestions after the session it compounds all of the suggestions that you have given her. Running a first session this way is done in order to improve the probability of success during Phase II, for the following reasons:
8. You have conditioned your client to reach a state of somnambulism that is the required depth of hypnosis for a successful hypnotic age regression and other therapies to come.
9. Your client has experienced some success and so she will be confident and relaxed during this next phase, which is usually conducted during a second session.

Again, let me remind the reader that Phase I and Phase II can be conducted during the first session if there is time to do both well. But in most professional office situations where only a single hour or up to an hour and a half is scheduled for an appointment, only the first phase is likely to be accomplished.

Phase II - Age Regression

Every problem, for which our clients come to see us about have an origin or an initial event that started it. The use of Age Regression Therapy is probably the most powerful tool available to a properly trained hypnotherapist. It is an essential part of 5-PATH™. In addition to uncovering information from the past that might have become unavailable to the conscious mind, regression allows the therapist to "undo" the effects of the incident or incidents that have formed the problem.

The age regression process is so important, that much of what was done in Phase I was done so that we can have a successful Age Regression Session virtually every time we conduct such a session. As I mentioned above, somnambulism is required for a successful age regression because it is a reliving of the events from the past (revivification). If your client is not sufficiently deepened she may experience enhanced memory because of the hypnosis (Hypermnesia) but be unable to experience revivification.

Phase II contains the following steps:

1. Discuss last session with your client. You will learn about your client's subjective experience of the last session and how she has responded to the hypnotic suggestions after the session was concluded.
2. Use post-hypnotic suggestion for rapid re-induction of hypnosis to somnambulism. Once your client has experienced somnambulism, it is very simple to take her from the normal waking state back into somnambulism if a suggestion for re-inductions was provided in the first session, i.e., "The next time we do hypnosis together, all I will have to do is drop your hand and you will close your eyes and return to this state."
3. Deepen the state of hypnosis. Although the hypnotherapist can overdo this, it is recommend that you take some time to deepen the hypnotic state using some simple procedures such as counting from one down to five with suggestions for going deeper.

4. Use the Affect Bridge technique to uncover the initial sensitizing event (ISE) which is the first event in your client's life that initiated the problem or issue. This is done by suggesting to your client that the feeling/emotion associated with the problem comes up as you count from one up to five. When your client exhibits signs of experiencing the emotion, it is time to regress. Signs that your client is experiencing the emotion include, but are not limited to: breathing faster, increased muscle tension, face turning red and crying.
5. Find the ISE by suggesting that your client follow that feeling back to an earlier time that she felt that way. Let the event be relived by your client. Then ask if the feeling is new or familiar. In addition to asking if the feeling is new, there are several other ways to validate whether an event is the ISE or a subsequent sensitizing event (SSE). Covering all of these validating techniques would require a separate article. Having said that, establishing whether the feeling is new or familiar is certainly one of the most important ways to validate an ISE.
6. When your client relives the ISE and SSEs she should be encouraged to fully experience the emotions associated with the situation. This discharges this emotion which helps to remove internal stress and will make your client easier to work with when doing the Informed Child Technique that follows. If your client is not allowed to experience and discharge these emotions she may resist the logical approach of the Informed Child Technique.
7. Use the Informed Child Technique once you have uncovered the ISE. The Informed Child Technique is accomplished when you have given the regressed client (usually regressed to a time in childhood) all the information that she needs to go through the ISE once again without being negatively affected by it. By that I mean, without becoming afraid or taking on an erroneous belief about herself, others or her world in general.
8. The Informed Child Technique uses the wisdom of the "adult" client with the help of the hypnotherapist to achieve insight into the situation. So many times in our adult lives we have said, "Boy, I wish I knew then what I know now." Using this technique involves going before the ISE and then having her relive it knowing what the adult client knows now. This removes the fears and erroneous beliefs.
9. Then have your client go through the ISE to ensure that the new information was accepted. She should be able to go through the ISE without becoming fearful or taking on erroneous beliefs. This demonstrates that the effect of the event has been neutralized. It has not been forgotten, it is now an experience that the client has learned from rather than being the cause of a problem.
10. If your client is unable to go through the ISE without becoming fearful or exhibiting erroneous beliefs, repeat the Informed Child Technique again. Give her whatever information that she needs to go through the event as it actually happened without being negatively affected by it.
11. Proceed forward in time from the ISE through some of the SSEs to make sure that the change has been fully accepted. If your client has difficulty with a particular SSE, you can repeat the Informed Child Technique for the SSE just as you did with the ISE.

12. Always finish each session with direct suggestions for the issue that the client came in to see you about. Tie in what happened during the age regression with the changes that she is going to experience. The age regression is an insight therapy, and as such caused the subconscious mind to go into a state of reorganization and for a short period of time will be highly suggestible for suggestions that are consistent with the insights gained during the age regression. Prior to this, the subconscious mind may have been resistant to suggestion and only reject it or only accept it temporarily. But, after having had the insights gained in the age regression she is now in a state of heightened suggestibility beyond what can be accomplished using direct suggestion alone.

Having done the age regression work, not only have you removed fears and erroneous beliefs, you have uncovered the situations, events and individuals that are associated with your client's issues. By doing this you have improved the probability of success of the next phase, Phase III: Forgiveness of Others, because now we know who needs to be forgiven and what they did.

Phase III - Forgiveness of Others

The Age Regression session (Phase III) has provided us with great opportunities. The negative impact of the client's ISEs and SSE has been removed. You and the client have a much better understanding of the history of the problem. And, most importantly to this phase, we know who was associated with the ISE and SSEs. We know about the people in our client's life that have been a part of the problem. In addition to gaining insight, and neutralizing some of the emotions associated with the problem, it can now be further healed by using forgiveness techniques. Used after the age regression process, forgiveness therapy provides for a much greater reduction in emotion and erroneous beliefs regarding the problem and a more complete releasing of the past regarding the problem.

The 5-PATH™ hypnotherapist understands that it is these emotions, especially fear, anger and guilt that drives the problems that her client has experienced. It is these feelings, often repressed outside of consciousness, that drive the psychosomatic illnesses, bad habits or addictions. Age regression is an excellent way to remove old fears and erroneous beliefs. But it does not adequately address anger, which will be addressed in Phase III: Forgiveness of Others, and feelings of guilt addressed in Phase IV: Forgiveness of Self.

Phase III: Forgiveness of Self has the following steps:

1. Do the induction and deepening.
2. Set up for "Chair Therapy" where the client can communicate with the person who contributed to the problem, i.e., abuser, parent, rapist, etc.
3. An environment is suggested to the client, in which she will be completely safe in expressing her feelings. Usually it is suggested that she is now in a room with two chairs, where she is to sit in one chair and the offender (the person she is angry toward) will be in the other. In this case, the offender cannot get out of the chair, or speak, unless either she or the hypnotherapist directs the offender to do so. I like to further suggest that when the offender leaves the room, the offender will forget everything that happened. This is done in part so that the forgiveness is not construed to

benefit the offender in any way. This forgiveness is being done to benefit your client.

4. The client is encouraged to express how she feels or felt about what happened. The client is greatly encouraged to really let it all out. This further discharge the feelings of anger that have been held inside the client and will enable her to follow the suggestions that the hypnotherapist will give her that will lead to insight and eventual forgiveness in the session.
5. Once the client has fully expressed her anger, the therapist has the client take the place of the offender, and will speak from that perspective. This event will unlock a great deal of insight into the event. This is accomplished by saying to your client, "Now be (insert name of the offender)."
6. The hypnotherapist then confronts the offender with what was said by the client to the offender (who is of course the client hallucinating being the offender). The hypnotherapist reads through all the things that the offender has done to the client, including how it made her feel and what it made her think. When the offender attempts to defend herself, she will access more information and insight held within the subconscious mind of your client regarding the events that have angered the client and caused the problem.
7. This new material will often cause new insight in the client with regard to the situation to occur, which will be useful in accomplishing the forgiveness.
8. Dialog is encouraged between the client and the offender (the client will speak from both perspectives).
9. The client is then guided into forgiving the offender. It is explained to the client that this is for her own benefit and not for the benefit of the offender (remember that the offender will forget what has transpired in this situation).
10. Once the forgiveness is complete, then additional suggestions are used, regarding the problem/issue.

This process of forgiveness may be repeated for additional individuals from your client's life who contributed to the problem. Your client may also be encouraged to continue to forgive less significant persons on her own for a period during the session.

Notice the use of suggestion at the end of the process. Again, I want to remind the therapist that powerful techniques such as this, forces the subconscious mind into reorganization, and as a result your client becomes exceptionally suggestible for suggestions that are consistent with the experience. Don't overlook this opportunity!

This phase again sets us up for increased success in the following phase. Once your client has forgiven these offenders who have hurt her so much in the past, she will now feel a great sense of relief. Then she will be much more inclined to believe that she can be forgiven and experience the healthy feeling of relief that comes after self-forgiveness. So now the process of self-forgiveness that comes next will be much easier.

Phase IV - Self-Forgiveness

Most of my clients report that this phase of forgiving themselves was the most important. I often wish that I could just go there first. But of course, the reason that this phase is so successful is because of the work and preparation that was done in the preceding phases.

Phase IV is nearly the same as Phase III, except this time the client takes on two roles in which the first role will be that of the "Self" and the other is the "Mistake-Making-Part." The Mistake-Making-Part is worked with, and forgiven, in the same way as the offender was in Phase III. This approach allows the client to see herself in a more detached and objective way.

Here are the steps involved in Phase IV:

1. Do induction and deepening.
2. Set up for "Chair Therapy" where the client can safely communicate with the Mistake-Making-Part, who will be blamed for every mistake she has ever made in her life.
3. The client is encouraged to express how she feels or felt about the mistakes made in her life. Once again, your client is greatly encouraged to really let it all out.
4. Once the client has expressed all the painful feelings that she has toward that Mistake-Making part of herself, the therapist has the client take the place of the Mistake-Making-Part, and will speak from that perspective. Before this she was speaking from the perspective of the "Self."
5. Therapist then goes after the Mistake-Making-Part, similar to how the client did, but perhaps even more emphatically.
6. This will cause new insight in the client with regard to the situations from her life, and will be very useful in accomplishing the forgiveness of herself.
7. Dialog is encouraged between the Self and the Mistake-Making-Part (the client will speak from both perspectives).
8. Because of the new insight, about the situation, the Mistake-Making Part can be reframed as the Protective Part, also making her more forgivable.
9. The client is then guided into forgiving the Mistake-Making-Part.
10. The two parts are then reintegrated into one.
11. Then additional direct suggestion techniques are used regarding the problem/issue.

This is usually a tremendous experience for the client. By this time in the therapy, the cause of the problem has been completely resolved/healed. The work is usually done at this point and no further work is required. However, sometimes more work may be needed because of a special circumstance. This will be addressed in Phase V.

Phase V - Parts Mediation Therapy

The vast majority of clients do not need this Phase of 5-PATH™. Phase V, Parts Mediation Therapy, was designed to be used for special cases. Some clients will not experience a complete resolution of their problem by resolving and neutralizing the cause of the problem. This is usually because of Secondary Gain Issues. It must be kept in mind by the well trained and experienced hypnotherapist that even some of the most painful problems can have benefits!

Secondary Gain Issues exist when a condition, problem or illness has been dealt with at the causal level, but it is being reinforced or demanded by present circumstances. The problem continues because to change would cause the individual to lose something or someone of value to her.

Phase V will enable you to effectively work with individuals who would otherwise be unable to overcome their problems.

It is patterned after two procedures, Parts Therapy and Mediation. Together they become Parts Mediation Therapy. It differs from Parts Therapy because it does not focus on descriptive characteristics of the individual such as the Joy Part, or Creative Part, etc. In that kind of therapy, the hypnotherapist suggests to her client that she will "bring up" these different characteristics or abilities that have been suppressed, lie dormant or are otherwise out of balance. There may even be an interaction between these parts as the client speaks from each one's particular perspective. But rarely does the interaction become as focused as it does in Parts Mediation Therapy.

In Parts Mediation Therapy, we utilize the principles of mediation, where the goal of the hypnotherapist is to act as a mediator and help the client work toward building agreements between the parts of herself that are in conflict. The 5-PATH™ hypnotherapist uncovers issues and focuses on helping the parts of the client who are in conflict to create a win-win situation. These new agreements include doing more beneficial or healthy behaviours in the future.

The steps for conducting a Phase V session are as follows:

1. Induce hypnosis and deepen.
2. Suggest that you are the mediator and not the judge (mediators are only facilitators and can make no final decisions).
3. Bring up the subject of the conflict (the problem/issue that has not been completely resolved).
4. Suggest that more communication may be in order to achieve an agreement in which the needs of both parts can be met.
5. Suggest that there is a part of her that is aware of a benefit of continuing to have the problem. For example you might say, "There is a part of you that would like to continue to (insert problem or issue). What is good about continuing to (insert problem or issue)?"
6. Find out why the problem is useful without becoming critical. The hypnotherapist in the role of mediator has the goal of creating an environment where the client can openly express why she wants either change or remain the same.
7. Name the part, such as The-Still-Wanting-To-Smoke Part. The part that wishes to change will be called the "Self."
8. When the needs of the part that did not want to change are fully understood, the name of the part is changed. For example, if you find out that the Still-Wanting-To-Smoke Part was doing what it was doing because smoking helped your client deal with stress by causing her to take a break from work, then we can rename that part as the Rest-and-Relaxation Part. The Rest-and-Relaxation Part can then be persuaded to do something else rather than smoke to provide your client with the breaks that she feels that she needs. On the other hand, if left with the old name, the Still-

Wanting-To-Smoke Part would be resistant to such suggestions or persuasion.

9. Have the Self discuss the benefits of making the change.
10. Begin a "brainstorming" process to uncover and discuss alternative behaviours that will provide the same benefits as the problem behaviour.
11. Assist both Parts in coming to a win-win agreement where both sides have their needs met.
12. Do any forgiveness work that needs to be done between the two sides.
13. Merge the two Parts back together as one person.
14. Finish up with direct suggestion techniques for change based on the agreement that was made during the Parts Mediation Therapy procedure.

As usual, the process ends with appropriate suggestions for change. Here we have uncovered the cause of the inability of the client to come to full resolution of the problem. And, we have provided an alternative plan of action that is designed to fulfil all of her needs. This is set up as an agreement between the parts. If there is any reluctance between the parts in this intra-psychic mediation, then a trial period can be agreed upon, where a next session can be set up to evaluate the success of the agreement and make any further changes that may be need to encourage ongoing success.

Summary

This has been a brief overview of 5-PATH™ a systematic approach to doing hypnotherapy, which is almost universally effective in the problems that our clients face. It can be modified to suit the client and application by the therapist. For example if it becomes evident that a particular phase of the therapy process was left incomplete, you may return to that phase and continue to do the hypnotherapy there until you are satisfied that it is complete. Then move on to the subsequent phases.

Therapeutic Metaphor for the Smoker

By: Joann Abrahamsen

There are times when it is necessary to construct a structured "story line" to deal with persistently resistant aspects of the client's problem. These are called "Therapeutic Metaphors" and their construction requires more thought than the simpler kind used in imagery (i.e.," imagine yourself sinking deep into a soft fluffy white cloud... " A therapeutic metaphor is a "story" that you tell a client. It can be an anecdote, a fable or even a fairy tale. The choice depends upon what form would be most acceptable to your client. A therapeutic metaphor is particularly effective, because the suggestions bypass the subject's "mindset" and allows acceptance of new concepts of behavior. Without the "bypass," those new concepts would come into direct conflict with old, deeply rooted behavior patterns. Metaphors widen the client's choices by illustrating new ways to solve a problem. Metaphors enable the client to identify with something familiar and make the connection with their own behavior.

In the imageries, you place your client in the setting and involve the client in the activity as characters in the story. The client perceives himself or herself to be part of the action. The action itself is often metaphorical in nature, but since the client is not personally involved, the situation is not threatening.

The script and characters must be carefully constructed to be comparable to the characters involved in the problem, their relationships to each other and to the events that comprise the problem.

As an example, consider the case of a woman who said she wanted to stop smoking. The usual imageries were only minimally effective and, after two hypnosis sessions, she was still experiencing a great deal of difficulty. She would "forget" to do the reinforcement exercise. She would "forget" to do the other behavior modification techniques that should have dealt with both the physical habits and the triggers. Each time she came back for a session, she would have some new rationalization for her behavior (we were using a four week stop smoking program of gradual withdrawal.)

It became more and more obvious that the problem was her inability to let go of the conviction that cigarettes enabled her to deal with the world. She had allowed herself only two choices: To smoke and continue to be effective in her life or not to smoke and be unable to cope. Suggestions and metaphors that characterized cigarettes as a crutch had no effect because she accepted the crutch as a necessity. It became necessary to construct a special metaphor that would allow her to accept the idea that cigarettes were unnecessary and that she was fully capable of coping without them.

Because of her well-developed appreciation of fantasy, a fairy tale setting was chosen. The characters were the Princess/Queen (the client), the King (a personification of successful control of all situations), the Prime Minister (the hypnotist) and the Crown (symbolic of the cigarette habit). Under hypnosis, she was told the following story.

Once upon a time in a very important kingdom, there lived a powerful King and his daughter, the Princess. From the time, the Princess was very little, she had always admired her father, the King, because he was strong and wise and good and ruled his kingdom well. The Princess would follow the King around as he dealt with this problem and that problem and made wise judgments for his subjects. Moreover, always the Princess wondered how he was able to do it. **She did not feel very wise, you see, or very capable**. Many times, she found herself unable to decide even simple things, like whether to wear a blue gown or a yellow one. She worried that, when it came time for her to rule, she would be unable to do it well. She did not understand what it was that set her father apart from the other men of the kingdom. There were others as strong. There were others as handsome. There were even others who were wise. And there were many others whose dress was as rich and whose belongings were as varied. However, none who could rule as well as the King.

Then, one day, it came to her. The only thing that she could find different about her father was the fact that he wore the Crown. "Of course!" She thought, in great relief. **"It's the Crown that gives him his great power** to rule! And when the time comes for me to rule**, I, too, will wear the Crown and I will have the power"** The Princess was greatly comforted by her discovery and ceased to worry about the future. Everything would certainly be all right when she wore the Crown.

And, in time, the King died and the Princess became Queen. The Crown was placed upon her head and in that very moment, she felt strong, wise, and capable. No longer did she worry whether or not to take some particular action**. With the Crown on her head, she knew her decisions would be good ones**. And she was, indeed, an excellent Queen. Just like her father before her, she was strong, wise, and good and ruled her kingdom well.

But, as time passed, she realized that wearing the Crown was not quite as simple as she had assumed. For one thing, it was rather heavy. But she gradually became used to the heaviness... at least she thought she had. Besides, what was the alternative? She had to rule. Therefore, she had to wear the Crown. In fact, she came to depend so much on its power that she removed it less and less often. After a year or two, she had formed the habit of wearing it every waking hour, even in her bath! She took it off only to sleep.

And the heaviness of the Crown began to take its toll. At first, it was just an aching in her neck and shoulders. Then, she began to have rather severe headaches. Soon, her face was permanently drawn in lines of pain and discomfort and she began to lose the beauty for which she had once been famous. Also, her shoulders and back began to stoop under the weight of the Crown. Although she was still quite a young woman, she began to look like a very old woman. What was worse, she began to feel like a very old woman as well. Her muscles ached, she became short of breath after only mild activity and she tired more and more quickly each day. Soon, she found herself having to take naps during the day, just to keep from falling asleep on her throne.

But the Queen failed to see that it was the Crown that was making the changes in her. After all, the Crown was the source of her power. It could not possibly be a bad thing. And so she remained in ignorance as to the cause of her physical problems.

As time went on, her advisors became worried and convinced the Queen that it must be some terrible sorcery that was making her ill. They called in the Prime Minister to see if he could recommend a wizard who might tell them who was doing this terrible thing to the Queen. The Prime Minister came to the Throne Room and bowed before the Queen. Then he simply looked at her for a long, long time. Finally, he said, "Your Majesty, you have no need of a wizard. Your problem is very easy to understand. You are doing this to yourself."

The Queen was appalled and very, very angry. "How insolent!" She exclaimed.

The Prime Minister only nodded. "Insolent it may be, but it is still quite true. The problem lies with the Crown on your head. It is much too heavy for you. I cannot understand how you have managed with it all this time. You must be getting terrible headaches. And I am sure your back and shoulders ache with the weight. In fact, they seem quite bent under it."

"That's ridiculous!" exclaimed the Queen. "There's nothing at all wrong with my Crown. Besides, I have to wear it. I'm the Queen!"

"It's true enough that you're the Queen -- and quite a good one, too," responded the Prime Minister. "But everyone in the Kingdom knows you're the Queen. So there doesn't seem to be any really compelling reason to wear a Crown that's obviously too heavy for you!"

The Queen was too upset at the Prime Minister's attack on her Crown to listen. She dismissed him from her presence without another thought. But the Prime Minister felt very sorry for the Queen and took to hanging around the Royal Apartments. Whenever he saw her, he would point at the Crown and shake his head sadly. The Queen was becoming more and more annoyed at his behavior and was seriously thinking of banishing him. But before she could act on her thought, something truly remarkable happened.

One afternoon, the Queen was taking her usual nap. On the table beside the bed rested her Crown, which she only removed when she slept. Suddenly, it seemed as though the entire castle shook and trembled and shifted. The Queen awoke with a cry to see great cracks appearing in the walls of her chamber. The furniture was tossed about, the table beside her bed had overturned and, unknown to the Queen, the Crown had rolled under the bed.

She was barely awake when her advisors rushed into the chamber. "Your Majesty," they cried, "a terrible earthquake has struck the kingdom! We could see from the battlements that many of your subjects' homes are destroyed, great trees have fallen and the river seems about to change its course to go right through the middle of the city!"

Immediately, the Queen jumped out of bed, snatched up a robe and began issuing commands. Advisors, courtiers, generals ran to obey. Rescue teams were sent out, food and pure water were distributed among those in need, a levee was begun to contain the river and all precautions were taken to prevent fires and looting. By nightfall, things were under control. The advisors praised the Queen (who still had not had time to dress properly) as she sat at her desk, still signing orders to deal with the catastrophe. "Thanks to your strength and quick thinking, much tragedy has been averted," they told her. "Your Father couldn't have done any better."

The Queen smiled, quite pleased with herself, now that she had a moment to think about it. And just then, she saw the Prime Minister standing in the doorway, grinning widely. 'What are you grinning about, Prime Minister?" She asked, still annoyed with him. "Why," answered the Prime Minister, "I'm just so pleased with the way you look this evening. Your face is unlined as it should be, your back and shoulders are straight as they once were and you look as fresh and alert after a whole day of activity as you were when you first awoke this morning." The Queen was so pleased that she forgot her annoyance. And she did feel very well, considering all she had had to do. She said, "Thank you for the compliment. I hope this means you have decided to stop nagging at me because of the Crown." "Of course," said the Prime Minister. "There's no need to nag you, now you've stopped wearing it."

The Queen stared at him in horror as she reached up to her head. He was right! She was not wearing the Crown! She looked around wildly, trying to find it. "Don't worry, it is quite safe, your Majesty. I found it under your bed. The earthquake must have toppled it there. I had it put in the Royal Treasury for safekeeping. It's not as though you need it for anything."

And the Queen realized how well she had handled the extreme emergency of her entire reign without the Crown on her head, and understood that the Prime Minister had been right all along. And she knew that from that day forward, the Crown would remain in the Royal Treasury, under lock and key, while she continued to rule her kingdom with strength and goodness and wisdom."

The sentences in bold type in the first three paragraphs refer, of course, to the subject's belief that cigarettes are necessary to her effectiveness. As far as she is concerned, this is absolute truth -- therefore, it is not resisted.

The next three paragraphs are a metaphorical restatement of the fact that, though she realizes consciously that smoking is detrimental, the alternative is unacceptable and so, she cannot allow herself to use that realization as a reason to stop. Then, the introduction of the Prime Minister and her refusal to accept his advice is just another way of reaffirming her resistance to the hypnotic suggestion.

All of the above is incontrovertible. It has already happened. And the fact that she has no reason to resist those analogies leads her closer to the acceptance of future analogies.

The balance of the metaphor was constructed so as to open up the client to the possibility of functioning without her "Crown." The fact that the "heroine" of the metaphor was someone else allowed her to listen to and accept the "story" without feeling threatened. She was then able, on the subconscious level, to connect the possibility in the story with her own situation.

The effect of the total metaphor was to make it possible for the client to accept that she was capable of dealing with the world just as well without cigarettes as she had done with them. This kind of metaphor requires careful construction. Not only must all aspects match the client's situation, but also it must be created to keep the client's attention. It has to be a good story. The insertion of detail helps to make it more interesting and, within that detail, you can often insert other suggestions that will be helpful in alleviating the client's problem.

If you wish, you can use almost the same metaphor for weight. Substitute another item of royal power and authority, such as a heavy cloak, for the crown and change some of the wording. For further and more in-depth study of the creation of therapeutic metaphors, you will find David Gorton's book *Therapeutic Metaphors* an excellent guide to further study.

Can Hypnosis End Bulimia?

By: Bryan M. Knight. MSW, Ph.D.

The short answer is yes. The longer answer follows.

Bulimia (usually defined as binge eating followed with laxatives, vomiting, diuretics or compulsive exercise to purge the body) is a life-threatening malaise. There are several theories about why people become trapped in this cycle of self-abuse. These fall into three main categories:

- Social
- Family
- Individual

Each, of course, is intimately linked with the others. Hypnotherapy helps on the individual level that, in turn, can influence the family and the social aspects.

Society

It is not society's fault that a particular person is bulimic. However, society certainly reinforces their dilemmas. How does it do this? Through its emphasis on food - and thinness. Ever watch television and *not* see a commercial for food? Read a magazine and *not* see an advertisement for food? Yet the cover most likely features a very thin woman. And on television you'll see skinny models and infomercials for weight loss.

So society says thin is good - yet promotes junk food. On top of this, we receive the message that some foods are "bad" and others are "good."

Similarly, drinking alcohol is adult, drinking alcohol is dangerous.

These contradictions lay a foundation of inner conflict. Especially for emotionally vulnerable adolescents.

If you eat "bad" foods, you feel guilty. If you force yourself to refrain, you feel deprived. No wonder some people turn to stuffing themselves, and then vomit the guilt.

It often seems that society is telling us we can't be thin enough. Not surprising then, if you try to be as thin as possible as to gain validation from outside.

Or, if overweight, feel unaccepted and unacceptable.

All of society's contradictions are further underlined in the school system. We teach children (especially girls) to be compliant, rather than independent. We do not teach children to question, to think critically. We teach them to conform -- and to regurgitate!

Family

A lot of people with eating disorders come from families that have difficulty in expressing emotions. It may be that the parents bury their own conflicts, or it may be that their religious or cultural beliefs preclude speaking openly about emotion.

Whatever the reason for the restriction of open expression, the result is often that the children absorb the family's silent pain. And one way in which a child deals with this unexpressed pain is to punish herself through the misuse of food.

Abuse -- emotional, physical, psychological or sexual -- within the family can also be a cause for an eating disorder later in life. The child, now grown up, continues to perpetuate abuse only now in the form of harming herself physically, psychologically and emotionally, through bingeing and purging.

In both lack of expressed emotion and overt abuse, the child's body expresses the family's dynamics.

Individual

Bulimia may begin as a person's reaction to the fear and sense of loss of control when a mood disorder such as depression occurs. When this is the case, treatment of the biologically caused mood disorder is essential -- another reason to involve a physician.

More often, bulimia is an ineffective way a person responds to the social and family cues described above or to other events.

Anything that causes severe emotional pain may lead to a person using bulimia in a frantic attempt to regain a sense of control. There may be a single originating trauma such as an abortion, divorce, rape, death of a friend. Or the psychological or emotional pain may have come from a series of traumas. Or even from an intolerable, ongoing experience such as a dispiriting marriage, or having grown up in an alcoholic family.

Some individuals become bulimic because after years of being givers, they tire of always pleasing others but don't know how to deal with their frustration and resentment.

Yet another possible cause of bulimia can be that your feelings were not validated. That is, when you felt angry, for example, you were told it that it was wrong to feel that way, or that you were selfish, or even that you didn't really feel angry.

The resulting confusion (because of course, you did feel angry) would likely result in you turning the anger and frustration inward.

Since you had been taught not to express your emotions through words, or to trust your own feelings, one way to deal with the resulting sense of badness or craziness would be to overeat -- and then to purge the guilt and shame.

Most bulimics think in "either-or" terms. This leaves no room for the acceptance of mixed emotions. For example, most people have mixed feelings towards their parents. But a bulimic would likely condemn herself for even a fleeting thought of disloyalty or anger toward a parent. Either you love, or you hate. Either you are good, or you are bad. Either you are thin, or you are fat. Either you eat well, or you eat badly.

Such thinking prevents a person from self-understanding and self-acceptance. It goes along with the uncritical absorption of television commercials and magazine ads. It keeps the bulimic's self-esteem at a low level.

Symptoms

In a futile attempt to soothe herself, the bulimic falls into a seesaw ritual as she tries to regulate the opposing tensions of emptiness and guilt.

Shame increases as the physiological effects of either overeating or malnutrition take effect.

The ritual of binge/purge can also be seen as a sad attempt to exercise control in what may be the only available arena in the bulimic's life: her body. Often, though, the body image is distorted. Where others see emaciation, she may see obesity. Desperately, the bulimic comes to define herself through this preoccupation with food and size. Self-esteem is consequently very low because the bulimic can never be thin enough in her own eyes, nor good enough in her own estimation.

There is, of course, a constant preoccupation with food and weight. This focus serves to protect the bulimic from facing the buried unacceptable, or terrifying, emotional conflicts within her or within the family.

Prescribed, or illegal, drugs to lose weight may exacerbate the physical damage and the shame.

These symptoms are not the problem. They are just that, symptoms. Hypnosis can be used to deal not only with these symptoms, but with the underlying problems that give rise to the symptoms.

Hypnosis to Get to the Cause

Hypnosis provides a quick route to the cause of an individual's bulimia. This is because hypnosis allows direct communication with the sufferer's subconscious. And the subconscious knows what is at the root of the problem. Sometimes this is a single event (terrifying sexual abuse, for example); more often there is a series of traumas or conflicts. Each such event builds on the previous ones until the psychological torment becomes intolerable.

Bulimia can then be seen as Both a Way to Exercise Control over Out-of-Control Feelings, and as a Scream for Help.

There are several techniques that a competent hypnotherapist is trained to use to help bulimics tackle the causes of their suffering. None involve gadgets or touching the client. They may include relaxing music but they are basically verbal. They concentrate on encouraging the bulimic to use her imagination in a creative manner.

To the subconscious, all events, imagined or actually experienced, are "real." This is a wonderful attribute of the mind.

It means that the bulimic can take some traumatic event that has deeply upset her and, in her imagination, re-write that event so the movie in her mind turns out the way she would prefer.

This results in her subconscious holding the two versions of "reality." The second gives relief to what has become popularly known as the "inner child."

It is not that the traumatic event is wiped out. The conscious mind still knows what happened. But the negative emotional impact is diminished. The person no longer needs to purge. She is freed from the self-punishment.

Hypnosis to Deal with Symptoms

Symptoms, apart from the major one of purging, vary from one person to another. Hypnotherapy enables the bulimic to imagine herself behaving differently. Thus, the people-pleasing bulimic mentioned above, who is tired of always being a giver, could use hypnotherapy to imagine herself instead dealing with her rage and resentment in constructive ways.

Freedom from the need to purge can be encouraged with *post-hypnotic suggestions.* That is, suggestions given while you are in hypnosis but that take effect after the session.

Usually more than a post-hypnotic suggestion would be necessary to eliminate bulimia. Even the most powerful post-hypnotic suggestions fade over time unless there is reinforcement (by you or with the therapist) or a profound change in lifestyle.

A main factor in the healing of a bulimic is the attention and validation offered by the therapist to the person seeking help. So, even without hypnosis, simply enjoying the experience of the professional encouraging and endorsing your feelings, is therapeutic.

What hypnotherapy offers you is a method to continue the healing by yourself.

Psychotherapy While You are in Hypnosis

"Either-or" thinking, characteristic of bulimics permits no room for the imperfections we all possess. Limited thinking prevents a person from self-understanding and self-acceptance. It's a mind trap with only two gates. It ignores the reality that we can choose to add as many gates as we wish.

"Either-or" thinking is the delight of the sponsors of television commercials and magazine ads. They can more easily persuade a limited-thinking viewer that such-and-such a food is "good."

Or, conversely, that you should feel guilty about eating this other product because it brings pleasure to your palate, and fat to your face. Thus is the uncritical-thinking bulimic's self-esteem kept at a low level.

The "either-or" thinking pattern of most bulimics can be transformed by using cognitive therapy while you are in hypnosis. This simply means the therapist helps you to think more clearly, with a wider variety of options than you have been used to. Also to question, to be sceptical.

This happens more quickly when you are relaxed in hypnosis than it would during ordinary psychotherapy. Such a change in patterns of thinking allows for the acceptance of mixed emotions. And for the evaluation of what others tell you. Ultimately, critical thinking makes freedom from bulimia possible.

Hypnotherapy can increase your self-control, your self-liking, your self-esteem and therefore, your self-protection.

Hypnotherapy provides a safe, healthy way to soothe yourself.

Distorted body image is characteristic of the bulimic, who often feels she cannot be thin enough. Hypnotherapeutic techniques can gradually help her adjust her perceptions to reality.

Similarly with unexpressed emotion. With hypnotherapy, you can unlearn messages the family may have implanted about keeping feelings in. You can learn how to safely express emotion, instead of stuffing it down and purging it out.

In the therapist's office, relaxed in hypnosis, you use your mind to allow yourself to feel and to imaginatively rehearse the safe expression of emotion.

This purging of emotion in a safe environment can translate into your not needing to purge food. You have undercut the need for the metaphor (food-purging) by experiencing the reality (emotion-purging).

You can also use hypnosis to give yourself post-hypnotic suggestions about eating normally, being free from the urge to purge food, being in control in healthy ways, etc. In addition, you could use hypnotherapy to provide yourself with a "trigger" (a word, a gesture, or an image) that automatically stops you from harming yourself.

Hypnotherapy can help you use your inner strengths to stop your body being the vehicle that expresses your family's disturbed dynamics.

Hypnotherapy can also strengthen your resolve to be your own person -- to resist the impact of the diabolical and paradoxical TV and magazine advertising that advocates both food and thinness.

Ultimately, hypnotherapy helps you achieve what all psychotherapy seeks: that you attain enough independence to trust your own judgement, and retain enough interdependence that you contribute the most to society that your unique personality can offer.

Hypnotherapy does this by enabling you to tap into your subconscious resources, and thus to strengthen your self-control.

Hypnosis and Sex

By: Bryan M. Knight, MSW, Ph.D.

A client asked:

"My girlfriend dumped me because she says I 'wasn't there' when we made love. She's not the first to say this. I know something's wrong. Can hypnotherapy help me?"

My reply:

"Your sexual dysfunction means you engage in sex more as an observer than as a participant.

You hold yourself back from entering a trance state; you have difficulty "letting go."

There are several ways in which a qualified hypnotherapist can help you to conquer this problem. Before using hypnosis it is essential that you receive competent medical advice. Hypnotherapy will have a particular focus depending on whether the problem is organic or psychological.

Organic sexual problems require medical intervention. Hypnotherapy may be used as an adjunct, for instance, in helping you to heal faster after an operation. More frequently, sexual difficulties treated by a hypnotherapist involve psychological issues.

Since the process deals with your mind, all sexual activity during hypnotherapy takes place only in your imagination. What you learn through hypnotherapy is practised privately elsewhere. Hypnotherapy may be used to heighten your sensual involvement and to help you to be fully present while engaging in sex.

A common, effective use of hypnotherapy is to lower your anxiety. The anticipation of failure (particularly for men anxious about their ability to have or to maintain an erection) brings on anxious feelings.

These in turn bring about the failure. Hypnotherapy ends this vicious circle and replaces the anticipation of failure with the certainty of success and confidence.

Traditional sex therapy methods are more readily accepted by you when in hypnosis because the conscious, judgmental, analytical part of your mind is temporarily set aside. Your subconscious then absorbs the new, positive messages you've asked the hypnotherapist to create.

Precisely because hypnosis taps into the autonomic nervous system, a person can use it to improve or alter functions that normally happen without conscious control, e.g., a man's erection.

Following are two case histories to illustrate the process:

Case 1: Charles, a 27-year-old former sailor and currently an electrician, consulted a hypnotherapist because he was too fearful to have sex with his wife. They'd been married three years and had had sexual difficulties since the birth of their daughter eight months previously. Charles was afraid he'd been embarrassed once again if he tried to make love.

"Kim laughed at me the first time and now she just gives me a look of disgust. Why? Because he couldn't maintain an erection."

Charles felt humiliated and frustrated; he worried that he'd never again have satisfactory sex with his wife. His dream of fathering a son seemed unattainable. He told the hypnotherapist that he had no problem masturbating when alone. This was a likely indicator that Charles' problem was psychological, not organic. As was Charles' report that he always had a firm erection when having sex with the occasional housewife in whose home he was doing electrical work. To be on the safe side, the hypnotherapist advised Charles to be examined by a medical specialist to be absolutely sure there was no organic cause for his ED. The doctor confirmed that Charles' trouble was "100 per cent psychogenic," meaning that for some emotional or psychological reason, he could not maintain an erection.

Of course, the more Charles tried and the more he worried, the more flaccid was his penis.

The hypnotherapist explained to Charles that hypnosis could be used to uncover the cause of his trouble, or to tackle the symptom, or both.

Charles, being the impatient type, and of course eager to end his humiliating experiences, opted for the "quick fix."

Over the course of three sessions of hypnotherapy, Charles relived successful love-making episodes from his younger years as a Navy "stud." Then the therapist used a melding technique to encourage Charles to see himself (in his imagination, while hypnotized) from now on once again enjoying a full, firm erection well beyond the time needed to satisfy his partner.

Positive suggestions were also made by the hypnotherapist to Charles about his prowess, his confidence and his desirability to his wife. For three months Charles and Kim had a wonderful sex life. Then he lost an erection just as foreplay had become hot and heavy.

Kim, hurt and disappointed, reacted with sarcasm. All Charles' fears and anxieties rushed back. He returned to the hypnotherapist. This time Charles agreed to investigate the cause of his impotence. The hypnotherapist used various approaches: age regression, age progression (in which the "future" Charles was to explain how he'd conquered the problem) analogue symbolic imagery, but nothing worked.

In a subsequent session, with Charles relaxed in hypnosis, the therapist told Charles he'd have a dream. His subconscious would provide this dream as a way, either directly or symbolically, to explain the origin of his impotence.

Three nights later Charles dreamed he was outside a factory. It was night time and the factory loomed dark and mysterious.

Charles felt a strong urge to scale the steel fence that surrounded the factory. Then he tried to find a way in. All the doors were shut and padlocked. A security guard ("very scary, because he had my face," said Charles) told him to go away.

But Charles persisted in his eagerness to enter the factory. He ran from the guard, to the back of the building. Here was the loading dock. Charles saw a bulldozer there. He jumped into its cab and began to operate the controls.

The guard reappeared, feebly told Charles to get off the property, to go to his own place. In the distance, Charles could see a stately castle that he somehow knew belonged to him.

But his only interest was in the dark factory. The guard shrugged. Charles started up the bulldozer and charged the heavy machine toward the small backdoor of the factory. As the bulldozer began to rumble forward, Charles awoke, with a massive erection.

The dream puzzled Charles. But it enlightened the therapist. To him it revealed that Charles was in the grip of the Madonna/Whore complex. This is the attitude that divides women into "good" and "bad." Thus, a man's wife and especially mother, are "good." Prostitutes, other men's wives and women of ethnic groups other than the man's own, are "bad". "Bad" women are exciting; "good" women are boring. Sex is forbidden with "good" women but possible with the "bad."

A man with this complex may have sex with his wife occasionally, or until she becomes a mother, or while a post-hypnotic suggestion lasts. But his heart is not in it. Neither is his penis. However, with a "bad" woman he has no commitment, no respect. She is there to be used.

His conscience (the security guard) barely bothers him about penetrating the stranger (the dark factory) but, perversely, does prevent him enjoying "his" woman (the castle).

When Charles heard this explanation, he nodded in agreement. This was indeed his view. And that of his father, uncle and most of his friends. He had no serious interest in changing this outlook, especially since Kim had announced she was pregnant. The hypnotherapist's suggestion that Charles and Kim seek marriage counselling fell on deaf ears.

Case 2: A female lawyer we shall call Mathilde did seek help from a psychotherapist. She had told the referring doctor that she rarely had an orgasm. The truth was that Mathilde *never* had an orgasm, with her husband. She'd been faking it for years. But she had climaxed with previous boyfriends. Also during a two-night stand a few months ago.

Mathilde had been a speaker at a lawyers' convention a thousand miles from home. There she met Roger, a brooding electrical engineer who had been trouble-shooting the hotel's elevators.

"He was not particularly good-looking but he had these soft grey eyes," Mathilde confided to the therapist. She smiled. "He was brutal in bed."

Mathilde was mildly surprised to find herself telling the male therapist details she had not felt comfortable confiding to her female doctor.

There was no question of her wanting to leave the marriage. She loved her husband, had a marvellous life. All that was missing was the joy of orgasm. It was something she yearned for. Until she met Roger the lack of orgasms with her husband had not bothered her much. Mathilde had become used to pretending -- and to satisfying herself in secret.

The therapist faced two dilemmas:

1) Perhaps, despite Mathilde's conscious denials, there was some problem between her and her husband

2) The therapist usually worked with couples, not individuals, on such sexual challenges.

He decided that, given the husband was not present and would be unlikely to come to future sessions, he would work with Mathilde, and he would use hypnotherapy. If the outcome was successful, there would be no need to explore possible conflicts between husband and wife.

First the therapist explained a little about hypnosis and how it could help Mathilde. Her first session was devoted to her simply relaxing into hypnosis, and becoming familiar with how safe and peaceful it felt.

In Mathilde's second and third sessions of hypnosis the therapist suggested Mathilde silently relive an earlier experience of orgasm.

In her mind she was to take particular note of the physical and emotional feelings that allowed her to climax. When the orgasm in her imagination was over she would open her eyes, though remain in hypnosis.

Then the therapist pointed out, and Mathilde confirmed, that she had been internally very relaxed just prior to making love. And that during foreplay and intercourse, she became "lost" in the pleasure.

The therapist asked Mathilde to again close her eyes and this time to imagine herself in bed with her husband. Again she could relive the details silently, no need to tell the therapist anything, except when the imagined lovemaking was over.

When Mathilde compared the earlier experience with how she felt when making love with her husband she immediately noticed her tension. "I am not relaxed and I don't get lost in the act." Sometimes she thought about cases she was working on and at other times she focused on making sure her husband was satisfied.

In the next part of the session the therapist first gave Mathilde suggestions that she could allow herself to relax with her husband that she could allow herself to climax with him.

The therapist again waited silently while Mathilde played the scene through in her mind. When she signalled (with a broad smile) that the scene had reached a successful end, the therapist closed the session with positive suggestions about Mathilde allowing herself to be relaxed, focused on pleasure and allowed to climax when making love with her husband.

And so it was. Hypnotherapy has also been used successfully to overcome other sexual problems such as over lubrication, exhibitionism, and to uncover the reason a client became a transvestite.

Before seeking help with a sexual difficulty it is important to be sure it really is a problem. For example, a man may go to a therapist because he believes he suffers from premature ejaculation. But if the man is married to a woman who dislikes sex, indeed "wants it over with as soon as possible," that's exactly what is happening, so where's the problem?

Case 3: Twenty-five-year-old Eugene's problem was real enough: he could not become erect. A handsome, single, bus driver, Eugene had had several medical examinations; all the doctors had concluded there was no medical cause for his impotence.

At first, hypnotherapy did not help Eugene. He became more and more despondent about his failure, scared to date and unable to sleep at night. The hypnotherapist had used approaches one or more of which usually resolve psychogenic impotence: Positive suggestions, aversive therapy, satisfying imagery, arm rigidity. But nothing worked.

The hypnotherapist finally decided to enlist the guidance of Eugene's subconscious mind through finger signalling and direct relay of images in response to questions (ideomotor response. With finger signalling, also known as an Ideodynamic technique, a hypnotized person allows the subconscious to answer questions with pre designated fingers that represent *"Yes," "No," "Don't Know,"* and *"Not yet ready to answer"*).

This approach proved fruitful, although at first puzzling.

Hypnotherapist: "I'm going to ask your subconscious some questions. There's no need for you to think about the questions or the answers. Simply allow your subconscious to respond through the fingers it has selected.
You will probably feel a tingling begin in the finger that the subconscious selects. Then it will lift as though of its own accord. Now, I'd like to ask your subconscious if there is a purpose served by Eugene's impotence." [This question is often answered "yes" and subsequently leads to an explanation such as a desire to punish self or partner for some reason].

[Finger responses are indicated with brackets ()].

Eugene: (No).

H: "Does the cause of the problem lie in Eugene's past?"

E: (Yes). [This response steered the hypnotherapist along the wrong path. He took no account of the literalness with which the subconscious absorbs information. Consequently, the hypnotherapist understood the "Yes" response to mean that there was a specific event, a trauma or a message, that began Eugene's impotence. As was later revealed, the "cause in the past" referred, not to a particular event, but to an ongoing process.]

H: "Did the cause happen before Eugene was 20?"

E: (Yes).

H: "Did the cause happen before Eugene was 15?"

E: (Yes).

H: "Before 10?"

E: (No). [Now the hypnotherapist, who erroneously assumes some single event happened, switches from finger responses to image responses].

H: "Okay. I'm going to ask the subconscious to present to your mind an image that is somehow connected to the problem we're dealing with."

E: "I'm in a shop. I don't know how old I am but a man picks me up. I'm very scared. He holds me to him. Someone else comes in and tells the man to put me down." [The hypnotherapist thinks that it is possible something happened in the shop to subsequently cause Eugene to become impotent. However, further questioning reveals that Eugene sees little more than he has already reported. There appears to be no abuse, no negative messages (such as "You'll never be a man.")

The session is drawing to a close so the therapist reverts to idiomatic questioning. He decided to check the medical verdicts].

H: "Does the problem have any medical basis to it?"

E: [Long pause]. (No).

H: "Is there something physical that would help?"

E: (No).

H: "Is there something missing in Eugene's diet, or something he should not be eating or drinking?"

E: (Don't know/don't want to answer yet). [Eugene snaps out of hypnosis, much to his own surprise. In previous sessions for other problems Eugene had enjoyed hypnosis so much he had been reluctant to emerge. He puts himself back into hypnosis.]

H: "Okay. Our time is nearly up. I want to thank your subconscious for its help. I'm now asking it to provide you with a dream that will give you a strong indication on how to solve the problem that brought you here." [Eugene once again snaps out of hypnosis].

H: "Wow. We're clearly close to something significant; otherwise you wouldn't come out so suddenly."

E: "I don't understand why. But while you were talking about me having a dream something floated into my mind: smoking."

H: [Incredulous]. "You smoke!"

E: "Yes, a lot."

H: "There you are. That's what your subconscious was telling us: the cause of your impotence is smoking! Have you stopped before?"

E: "Yes. For a while."

H: "And did you have erections okay then?"

E: [Thinks back]. "Yes, I did. I did." [And the shop? Why did the subconscious throw that memory into Eugene's mind? Perhaps because the shop sold cigarettes.].

Sexual Difficulties as the Result of Negative Self-Hypnosis

By: Dr. Daniel Araoz

If we put the title above in the form of a question, the simple answer is that at times, yes and at times, no and that in all sexual difficulties there is the possibility of negative self-hypnosis (NSH) (Araoz, 1981). When dealing with sexual problems I have called it the hidden symptom (Araoz, 2001). NSH depends on the personality of the individual, not on the type of problem. In other words, besides the obvious diagnosis there is the perception and interpretation of the problem that the person uses mentally. What follows is intended to serve as a guide to avoid NSH in general and especially in many human sexuality aspects including in psychogenic sexual dysfunctions. Therefore, we have two main concepts to deal with NSH and human sexuality.

NSH is the mental process, mostly unconscious, by which humans devalue and put themselves down without recognizing their own assets, successes and accomplishments. It is negative thinking and self-talk, a way of looking at the glass half-empty, not half-full. A way of searching for what is wrong and negative in situations, people and future events. The reason I call it self-hypnosis is that by bypassing reason, it has the same effect of post-hypnotic suggestions and influences the person to act as if hypnosis had been used. Without mentioning hypnosis, Seligman (1975) researched "learned helplessness," that results from the same negative mental activity.

On the other hand, when human sexuality is mentioned, most people think of *sexual activity*, often referred to as sexual *performance,* with all the different technical, entertainment and athletic connotations the word performance has in English. However, sexuality in humans has, at least, six different dimensions. These are sexual identity, orientation, preferences, functioning, meaning and socio-cultural mores. In each of these dimensions, NSH may sneak in. Once discovered, the person needs to learn new hypnosis and apply it to stop and undo the NSH. New hypnosis (Araoz, 1995), based on Erickson's teachings and practice (Zeig, 1985), naturally and centered on what the person is experiencing at the moment, leads her or him to a vivid, imaginative experience of what he or she can change, do or be that seemed impossible without hypnosis (Araoz, 2002). Of the multitude of hypnotic techniques, we select three that are highly effective for the enrichment of human sexuality: mental rehearsal, personality parts and inner wisdom (See Appendix).

Sexual Identity

The large majority of the population can truly say that they regarded themselves as male or female as far as they remember. A small percentage (mostly males) come to the realization that they "are trapped in the wrong body," (officially called *gender* dysphoria) or that their sexual identity is opposite to the biological sex. There seems to be true that some of these people benefit from the prolonged and difficult surgery that changes their sex but other treatments, both pharmacological and psychotherapeutic must be tried first and thorough screening should precede any surgical intervention (Abel and colleagues, 1992). Cross-dressing gives them a sense of comfort and inner peace, not sexual excitement (Crooks & Baur, 1999). Many children and adolescents question their sexual identity at some point or other. Without help, they end up using NSH, convincing themselves that the only solution is surgery. In other parts of the world it is easier than in the US to obtain the operation for sex change and there are reasons to suspect that a number of these patients become victims first of their own NSH and then of the knife. Some, like Roberto (1983) assert that biological alteration is the only solution, while Pauly (1990) and many others agree with my preference for psychological and hypnotic interventions.

With hypnosis, the pseudo-transsexual can imagine him or herself enjoying his biological sex, feeling the pride of being what she or he anatomically is. This approach has proven effective with young people when encouragement to join a group for those with this condition is added to hypnosis. It must be stressed that the person has to practice self-hypnosis every day until he notices a weakening to his conviction about changing his or her body.

Sexual Orientation

This refers to the people we are attracted to sexually: most of the time men want women for sex and vice versa. True homosexuals find their same-sex attraction natural and comforting. The important studies of Bell and colleagues (1981), of LeVay (1991) and many others seem to give us reason to accept a biological disposition for the explanation of homosexual orientation as being similar to left-handedness. Others (Peplau and colleagues, 1998) point to socio-cultural influences. However, no serious scientist believes today that a mentally healthy individual chooses to be gay, as Schmalz (1993) indicated. True homosexuality seems to be the result of biological, psychological and environmental factors and it cannot be attributed to one simple cause.

However, many have asked themselves the question about being gay. Those who are troubled for their sexual attraction to people of the same sex often use NSH and end up believing they are gay. When this comes up, the person must start being fair to him/herself by using the new hypnosis and forcing the self to experience internally being fully a man (if he is a man) or a woman (if that is her sex). If, on the other hand, the person is truly homosexual, hypnosis helps in making that new life style mode attractive and comfortable.

Sexual Preferences

These "things" (actions, sights, smells, etc.) arouse the individual. Many worry and consider their preferred stimuli "abnormal or crazy." The fact is that since the serious research of Masters & Johnson (1966) and Kaplan (1979) the professional consensus is that nothing is abnormal as long as it is not damaging to self or others, either physically or psychologically. Here too, new hypnosis techniques help people to stop the NSH and accept themselves with their idiosyncratic preferences.

Sexual Functioning

This is the traditional area of sex therapy comprising the entire sexual response, from desire to resolution and mental processing. The uses of hypnosis in sexual dysfunctions are well-documented (Araoz, 1998; Araoz & Bleck, 1991). Two highly effective hypnotic techniques are mental rehearsal and personality parts (See Appendix).

Meaning

Yes, the biological meaning of sex for the human race is reproduction. However, because sex is a highly subjective experience, there are at least three meanings human individuals find in it. The physical, psychological and spiritual meanings often overlap and can be experienced with the same partner in different times. Simply put, physical sex cares about its own orgasm; psychological sex cares about the self and the partner's orgasm. Spiritual sex cares about communion, the fulfillment of two souls becoming one, for which the physical union is a metaphor. The three meanings of sexuality are important and part of one's personal development, which may reach the top level to savor it every time one returns to it. Zen (Sekida, 1975) and Taoist (Huanchu Daoren, 1600/ 1990) traditions have recommended the highest sexual experience for centuries. In our culture Frattaroli (2001) and Sardello (1999), among many others, are insisting on the enrichment of spiritual sex for the individual and for society.

With self-hypnosis, one can facilitate the development from physical to spiritual sex and accept the limitations and imperfections of human relationships and unions. This is where sex, considered "animal" and purely physical by many becomes the springboard to the spiritual dimension of being human. Perhaps in many cases the altered state of consciousness that hypnosis is supposed to be is really a spiritual experience, a reaching for and touching our soul.

Socio-Cultural Mores

The social and sexual rules of each culture and historical period in which every human being lives determine the behavior, limitations and expectations of each person, man or woman (Laumann and colleagues, 1994; Beuka, 2003). Men can be topless in the beach or the backyard; women can wear men's clothing, cry in public and hold each other in their arms; men are expected not to hesitate and to make decisions on their own, and so forth. You can complete a pretty long list of rules, different from those a century ago in the same culture. Other countries are less (Power, 1998) or more (Swedish Institute, 1997) equalitarian than the US.

Rebels, including cross-dressers and other sexual nonconformists, are socially punished when they do not abide by the "official" rules and end up isolating themselves in communities not respected by society at large. When these people are unhappy about their situation, self-hypnosis is an effective method for changing, even though often it must be preceded by Hypnoanalysis. When used, the techniques of inner wisdom and mental rehearsal are powerful to change many behaviors and attitudes of the nonconformist.

In sum, hypnosis is especially useful to resolve sexual difficulties because very often NSH is at work when a person experiences them. To stop NSH the new hypnosis deflects the person's attention to fresh, creative and positive possibilities or to a more hopeful acceptance of what has become the center of concern. The Appendix outlines three valuable approaches or techniques for resolving human sexuality difficulties.

Appendix

Each practice takes about 20 minutes and requires concentration in what you are doing without interruptions of any sort. Always decide to repeat each practice often. During the time you are practicing self-hypnosis, you will pay no heed to the surrounding world [except if there is any sort of emergency that requires your attention] and will concentrate on your inner world.

Mental Rehearsal

1) Relax physically and mentally by using your breathing until you feel at peace with yourself and the world.

2) Visualize yourself doing, acting, being what you want to accomplish. Take your time to include as many details as possible, involving all sensations that you regularly experience through your five senses. Become aware of your body sensations and enjoy the experience vividly. Become aware of your partner's active presence to enjoy every miniscule aspect of it. Become aware of the surroundings.

3) If you find it difficult to "see yourself" in the situation you want to experience, imagine someone you admire acting as you want to act. Once this is vivid and detailed in your experiencing mind, try #2 again. Repeat until you can comfortably accomplish #2.

4) Once you find yourself experiencing comfortably what you want to do in reality, say to yourself, "This is me. I can enjoy this to the fullest," etc.

5) Return to the relaxation of #1 above. Enjoy the feeling for a moment.

6) Prepare yourself to go back to the ordinary way of using your mind, knowing that you can and will come back to this special way of thinking anytime you decide.

Personality Parts

1) Relax, as before.

2) Think of one part in you that wants to change and improve. Imagine yourself as that part:" Where are you, how are you dressed, what are you doing? In addition, listen carefully to what you are saying about this issue or problem.

3) Then allow the other part who does not allow you to change to step into the picture of the first part. Pay attention to all the details of you as the negative part. In addition, listen carefully to what this part of you is saying about the same issue.

4) Now let the two parts of you discuss the issue, argue, verbally fight. Listen very carefully: it is *you* in both parts.

5) Let one part win. You decide which one of these two parts in you shall prevail.

6) Go back to the relaxation, allowing the part that won to become one with you.

7) After a few moments remind yourself that you will repeat this practice soon. Then return to the ordinary mental channel and connect with all the outside surroundings.

Inner Wisdom

1) Relax as in the previous practices. This time concentrate on the mystery of your living body. The unconscious part of your mind (the brain activities that you are not consciously aware of) is keeping you alive, directing and producing all the complicated functions in the functioning of your body. Think of them in detail.

2) Linger on the mental images that come spontaneously when you consider your unconscious mind. And say to yourself, "I can trust my unconscious: it keeps me alive, it fights disease, and it restores my body."

3) Go a step further and think of all the memories and information that your unconscious has accumulated in your lifetime. All the things and skills you have learned and are now part of you without you realizing it. Say and repeat to yourself," My unconscious knows more than I know."

4) Now concentrate on the issue you want to change or improve, and relax gain.

5) Still relaxed, tell your unconscious to use its Inner Wisdom and to advise you now or later, perhaps when you least expect it, on the issue at hand.

6) After a few moments of relaxation trusting your Inner Wisdom and promising yourself to repeat this practice the next day, get ready to connect again with the ordinary mode of thinking.

7) Now you are back in full contact with all your surroundings.

References

Abel, G., Osborn, C., Anthony, D. & Gardos, P. (1992) Current treatment of paraphiliacs. *Annual Review of Sex Research,* 3, 225-290.

Araoz, D. L. (1981) Negative self-hypnosis. *Journal of Contemporary Psychotherapy.* 12: 45-52.

Araoz, D. L. (1995) *the New Hypnosis: Techniques in Brief Individual and Family Psychotherapy.* Northvale, NJ: Jason Aronson Inc.

Araoz, D. L. (1998) *the New Hypnosis in Sex Therapy*. Northvale, NJ: Jason Aronson Inc.

Araoz, D. L. (2001) the Hidden Symptom in Sex Therapy. In *The Handbook of Ericksonian Hypnosis* by B. Geary & J. K. Zeig, eds. Phoenix: The Milton H. Erickson Foundation Press.

Araoz, D. L. (2002) *Self-transformation through the New Hypnosis.* New York: The Milton H. Erickson Institute of Hypnosis.

Araoz, D. L. & Bleck, R. T. (1991) *Sexual Joy through Self Hypnosis.* Glendale, CA: Westwood Publishing Company, Inc.

Bell, A., Weinberg, M. & Hammersmith, S. (1981) *Sexual Preference*: *It's Development in Men and Women.* Bloomington: Indiana University Press.

Beuka, R. (2004) *Suburbia Nation.* New York: Palgrave/Macmillan.
Crooks, R. & Baur, K. (1999) *Our Sexuality* (seventh Ed.) Pacific Grove: CA: Brooks/Cole Publishing Company.
Frattaroli, E. (2001) *Healing the Soul in the Age of the Brain.* New York: Penguin.
Huanchu Daoren. (1600/1990) *Back to beginnings: Reflections on the Tao.* Boston: Shambhala.
Kaplan H. (1979) *Disorders of Sexual Desire.* New York: Brunner/Mazel.
Laumann, E., Gagnon, J., Michael, R. & Michaels, S. (1994) *The Social Organization of Sexuality: Sexual Practices in the United States.* Chicago: University of Chicago Press.
LeVay, S. A difference in hypothalamic structure between heterosexual and homosexual men. *Science*, 253, 1034-1037.
Masters, W. & Johnson, V. (1966) *Human Sexual Response.* Boston: Little, Brown.
Pauly, I. (1990) Gender identity disorders: Evaluation and treatment. *Journal of Sex Education and Therapy,* 16, 2-24.
Peplau, L., Garnets, L., Spalding, L., Conley, T. & Viniegas, R. (1998) A critique of Bem's "exotic becomes erotic" theory of sexual orientation. *Psychological Review,* 128, 140-156.
Power, C. (1998) the new Islam, *Newsday*, March 16, 35-38.
Roberto, L. (1983) Issues in diagnosis and treatment of transsexualism. *Archives of Sexual Behavior*, 12, 445-473.
Sardello, R. (1999) *Freeing the Soul from fear.* New York: Riverhead Books.
Schmaltz, J. (1993) Survey finds U.S. divided over gays. *The Oregonian*, March 5.
Sekida, K. (1975) *Zen training: Methods and philosophy.* New York: Weatherhill.
Seligman, M.E. (1975) *Helplessness: On Depression, Development and Death.* San Francisco: W. H. Freeman.
Swedish Institute (1997) In *Our sexuality* by R. Crooks & K. Baur as a "personal communication."
Zeig, J. K. (1985) *Experiencing Erickson: An introduction to the man and his work.* New York: Brunner/Mazel.

Forensic Hypnosis vs. Therapeutic Hypnosis

By: Inspector Marx Howell, BS (Ret.)

While there are a number of similarities between the application of investigative and therapeutic hypnosis, there are distinct and important differences. This article will delineate the salient factors associated with both approaches.

Initial Interview

The initial interview, rapport- building and evaluation of the witness/victim or client/patient are similar, but an investigative session is more demanding regarding the keeping of records. In an investigative session, it is imperative that all contact between the witness/victim and the hypnotist be audio and/or video recorded. While most, if not all clinicians, keep a patient file and records of contact, there is no compelling reason, in most cases, to keep an audio and/or video record of all patient contacts.

Induction

The induction phase of the sessions could be the same in both therapeutic and investigative applications. It is recommended that a standard induction, such as progressive relaxation be used in a forensic session and this is also commonly used in therapeutic sessions. Esoteric and "showy" rapid inductions are not recommended for investigative sessions. You need to remember that everything you say and do is being recorded and may be viewed by a jury. You may also be required to explain why you did what you did at any given time during the session. The same thing holds true regarding the use of deepening techniques. There is no reason that deepening techniques cannot be used in a forensic session; however, if such techniques are employed, they should involve counting, silence or other common and straightforward approaches as opposed to pressure techniques, which may be subject to misinterpretation as wittingly or unwittingly cueing the witness/victim. This admonition is also true regarding the use of depth scales and challenges. As a general rule, permissive techniques are preferred over authoritarian ones in a forensic session.

Purpose of Session

The purpose of a forensic session is to refresh the subject's memory. The purpose of a therapeutic session is to assist the patient/client in resolving conflicts and achieving therapeutic goals. In an investigative session it is imperative that you use neutral non-leading questions and do not contaminate the subject's memory. Clinicians are typically not accustomed to this approach and thus may resort to using their clinical skills during the session. This is, of course, the right thing to do in a therapeutic session, but the wrong thing to do in a forensic session. This is the portion of the procedure that holds the most risk for the integrity of the hypnotic interview. If the proper procedural guidelines (See Zani for Texas) are not followed, the witness/victim post-hypnosis recall may not be admissible in court regarding their recollections of the crime. This may vary depending upon the state in which you practice.

The emerging portion of the therapeutic and investigative sessions is similar, if not identical. Simply counting the subject up from one to ten is a common technique in both approaches. It is also common to give suggestions for well-being during this part of the session. This is permissible in both forensic and therapeutic settings. Again, acceptable techniques should always be employed.

Post-hypnotic Differences

Finally, the post-hypnotic portions of both the forensic and therapeutic sessions are similar but there are distinct and important differences. Clarification of questions is permissible during this part of the forensic session, just as it was during the pre-hypnotic interview. However, you need to be careful not to ask leading questions or be suggestive during this final part of the investigative session as was true during the information-eliciting phase. This is, of course, not an issue during a therapeutic session. Another important difference is typically associated with the closing of the session. In a therapeutic session, the clinician will usually answer the patient's questions, clarify and discuss clinical issues and finally make an appointment for the next visit. In a forensic session you will most likely only see the subject once. You should tell the subject that he/she should contact the case investigator in the event of recall of additional information or any questions regarding the case. In the event they do contact you, it is mandatory that a record of that contact be made.

The pictorial depiction (see Exhibit #1) of an investigative and therapeutic session may be helpful in clarifying the overall relationship between the two approaches. In an investigative session it is necessary that all contact between the subject and the hypnotist be recorded from hello to good-bye. Failure to follow the proper guidelines may result in information that has no legal status in that it is not admissible. As a forensic investigator, it is your goal to elicit and uncover memories that were not readily available before; however, it is also your goal to do this in a way that will not jeopardize the witness/victim's opportunity to testify about the crime. Proper training and knowledge of legal requirements will assure that the forensic hypnotist does not jeopardize the witness/victim's right to a day in court.

EXHIBIT # 1

INVESTIGATIVE VERSUS THERAPEUTIC HYPNOSIS

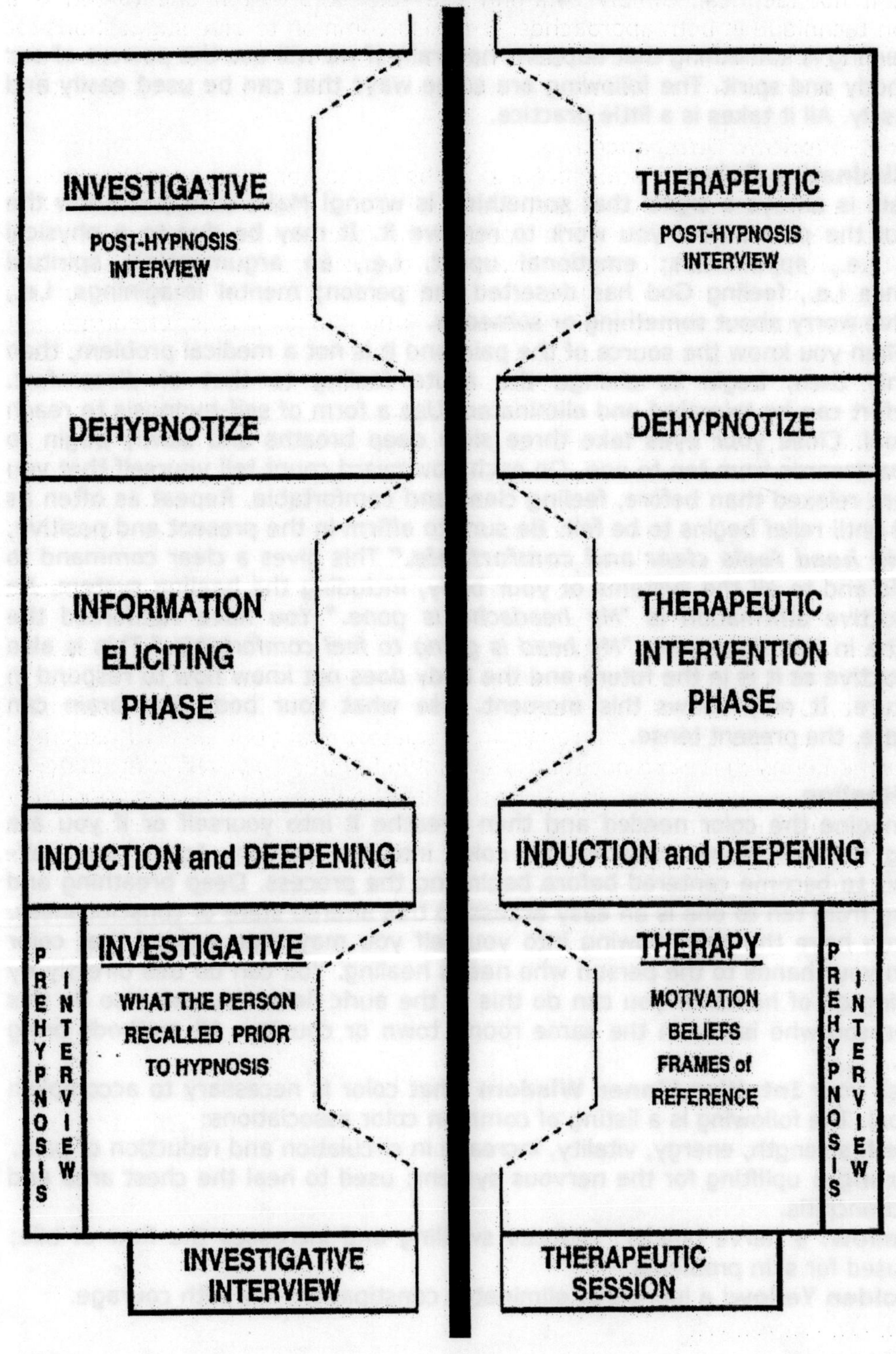

Healing, Inner Wisdom and Hypnosis

By: Anne H. Spencer- Beacham, Ph.D.

Healing is something that happens naturally if we will use the powers of our mind, body and spirit. The following are some ways that can be used easily and effortlessly. All it takes is a little practice.

Eliminating Pain

Pain is always a signal that something is wrong! Make sure you know the cause of the pain before you work to remove it. It may be due to a physical illness, i.e., appendicitis; emotional upset, i.e., an argument(s); spiritual imbalance i.e., feeling God has deserted the person; mental imaginings, i.e., excessive worry about something or someone.

When you know the source of the pain and it is not a medical problem, then and only then, begin to change the acute feeling to that of discomfort. Discomfort can be tolerated and eliminated. Use a form of self-hypnosis to reach your goal. Close your eyes take three slow deep breaths and slowly begin to count backwards from ten to one. On each downward count tell yourself that you are more relaxed than before, feeling clear and comfortable. Repeat as often as needed until relief begins to be felt. Be sure to affirm in the present and positive, i.e., ***"My head feels clear and comfortable."*** This gives a clear command to the cells and to all the systems of your body, including the healing system. An unproductive affirmation is *"My headache is gone."* You have reinforced the headache in this statement. *"My head is going to feel comfortable."* This is also unproductive as it is in the future and the body does not know how to respond in the future. It only knows this moment. Use what your body and brain can assimilate, the present tense.

Color Healing

Imagine the color needed and then breathe it into yourself or if you are working with someone, channel the color into the person. Again, use self-hypnosis to become centered before beginning the process. Deep breathing and counting from ten to one is an easy access to this altered state of consciousness. Once you have the color flowing into yourself you may then extend that color through your hands to the person who needs healing. You can do this directly by the laying on of hands or you can do this in the auric field. You can also do this for a person who is not in the same room, town or country. All methods bring results.

Ask your **Intuition/Inner Wisdom** what color is necessary to accomplish your goal. The following is a listing of common color associations:

- **Red:** strength, energy, vitality, increase in circulation and reduction of pain.
- **Orange:** uplifting for the nervous system; used to heal the chest area and bronchitis.
- **Yellow:** a nerve builder; reduces swelling and increases the flow of bile; used for skin problems.
- **Golden Yellow:** a lubricant; eliminates constipation, fills with courage.

- **Rose Gold:** use for relief of stress; brings joy to the spirit and soothes the soul.
- **Green:** increases vitality; dissolves blood clots; restores balance.
- **Blue Green:** calming and reduces fevers, cools tempers.
- **Turquoise:** tranquilizes; relieves headaches and muscle spasms.
- **Blue:** anesthetizes and reduces fevers; lowers blood pressure, invites relaxation.
- **Violet:** soothes, relieves cramps and induces sleep; relieves psychological distress.
- **Magenta:** good for problems of the heart and promotes emotional equilibrium.
- **Indigo:** purifies; relieves swelling; ear and eye problems; sedative.
- **Purple:** stimulates veins; relieves indigestion (physical and mental), invites sleep.
- **White:** overall feeling of well-being; from the **Source**; Angelic protection.

Healing Energy, Sensing and Flowing

Healing energy is within and without of your body. It is everywhere. If you are alive then you have healing energy working for you day and night. The normal state of the body is health. In order to become aware of your healing energy, sit in a comfortable position. Place your feet firmly on the floor/ground. Close your eyes and imagine that you are connected to the earth's energy, feeling relaxed and calm. Take several deep breaths and put yourself into that altered state of self-hypnosis using the techniques discussed above. Deepen that feeling by using a color or other images to relax yourself even more. Ask for spiritual help. Say a prayer, mantra, or repeat the word love, which will bring a sense of divine presence.

Next, imagine yourself surrounded by this divine healing presence. Rub the palms of your hands together to get the energy flowing through you. Now inhale and draw that healing energy into you, exhale and let go of any tension. Imagine it flowing out of you as it goes into the ground, where it is transformed by the earth. Inhale again and imagine the earth sending healing energy up through the soles of your feet filling you very slowly. Exhale and release tension. Continue to do this until the energy inhaled and exhaled is balanced. You will have healing flowing into you, through you and out from you. Imagine that it is forming a cocoon around you. Notice how good you feel.

On purpose, inhale and send the exhale out your arms and fingertips. Notice how that feels. Hold the palms of your hands together, but not touching. Notice the sensations between your hands. Continue to examine this energy, play with it, extend your hands farther apart, what do you feel? Now move them closer together. What do you feel, any differences? Are you aware of something? Whatever you are sensing is your healing energy. It may appear in the form of color, it may feel cool, warm, tingle, etc., or you may just know that something is there. Accept your intuitive awareness. It is correct. Once you have an awareness of this energy you can then begin to project it to another person/animal/plant, etc. When the healing is sent then easily bring yourself back to your usual awareness, balanced: body, mind and spirit.

Healing and Others

When someone requests a healing then it is time for you to go to work. If the healing was requested by a loved one, for their beloved, then you must ask intuitively if you may send the healing energy. Go into that quiet altered state of self-hypnosis and ask your higher self to connect with the higher self of the person in need. The next question is ***"Do I have your permission to send you healing energy?"*** If the reply is ***"Yes"*** go ahead. If it is ***"No"*** then you must respect that reply. When you send energy you are helping the person heal herself. Some people do not wish to get well. Let it be.

Let people know that you are available to help. There is an old saying "When the student is ready the teacher will appear". It is good advice for anyone who enters this field of hands-on healing. You do not want to throw pearls among the swine, as they would have no use for them! Remember: "It is not I, but a power greater than I, that works through me." You are aligning yourself with universal divine energy and the person who is to receive the energy. You are a channel. It is as though you are a conductor. You attract the energy that the ill person is unable to attract. This energy mixes with the patient's energy and gives her healing system a boost. You have become a ***"Jumper Cable"***! What a great way to use healing energy!

Laying on of Hands

Laying on of hands may be used by everyone who will to learn to become quiet and has the intent to help heal. It is not reserved for some special doctor, nurse, priest, healer, etc. It is your birthright, one of many that you may choose to exercise.

Ground yourself by using self-hypnosis to get into a receptive state. Relax and deepen your state. Say a prayer and surround yourself with healing energy. Rub your hands together to get the energy flowing.

Intuitively place your hands where they are guided, on the front and back (if you can) of her body. A good place to start is the head or the belly/spine. Send the energy through your right hand to the left hand. Hold it there until you intuitively know that you have done enough in that area. Go to the next area that your hands are called to work. Remember to breathe the healing energy into yourself and exhale it out into the body of your patient through your hands. Join with her mind and imagine her healthy, full of vitality and smiling. Imagine her exactly the way she wants to be. When minds are joined there is greater power for healing. This is how all of the ancient healers of the Mystery Schools did their work. You must remain present to the task at hand for it to be effective.

Healing at a Distance

Often this is called Absent Healing. Sit in a comfortable chair, ground yourself and use self-hypnosis to get into a receptive altered state of consciousness. Relax and deepen your trance. Say a prayer, surround yourself with the healing energy and rub your hands together to get the energy flowing.

Energy flows where attention goes! It is not bound by time or space. It just is. Imagine the person is in front of you. Ask your Inner Wisdom where you are to send the energy. Extend your hands and place them on the person's body where you are guided. You may also imagine the energy extending from your third eye, your heart and solar plexus coming to a point, like a triangular beam of light. Direct that beam of light to the place on the body of the person who is in need of the healing. Use color or a white light beam, which has the full spectrum of rays within it. Intuitively you will know when you have done all you can do for the patient. When you feel you are finished, say a short prayer of thanksgiving and return to normal awareness.

If you are doing this healing work at night and should feel sleepy, there is a way to continue. As a child my teacher told me that if I fell asleep saying my prayers my Guardian Angel would finish them. Angels have made a big comeback in this last decade of the 20th century. It is said that they are waiting for you to ask them for help. What a great way to engage the help of these great spiritual beings. So, when you are tired, go to bed, begin the process and then ask your Guardian Angel to continue the work of sending the healing energy and go to sleep. This simple request allows you to get your rest and relaxation that is vital to your good health, while doing the work you have agreed to do.

Body Language

How to hear the messages from your inner guidance system - by Christine Northrup, MD -*Adapted from* **Woman's Bodies, Women's Wisdom** *(Bantam)*

Learning to ***listen to*** and ***respect*** your body is a process that requires patience and compassion. You can begin this process by paying attention to your body as you practice the following steps. Go slowly and come back to it as needed.

1. Make note of those things in your life that are difficult, painful, joyful, relaxing and the like. As these things come up, notice your breathing, your heart rate and your bodily sensations. What are they? Where are they? What do they feel like?
2. Pay attention to what your body feels like. Do certain parts feel numb, tired, heavy or sore? Do you feel like crying? Do ***parts*** of you feel like crying? These feelings are your body's wisdom. They are part of your inner guidance system, your Inner Wisdom.
3. When you experience a bodily sensation such as back pain, "a gut reaction," a headache or abdominal pain, pay attention to it. Are emotions, such as anger, fear, guilt, resentment, sadness, etc., connected with certain parts of your body? When a sensation arises in your body, **stop** what you are doing, lie down, breathe slowly and wait with the symptom, emotion or feeling. Relax into it. You may be surprised at what other feelings and/or insights come up.
4. Notice how you routinely talk to your body. What happens when you look in the mirror each morning? Do you criticize your face, your legs or hair? Do you routinely apologize to others for how you look? Or do you give your body positive messages, such as ***"Thank you very much for digesting last night's dinner without any conscious effort on my part."*** Cultivate the link between your mouth and your ear - and the rest of you - so that you get used to hearing yourself with your inner ear, your inner wisdom.
5. Understand that your health is at risk if you are constantly undermining certain parts or functions of your body. Is it possible that, if someone at work

has a cold, and you are obsessing about how many germs you are exposed to, that you automatically undermine your body's ability to stay healthy? Instead say to your body, ***"Don't worry - I know you have the ability to stay healthy when I nourish and rest you optimally."*** Then you must follow through with what you have just told yourself.

6. You can learn to accept your body unconditionally right now, regardless of where you are starting. Stand in front of a mirror regularly, and thank your body for all it has done for you. Notice what comes up when you do this. Write the following sentence down on a piece of paper and tape it to the mirror: ***"I accept myself unconditionally right now."*** I often write it on a prescription blank and hand it to my patient with the following instructions: **"Say this sentence out loud to yourself in the mirror while gazing into your eyes. Do this twice a day for 30 days."** (Self-hypnosis at its best!)
7. Remember that 90% of your bodily functions take place without your conscious input. Who keeps your heart beating? Who metabolizes your food? Who heals your skin when you get a cut? Who tells your ears to listen to beautiful music? Acknowledge that your body is a miracle.

In Summary

If you follow your **Inner Wisdom** it will guide you to a life filled with wellness: body, mind and Spirit. Your ability to heal yourself is inherent. The body wants to function as it was designed to do. Pay attention and when you get out of balance use the techniques above to heal yourself. Take the time on a daily basis to practice self-hypnosis.

CHAPTER 9: MISCELLANEOUS ARTICLES BY NOTABLE CONTRIBUTORS

Introduction to Electronic Hypnosis

By: Larry Garrett

What you are feeling emotionally when you are hypnotizing a client is very important in accomplishing successful hypnosis. Imagine that you are running late, walk in 10 minutes after your client and they are stressed. You are attempting to calm them down sufficient enough to hypnotize them. *Good luck, your humanness has just gotten in the way.* To even consider, that 50% of our hypnosis inductions are superior would be difficult for most to acknowledge. You might want to tell others that you have a high rate of success, but the human element can get in the way often. Especially on one of those bad days. Now of course if you never have a bad day, then you can tell all of your peers that you have 100% success. Hypnosis is like art or music; it has a variable to it that can be better one day than another day. However, our clients do not want to hear that we are having a bad day.

Most consumers purchase services or products that are consistently superior and hypnosis needs a more superior sell then most other businesses. Most consumers know very little of hypnosis. It is up to us to educate them fully to allow them to achieve their greatest potential. If a consumer purchases pair of shoes, they have worn shoes before. If they have never flown before, there are enough people that have that, they can ask most anyone and receive a description of flight. How many potential clients even know someone who has been hypnotized? Maybe more today than a few years ago, but still most of our society knows absolutely nothing about hypnosis, nothing! Sure, many of your clients are referrals from other clients, and many finally decided to try hypnosis. They then call you.

However, even with many more people using the services of a hypnotist, nothing can say it will be a consistent venture like buying a pair of shoes or even flying is more consistent. Each hypnotist is different; each experience is different even if the client sees the same hypnotist. Even if they ask their friend that sent them to you, the friend's experience might have been much different than the new client may experience. How many hypnotists hypnotize individuals the same way? How many planes fly in a similar fashion? Not all hypnotists, but most planes have a consistent pattern of flight. Consistency is the key and hypnosis is much like an art, it lacks the ability to be exact each time.

Because we are in a very creative and unique profession, we must express our individuality. The style of hypnosis that we incorporate must match our personality. Attend the National Guild of Hypnotists Conference and observe how many hypnotists incorporate a technique that you would never consider using.

Guess what? It works for them. We can even sit in on a lecture and hear a speaker telling the audience that their way is the only way to achieve success and then the next speaker says, "No, not that way, my way is the best!" Which is the best? Your way is the only way that you will achieve great success, because it is a reflection of you. At this moment, create an awareness that people seek out the services of this hypnotist, as many would seek you out. How can we offer success to our potential client with so many different directions of hypnosis available? Can we offer hypnosis in a somewhat consistent from? Are we able to predict that there will be a potential success, as the plane has a prediction of landing at its destination? We do not want to crash 50% of the time. We want to look at our client/patient in the eyes and say, "You will be successful and know that it is true. We as the practitioner need to know a potential end result. We need to be in control of the experience each and every time.

I recall an early moment of my hypnosis career in 1970. I was at an AAEH (Association to Advance Ethical Hypnosis) meeting. I was young, naïve and full of "I'll show them attitude." Of course at that moment there were some issues that I was not aware of.

1) They did not want me to "Show them".

2) I had very little to show them.

Of course I did not realize either of these issues at the time, but like most hypnotists, I thought I knew everything I needed to know to hypnotize someone. I could, in the snap of a finger, show my stuff to all these members. In our earlier career of hypnosis, we have hypnotized a few people and as they responded we were impressed with our selves. Most of those in attendance were masters; they had been around for many years. They would look at me and say "Larry who"? At that time in hypnosis, very few hypnotists were open to something new any way. Who was I to think that I could influence their minds that I knew something? Their ideas were limited by what they knew. They had however been involved in hypnosis for many years. I had not. They were going to use their old techniques, as that is what they knew would work for them. Many were still using techniques that James Braid used in 1865.

My very special friend, who also happens to be my mother, was in attendance with me at that meeting. In my earlier career of hypnosis, my mother was also very active in hypnosis with her nursing career. My mother has always been very wise. She has always been advanced in her thinking. She wore slacks as a young woman in the '30s and her own business and was a single mom in the '40s. I even recall when I was a child that she would say to me, "I know everything, because I am your mother." It is amazing how those anchors hang on, even if we don't believe them any more, they seem to ring a bell of truism. Hypnosis was just another cog in the wheel of advancement for her in the '70s in nursing. She did not always express, but when it was appropriate, my mother seemed to always know what to say. Isn't that called something like, "When the student is ready, the teacher will appear."? I must have had one of those "I am ready" looks that night at the AAEH meeting. My mother said these very special words that have stayed with me since that day in 1970. She said with a gentle reminder, "Don't compete with them, as you will lose. Just be the best Larry Garrett that you can and no one can be a better Larry Garrett than you."

That was many years ago, but I remind myself of this statement often in many areas of life. In communications with others, in real estate or investments, in love and especially in life, I have found it best to not attempt to be better than anyone or do what they do, but to be the best Larry Garrett that I can. I have found that no one can do it as well. Wow, what a great feeling to believe that we can do something better than anyone else. Be ourselves!!!!

You need to enter into that direction with yourself. Be the best that you can all the time. Each and every induction needs to be superior. No flubbing or doing a mediocre induction, only best ones will be accepted. I know that you can do this, as we have already determined that you can hypnotize well. The only criteria that I am suggesting, is to do it well each and every time. Your client deserves the best. They respect you as the professional; they have paid you and have expectations that you will deliver. Have you ever had the client call or come into your office and say, "I have tried to be hypnotized before and it didn't work"? Of course the best comment to make, is, "Well I do it differently than that other hypnotist did." Maybe that other hypnotist did a great induction, but was a little fatigued or preoccupied that day. Hypnotists are allowed to be fatigued are they not? That hypnotist could be a great master, but was on their fifth client of the day and had used up a lot of their own energy. Actually this previous hypnotist usually does great hypnosis, but this was just one of those days, when nothing goes well for them. Your new client went to this other hypnotist on such a day. Hopefully your day is not one of "those days." Then that client will say as they leave, "I have tried to be hypnotized twice and both hypnotists had difficulty."

This is not an uncommon story. We just have not come up with an idea till now that can create the consistency that we all need. The skill will be to do as good an induction on your last client of the day, as good as your first client received. Imagine if two clients that have seen you compare notes. The first client and the last one. I would speculate that they would become dissatisfied or discouraged after comparing notes. The last one will be saying, "The hypnotist didn't say that to me" and your first client will be thinking that they could have had something different, as the last client had a different experience. Right or wrong, good or bad, those are not the issues here. Creativity has no barriers or value judgments. Only the perception of the client is at stake here. The client needs to accept and trust you at all times. You will need to be consistent and good each and every time that you hypnotize someone. The human factor is often in our way for this consistency. There is, however, a way to be consistent and excellent on every induction.

Time for a Change

Hypnotists more than many other professions have a difficult time with new technology and change. In most other professions, what was used last year is already obsolete. With hypnosis, many are still swinging the "Proverbial watch" or using the "hypno-disk." No disrespect is intended to traditional techniques that work; however, matching society's needs is imperative to creating success and consistency. By matching your client's expectations, you will offer to them something that does not challenge their intelligence. To continue the progression and acceptance of our profession, we need to appear as though we have advanced. We actually need to be advanced to appear as though we are.

New Technology for Hypnosis

In 1974, I was introduced to "Electronic" techniques of hypnosis. I had the great opportunity to meet a very skilled physician, Dr. Laurence Beuret MD. Dr. Beuret practiced in Rockford and had studied the Dr. Bryant method of Electronic hypnosis. I have taught many hypnotists techniques of "Electronic Hypnosis." I have also established and built many successful Electronic Hypnosis setups. There are still very few hypnotists in the country using an electronic application of hypnosis. I realize that his method is not for everyone. Many hypnotists enjoy the process of the induction. There is a certain romantic feeling with the relaxation part. Then of course there is the other hypnotist, as myself.

This is my primary profession and livelihood; I have an overhead to pay and the need to feel prosperous with what I do. Imagine hypnotizing five clients a day at $50.00 each client and fulfilling your financial obligations of a typical private practice. Remember that there is an element of professionalism in establishing an appearance that is comfortable. You will do best if you appear as a professional to accomplish professional results. Looking like a professional is a costly venture. You will need to hypnotize many more than five clients a day to make your overhead expenses. Of course if this is just a hobby with you, then a few clients a day will satisfy your needs and you do not need to read on. For most though, I am sure that you are ready to begin a good earning using hypnosis. Remember this is a profession and your earnings will reflect that. Sure you can do public speaking or groups at the local hotels. You could be one of the fastest hypnotists in the country and hypnotize 20 clients a day only taking five minutes per client and having great success. I am not sure how your client will feel paying $50.00 to $100.00 for a five- minute induction, but you can do it. It is all up to you what your desires are for a successful hypnosis practice. I have always felt that hypnosis is a very intimate experience. Much like lovemaking, who would want to spend only five minutes with such a great feeling or be in a group with 100 other individuals? Yes, there is a way to hypnotize more individuals, for longer periods of time and everyone is satisfied.

Personally speaking, I happen to like the idea of a client coming into my office and spending anywhere from 1 ½ to 2 hours for a session. They often are amazed that I took so much time with them. They usually do not spend much time at any professional's office. Maybe a massage therapist might spend an hour, but few others will. I enjoy the special feeling that they leave with. Seldom can a client say to me that I did not spend enough time with them. It becomes a very special experience. Very few people have time in life to spend 1 ½ to 2 hours in a professional's office. When they do, it becomes a very memorable experience. It becomes much akin to the restaurant that serves a large quantity of good quality food. When your client spends more time in your office, they become more familiar with the experience and setting and feel more comfortable coming back for a follow- up session. I also personally enjoy the fact of being able to have many clients in my office at the same time. There is a certain appearance of prosperity and success when a client walks in and other clients are there. It is also very exciting to be able to see three clients or more per hour and each and every client is hypnotized for an hour. Nice trick, isn't it?

With the addition of some techniques that I will be explaining to you, you will be able to increase your success to be somewhat consistent with each and every client and earn a comfortable living that would be unheard of in a private practice of hypnosis previously.

To do this, you need to reproduce yourself. I recall a very special friend of mine saying to me, "Unless I was willing to train others to do what I do for me, it would be difficult for me to earn a comfortable living without working many hours." I did not know who I could trust to hypnotize as I did. Who would you trust with your very special clients? I have many hypnotists that work in the same office as I do. They contribute to the overhead and have a very professional office to use. They hypnotize their clients and I hypnotize mine. If you trained someone, how could you trust your reproduction other than using your own voice to hypnotize others? How can you have someone else using your techniques and your voice? I recall many years ago, thinking of hiring other hypnotists to assist with my practice. My discomfort with this was that they were not me. I could not imagine a client that was referred to me and needed to see someone else. A client comes in to see me the first two times and then I refer them to my associate on the third visit. What a great way to sabotage your own success. Do what works and then stop. You would need to reproduce yourself.

There are many methods of reproducing yourself, but none to match your own voice at its best. What a great fantasy! Save your voice at its very best moment and then use it later together with your personal direction when your client arrives. Similar to a restaurant that has the lunches precooked, waiting for the customer to arrive. When the customer orders, the precooked food is warmed up with a little fresh greens and dessert and the whole dinner appears as though it was just prepared for you. Seldom do we wonder how so many were served at the same time and with such personal care. Why we even can make substitutes in some restaurants if we choose.

By learning techniques of "Hybrid Electronic Hypnosis," we can do something like the restaurant does. We can personalize our hypnosis to match the client's needs and expectations with customized success. By making tapes of some of our favorite inductions or deepenings and using them together with our personal direction at a very precise timing, we will have consistency in our success. Tapes or CDs that are made when we are at our best and used when needed can add so much to our continued success. By making a tape when you are up, you can be more creative with your suggestions. Your words will flow; you will be "on" continually. You will imagine yourself successful each and every time that you do an induction, because you only made the inductions when you were at your best.

When I was first introduced to tapes, I was shocked that someone would even think of using a tape to hypnotize someone compared to speaking to them personally. I was so upset at first that I would not even speak about it except with anger. A physician from near the Chicago area originally introduced me to electronic hypnosis in 1973. Later we became great friends. It was most likely more the friendship that eventually turned me on to using tapes, than the practical side of tapes in hypnosis. I hated the concept of using tapes to hypnotize people, but admired who he was. I listened, and he taught.

My first introduction to this physician was on a TV show that we were both guests of. There was a third medical person that was anti hypnosis. I spoke of "Stage Hypnosis," he spoke of "Medical Hypnosis" and the third person spoke of the inadequacies of hypnosis. Since we were both interested in hypnosis we sided on the TV show and later began to exchange methodology. He was amazed with "Stage Hypnosis' and I was hungry for the academic side of hypnosis. Never had I met a real live physician that used hypnosis. In 1973, it was rare to meet professional that felt positive with hypnosis. He drew me to him like "Mesmer's Magnets."

He was trained by the Dr. William Bryant method. This method was a system that in 1972 cost well over $10,000 to learn. For that cost, it was obviously a very extensive course and had an Analytical approach using hypnosis. The hypnosis however was done with tapes called programs. The basics of the complete program were an extensive intake on the first session that consisted of the patient taking an "MMPI" and consultation with the Doctor. A complete history of the patient was part of the first visit and then in some cases a short hypnosis session may have been used.

After the first session, a complete program of many weeks was established and the patient began treatment. The treatment was determined by the first appointment. It would consist of a set amount of time and sessions that was determined to be most beneficial to the patient. Many patients came in a straight year for treatment. Some patients came in twice a week and others once a week. It was unheard of to see a patient once.

When the patient came in for their regular treatment, they would be escorted into another room, called the treatment room. This room consisted of very low light cameras (high-tech for the time), headphones, a recliner and a microphone for the patient to speak back to the doctor. The rooms were very comfortable, although somewhat sterile in nature. I guess this must have added to the professionalism of the whole system. There were 12 treatment rooms in a high-rise professional building. I was shocked as I walked down the halls, which seemed an eternity, and inspected each room. It reminded me of *Space Odyssey 2001*."

All this was controlled from a room called the "Control Room" which put to shame many a TV studio. It was sophisticated and could control any treatment room with the flip of a switch. Lights and meters were everywhere. The master was behind these controls. He could create any effect he wanted. A deep level of hypnosis was easy, a regression was another switch and still another could add a few suggestions to eat fewer sweets. Use your imagination and it was immediate with a switch and a tape. I was in awe and as I had mentioned earlier, I was angry that such a mockery of hypnosis was allowed. Which was it to be, anger that he would even consider such a technique, or was I going to open my mind and eyes to see the future. We as hypnotists in general are pretty stuck sometime. Notice during a training session, that techniques that are 50 or 100 years old will be used. Of course we all know that hypnosis is hypnosis. There is not much different that you can do, is there? After you have had your traditional training, it will be time to fly.

My good fortune was that I later was able to work alongside this genius. He was a master and I needed to drop my prejudices to learn. My thoughts were that I knew everything that I needed to know to hypnotize someone, what could I possibly learn from this person. I obviously knew that there was more, I just wasn't sure what it was. I was after all very addicted to hypnosis. I was always amazed as to what could be accomplished with hypnosis. I just wasn't able to be successful every time. I wanted more success and this person was willing to teach me. Should I hold my own and say, "Oh no you don't," I am not going to use those tapes to hypnotize my clients, they would know." Of course I did want to hypnotize more than five or six clients a day. Maybe not 12 at the same time as he did, but two could be appealing. At the time in my life that I met him, I was just beginning to take hypnosis serious and earn what I thought to be a living at it. Can you recall that time? I was making a transition from "Stage Hypnosis" to hypnotizing someone in an office to accomplish a goal. I was beginning to fly. I was becoming a "Professional."

To become involved in hypnosis, I had given up a profession that I had earned a comfortable living at. I realized that hypnosis was in my blood, though. I had to search for a better way to make a living at hypnosis that was comparable to my previous position. I loved hypnosis so much and I wanted so badly to make it work. I could taste the success. I just didn't know how I would do it. I had been doing hypnosis for about three years. I had a small storefront establishment with a small office and a larger room to instruct others. I really wanted to do more private hypnosis, but the classes helped pay the rent. It was time to grow, but I wasn't sure as to how. I had a very special friend and associate of mine, Diana Barrar. She was alongside my every move and a great motivation for growth. Diana Barrar presently operates two very successful electronic offices near Chicago. Diana Barrar is the first woman to do hypnosis as a full-time career. She began hypnosis as her only livelihood in 1970. Excuse me for digressing, but it is a part of my beginning in "Electronic Hypnosis." Diana Barrar operates two very successful "Electronic Hypnosis Centers."

We all need a partner or motivator. Someone to bounce ideas off. Someone to experiment with, anyone, just so we are not alone in this venture called Hypnosis. To be alone sometimes is like to think and forget what we just thought of. You get an idea and poof, it is gone if you don't implement it immediately. We all get ideas everyday, unless we share them or write them down, we often forget them. The importance of conferences such as the National Guild of Hypnotists each year becomes a must if we wish to expand and develop one of the oldest known professions. Absorbing only is not enough; we must express what we have absorbed to learn what we know. I recall many years ago hearing a phrase, that we don't know what we have read until we share it. That is the way hypnosis is, we must share it to know it. The more people you hypnotize, the more you learn. Not by just the act of doing the hypnosis, but by the feedback that you receive doing the hypnosis. The feedback creates wisdom. Wouldn't it be great to hypnotize ten people a day and learn from each of them? Later I will explain a method of being objective while hypnotizing someone. A technique that with traditional hypnosis would all but be impossible.

After I was introduced to "Electronic Hypnosis," I relocated my office to a much larger facility and designed it exclusively for electronic hypnosis. I recall my electronic mentor saying to me, "Do you think that there is enough room in this building. It had more room than I could ever imagine using. I had been used to about 800 sq ft. with a small office and a larger room for groups. Now I was moving into 2,000 sq. ft with multiple rooms. Three years later, we reached our limitation for physical growth. I originally set up a mini system to his with five treatment rooms and a combination office/control room. The three of us, Diana Barrar, the physician that was training us and myself were able to alternate times and utilize the facilities. It was my first introduction to hypnosis and professional efficiency. The three of us designed and wired the complete facility for the exclusive purpose of "Electronic Hypnosis." We spent 18 months with that project and it still, till this moment, needs additions to improve and keep up to technology. I am presently operating my fifth system and beginning the next generation of "CD's."

The most successful way to initiate a system such as this is from the beginning. I have often written that you can synthesize your existing office and system with an electronic addition, but obviously wires, construction and design have no limitations with a new facility.

Since that first tour of this space age hypnosis office in 1973, many changes have occurred. One that has stayed with me is to recall the resistance that I had to electronics as well as change and realize that incorporating electronics into my hypnosis career was the one most successful move that I had ever made in hypnosis.

I have designed a system that matches my personality. I did not set up 12 rooms and, in fact, later eliminated two of my five rooms. Today, I coast with three clients an hour. All are consulted personally on every visit and then hypnotized for a full hour. It is a great pace, financially rewarding and allows for much creativity and personal attention. There are times when I will see only one client during that hour and have time to experiment and make some new CDs or tapes. Rarely a day goes by that I don't make a new recording. As I learn, I share, as I share, I learn more. With "Electronic Hypnosis," it is endless the experimentation that you can do. The learning that is available. Remember, you are not always producing and expressing energy. With Electronics, you are often on the observing end. It is a much different experience than always needing to keep your voice in control or chair from squeaking or worried about a distraction that might occur.

Vicarious Experiential Memory Machine

By: Brian David Phillips, PhD, CH

I would apply this to skill improvement - it's basically an associated visualization technique. It is particularly appropriate for physical skills such as sports, dance and the like.

The *Vicarious Experiential Memory Machine* is an adaptation of an approach to deep trance modeling commonly used in performance or stage hypnosis. Typically, the hypnotist will instruct the subjects that they copy and do everything they see a puppet or doll do that is being manipulated by the hypnotist. This seemingly straightforward "gimmick" can be combined with trance identification for very positive results in skill improvement.

Basically, the subject is given suggestions to use a trigger-response word post-hypnotically. The trigger "Memory Machine" helps the subject focus on visual information (photo series, film, video, and the like) in such a way that she actually feels the experience being observed as if it is a very powerful vicarious experience or secondary memory. Many subjects report actually feeling physical sensations that are observed in the video.

The purpose of the technique is predominately conditioning for physical skill improvement - along the lines of much of the work being done with visualization and skill progression.

The basic protocol is not overly complicated. The technique works best with somnambulism so it is best to use a standard induction - this author prefers the Elman protocol as it is simple, straightforward and has built-in tests. Deepen the hypnotic state and establish number amnesia (tested with the suggestion that the number seven is missing from the subject's vocabulary). Test the number amnesia in and out of hypnosis - once it's been established and a chain of compliance has been established, re-induce, deepen, and give the following suggestions as a simple patter:

You can create a Vicarious Experiential Memory Machine of your own anytime you like by using VCDs, DVDs, videos, photo albums or any other collection of images. All you need do is select images that describe or depict what you want to model, for those images will seem together in a way that really works for you, anytime you watch a video, a film, television, or looking at pictures, photographs, or images on the computer, you can use this wonderful, memory machine technique. All you need to do is simply breathe in, breathe out, relax, use your relaxation or hypnosis trigger about five times, each time with a deep breathing, your relaxation trigger really building, breathe out, relax, use your trigger and really let go, and just relax as your eyes close down, and let yourself feel the glow.

To feel very glad about this experience, really let go, and then, hold on to that relax section, you open your eyes, and once more breathing deeply, hold it for a moment, and breathe out, relax, trigger yourself again as your eyes shut, and you relax even more deeply, and really let yourself feel the glow. Once more you open your eyes as you breathe deeply, holding on to that wonderful feeling, hold that breath for a moment, feel really good as you relax, self-trigger, and breathe out, closing your eyes and relaxing so very much as you feel the glow and feel so wonderful, that's right.

Really let yourself feel loose, limp and relax as you feel the glow, that's right. Wonderful! Trigger yourself for deep relaxation at least five times, and let yourself really feel that glow, and when you feel that grow, you feel so wonderful. Give yourself the following suggestions:

Say to yourself, "I am using the Vicarious Experiential Memory Machine now, these images are me. I am watching my own vicarious created memories and experiences, and as I watch my own experiences, they become more real and more powerful, as I enjoy myself, and feel these experiences, desires and suggestions, sink deeply into my mind, going deeper and deeper with each and every breath."

Allow yourself to accept these suggestions and others now, wonderfully. The memory machine technique works for you. If you wish to at anytime of watching a film, you can activate the memory machine instantly by simply breathing in, holding it for a moment, and feeling real good as you self trigger. Relax, your eyes shut for a moment, and you feel the glow. Say to yourself "memory machine, memory machine, memory machine". That activates the memory machine. And, whatever you're watching on television or film, or on your computer, it could be video, it can be pictures, it doesn't matter whatever you see or read, activate the memory machine. And the images are you. And you are watching your own memories. As you watch your own memories, they become more real and powerful. As you enjoy yourself and feel these memories, desires and suggestions, seek deeply into your mind. Murmuring deeper and deeper with each and every breath, as you continue to use the memory machine. Whenever you use the memory machine, those memories you are watching, burn deeply into your mind. They become your memories.

As you watch the images, as you watch your memories, as you experience your memories in the memory machine, you can feel your body respond. You feel muscles working. You feel your body remembering the memories that are activated. You feel your mind remember the thoughts. You feel your body remember the feelings. You feel your motions contact, connect with those memories you are watching. And they burn even deeper in your mind. They become your past. They become your faded past. And they activate your present and mitigate your future. Your present actions and your future responses are all based upon these past memories. It is a habit. It is a compulsion. These memories run deep. These memories are automatic responses to your environment. Notice how good they make you feel. That's right. Wonderful! Listen to my voice, and accept my suggestions for your benefit. Surrender to my voice. Meet my suggestions. Let my voice guide you. Let my voice envelope you, let my voice surround you, and let my voice enter you. Deep, deeper, deeply into those secret places will you know things to be true as the memory technique works wonderfully for you. Take a deep breath. Relax. Self-trigger. Feel the glow. Allow yourself to say: "memory machine," and activate that memory machine. The images are you. You are watching your own memories. And as you are watching your own memories, they become more real and more powerful. As you enjoy yourself, these memories, desires and suggestions sink deeply into your mind, murmuring deeper and deeper, so wonderfully into your mind and you feel wonderful, that's right. Memory machine, rest now for a few moments, and relax.

And relax, breathe in, relax, breathe out and relax. Just relax, let go, surrender, feel the joy, the happiness, the contentment, the comfortable joy. Each time you practice the memory machine technique, every time you have a memory machine experience, feel these wonderful effects, stronger and stronger, feel the glow, each and every time. Just let go, and notice how good it feels and how much you'll enjoy having it become one of your daily activities.

It is very important that you deepen, repeat and compound suggestions. Make certain that the trigger for memory machine is set very powerfully and reinforce the positive suggestions.

This method is very effective with natural somnambulists who often report very powerful effects. Others may require further conditioning or repetitions for proper conditioning.

Profile of a Forensic / Investigative Hypnosis Interview

By: Inspector Marx Howell, BS (Ret.)

The use of hypnosis and extensive news media coverage of the kidnapping of 26 schoolchildren and a bus driver in Chowchilla, California, probably was one of the catalysts that stimulated the use of hypnosis in criminal investigations. On July 25, 1976, three persons kidnapped 26 schoolchildren and the bus driver. All occupants were buried alive underground. After the bus driver and children dug their way out of the makeshift grave and contacted law enforcement authorities, it was decided that hypnosis would be used for memory enhancement to develop investigative leads.

Dr. William S. Kroger (Clinical Professor of Anesthesiology, University of California, Los Angeles School of Medicine; Teaching Consultant, Department of Psychiatry, Cedars-Sinai Medical Center, Los Angeles; Consulting Psychiatrist, Department of Neurology, City of Hope Medical Center, Duarte, California), a leading authority on hypnosis, conducted the session on Frank Edward Ray, the 55 year old bus driver. He retrieved all the digits except one on the license plate of the vehicle used in the kidnapping. As a result of the information developed through the use of hypnosis and investigation of leads, three suspects were arrested and convicted of kidnapping the students and bus driver.

On September 13, 1979, Leo E. Gossett (Assistant Director of the Texas Department of Public Safety), established, by memorandum, a seven-member committee responsible for studying available data concerning law enforcement uses of hypnosis. And developing recommended guidelines and criteria to be used in the selection and training of DPS personnel in the use of hypnosis.

The Texas Department of Public Safety (DPS) hypnosis program was implemented in 1980 after the committee reviewed numerous articles, training material, and books on hypnosis; and met or consulted with numerous experts in the field. The committee then developed self-imposed guidelines and selected a 50-hour training course. The training course consisted of various lectures, demonstrations and applications as related to the history of hypnosis; basic psychodynamics; emotional development; the nature, theories, and laws of hypnosis; principles of suggestion, criminological versus psychotherapeutic use of hypnosis; myths, misconceptions, indications and deepening techniques; and information eliciting techniques; just to name a few. Personnel selected to receive this training were, veteran law enforcement officers with many years of experience and numerous hours of classroom instructions in criminal investigation and interviewing techniques.

The initial basic training for our investigators was conducted in the DPS Academy by the Therapeutic and Forensic Hypnosis Institute of Houston, Texas, after an evaluation of the availability and adequacy of various training courses.
Some of our personnel had received basic and advanced training at the North Texas Regional Police Academy in Arlington, Texas and at the Law Enforcement Hypnosis Institute in Los Angeles, California. We subsequently developed and coordinated two in-service hypnosis schools in the DPS Academy, emphasizing

practice session testifying in court, and advanced techniques to enhance the skill and confidence of our investigators.

From July 1, 1980 through December 31, 1990, 1,187 hypnosis sessions were conducted by DPS investigators resulting in additional information reported in 876 sessions (73.80%) and no additional information in 311 sessions (26.20%). The additional information gained in 876 of the hypnosis interviews varied from minimal information in some cases to additional information that led to the identification and arrest of the perpetrator. The cases in which hypnosis was used included a wide variety of offenses such as hit and run traffic fatalities, rapes, assaults, robberies, kidnappings and murders.

The DPS stresses that hypnosis should be used as an aid to investigations, not a substitute. Investigators have been cautioned to assure that standard investigative methods have been fully utilized before hypnosis is used.

The Texas appellate courts have upheld convictions where hypnosis was used with either a crime victim or witness for the purpose of memory enhancement. See, e.g., Vester v. State, 713 S.W. 2d 920 (TEX. Cr. App. 1986); Goudette v. State. 713 S.W. 2d 206 (TEX. App. -Tyler 1986); Walters v. State. 680 S.W. 2d 60 (TEX. APP—Amarillo 1984); Zani v. State. 758 S.W.2d 233 (Tex. Cr. App. 1988); Laird v. State.650 S.W. 2d 198 (Tex. App—Fort Worth1983).

Many police officers, prosecutors and civilians have limited understanding about what occurs during an investigative hypnosis interview to refresh recall of a witness or victim of a crime event. It is hoped that the profile and brief explanations of what occurs during an investigative hypnosis interview will provide a better understanding of the components of this type of interview.

The Profile Consists Of:

- Pre-hypnosis Interview
- Induction
- Information Eliciting
- De-Hypnotizing
- Post-Hypnosis Interview

(Refer to Exhibit #1 for details)

EXHIBIT # 1

VIDEO OR AUDIO RECORDING
1 COPY HYPNOTIST
1 COPY INVESTIGATING OFFICER
BOTH RECORDED DURING SESSION
TAPE RECORDING OF TOTAL TIME SPENT WITH WITNESS
TIME STARTED
TIME ENDED
2-22-82
9:05 A.M. "HELLO"
11:02 A.M. "GOOD-BYE"
32 MINUTES
1 HOUR 17 MINUTES
8 MINUTES
9:37 A.M.
TIME STARTED
10:54 A.M.
TIME ENDED
PRE-HYPNOSIS INTERVIEW
INDUCTION
INFORMATION ELICITING
DE-HYPNOTIZE
POST-HYPNOSIS INTERVIEW
ENTIRE INTERVIEW RECORDED
FROM HELLO TO GOOD-BYE

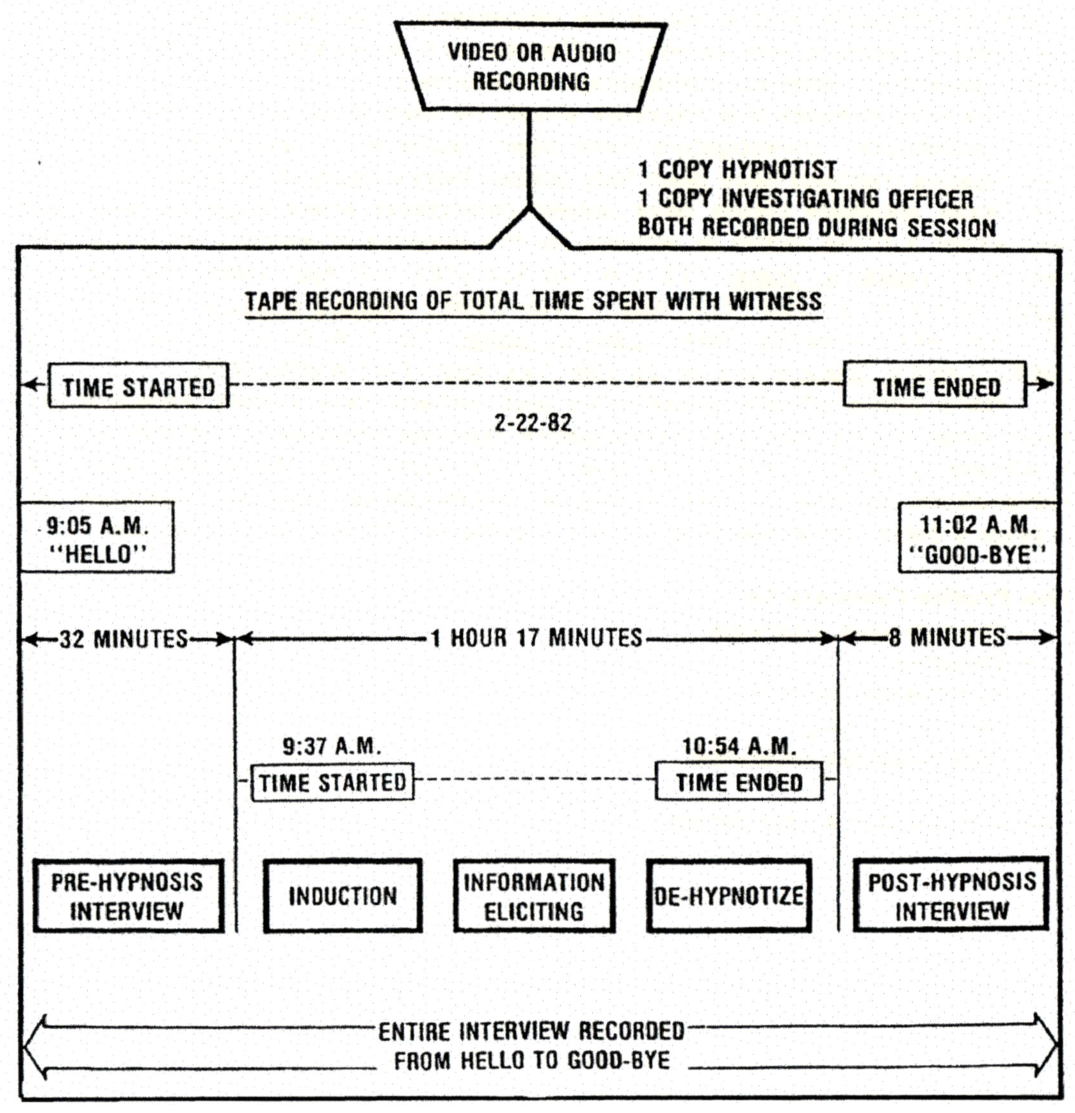

Pre-Hypnosis Interview

The pre-hypnosis interview consists of very important components that may negatively affect the outcome of the session if not handled properly. The police hypnotist is NOT a member of the investigative team assigned to the case and should have only limited knowledge of the facts, i.e., if the person to be hypnotized is a witness or victim, as well as the time, date, location and type of crime. There should be enough information to set the scene for the hypnotic review during information eliciting.

The investigator may be present but will not participate in the hypnosis interview of the witness.

Introduction to Witness/Victim

The first step is the introduction of the witness/victim to the police hypnotist at which time either an audio or video recording must be operating to document this initial contact. It is imperative that the entire contact between the police hypnotist and the witness/victim be audio or video recorded. In addition, it may be desirable for the investigating officer to make his/her own recording of the interview. The recording of the entire contact will provide the prosecutors, judges, defense attorneys, and jurors an accurate record of the interview; and to show that acceptable techniques were utilized and the interview was not impermissibly suggestive. If the police hypnotist is a uniformed officer, it may be desirable for him/her to be dressed in civilian clothes. Almost any location is sufficient as long as it is quiet, reasonably comfortable, and none threatening to the individual.

Rapport Building Session

One of the main tasks of the hypnotist is to establish and maintain rapport with the individual to be hypnotized by building a sense of trust in the hypnotist and the process.

Explaining Hypnosis

Explain the hypnosis process, what will be said and will be expected of the individual.

Discuss the Misconceptions

Explain the common misconceptions that most people believe about hypnosis, i.e., that the hypnotized person is not asleep or unconscious, will not divulge his secrets, cannot be compelled to tell the truth, will not get stuck in hypnosis, cannot be made to do foolish things, etc.

Many of these misconceptions come from the *Svengali-Trilby* novel by George Du Maurier (published by W. H. Allen-London A. Howard and Wyndham Company), and have been perpetuated over the years through television, motion pictures, and stage hypnosis.

It should be noted that a person could lie, confabulate or make up information while hypnotized if the person is motivated to do so. It is for this reason the Texas Department of Public Safety's policy prohibits the use of hypnosis with suspects and defendants.

Answer Any Questions

Allow the individual an opportunity to ask any questions that he/she may have and provide appropriate response.

Have the individual sign a voluntary consent to participate in a hypnosis session for the sole purpose of aiding in the criminal investigation. If the Witness/victim is a juvenile, obtain parental consent. (Refer to Exhibit #2 for details.)

EXHIBIT # 2

Hypnosis Consent Form

I, (name) ________________________ do hereby voluntarily and freely consent and agree to enter hypnosis with the assistance of

(name) ________________________ of the Texas Department of Public Safety, for the sole purpose of aiding in a current criminal investigation.

Signed: ______________________________

Date: ______________________________

Parent or legal guardian: ____

Hypnotist: (name & signature)

____

Witness: (name & signature)

____

Checklist

Utilize the appropriate checklist with the subject to determine if the person is under the treatment of a psychologist, physician or psychiatrist; wearing contact lenses; or has any phobias; etc.

By policy, the Texas Department of Public Safety prohibits a Department-authorized hypnotist from hypnotizing a subject who is under treatment for a heart condition, epilepsy, diabetes or other serious physical problem or is taking stimulants or sedatives, without the consent of the subject's physician. Consent is also required for persons who are under the care of a psychologist or psychiatrist. (Refer to Exhibit #3 for details.)

EXHIBIT # 3

Checklist for Investigative Hypnosis Session

Case No. ________

Subject ________________________________ Age ______ Sex ______

Persons Present ____

____

____

____

1. Was Consent obtained? ____________
2. Does subject appear to be fatigues or depressed? ________
3. Does subject appear to be emotionally upset or intoxicated? ________
4. Is subject under medical treatment? ____________ For? ________

   ______________ Medication ______________________________
5. Is subject under treatment by a psychiatrist of psychologist? ______
6. Has subject ever been treated for a mental problem? ______When? _____
7. Have subject remove contact lenses if worn.
8. Is subject known to be addicted to drugs or alcohol? ____________
9. Does subject have any phobias? _____ What? ______________
10. Does subject appear to be in good mental and physical condition? _____
11. Is someone from requesting agency present? ______________

If subject is under treatment for heart condition, epilepsy, diabetes or other serious physical problem, or is taking stimulants or sedatives, do not proceed without the doctor's consent.

Subject, who is under the care of a psychiatrist or psychologist, will not be hypnotized without the consent of the caretaker. The immediate supervisor will be fully informed of the reason for such care when authorization is requested.

Hypnosis Data Report

The hypnotist should keep notes or use an agency form to document the specific information relevant to the hypnosis sessions. Examples would be the names of all persons present, the time the initial interview started and ended, the time the hypnosis session started and ended the type of crime, and the results of the hypnosis session, etc. (Refer to Exhibit #4 for details.)

EXHIBIT # 4

TEXAS DEPARTMENT OF PUBLIC SAFETY
INVESTIGATIVE HYPNOSIS DATA REPORT

SUPERVISOR'S APPROVAL ☐ YES ☐ NO

C A S NUMBER ____

CRIME DATA

OFFENSE ____ COUNTY ____ DATE ____

VICTIM ____ PLACE ____ TIME ____

OFFICER REQUESTING ASSISTANCE | AGENCY/ADDRESS | TELEPHONE NUMBER

BRIEF SUMMARY OF OFFENSE

OTHER DATA WHICH MAY BE SIGNIFICANT TO STATISTICAL INFORMATION

HYPNOSIS SUBJECT DATA

NAME ____ SEX ____ DOB ____ AGE ____

☐ WITNESS ☐ VICTIM ☐ OTHER OCCUPATION ____

ADDRESS | HOME TELEPHONE NUMBER

SUBJECT HYPNOTIZED BEFORE ☐ YES ☐ NO | IF YES—NUMBER OF TIMES | REASON

PRIOR HYPNOSIS IN THIS CASE ☐ YES ☐ NO | IF YES—NUMBER OF TIMES | DATES/OFFICER CONDUCTING HYPNOSIS

HQ-124 ☐ YES ☐ NO | HQ-125 ☐ YES ☐ NO | VIDEO TAPED ☐ YES ☐ NO | AUDIO TAPED ☐ YES ☐ NO | ARTIST SKETCH ☐ YES ☐ NO ARTIST NAME ____

HYPNOSIS DATA

DATE | INTERVIEW STARTED ____ AM ____ PM | SESSION STARTED ____ AM ____ PM | SESSION ENDED ____ AM ____ PM | INTERVIEW ENDED ____ AM ____ PM

NAME OF HYPNOTIST CONDUCTING SESSION | NAME OF HYPNOTIST ASSISTING | LOCATION OF SESSION

WITNESSES PRESENT | AGENCY/ADDRESS & RELATIONSHIP IF CIVILIAN | TELEPHONE NUMBER

RESULTS DATA

BRIEF SUMMARY OF RESULTS ACCOMPLISHED (continue on back if necessary)

ADDITIONAL INVESTIGATIVE DATA ☐ YES ☐ NO

OFFICER'S SIGNATURE ____ ID # ____ SERVICE ____

Induction

The hypnotic induction starts with a series of suggestions to the witness/victim to allow the eyes to close, to become aware of breathing, to allow the experiencing of mental and physical relaxation, and to count numbers backwards slowly. Some induction techniques commonly used by hypnotists are progressive relaxation, confusion techniques, counting, fractionalization, Chiasson's method or some version of these techniques.

Information Eliciting

The various information-eliciting techniques are designed to permit the victim/witness to recall forgotten or repressed information if he/she is willing and able to have such recall.

Some of the techniques used for eliciting information are the movie theater technique, the calendar technique, ideomotor finger signal, the blackboard technique, automatic writing and artist composite sketch, to name a few. A commonly used technique for regression to achieve Hypermnesia is the movie theater. This technique is designed to regress a person back in time for the purpose of mentally reviewing the circumstances while experiencing a feeling of detachment. This technique is used to separate the event and the mental review process by time as it is well documented that tension, anxiety and trauma have a negative effect on recall and interrupts memory.

The procedure utilized in the movie theater technique consists of a series of instructions given to the subject, while in hypnosis, indicating they are going to review a special documentary film of the sequence of events as they occurred on the day in question. They are advised that the film can be stopped, reversed, fast-forwarded, freeze-framed, or played in slow motion to provide them an opportunity to make a closer review of any segment of the events. The person is told even though the event was traumatic; they will be watching the documentary and will be able to remain calm, relaxed and able to report the events as an investigative reporter.

The person is then directed, in imagination, to the inside of a theater and the review of the documentary film is started. While the person is in hypnosis with eyes closed mentally reviewing the events, they can verbally respond to the police hypnotist as to what is occurring or to questions by the hypnotist.
The witness/victim knows they are not in a theater while in hypnosis or after they are dehypnotized; however, this technique allows them to isolate some of the emotions attached to the event while they are mentally reviewing what occurred.

The calendar procedure is another regression technique, which would not be used with a witness or victim who has been traumatized. The witness/victim is instructed to imagine a calendar on the wall. The person is then instructed to look at the calendar and see that it is (month) __________ (date) ______________ (year) which is a __________ (day of the week). You should always start with the current date. The police hypnotist then starts regressing the witness/victim backwards by each day (seeing the previous day on the calendar) for recently occurred events. If it has been some time since the crime event occurred, one may want to regress the individual by months or even years. It may be necessary to regress the witness/victim back to the day prior to the crime event and have them seeing themselves go to bed that night and getting up the next morning, if that is what the person advised happened, continuing the mental review and verbalizing the sequence of events as they are occurring. The structure of the interview will depend on the circumstances surrounding the event as reported by the witness/victim.

An artist composite sketch can be developed while the person is in hypnosis or afterwards. The police hypnotist conducts the induction, has the witness/victim mentally review the events and then, while in hypnosis, asks the witness/victim to describe the physical characteristics of the perpetrator. The artist may be present and start the artist composite sketch of the perpetrator based on the description provided. The witness/victim should then be instructed to remain in hypnosis and open their eyes and compare it to the mental picture in their mind. It is permissible for the artist to discuss any changes that may need to be made with the witness as long as they are trained in forensic interviewing techniques. The police hypnotist may occasionally need to use deepening techniques between viewing of the sketch. Upon completion, the subject is told to close their eyes and then dehypnotize.

These techniques or a variation of these procedures are used by many practitioners for memory refreshment as reported throughout the literature.

Being an expert in the clinical use of hypnosis does not qualify the hypnotist to conduct the information-eliciting phase of an investigative hypnosis session with a witness/victim to a crime event for the purpose of refreshing recall unless he/she is also trained in the use of investigative hypnosis and forensic interviewing techniques.

It is imperative that the hypnotist use neutral non-leading questions, allowing the person to report in free narrative recall, and use compound or zeroing-in questions for specific details. An example would be if the witness/victim tells the hypnotist the suspect has a mustache while mentally recalling the characteristics of the perpetrator's face; the hypnotist may then ask the witness to describe the mustache, and then if it is thin, medium or thick.

De-Hypnotize

One of the most common techniques used to de-hypnotize a person is for the hypnotist to tell the subject that, "In a moment I'm going to count from one to ten and when I reach the number ten you will become alert, feeling refreshed and relaxed, opening your eyes on the count of ten."

The police hypnotist then counts from one to ten slowly while giving positive suggestions to the individual of feeling refreshed, relaxed, clear-headed, and having all of the normal sensations return to all parts of the body. Upon reaching number ten, the hypnotist tells the individual to open his/her eyes feeling refreshed and relaxed. It is important that the hypnotist makes certain that the person is fully de-hypnotized and reoriented before terminating the post-hypnosis interview, especially with individuals who achieve a deep level of hypnosis. In most instances, this takes only a short time.

Post Hypnosis Interview

The post-hypnosis interview may include questions, comments, or additional information. Whether or not the investigator uses standard interview techniques or hypnotic interview techniques, a witness/victim often will think of something else at a later time that may be important to the investigation. The police hypnotist should tell the witness/victim that if he/she recalls any additional information in the future, it should be reported to the investigator assigned to the case. The audio or video recording documenting the entire contact between the police hypnotist and witness/victim may be terminated only when the hypnotist and witness/victim separate.

Chain of custody of the original recording should be maintained by the police hypnotist until all appeals have been exhausted in cases where an offender was arrested and convicted or until the statute of limitations has run out.

For a more detailed accounting of the various aspects of hypnosis and its use for investigative purposes, refer to the *Handbook of Investigative Hypnosis* by Dr. Martin Reiser (LEHI Publishing Company) and *Clinical and Experimental Hypnosis* by Dr. William S. Kroger (J. B. Lippincott Publishing Company).

While this is a basic outline of the hypnotic interview, it is not intended to oversimplify the investigative hypnosis process, because all aspects cannot be covered in a condensed article on this topic.

It should also be understood that the law enforcement officer with years of prior experience, who receives training in hypnotic interviewing techniques, brings a wealth of interviewing skills and experiences in dealing with both traumatized witnesses and victims to crime on a fairly routine basis.

There are currently 24 commissioned officers within DPS who are trained, certified in compliance with state law and authorized by the Director to conduct Investigative Hypnosis Interviews. Texas is the only state in the USA that requires, by statute, mandatory training, testing and certification for police officers who use hypnotic interviewing techniques.

DPS-authorized hypnotists are prohibited from using hypnosis for therapeutic or public entertainment purposes. Although there is a considerable difference of opinion as to what constitutes therapeutic use of hypnosis, DPS policy includes weight reduction, stop smoking and similar applications of hypnosis as prohibited activity.

On June 29, 1988 the Texas Court of Criminal Appeals issued an opinion in Zani v. State, addressing the use of hypnotically enhanced testimony and establishing ten procedural safeguards.
In a case of first impression, the Texas Court of Criminal Appeals has approved the admissibility of hypnotically enhanced testimony under certain circumstances. This case involved the hypnosis of a witness 13 years after the murder of a convenience store clerk for which defendant Robert Zani was subsequently convicted and sentenced to 99 years in the Texas State Prison.

The Court of Criminal Appeals, the highest appellate court in Texas for criminal cases, held that in considering the admissibility of hypnotically enhanced testimony, a trial court should consider the four-prong dangers of hypnosis:

1. hypersuggestibility.
2. loss of critical judgment.
3. confabulation.
4. memory cementing.

The court listed several factors relevant to the trustworthiness of hypnotic recall, including:

1. The level of training in the clinical uses and forensic applications of hypnosis by the person performing the hypnosis.
2. The hypnotist's independence from law enforcement investigators, prosecution and defense.
3. The existence of a record of any information given or known by the hypnotist concerning the case prior to the hypnosis session.
4. The existence of a written or recorded account of the facts as the hypnosis subject remembers them prior to undergoing hypnosis.
5. The creation of recordings of all contacts between the hypnotist and the subject.
6. The presence of persons other than the hypnotist and the subject during any phase of the hypnosis session, as well as the location of the session.
7. The appropriateness of the induction and memory retrieval techniques used.
8. The appropriateness of using hypnosis for the kind of memory loss involved.
9. The existence of any kind of evidence to corroborate the hypnotically enhanced testimony.
10. The presence or absence of overt or subtle cueing or suggestion of answers during the hypnotic session.

Upon consideration of the totality of the circumstances, if the trial court should find by clear and convincing evidence that hypnosis neither rendered the witness post-hypnotic memory untrustworthy nor substantially impaired the ability of the opponent fairly to test the witness recall by cross-examination, the testimony may be admitted.

Of significant importance are the following statements contained in the concurring opinion by Judge White with Judges Davis and McCormick concurring. There are several factors that satisfy the test and support the conclusion that Magonye's testimony was admissible. The hypnotist, Ranger Carl Weathers, was independent of the law enforcement personnel who investigated the case, as well as the attorneys for the State and the defense. At trial, Weathers testified that he knew nothing of the details of this case prior to the hypnosis session. There was a record in the instant case, by interview with Jerry Magonye, Jr., of what Magonye recalled prior to hypnosis. The hypnosis session was tape-recorded. The majority concluded that the questioning was not overtly suggestive. Although two other persons were present during the session, they did not exert an influence on the subject during hypnosis. Lastly, there was sufficient corroboration, both direct and circumstantial, of the hypnotically refreshed testimony.

The court rejected the *Per Se* exclusion of hypnotically enhanced testimony based upon the opinion of the U.S. Supreme Court in Rock v. Arkansas.107 S.Ct.2704 (1987), which held that a trial court may not automatically exclude the testimony of a criminal defendant who has been hypnotized for memory enhancement prior to trial. The Court of Criminal Appeals also held that Zani was not entitled to the presence of counsel at the hypnosis session conducted prior to indictment. Finally, the court determined that a jury charge cautioning against excessive reliance on hypnotically enhanced testimony should not be given, since the requested charge would constitute a comment on the weight of the evidence unauthorized by Texas Law. Prior to considering the use of hypnosis for the purpose of enhancing recall with a witness/victim to a crime, it is recommended that the case investigator check with the prosecutor to determine the legal status of hypnosis in his respective jurisdiction.

Hypnotic Writing

By: Dr. Joe Vitale

How To Easily Use Certain Magic Words And Hypnotic Phrases To Persuade, Inspire, Inform, Entertain, Seduce Sell - and Much More!

I used to wonder how great authors could write novels that made people laugh, cry and even cause war or peace. They used the same words available to us all. Yet they wove them in such a way that we went into a waking trance. That's what I call "Hypnotic Writing."

I apply the same principles to writing sales copy. I put people into "buying trances." I get them to feel, see, taste and *want* whatever I'm selling. Here are some of the trademarks of hypnotic writing:

1. Personal.

Hypnotic Writing speaks to YOU. You'll find words such as '"you," "me," "I," "yours," etc. All of this makes you feel like the writing is speaking to you personally. In fact, it is. The more personal, the more hypnotic.

2. Active.

Hypnotic Writing is active. You'll find lots of verbs. You'll find little passive writing. It's the difference between saying, "The writing was hypnotic" and saying, "Joe Vitale weaves hypnotic writing." The first is passive, the latter is active.

3. Emotional.

Hypnotic Writing taps your emotions. You may find it doing so in a story format, or in a direct narrative. Either way, the writing will pull at your heartstrings. One of my most famous letters began, "I was nearly in tears..." That line engaged the emotions of readers. You had to read the letter to discover what the tears were for.

4. Sensual.

Hypnotic Writing involves your senses. You'll find descriptions of feeling, tasting, seeing, smelling, and hearing. All of this will help you become involved with the writing, and therefore susceptible to what it commands.

5. Commanding

Hypnotic Writing will command you to do something. You may not always detect the command as it may be embedded. But there will always be one. Ask yourself, "What do I want to do after reading this?" What you do next may be a result of the hypnotic command.

6. Curious

Hypnotic Writing plays on your curiosity. You may find it beginning a story- but not ending it until the end of the article. You may find it promising to tell you how to do something (like write hypnotically) - but it will only give you limited details, thereby urging you to order the book it said contains more information.

7. Hidden

Hypnotic Writing is hidden. You won't find any obvious clues that signal "Warning: Hypnotic Writing" at work. The writing will instead be smooth and personal, and the hypnotic aspect will sneak in below conscious awareness.

How do you put this all together and bring it to life? Some examples will help. The following are excerpts from the e-book, *The Hypnotic Writing Swipe File*.

31 Hypnotic Headline Words

You can generate headlines fast simply by using words from this list. Simply take words from below, add them to your product or service, claim or guarantee, and watch how easy it is to write a hypnotic headline.

Example: **Announcing: Astonishing Guaranteed Free New Way to Find Love Now!**

Announcing, astonishing, at last, exciting, exclusive, fantastic, fascinating, first, free, guaranteed, incredible, initial, improved, love, limited offer, powerful, phenomenal, revealing, revolutionary, special, successful, super, time-sensitive, unique, urgent, wonderful, you, breakthrough, introducing, new, how-to.

Hypnotic Openings

These will easily help you start any advertisement (or any sort of writing) without thinking. They are prompters, mind joggers and brain stimuli. Just read them and fill in the blank with whatever comes to mind. For example, in your opening sentence tell your readers what they will learn or what feelings they will get from reading your advertorial.

As you start reading the beginning of this article you find yourself...
As you sit there and read the beginning of this report you start to feel...
As you read every word of this report you will become (amazed, stunned, etc.) at...
As you analyze each word of this document you will shortly feel a sense of (calmness, joy, etc.)...
As you scan every word of this web page you will begin to discover new ways of...
After you read this short article, you will feel...
Can you imagine...
Picture yourself five years from now...
Just picture...
Just imagine...
Remember when you were in high school...
Imagine what it would be like if...
Wouldn't it be amazing if...?
And in those early years of existence...
Imagine what it would be like if you could...
See yourself...
Remember the smell of...

And you begin to notice...
Do you remember hearing...?
Can you recall what a (insert word) feels like?

Tip: Use statements at the beginning of the ad copy that your prospects already know to be true. This creates trust right away. Trust leads to sales - and to getting people to do anything else you may want them to do.
You probably know...
You're intelligent enough to know...
Of course you've heard that...
Everyone knows...
You probably already know this...
Rare thinking people like you already know that...

Psychological Copy Connectors

Copy connectors are ways to weave your sentences and paragraphs together to end up with a sales letter, ad or email that compels people to take the actions you want.

Tell your readers what they're thinking or feeling as they read your words. Most people will actually start thinking or feeling it because you brought it up. Only induce thoughts that will attract them to buy your product.

Ask questions to make your readers think about their problems. Make their problems seem bigger than they actually are by using "what if" questions. The more they think about their problem, the more they want to find a way to solve it. The bigger they see their problem, the easier it is for you to make a sale.
What if you...
Little by little you begin...
And as you absorb this information, you'll...
And as you are thinking about..., you become really interested...
Are you beginning to see how...?
As you read each word in this letter...
Have you noticed yet that...?
Now I would like to help you experience...
Wouldn't it be amazing if...?
And you will sink deeper and deeper...
And you will start to feel better and better about...

Verbal Implication

By: Steve Andreas, MA

Implication is one of the most common ways that we unconsciously make meaning out of events in everyday life. A speaker's statement *implies* something that the listener *infers*. Implication was used extensively and deliberately by Erickson, as shown in the following examples (some paraphrased) with the implication in parentheses:

"You don't want to discuss your problems in that chair. You certainly don't want to discuss them standing up. But if you move your chair to the other side of the room, that would give you a different view of the situation, wouldn't it? (From this different position you will want to discuss your problems.)

"I certainly don't expect that you'll stop wetting the bed this week, or next week, or this month." (I certainly expect that you will stop sometime.)

"Your conscious mind will probably be very confused about what I'm saying." (Your unconscious mind will understand completely.)

Examining these examples, we can begin to generalize about the structure of implication.

1. There is a presumption of a *categorical mental division* that is usually an "either/or"--here/there, now/later, conscious/unconscious, etc.

2. This categorical division can exist in space*, time* or *events* (matter and/or process).

3. A statement that is made about one-half of the either/or division (often using negation) implies that the *opposite* will be true of the *other* half. (Look back to verify that these three elements exist in each example above.)

SInce *implication* is often confused with *presupposition* (which, Erickson also used extensively) it is useful to contrast the two. Presuppositions have been well-studied by linguists, and 29 different "syntactic environments" for pre-suppositions in English have been identified. (See the Appendix to *Patterns of the Hypnotic Techniques of Milton H. Erickson, M. D. Volume I,* and (pp. 257-261). However, implications have not been studied, even though Erickson made *very* extensive use of them, so this is a very useful area to examine in much more detail.

Presuppositions

1. Can be identified unambiguously by examining a statement in written form. The simplest way to identify presuppositions is to negate the entire statement, and notice what is still true.

For example, "I'm glad that you have the ability to change quickly and easily." Negated, this becomes, "I'm *not* glad that you have the ability to change quickly and easily." Only gladness is negated, the rest of the sentence, "You have the ability to change quickly and easily" remains true.

2. Are usually passively accepted unconsciously.

3. Are usually processed and responded to unconsciously, yet can be identified consciously and challenged. "You are presupposing that I have the ability to change quickly and easily, and I disagree."

Implications

1. Can't be identified unambiguously by examining a verbal statement. For example: "Of course, it's difficult to change quickly and easily in your everyday life." (It will be easy to change quickly and easily here in my office.)

2. Are generated by the listener *inferring*, using their assumptions and worldview.

3. Are almost always processed and responded to unconsciously. Although they can be identified consciously, they can't be challenged in the same way that presuppositions can, because they do not exist in the statement. If a client were to say, "Are you saying that I can change quickly and easily here in your office?" it is easy to reply, "No, I only said that it is difficult to change quickly and easily in your everyday life, isn't that true?"

Summary: Implications are much *subtler* than presuppositions, they are *generated actively by the listener's process of inference,* they are typically processed entirely *unconsciously*, and they *can't be challenged.*

Creating and Delivering Implications (an algorithm)

Outcome: Identify your *outcome* for the client, what you want to have happen. (Example: The client will talk freely about their problem.)

Opposite: Think of the *opposite* of this outcome (not talking freely; keeping information secret, etc.)

Either/or Category: Use *space, time* or *events* (matter/process) as a way to divide the world into two categories (here/there, now/later, past/present, conscious/unconscious).

Sentence: Apply the *opposite* of your outcome to the contextual category that is *not* present (there, then, other) and create a sentence that will *imply* the outcome that you want the client to *infer*.

Space: "In your life outside this office, I'm sure that you would feel uncomfortable talking about private matters." (Here in the office, you can feel comfortable talking about anything.)

"If you were talking to someone at work, there would be many things that you would not want to discuss at all." (Here you can talk about anything.)

Time: "In the first session with me, there were undoubtedly certain matters that you were not comfortable disclosing." (In this session, you can feel comfortable disclosing anything.) "In your previous therapy, you may have been unwilling to talk about certain events that were relevant to your problem." (Now you are willing to talk about these events.)

Events: "I want you to carefully think about which matters are not relevant to the problem, and that you would like to keep entirely to yourself." (You can talk freely about anything that is relevant to the problem.) "In your normal waking state, of course, there are topics that you would be very reluctant to discuss with me." (In trance, you can easily discuss any topic.) Another way of thinking about this process is that the client's concern, objection or reluctance is completely acknowledged, at the same time that it is placed in a different context (place, time, or event) where it won't interfere with your outcome. Implications can also be delivered *nonverbally*, and since Erickson also made great use of that, it will be the topic of the next paper.

Nonverbal (Contextual) Implication

By: Steve Andreas, MA

In a previous article, I described verbal implication as follows: a statement is made that is the opposite of the desired outcome. This statement is made about a *different* context, which is one part of a categorical "either/or" that divides space, time or events into two categories. The result is that the listener (usually) *infers* the desired outcome in the *present* context. For example, "Your conscious mind will probably be very confused about what I am saying" implies that "Your unconscious mind will understand completely."

Nonverbal implication works somewhat differently, by creating a *nonverbal context* that elicits the desired response. Here are a few examples from Erickson's work.

With several women who were incontinent due to physical reasons, he put them into trance, and then had them experience sitting on the toilet urinating, and then imagine the bathroom door opening and a strange man's face appearing ("Strange man" is a context for *not* urinating, eliciting an autonomic response of constriction.)

A woman was in intractable pain due to inoperable cancer, and drugs and surgery had not helped. After considerable pacing, Erickson asked her, "Now tell me, madam, if you saw a hungry tiger in the next room, slowly walking into the room and eying you hungrily and licking its chops, how much pain would you feel?" (Extreme danger is a context for not feeling pain.)

A mother always spoke up and answered for her anorexic daughter when Erickson asked the daughter questions. Erickson told the mother to get out her lipstick and hold it very close to her lips and notice how her lips tended to move when he asked the daughter questions. (Putting on lipstick is a context in which the lips are kept motionless--and therefore unable to speak.)

A man who couldn't drive outside the city limits without passing out and vomiting was told to put on his best suit, drive to the city limits and stop by the last telephone pole he thought he could reach. Then he was to start his car, accelerate, and then put it in neutral so that it would gently coast to a stop when he passed out. If he felt faint, he was to stop the car, and get out and lie in the roadside ditch until he regained consciousness. (His best suit implies not vomiting, and not lying in the ditch where it would get dirty. Having to put the car into neutral implies some control, or at least delay in passing out, and passing out implies a delay in driving out of town, rather than its impossibility.) He passed out repeatedly in the car, but Erickson's report makes no mention of his vomiting or lying in the ditch. (An additional implication in Erickson's instructions is that passing out becomes the *beginning* of driving out of town, not the end of it.)

A "horribly fat girl," prudent and prudish, came in and said that even after she lost weight she would still be about the ugliest girl in all creation. In the first session, Erickson spent most of his time handling and looking at a paperweight, glancing up at her occasionally. At the end of the session he said to her. "I hope you'll forgive me for what I have done. I haven't faced you. I know it's rude. I've played with this paperweight; it's been rather difficult to look at you. I'd rather not tell you, but since it's a psychotherapeutic situation, I really ought to tell you. Perhaps you can find the explanation. But actually I have the very strong feeling that when you get reduced, at least everything I see about you, that's why I keep avoiding looking at you, indicates that when you get reduced you will be even more sexually attractive, which is something that should not be discussed between you and me."* (She is sexually attractive--nonverbal implication supported by verbal presupposition.) Since in the context of therapy, Erickson shouldn't notice or talk about her sexual attractiveness, the fact that he did, along with his rudeness in not looking at her, playing with a paperweight instead, etc., all imply the truth of what he says.

Nonverbal Implication

1. Is provided by the *nonverbal context*, or some element(s) of it.
2. This context can be either real, or imagined/hallucinated, but it must be Compelling.
3. The context *elicits* the desired response or understanding.
4. Is what Erickson often described as, "What you know, but you don't know that you know"--a dependable involuntary response to a specific context that you aren't consciously aware of.

Creating Nonverbal Implication (Algorithm)

1. Select the *response/outcome* that you want to elicit in the client.
2. Find a *context* that would naturally and powerfully elicit that response/outcome.
3. *Create* that context, either:
   - Vividly and compellingly in imagination (in or out of trance).
   - By "tasking," instructing the client to do a certain set of actions in the specified context in the real world.
   - Behaviorally, by your own actions in the present.

Summary

These different aspects of nonverbal implication, or what might better be called *contextual* implication, have been presented separately for clarity of understanding, but of course they can be used together. They can also be combined with verbal implication and presupposition, to elicit a stronger response, and this will usually be the case with behavioural elicitation, as in the last example given above.

Contextual implication will actually be a factor in *every* moment of therapy; since the therapist's office, clothing and especially nonverbal behaviour--speech, pauses, tonal patterns, posture, gestures, etc.--*all* provide a context for the meaning of what the therapist says.

There is yet another aspect of implication, how to create *intensity* of response to an implication through *drama* or *suspense*. Let's take another look at the last example. Erickson apologises for not looking at her, which she will certainly interpret as a response to her ugliness. He then follows with *five* more statements that she will surely interpret in the same way--each of which will confirm and intensify her unpleasant response. Then he suggests that she do what she is already doing, "Perhaps you can find the explanation," confirming her interpretation yet again, followed by a meandering sentence with *five* more phrases that seem to confirm her ugliness. Only after this build-up and suspense does he deliver his alternate explanation, which offers her a surprising, and much more pleasing, way to reinterpret the entire situation.

If Erickson had said something about her being sexually attractive without this hour-long nonverbal build up and suspense, it would have had very little impact, and would probably be understood as yet another confirmation of her ugliness: "Oh, he's just trying to make me feel better because I'm so ugly." How to create this kind of *intensity* of response will be the topic of a subsequent article.

**Conversations with Milton H. Erickson, Vol. III*, by Jay Haley, pp.18-21

Scripted Hypnotherapy

By: Steve Boyley

There are many scripts available. Scripts are a way to organize your thoughts and to transmit ideas and procedures to other hypnotists if desired. Induction and deepening scripts *are* useful; the intervention script may be a different story. Most hypnotherapy intervention scripts focus on behavior changes and that is all very well, *if* the behavior changes fit your client's beliefs about what reality is for them. If not, your client may return to their previous behavior. Changing the beliefs that support their behaviors is often the best way to create long-term behavior changes. Neuro-Linguistic Programming is a useful tool for discovering these beliefs and making each client intervention unique.

Once you can shift someone's attention inward, a script is unnecessary. However, a script is a useful way to make the ideas and concepts in the script into *your* ideas and concepts... using your words to 'customize' the script to fit your client. The most important part of using a script is keeping your eyes on your client. Here is how to accomplish that:

1. Print the script so it is formatted as two columns per page.
2. Highlight the key words or phrases that will remind you what to say.
3. Staple the pages of the script together in the top left hand corner.
4. Fold the script in half so that only one column is visible.

This format allows you to read the script easily without blocking your view of the client (your folded script will only be half a page wide). To keep your place in the script easily, simply slide your thumb down the column as you read. Hold the script up so that you can easily see your client beyond the script.

Remember where your focus is, *on your client* not the script. Professional communicators find the communication tools in the people they are communicating with. If you are learning a new process and use a script as a guide (highlighted key words/phrases), pull the folded script out and introduced it to your client as your notes on the *fantastically effective process* that they are about to experience.

Defining Hypnotism

Defining hypnotism as a function of the state that is produced by the hypnotist... seems like defining a light source by focusing on whatever it is shining on. It's confusing because the light can shine upon *many* different things and reflect in different ways.

A more useful definition may be as follows:

Hypnotism (descriptive) / Hypnotize (active): The process of using specific communication skills to change someone's state of mind. What a hypnotist does.

Hypnotist: A person who knowingly and artfully changes someone's state of mind using hypnotism.

Hypnosis: The effect produced by a hypnotist using hypnotism/while hypnotizing. Usually involves bypassing the critical factor of the conscious mind.

Hypnotherapy: Hype? No! Therapy (wink) and it works like magic!

Why Stage Hypnosis Is Important To Clinical Hypnosis

By: Jerry Valley

My office, in Methuen Massachusetts, is busy because of several sources. One, of course, is from referrals of satisfied clients. The second source is from the "Yellow Pages." It seems that if you are in the "Yellow Pages," the public assumes two things:

1. You are good at what you do.
2. You are ethical and reliable.

Then there is advertising in the newspapers, magazines, flyers etc.

However, in the last ten years and particularly in the last two years, one of the driving forces in attracting new clients has been the stage shows. People have been attending stage hypnosis shows in greater numbers than ever before. Right now, there are many very good stage hypnotists, "One on Every Corner," who do promote the clinical opportunities at each and every show. At first glimpse, it appears that having so many stage hypnotists will flood the market. Let me tell you that we, and many stage hypnotists, are busier now than we have been in the past. Why? Because when hypnosis is getting public exposure, it whets the public's appetite to see more. Many will also seek out a good, certified hypnotherapist. Even when there is a "raunchy" show, people are prone to go and see another hypnotist performing in the area. Whether it is curiosity or just to compare, they go.

Stage shows today are generating more discussion and interest amongst people than ever before. It is a catalyst for the acceptance of hypnosis when done in an ethical manner.

Yes, yes, we do have some idiots running around doing horrendous stage show, but that is what you will find in just about any profession. After all, this is America with free enterprise.

So why is stage hypnosis so popular today? Because people want to try it, and where can they do it so easily than with a professional stage hypnotist? Then they become curious.

Many have taken our "Masters Ultimate Stage Hypnosis Seminar" and are doing well. They enjoy the fun of a good, ethical and classic show and get paid as well. They have learned that stage hypnosis is actually easier than clinical hypnotherapy because we can pick and choose the best subjects for the show while the hypnotherapist has no choices at all.

What is happening now in the year 2003 is that the exposure of hypnosis via the stage is, more than ever, calling the public's attention to a viable and powerful source within a person that can be tapped for greater achievements. Of course, we have fun on stage, but we also we also endeavor to treat subjects with courtesy and respect yet, at the same time, unleash their innermost, subdued talents.

There are more stage hypnotists performing now than in any time in history... and why is that?

The hypnosis show has charm, wide appeal and lets the audience in on what is going to happen. The audiences love it! Nothing is funnier than audience participation. Art Linkletter had a television show called "People Are Funny." He would put people into funny skits, like we do, and just give them some room to become someone who they normally are not. He literally gave them a license to perform.

When people volunteer for a show, they put into the stage hypnotist's hands their most prized possession... their minds. If the hypnotist is ethical and professional, he/she does everything to ensure that the subjects, as well as the audience, have a great time.

Therefore, we as stage hypnotists have the duty to perform and enthrall those audiences that seek enjoyment, and if in the process we are able to convince a few skeptics, then we get a bonus.

These are some of the great hypnotists who have influenced me in developing the show; I had the pleasure of performing on the award-winning television show "20/20."

Sam Vine, who passed away in 1992, was perhaps the finest stage hypnotist that I have ever had the pleasure to observe, follow and borrow routines from. Sam was my friend and my mentor. He had a unique quality in that he never presented any magic or jokes, just pure and simple hypnosis. He had the ability to put subjects more deeply into hypnosis than I have ever seen in any other stage show. He was a gentleman.

Harry Arons, founder and leader of the Association to Advance Ethical Hypnosis was my first classroom teacher and he really got the ball rolling. He was a fine man and had many, many years of invaluable experience that he shared with many.

Ormond McGill, the "Dean of American Hypnotists," has traveled the world more than any other stage hypnotist and has authored over 32 books on hypnosis. It is my distinct pleasure to be teaching with this "Giant." In addition, he is such a great humanitarian.

In summation, may I suggest to those hypnotherapists who have not utilized any stage shows, to consider doing lecture/demonstrations that are appropriate for smaller groups like Kiwanis, Lions, K of C, Exchange Clubs, Sons of Italy and many other groups that are always seeking speakers.
When you show them just some very simple experiments, you will motivate them to seek self-improvement through your clinical programs. Try it. It works!

Mind Power Is Energy

By: Anne H. Spencer-Beacham, Ph.D.

Begin with a rapid induction and then proceed with the following:

You are now aware of the truth and vastness of mind power that flows throughout your body at all times. Your entire being is now open to a harmonious flow and it manifests in all your activities. You now have faith in the power of your mind, in the power of your word. You speak that word and send it forth charged with mind power. It accomplishes that for which you send it. The affirmations you now accept and make your own register throughout every fiber of your being on all levels of consciousness and mind activity. They perfect and heal your entire being, physical, mental, emotional and spiritual. You are now living a New Age.

Einstein has proved with his formula "E equals MC squared" that energy and matter are one and the same. One can be converted into the other. From the farthest star to the most infinitesimal part of the atom, the only thing that scientists have been able to find is energy. Everything that exists is energy at one level of activity or another.

Mind power is energy; perhaps the most powerful form of energy known. It is the storehouse of all knowledge, all intelligence, all wisdom and all power. It is subject to **your** will. It is at **your** command. It is your responsibility to direct the energy of brainpower into the best and most constructive and useful forms of activity on all levels of consciousness that you can conceive. As you do so, you prosper in all aspects of your existence, and this is so.

Your thoughts govern the condition of your body, and your body responds to all of your thoughts. Your body is a combination of what you eat and what you think. Good health, happiness and youthfulness are its normal state. Abundant life and substance and energy are everywhere. They manifest themselves in all their beauty, in you.

Your hair is flooded with pure life, energy and substance. The original color is abundant in every hair. Its growth is normal, its color natural. Through all-seeing mind power, you have perfect vision. Your eyes are relaxed and strong; your vision is acute and keen, clear and perfect. Your hearing is acute. You can hear perfectly. Your ears are alert and responsive to all the sounds of nature. The all-knowing, all-informing, all-understanding mind power is now expressed in you as perfect hearing. Perfect order and harmony are now established in your heart. It is filled with perfect love. You are at peace with all men. Your heart is strong and healthy.

Your stomach and digestive organs are the biological chemists of your body. There it is converted all foodstuffs to energy, both physical and mental. They are now in harmony with mind power; they are strong and well. Your appetite and the assimilation and elimination of your food are in balance and in harmony with mind power. Your diet is in balance between proteins, fats, starches and carbohydrates. The necessary vitamins and minerals are included in the foods you eat. Your body is perfect and that is so.

The all-powerful mind power flowing through you perfects the glandular functions of your body. It creates harmony in your arms and hands, in your thighs, knees, legs and feet, in every cell of your body and throughout every fiber of your being. Your skin is strong, healthy and resilient. It is the natural protective barrier between you and your environment. It easily resists biological, chemical and physical forces that come against it from your environment. Your skin is smooth and clear, soft and clean, strong and healthy. Your skin is perfect; your nerves are quiet, harmonious, peaceful and healthy.

In the midst of the crowd, you maintain your independence and solitude with calmness and serenity. You are tuned to mind power, from which all knowledge flows. You know what you need as you need it, and you supply it through mind power.

All the issues of your life are resolved by the wisdom and energy of mind power, which flows through you. You are fed, satisfied and guided by this infilling, nourishing wisdom. There is now harmony in your mind on all levels of activity... your business, your personal, your social and your family life. What you have been seeking from without, you have found within.

The ever-new, ever-unfolding expression of mind power... life and youth... is now manifest in every cell of your body. New perfect order and wholeness are established in every part of you. You are filled with vigor, vitality, youth and strength. Your body is perfect, you are happy. You live with nature above time. The tide of mind power and life energy sweeps your body, through every organ, every tissue, and every cell and charges them with power, life and energy.

The peace and power of universal energy falls and surrounds you. That peace and power go with you as a pillar of fire by day and by night. It is in that peace that power, that health and that harmony that you dwell. The in-dwelling power of universal energy guides your path. It has opened the way for your true prosperity, your freedom and unlimited physical, mental, emotional and spiritual growth.

It is establishing you in your true place. The inspiration from this power is now enabling you to visualize yourself in this true place. Into your life come people who can and do help you to maintain health, happiness and prosperity. Every manifestation fills you with gratitude and you are richer for it. You are thankful for all challenges, successes, all fulfillments and accomplishments.

Imagine yourself this way - project yourself into the future one-month from today and see what you see, feel what you feel, hear what you hear, know what you know. This is you in all of your glory. Next project yourself six months into the future... and now one year from today... Notice how good you feel – you are in charge of your life and this is so.

Continue to relax until at the proper time to be awakened, feeling refreshed, happy, rested and restored with abundant energy for the work you have to do.

Hypnosis and Religious Faith

By: Chaplain Paul G. Durbin, Ph.D.

Though the title of this presentation is "Hypnosis and Religious Faith," I will be dealing primarily with "Hypnosis and Judeo-Christian faith". It matters not whether you are a Christian or not, whether you are religious or not. Many of your clients come to you as religious people. Most of whom, will have a Judeo-Christian background. The better you understand the client's religious history, the better you can relate to that person and help that person. This article will give information that will help you answer questions that people of religious faith may present concerning hypnosis. What does the Bible say? What is the position of various Christian churches in regards to hypnosis? What is the position of the major non-Christian religions concerning hypnosis?

A few years ago, I read an article by Kathleen Dohney, (*Family Weekly*, August 19, 1984) titled, "Boom Days For Devil Hypnosis" Hearing that title: what ideas, images, thoughts come to you? Though the article had what I considered a very negative title, it was a very positive article on hypnosis in the health care field. The only reference to the devil was in the last paragraph, "Some conservative religious groups consider hypnosis to be the work of the devil."

Hypnosis is mistakenly viewed as mind control or demonic by many people. Recently I received a physician consult to work with a woman for pain management. As I explained the process of relaxation, imagery and hypnosis, I could see that she was very responsive. As I concluded my pre-talk, she said, "I am really looking forward to this experience, but I need to tell you that my daughter is a self-proclaimed born-again Christian and she may say something negative to you about this. If so, do not pay any attention to her, for I am the one who is hurting and I want this."

As I completed the induction, the phone rang. I told the patient, "Just allow the ringing of the phone and my answering it to add to your relaxation." I answered the phone, "This is Mrs. Doe's room. As she is in therapy, please call back in 30 minutes." and hung up the phone.

When the procedure was completed, I walked out of the room and there was her daughter standing in front of the door with arms folded over her chest. She said, "What have you been doing to my mother?" I explained that I had brought her mother relaxation, self-hypnosis and pain reduction. She responded, "I am a born-again Christian." Before she could continue, I raised my hands and said, "Praise the Lord, so am I." She was speechless, so I continued, "I will bring you some information on hypnosis, but regardless of how you feel about hypnosis, your mother has found it very helpful in the reduction of pain."

I believe that hypnosis and religious faith can work hand-in-hand to bring about a better life. Jesus said in St. John 10:10, "I am come you may have life and have it more abundantly." Though the title of this presentation is "Hypnosis and Religious Faith," I will be dealing primarily with "Hypnosis and Judeo-Christian faith." In our study of hypnosis and religious faith let us look at the history of hypnosis. Now I am not going to review the entire history of hypnosis, but would like to point out those incidents that relate to religion. ***What is the***

first written record of the use of hypnosis? The first written recorded use of hypnosis is found in the book of Genesis 2:21-22, "So the Lord God caused a deep sleep to fall upon man, and while he slept, took one of his ribs and closed up in its place with flesh, and the rib which God took from man. He made woman and brought her to the man." In this incident, God used hypnosis as an anesthesia so that Adam felt no pain during the removal of his rib. (Durbin, 1993)

In addition to the reference in Genesis, mention of hypnotic techniques is found in other ancient sources concerning the Egyptian "Sleep Temples." In the temples, Egyptian priests used hypnotic-like procedures to improve health. These temples were so popular that they spread to Greece and Asia Minor.

Paul speaks of going into a trance while praying in the temple (Acts 22:17). Peter "fell into a trance" and from that experience came to see that God loved all people and accepts all people who come to him. Peter had been invited to the home of a centurion who was devout in his faith, but was not Jewish. At that time, it was religiously unlawful for Peter to visit the centurion's house. After the dream, Peter went to visit the centurion (Acts 10:1-48).

The practice of "laying on of hand," mentioned in the *Bible*, uses some of the techniques of hypnosis. In the Book of Acts (28:8) we read, "And it came about that the father of Publius was lying in bed afflicted with recurrent fever and dysentery; and Paul went in to see him and after he prayed, he laid his hands on him and healed him." Elsewhere in the Book of Acts, there is a reference to an apostle looking into the eyes or gazing into the eyes of a person that resulted in the person being healed. "This man was listening to Paul as he spoke, who when he had fixed his gaze upon him, and had seen that he had faith to be made well, said with a loud voice, "stand upright on your feet." And he leaped up and began to walk." (Acts 14:9-10)

In the Eighteenth Century, two Roman Catholic priests used hypnotic procedures and gained a reputation as healers. Due to their influence on *Dr. Franz Anton Mesmer*, they played a significant role in the history of hypnosis. *Father Gassner* would have those desiring to be healed brought into a room where they were told to wait. As their expectations mounted, Father Gassner would then majestically enter the room, lower his cross on the head of a patient and command him to sleep. The patient would collapse and upon command would rise praising God for healing. *Father Hell* used hypnotic techniques and metal plates. He believed that illness occurred when the magnetism of the body was out of polarization. He would have his patients lie down and pass mental plates over them. His suggestions and the passes of the metal plates seemed to cure those who came to him for healing. Dr. Franz Anton Mesmer (1735-1815) came to the conclusion that it was the metal in Father Gassner's cross that caused the cures as well as the religious significance of the cross. If the metal in the cross could bring cures, perhaps any metal could be used for healing. With this information and experiments conducted by Father Hell in mind, Mesmer began to develop his theory of "animal magnetism." (Durbin, 1998)

The foundation of my work in hypnotherapy is based on what I refer to as the human trinity. I also believe each of us is a trinity within himself or herself. I am a trinity. You are a trinity. What is the human trinity? We are physical, emotional and spiritual beings. These three aspects of our being are so different and yet so integrated that one part of the human trinity cannot be affected without having some affect on the other two. If you have a physical problem, it affects you spiritually and emotionally. If you have a spiritual problem, it affects you physically and emotionally. If you have an emotional problem, it affects you spiritually and physically.

With this understanding of the human trinity, hypnosis can be used as a bridge between the conscious and subconscious mind. Though you only have one mind, you have two parts to your mind: conscious and subconscious. The conscious mind is the logical, reasoning, analytical two plus two part of the mind. The conscious part of the mind makes up about 10% of your thinking power. The subconscious part of the mind makes up about 90% of your thinking power. It does not think logically and is concerned with bringing about your deepest wishes, desires and expectations even if they are contrary to logic and your own well-being. The subconscious mind does not care if your body hurts but rather that your deepest needs are met. If your greatest need is for affection and the only time you experience affection is when you are sick, you may get sick in order to receive the affection you need. This occurs even though you do not like being sick and the reason is unknown. It is interesting to note that the subconscious mind cannot tell the difference between a wish and a fear. If a fear becomes dominate, the fear is received by the subconscious mind as wish.

A woman was in the hospital because she had lost the use of her right arm. As she had gone trough many tests and none had shown any reason for the cause of her problem, I was consulted. Through counseling, I discovered that she had been physically abused, (not sexually) as a child. As a young child, as a teenager, as a young wife and mother, she vowed that she would "never ever" hit her child in anger. She had a five-year-old son and she had disciplined him when needed, but she had never hit him in anger. A few days before coming to the hospital, her little five-year-old son had been especially aggravating. He did one more thing and in anger, she hit him. As this was such a shock to her, her subconscious mind protected her against hitting her child any more by making her arm useless.

As I felt that she needed to experience forgiveness, I used the following imagery. I suggested that she visualize herself walking down a country road. "On your back is a heavy backpack, but there is nothing in that backpack that you need for this journey. In fact, that heavy backpack contains the guilt you have been holding on to since you hit your son. God has forgiven you. He is telling you that you can now forgive yourself. You can be free of the heavy backpack. It is a decision for you to make. If you are ready to be free of that heavy load of guilt, one of your fingers will rise indicating that you have released the backpack and your guilt.

The first finger of her right hand jerked upward and I said, "The backpack with all your guilt is gone. God has forgiven you and you have forgiven yourself. You are forgiven." I added the following post-hypnotic suggestion, (Note: I seldom use negative words in suggestions but this time I used some of her own words.) "Since as a little girl, teenager, young wife and mother you vowed that you would 'never ever' hit your child in anger and because of the trauma you have experienced, you need 'never ever' hit your child in anger again, and therefore you have no need to be paralyzed." She left the hospital two days later completely cured.

Accepting the theory of the human trinity, one understands that life is more than just being alive mentally and physically. To be the whole person that we were meant to be by our creator, we have to be alive spiritually as well as physically and mentally. An airplane does not cease to be an airplane when it sets in the hangar or taxies along the runway, but its true nature as an airplane becomes apparent only when it is airborne. Similarly, a person is a human being when he or she is functioning only on the physical and psychological plane, but one shows his or essential humanness when he rises to the spiritual dimensions.

A man asked his three daughters how much they loved him. The oldest of them replied that she loved him more than all the gold and silver in the world. The father was noticeably pleased with her answer so he threw his arms around her and thanked her. The second daughter responded, "I love you more than the most valuable jewels in the world." He was pleased with her response so he threw his arms around her and thanked her. The third and youngest said, "I love you better than salt." The man was not especially elated with her remark and dismissed it lightly as an indication of her immaturity, but nevertheless threw his arms around her and thanked her. His wife, their mother, overhearing the conversation, left salt out of her husband's next meal. As he ate his food, he was confronted with the deep meaning of his youngest daughter's statement. She was saying that he was the flavoring, the spice and the seasoning of her life. Developing the spiritual aspects is like salt is to food. The spiritual dimension gives flavor, spice and seasoning to all of life.

When one is functioning in all three levels (physically, emotionally and spiritual), life is more joyful, more productive and more healthy. Accepting this position, one can see the important place that hypnosis can have for us; physically, emotionally and spiritually.

Hypnosis is neither anti-religious nor pro-religious. It can be used for good or bad depending on the hypnotist and the subject. Today, most religious groups accept the proper ethical use of hypnosis for helping people. Exceptions are Christian Science, Seventh-Day-Adventist and some individuals of various churches. In recent years, the Seventh-Day-Adventists have lessened their resistance by using relaxation therapy and suggestion therapy. A hypnotist by the name of Quesby greatly helped Mary Baker Eddy overcome an illness and she used many of his teachings and techniques in developing the Christian Science Church. (Morton 1980) Though Quesby used hypnosis to help her, she denounced hypnosis while using its techniques. Though many in various churches opposed to hypnosis are using the principles of hypnosis (relaxation, concentration, suggestion, repetition) in their healing services, they denounce hypnosis. (Durbin, 1998) For those who oppose hypnosis on religious grounds, I remind them of the words of Baptist Van Helmont, "Hypnosis is a universal agent... and is a paradox only to those who are deposed to ridicule everything and who ascribe to Satan all phenomena which they cannot explain." (Pratt, Wood, & Almon 1988)

The Roman Catholic Church has issued statements approving the use of hypnosis. (Morton, 1980) In 1847, a decree from the Sacred Congregation of The Holy Office stated: "Having removed all misconceptions, foretelling of the future, explicit or implicit invocation of the devil, the use of hypnosis is indeed merely an act of making use of physical media that are otherwise licit and hence it is not morally forbidden provided it does not tend toward an illicit end or toward anything depraved."

The late Pope Pius give his approval of hypnosis. He stated that the use of hypnosis by health care professionals for diagnosis and treatment is permitted. In 1956, in an address on hypnosis in childbirth, the Pope gave these guidelines.

(1) Hypnotism is a serious matter, and not something to be dabbled in.

(2) In its scientific use the precautions dictated by both science and morality are to be used.

(3) Under the aspect of anesthesia; it is governed by the same principles as other forms of anesthesia. This is to say that the rules of good medicine apply to the use of hypnosis. (Bryan, no date)

Except for exceptions noted, no other Protestant or Orthodox Churches have any laws against the proper ethical use of hypnosis. To the best of my knowledge, there has been no opposition to the use of hypnosis in the Jewish faith when it is used for the benefit of mankind. Many of the Eastern Faiths: Buddhism, Yoga, Shintoism, Hinduism and others approve the use of hypnosis and they often use hypnosis in their worship. The Moslem religion has no opposition to hypnosis that I have been able to discover.

In their book, *The Holy Spirit and You*, Dennis and Rita Bennett (1998) have shown a profound dislike and misunderstanding of hypnosis by declaring, "Hypnosis is particularly dangerous because it is thought to be a valid form of therapy in psychology and psychiatry, or an alternative anesthesia in medicine and dentistry." The Bennett add, "The fact is the hypnotist, by placing the soul in a passively receptive state even when the hypnotist has no such intention, opens the door to morbid spiritual influences that may bring oppression that lasts for years. Until the person is delivered by prayer and exorcism... Do not allow yourself to be hypnotized for any reason whatsoever." By these statements, the Bennett's show their prejudice and total misunderstanding of hypnosis. If their interpretation is correct, the Bennetts should also be concerned about prayer, meditation, chemical anesthesia and going to sleep (for that period just before you go to sleep is a natural state of hypnosis) for the individual is in a similar state to hypnosis in all those situations.

Hypnosis should not be condemned as anti-religious just because some people misuse it. Some oppose hypnosis because they say it is used by the occult, but do they condemn prayer because prayer is used for occultist purposes? Hypnosis can be a very helpful tool in counseling. Without apology and when appropriate, hypnosis can be used for growth, health and the benefit of people.

During counseling and hypnotherapy, I often tell a story to bring home a point or allow the client hearing the story to come to his or her own meaning to the story. Roger Ring in a seminar conducted at a past College of Chaplains convention called these "Parables, Metaphors, and Healing Stories." Jesus often spoke in parables or used stories that still bring to mind vivid word pictures that teach something important about life.

Until there is an image in the mind there can be no reality. All great inventions began with a thought in the mind. The inventor was able to visualize or imagine the invention before he could bring it to reality. The same is true of great music, great writing, and great living. The author of Proverbs 28:18 also wrote that where there is no vision, the people perish.

I would like to share with you a healing story and how it may be used when working with someone who would respond well to religious or spiritual imagery. You can use this story to help a Christian client regardless of your religious views.

IN THE MIDST OF THE STORM: (Can be used with Christian in the midst of a crisis or having trouble dealing with stress. I say to the client: "Let this story speak to you the message it has for you"). For just a moment, let this story of the disciples in the midst of the storm speak to you the message you are ready to hear. Just imagine that you have been with Jesus all day and he has been teaching from a boat because there were so many people there to hear him. Jesus concludes his message and needs a rest so he tells you and the other disciples to sail with him to the other side of the sea.

As the boat sails for the other side, Jesus lies down and goes to sleep. All of you are happy. The gentle waves rocked the boat back and forth, back and forth, which allows Jesus to sleep soundly. As so often the case in this region, the weather can change drastically in a very short time. Suddenly the sky turns black and winds began to blow. The storm winds intensified and the waves now rock the boat violently. Lightening struck the water near the boat and the boat rocks and water leaps over the side into the boat. You are afraid that the boat will sink. One of the disciples who is also afraid cries out, "Wake up Jesus! Don't you care that we perish?"

As you use your imagination, let that storm on the Sea of Galilee represent any storm that my be going on in your personal life. Do you feel like the disciples? Can you cry out, "Wake up Jesus!"

Jesus responded to the cries of disciples by reassuring them of his presence. "Peace be still, I am with you." When the disciples heard those words, the heart of each disciple began to grow calm. At almost the same time, it was as if the storm was listening for the storm itself became calm.

If you listen now you can hear Jesus say to you, "Peace be still, I am with you." Peace can come to you with or without a change in your circumstances. In the Bible, the word "peace" never simply means just the absence of trouble or discord. When Jesus comes to us and speaks "Peace be still, I am with you," he is offering the gift of his presence -- not just to resolve disharmony but to assure us that he with us to help us overcome or endure.

No, you are not on the Sea of Galilee, but you feel the winds of the storm and perhaps you are questioning your resources to cope with the situation. The storm in your life may be caused by unrealized dreams, dashed hopes, impairment of health, domestic difficulties, tension on the job, insecurity of position, inadequate finances or conflicts with family or friends. When the storms of life come, we want to cry out, "Wake up Jesus! Don't you care that I perish?" Then we hear him say, "Peace be still, I am with you." When the uncertain winds of anxiety blow, there is a steady safety in the presence of Jesus. When the harsh winds of illness or injury blow, there is calm and comfort in the presence of Jesus. When the cold, bleak winds of sorrow and grief blow, there is peace and security in the presence of Jesus. I am not saying that Jesus is a magic cure, but He is with us to either still the storm or help us cope with the storm. To experience the presence of Jesus is to experience peace in the midst of the storm. May you experience peace today.

As therapist, it is our job to help people move from an area of dissatisfaction to one of better dealing with life. If you listen to the broadcast of baseball, football or basketball game, you have surely heard the announcer say, "It's a brand-new ball game!" If you are a sports fan, you know the announcer means that the score is tied. It is like starting over again. The past is still there, but we can begin where we are. In a baseball game, if a team ties the score in the sixth inning, they do not go back to the first inning to start over again. For they keep playing from where they are. See we began where we are, but with the proper use of relaxation, imagery, hypnosis and hopeful expectation comes a "brand new ball game."

In the years ahead, may those who discount hypnosis, come to see its value. May those who oppose hypnosis on religious grounds come to view it as a gift of God to help us attain the more abundant life.

Jesus said, "The spirit of the Lord is upon me, because He hath anointed me to teach the gospel to the poor. He hath sent me to heal the brokenhearted, to preach deliverance to the captives and recovery of sight to the blind, to set at liberty them that are bruised." (Luke 4:18) Following this guidance and with the proper use of hypnosis; we can heal the brokenhearted, bring deliverance to those in captivity to pain, fear and phobias; give sight to the emotionally and spiritually blind, and set at liberty those who are bound by unwanted habits. As members of different denominations and religions, let us join hands in brotherhood to share the blessings of hypnosis with others.

HYPNOSIS AND RELIGIOUS FAITH BIBLIOGRAPHY:

Bennett, D & R. (1998) *The Holy Spirit and You* Gainesville, Fla. Bridge-Logos.

Beveridge, I. (1992) *Hypnotherapy: Its Christian Aspects*. Columbus, GA. Brentwood Christian Press.

Bryan, W.J. (1988).*Religious Aspects of Hypnosis.* Ann Arbor, MI: A.I.

Durbin, P.G. (1993) *Human Trinity Hypnotherapy.* Ann Arbor, MI: A.I.

Durbin, P.G. (1998) *Kissing Frogs: The Practical Uses of Hypnotherapy* Dubuque. Iowa: Kendall/Hunt

Kroger, W. (1977) *Clinical and Experimental Hypnosis*. Philadelphia. J. B. Lippincott

Morton, R. (1980) Hypnosis *and Pastoral Counseling.* Los Angeles, CA. Westwood Publishing.

Pratt G. & Wood D. & Almon B. (1988) *A Clinical Hypnosis Primer*. NY, John Wiley

Wittkofski, J. (1971) *Pastoral Uses of the Hypnotic Technique,* Springfield, IL Charles C. Thomas, Publisher.

Hospital Job Description for Hypnotherapist

By: Chaplain Paul G. Durbin, Ph.D.

(From an interview): Chaplain Durbin said: "I have been working with hypnotherapy at PMMH since 1982, and one of my goals has been to have a position of hypnotherapist at Methodist Hospital. I desired the position for two reasons: First, I believe that every hospital should have a hypnotherapist and second, I wanted hypnotherapy to continue after I had retired. I am now retired, but work three days a week as Director of Clinical Hypnotherapy. Thanks to a forward-looking CEO, Mr. Fred Young, Jr., who encouraged me to stay on after retirement and approved the Department of Hypnotherapy in 2001, that dream is now a reality.

I consider myself very fortunate for since 1982, I have had full support for the use of hypnotherapy by both the Administration and Medical Staff of our hospital. I receive many consults from our doctors for both inpatient and outpatient hypnotherapy. I am consulting for stress management; pain management, personal problems, and habit control such as stop smoking, stop nail biting and weigh control. Most of my inpatient consults are for pain management and most outpatients are for stop smoking. The dream of having a hypnotherapist in every hospital is a dream that has been shared by Anne Spencer Ph.D. of IMDHA and the late RD Longacre, Ph.D. I wish to thank them for their support and backing over the years.

For those of you who have a chance to work as a hypnotherapist in a hospital and need a guide for a hospital job description or for those who want a guide for working with a hospital, I share with you the following Hypnotherapy Job Description:

HOSPITAL JOB DESCRIPTION SPECIFICATIONS

DATE: ____________ Exempt (X) Non-Exempt ( )
JOB TITLE: Hypnotherapist
REPORTS TO: (CEO/President or a Vice President)
APPROVED: (President of the hospital)
SUMMARY OF FUNCTIONS: To assist the CEO in providing hypnotherapy for patients of Hospitals and others in the community.
To provide hypnotherapy and hypnosis, guided imagery, relaxation education to the community.

DESCRIPTION OF REQUIRED DUTIES:

1. Provide hypnotherapy to patient, families, staff and others. (Note patient/client are used interchangeably)
2. Provide relaxation therapy, guided imagery and the use of the imagination for enhancement of healing for patient family and staff.
3. Provide hypnosis for pain management. (The hypnotherapy should provide pain management only upon referral from a physician.)
4. Provide hypnosis for overcoming habits, fears and phobias.
5. Provide hypnotherapy and hypnosis, guided imagery and relaxation education to the community.

6. Participate with physicians and members of the health care team in providing total patient care.
7. Participate in classes on appropriate subjects for in-service education.
8. Speak, present seminars and workshops for civic organizations, Churches, institutions and businesses.
9. Serve on hospital committee as assigned.

SUMMARY OF QUALIFICATIONS:
1. Certification from one or more of the following organizations:

- International Medical and Dental Hypnotherapy Association
- American Counsel of Hypnotist Examiner
- National Guild of Hypnotists
- American Board of Hypnotherapists
- International Association of Counselors and Therapists
- (Other recognized hypnotherapy organization)

2. Proficient in the use of hypnosis, relaxation techniques, visualization and guided imagery.
3. Ability to interact with all levels of the health care team for the welfare of the patient.
4. Respect for confidential material and confidentiality concerning patient Information is required in line with the physicians' referral.
5. Ability to talk with patients, explain procedure, establish rapport. Determine if patient is receptive and agrees to the procedure. (Note: As all inpatient hypnotherapy is by physician's referral, should the patient refuses procedure, note in patient's chart
6. Ability to solicit information from patient that will be helpful in developing and using hypnosis, relaxation procedures and/or guided imagery.

EXPERIENCE REQUIRED:
1. College Degree or above with special training in hypnosis, relaxation procedures, guided imagery and visualization.
2. A minimum of 120 hours of training specific to hypnosis, relaxation, guided imagery and visualization.
3. A minimum of 25 hours of instruction specific to hypnotic pain management.

EXPERIENCE PREFERRED:
1. Ability to make independent judgment.
2. Must be accurate in reporting information to other health care professionals.
3. Must be able to work with other health care professionals for the well-being of patients, families and staff.

POSITION KNOWLEDGE AND PERSONAL ATTRIBUTES REQUIRED:
1. Must have knowledge of hypnosis, relaxation procedures, guided imagery and visualization.

2. Must be able to work with people of different religions and cultural backgrounds.
3. Must be able to work with other health care professionals for the well-being of patient, families and staff.
4. Ability to help patients and clients:

- To reduce patient's tension, anxiety and fear.
- To help reduce pain and discomfort.
- To enhance healing.
- To prepare for surgery by relieving anxiety and creating confidence.
- To help patient following surgery by reduction of pain and by proper suggestion enhancing healing.
- To reduce pain and anxiety during childbirth.
- To reduce nausea and other side effects of chemotherapy.
- To reduce the harmful effects of stress.
- To help patient overcome unwanted habits: smoking, nail biting, hair pulling etc.
- To use for weight control.
- To help patient improve memory, concentration and study habits.
- To help enhance athletic ability.
- To increase self-confidence and ego strengthening.
- To overcome insomnia.

AREAS OF USE:

1. Use hypnosis and guided imagery for pain reduction and teach self-hypnosis, relaxation and visualization for pain management.
2. Use hypnosis and guided imagery for reducing the side effects of cancer treatments and teach self-hypnosis, relaxation, visualization and stress management.
3. Facilitate the reduction of anxiety, fear, nausea and other side effects of chemotherapy.
4. Teach pain management and the reduction of anxiety and stress for those in rehabilitation.
5. Stress management and teach techniques to facilitate relaxation, blood pressure regulation, weight control, and medication support.
6. Facilitate the reduction of fear, anxiety and pain.
7. Use hypnosis to reduce pain, anxiety, fear, bleeding and stress in emergency room.
8. Facilitate the reduction of time the patient requires ICU care through pain management, stress management, providing positive mental expectation to encourage healing and stabilizing vital signs.
9. Teach techniques for pain management, anxiety and nausea during pregnancy, labor and delivery and giving positive suggestions to reduce or eliminate post-partum depression.
10. Use hypnosis and guided imagery to reduce anxiety and fear before surgery with suggestion for the success of the surgery and healing. After surgery use hypnosis and guided imagery to reduce pain and enhance healing.

11. Use hypnosis and guided imagery and teach self-hypnosis, relaxation and visualization to help patient deal with medical procedures such as receiving injections, physical therapy, MRI, respiratory therapy and other procedures.
12. Teach staff relaxation techniques, self-hypnosis, and visualization for stress management to help them cope with their jobs and reduce burnout.
13. Use hypnosis to overcome unwanted habits.

The Troubled Squirrel Metaphor

By: Steve Andreas M.A.

The troubled squirrel is a general-purpose problem-solving metaphor, with an unconscious access via the old squirrel, and a lot of suggestion for rearranging resources in order to find a solution. Properly and slowly delivered, it can be very powerful.

Once upon a time, or twice down within a time, there was a very troubled ground squirrel. His troubles were not simple ones, like his fear when the shadow of a hawk swept across the ground nearby, or when a coyote's yelp split the night. Nor was his pain like the ache of an injured leg, for at all those times he knew what to do or what not to do.

Often he felt very young and very, very small; at other times he felt very old, and bone-weary. But mostly he felt confused, and frustrated, and very lost. When he thought about his troubles, it was as if he were at the shady side of the pond in the meadow, groping in the muddy water for a slippery bottom-dweller. At times he would feel a tantalizing touch within his grasp, and seem to be at the brink of understanding, before it slithered away into the swirling gloom.

At other times his troubles were like a cloud, muting the colors around him and casting a dark shadow over all his days. Yet when he searched the heavens for the source of this shadow, the wide blue sky gave him no answer.

At other times his troubles seemed like soft voices, as if just out of reach, and he strained his ears to hear what meaning they might reveal to him. But always it was only a breeze or a large insect rattling the stems of the dry grasses or the leaves over his head.

After much thought and anguish, his mind turned to the many stories he had heard of the oldest and wisest squirrel who, it was said, lived alone in the deepest burrow in the meadow. All the stories about the old squirrel were curious and puzzling, full of strange twists and unpredictable behavior. Some said the old squirrel was wise beyond imagining, while others said that he was crazy, or worse. Others said he was both, but there was no telling one from the other. When he thought of all these stories his mind swirled with images, sounds and feelings that reached no resolution.

At last, one evening when the weight of his troubles pressed down particularly heavily upon his shoulders, he decided to seek out the wise old squirrel, come what may. As he slowly descended to deeper and deeper levels, the activities of the other squirrels and the sounds of their comings and goings gradually faded away. As he crept though these burrows where the dust and dampness had not been disturbed--for who knows how long--the sound of his soft breathing and his footfalls echoed in the long-abandoned chambers. Sometimes when he paused, he thought he could hear the gentle heartbeat of the earth itself.

As he explored burrows he had never visited before, in some he found only cobwebs and old nests made of leaves and twigs, the hulls of nuts and seeds, and other signs of the life that had once occupied them. In others he found the walls sparkling with tiny grains of some shiny crystal that he had never encountered in the shallower burrows nearer the surface. In yet others he found fragile patterns of roots and spider webs that seemed to welcome him and beckon him deeper and deeper.

As the soft light faded into almost total darkness, he seemed at the same time to be traveling deeper and deeper into himself, into unseen and unheard realms that began to whisper soft and poignant meanings to him.

Eventually he reached a level where only one burrow still angled downward. It was a large burrow, free of dust and cobwebs, and the smell and warmth of life radiated from its walls, a little like the sound of a soft choir in a great cathedral. As he reached the end of this burrow and his eyes slowly adjusted to the darkness, he saw before him an immense squirrel whose eyes were closed, and whose fur was almost completely white with age. Without opening its eyes, the great white squirrel muttered, "What do you want?" As the troubled squirrel began to pour out his misery, he was astonished to feel his unhappiness empty out of him as cleanly as if he were a pants pocket that someone had turned inside out to see what was there, spilling its contents out into the sunlight where they could be seen clearly. It seemed as if the old squirrel was picking through the jigsaw puzzle of his life with gentle, loving hands, carefully separating pieces that had been jammed together, and rearranging and uniting pieces that had been long been separated, simply curious to see what image would slowly emerge from the scattered bits of color.

He remembered a time when he was much younger, watching other squirrels playing in the pond, fascinated by the fragmented reflections flashing on the surface of the water. And when the squirrels left the water, watching the scattered dancing bits of light slowing their dance and gradually coalescing into larger patterns of color and shape, until finally he saw an image of himself, still moving. And as he watched this image of himself slowly move toward stillness, he felt the calmness of the quieting water enter his body and refresh him.

After what seemed to be an eternity, the great white squirrel's eyes opened and he began to hum a soft low sound. As he gazed into these eyes, he felt a comfort and safety he had never known before, and he seemed to be drawn into the heart of life itself. He felt himself welcomed to slide into their depths and into a peaceful reverie in which he lost all track of time.

In this timeless realm some of his thoughts seemed like soap bubbles riding within a gentle breeze, until they popped and vanished, while others gradually became so tangible that they seemed to pervade throughout all space and time, and through every fiber of his being.

At the same time, the myriad sounds of his nature rose and fell around him and gradually become a quiet, yet joyous song that conveyed the courage and majesty of his simple life. Tiny imperceptible movements--like tiny eager minnows swimming in his body releasing tensions into fluid movement, told him that his body, too, was participating fully in this joyous learning, changing, rearranging.

These movements, images and sounds stirred each other to greater searching and expression, and gradually melded into a subtle dance that resonated with every particle of his being, a moving that he would carry reverently in his body to the end of his days.

Some time later, as he found himself crawling slowly upward through the burrows, he felt a new lightness that told him that so much had changed in a delightfully solid way, though exactly what it was, or how it had happened, he could not begin to describe.

Negative Suggestions? An Apology.

By: Jillian LaVelle CH

For the last 15 years I have presented classes that often promoted the concept of using only positive suggestions with clients. I told students that there was no research showing negative suggestions to be of greater benefit. "Therefore," I theorized, "practice using only positive ones." This made me feel comfortable. It was politically correct thinking. Other teachers have also promoted the theory, so surely, they must have the data. There was a problem: I was not being very successful with my stop smoking clients (only 40% success rate). I found this out after I contacted the clients with a follow-up phone call. This interview was done a few months after being released from treatment. This concern motivated me to conduct a review of all the available research studies. Guess what I found out. In many therapies, negative suggestions worked very effectively. In fact, success rates in behavior modification were significantly higher when negative suggestions were included.

Oops, I goofed in the prior teachings. The only thing I can do is to correct it by speaking out.

When I began using negative suggestions, my success rate soared. People actually stopped smoking (almost an 80% success rate). If you review the Hammond's book, *Hypnosis Suggestions and Metaphors*, it clearly shows increased success rates coupled with dialogue that includes negative suggestions. I do tell people that they would "no longer support a habit that was robbing you of three minutes of life every time you lit a cigarette," "You will never want to smoke again," or that "smoking would taste like you were placing your lips on the exhaust tailpipe of a running car." These negative imagery statements, and others like them, get people to stop smoking. Of course, I do "future pace" them to a time within three months of being an ex-smoker. I tell them that they can breathe easier (instead of labored), have more energy and feel proud of their achievement of being an ex-smoker. When you are reading suggestion technique literature and find the author using negative suggestions, it is probably because it is indeed an effective method. Strongly consider using it. When I decided that my private practice needed to be of true service to the clients, I became a better therapist.

In addition, I found that the subconscious mind fully understands the words "no, never and not." There is a theory flying around that the subconscious mind does not hear those words. Actually the subconscious mind does hear them and people have been conditioned to respond to them since childhood. Frequently "no" is a child's first word. The mind has been trained to accept those words, so feel free to include them into the suggestions you give your clients. Now, I did recently get into an argument over this very concept by a New Age practitioner who is trying extremely hard to eliminate all negativity from her life. She feels that it helps humanity to correct other people during the simplest conversations. It reminded me of where I was several years ago. I thought that in order for me to have a perfect world, all negativity needed to be removed. Whenever an absolute, inflexible idea crops up, then a learning experience was about to take place in my life. Within a month, of striving to only be positive 24/7, I had the pleasure to attend a lecture by Deepak Chopra. In a question and answer session, a man in the audience asked Dr. Chopra how he could eliminate all negative thoughts from his mind. He, too, was on the same quest. I smiled. A kindred spirit. Deepak took a breath and said that he thought it would be too stressful to do that. He thought that it was not in the best interest of any person to undertake such a task. I have begun to realize that to be spiritually mature means that you can accept the imperfections in life. This does not mean that you are sacrificing your goals. It means that within life, the imperfections are not to be immediately declared "the enemy."

It is amazing how much more peace I have in my life as I learn to simply accept the imperfections. If I waited for all negativity to leave my every sinister thought that crops up, I would never leave my room. Life is too short. Sometimes my negative thoughts have led to positive experience. I often now view them as an early warning system that something is off-course. I also want to be clear that I am in no way endorsing living only in the negative state of mind. The majority of my time is positive in thinking. In all honesty, it is about a 75% positive/25% negative mix. I lean towards positive thinking, but it is no longer my obsession.

As for you clients: Use the negativity, where appropriate, to produce the positive result of elimination of habits/behaviors that are truly detrimental to their lives.

The Magic of Thoughts

By: Ormond McGill

Man (which term is used to include both genders of the human species) can be looked upon as having a trinity of awareness; SELF, MIND, THOUGHTS. Self is our consciousness that uses mind to produce thoughts, and thoughts are the way we think, which is the way we perform in the physical world. To give a quote, "As a Man Thinketh in His Heart So Is He."

Let us start with Mental Equilibrium.
Mental Equilibrium is mental discipline that is a paramount factor in life's achievements. In mental equilibrium all things are met with calm detachment, being free of judgments neither for nor against. **Mental equilibrium is the balancing of thoughts.**

Next, let us move on to Logical Thinking.
Logical Thinking is scientific concentration. Logical thinking prevents one from making mistakes and often leads to success. Remember, the beginning of success is the knowledge of one's faults. Learn to control your thoughts - for thoughts are forms of energy - and energy makes things happen.

Make use of the Psychological moment.
Psychology is a study of the mind, and mind is the creator of thoughts. Psychology is really instruction in mental discipline. There comes a moment in every thought when it has its greatest impact. Such is known of "the psychological moment." To become consciously aware of these moments is part of the mastery of mind. How? **Learn by experiencing.**

Let us apply some Scientific Concentration.
Science aims to explain and make things logical so such can be useful in organized ways. Concentration is mental attention. Combine with science to make forms of mental effort become an act of pleasure that you enjoy. **Do it until it becomes a habit of the constructive way you use your mind.**

On now to the Power of Imagination.
Imagination is the creative power of the mind. Everything that is, first started in imagination. It is well to understand this power, for it can be both productive and destructive depending on how it is used. Understand that every thought we think starts a matrix in space leading to its physical creation (its creation depending upon the concentration and will is placed upon the thought). As imagination is the creative power of the mind its use should be constructive.

A bit about attention.
Attention brings into your reality that which you most strongly think about. To deliberately be able to control what you think about is a great skill. It is based upon concentration of attention. Concentrated attention is attention to specific

objectives. This power of concentration can be raised to a high polish of perfection. Here are some tips that will help you along the way:

Avoid the Hurry Habit.

Much of the way of the modern world is the way of hurry, hurry, hurry. Hurry becomes a habit that is often the source of accidents and mistakes. Hurry causes ceaseless agitation. Hurry is a matter of time, and there is no time in eternity. So slow down remembering you have eternity for doing whatsoever you have to do. **Without hurry you will actually get more done than if you hurry.**

The Way of Optimism.

Mind has an instinctive Center of Right Knowledge. Knowing what you know is right, is optimism. **Optimism is like a bright light that removes the shadow of doubt.**

The Demise of Doubt.

Doubt is the opposite polarity of knowing. It is pessimism. To dwell in doubt undermines your confidence. Use Mental Equilibrium, Logical Thinking and Less Hurry to make it disappear.

Mentally Picture the Way you Want to Be.

When you become at peace with yourself you become at peace with the world. A peaceful mind brings serenity and creative mind power. Just let it happen without trying to make it happen. That is, make the effort without effort. All the inner operations of your body function of their own accord. Allow your mind that freedom. **Just form a mental picture of the way you want to be, and let it be.**

Thought on Self Control.

Thought Control is Self-Control, and vice versa. Use your Will to achieve this strength of character. Freedom of Will is a divine gift. It has great power. **Use it wisely to produce the thoughts you wish to think rather than a continual jabbering of thoughts.**

Making your mind think what you **want** it to think and **when** you want it to think is mastery of the mind. **Mastery of your mind makes you a MASTERMIND.**

Claim What is Your Own.

Whatever you elect to create by your thoughts is your own. Your thoughts belong to your private world, unless you choose to share them. They are exclusive. They belong to you alone. As Emerson expressed it...

"Whatever in nature is thine own
floating in air or pent in stone.
Shall rive the hills and swim the sea
and like the shadow follow thee."

You can form what you have considered in this brief dissertation into a SELP-HYPNOSIS process, if such is your wish.

Buried Treasure

By: Cork Graham

Post-traumatic stress disorder (PTSD) was the hell I suffered through from age four to 19, a hell that I would never wish on my worst enemy. The symptoms were so bad that while others my age were playing with dolls and trucks, I was thinking of a way to die.

By the time I was 13, I was overweight, shy and insecure, still wetting my bed out of some unclear, subconscious fear, and never getting a really good sleep because of repetitious nightmares in a surreal splash of whites, reds and pinks. And the fits of near-homicidal rage! I spent many a moment after an emotional outburst realizing how close I had come to making the rest of the world see what I saw and feel what I felt. If I had not controlled myself, Columbine would not have been the first time teenagers had gone too far.

And if it weren't for the opportunity, of jumping on a plane and heading to Bangkok with the idealistic dream of becoming a combat photojournalist, I'm sure that you would have seen my mug on an FBI wanted poster, instead of on the front page of the *San Francisco Chronicle*, and so pleasantly interviewed by Joan Lunden on *Good Morning America*.

What strikes me to this is day is that while everyone was so interested in how a 19-year-old became the first American political prisoner held in a Vietnamese re-education camp eight years after the United States lifted off in a helicopter from its embassy in Saigon, they never touched on the real reason why I was in Vietnam in 1983 in the first place, and never learned why I would remember that year of solitary confinement as a healing experience!

It is common knowledge that people do not make profound change if they do not have profound impetus. Even before high school was over, I was telling friends that I was going to Southeast Asia to cover the big story at that time: American MIAs. Everyone thought I was crazy, at times even me. But, that is the thing about the subconscious: it leads us to things we do not recognize as important until we are in the middle of it, or more importantly, after we are done.

Three months after I arrived in Bangkok, I found my first big story: an Englishman by the name of Richard Knight needed a photographer to cover his treasure-hunting expedition onto *Iles des Pirates*, an island forbidden to non-Communists.

After three months of interrogation, we were moved from the Kien Giang Provincial Prison in Rach Gia on the Thai Gulf side of Vietnam, to Saigon.

In Saigon, the beatings as part of interrogation finally stopped, which made my interrogators seem much friendlier and helped me feel more willing to open to introspection. Part of that introspection was a regimen of self-hypnosis I had started in the first prison to alleviate the physical and psychological torture I had undergone there. Now, in the more relaxed situation of solitary confinement that was interrupted only by an occasional interrogation once every week instead of every day, I found myself using self-hypnosis to follow the threads of memory revolving around my childhood experiences of living in Saigon as the son of an

American businessman during some of the worst years of American participation in the war in Vietnam.

My impetus was the nightmares that had come back in the form of swirling red, white and pink. I had not had these dreams since I was 13, a year after I had moved with my family to the United States from Southeast Asia.

Four years later, the nightmares returned to haunt me in Bangkok within a month arriving there, looking for my first big photojournalism assignment for the Associated Press. I had attributed the return of the psychedelic nightmare to living in an area that was offering me the same sensory experiences of living in Southeast Asia as a child. But, unlike the nightmares while in prison in Saigon, these nightmares seemed to have much more of a psychological and emotional impact. That is when I started looking at the nightmares as a possible link to some traumatic experience during my childhood in Saigon; experiencing the anchors to the past (sights, sounds, smells) were having a more profound effect.

Instead of avoiding them I began asking myself what they meant and, more importantly, what my subconscious thought them to be!

In my cell at the first prison in Saigon, I was offered a traditional Vietnamese bed: a wooden bed frame, four posts from which stretched a mosquito net, and a thin straw mat that served as a mattress. The bed was my therapist's couch, and I was doing double-duty as client and therapist.

Mr. Al Stewart, my history teacher at Carlmont High School in Belmont, California was also a trained hypnotist who ended up teaching me hypnosis back in 1981, the year before I graduated. He taught me about direct suggestion, how to take myself down, and described it like floating on a raft at sea—self-hypnotic age regression and abreaction I would learn myself.

As you can imagine, floating on a raft on a nice warm sea was definitely more attractive than being locked up in a cold, dank concrete cell waiting for a judgment that could easily result in being taken out and shot as a spy for the CIA. At one point, my interrogators even put me through a mock execution, with a blindfold and a firing squad!

My daily self-hypnosis session would always begin by counting down from five to one, drawing and releasing a breath with each number, tuning into my heartbeat as I slipped further into trance. After taking five deep breaths, my heart would be beating about once a second. The outside world would become non-existent. I would then leave my body, feeling as though I was rising and the Earth was falling away. The hard bed became soft like water. Waves, actually. Slow, rocking waves, like lying out on that raft at sea. A smile would come across my face. Warm sunrays seemed to come right down through the ceiling, touching my skin, my chest and my body. Free from my cell, the sea was wide open around me. There were no crests on the waves. These were early morning waves, slick as glass. Bright sun, lapping waves; my consciousness was free!

Completely bypassing my critical factor, I would direct my attention to an imaginary calendar, and then I would imagine the calendar becoming a clock, where the 12 months from the calendar had changed into 12 hours. I had programmed myself with the intent of getting out within 12 hours. Hypnotizing my subconscious into thinking I was in prison for only "11 hours" would enable me to later tell reporters that prison was not so bad, that it was just part of the job of being a journalist in a hostile country. After my three-hour trip, I would come back out of hypnosis by counting up my breaths, recharging with the revitalizing *Chi* that I had learned to modify through the instruction of a Buddhist monk back in Bangkok. Then I would go over to the cell window for my physical attempt at escape.

I never did make it out through physical escape, and I tried three times, bearing the repercussions when my attempts were discovered. But, as the self-hypnosis settled into my subconscious, positive affirmations of self-improvement finally began to surface, maybe not as fast as might have occurred had I actually had a properly trained clinical hypnotherapist in the cell with me, but no less effective, especially removed from the distractions of modern society, like television and radio.

Abreaction is truly a powerful and loaded word: "To release (repressed emotions) by acting out, as in words, behavior, or the imagination, the situation causing the conflict." To do this in prison, where physical escape from the emotional memory of Saigon was impossible, was even more powerful, like being held in place by an almighty hand, forced to confront a past I had so skillfully evaded until then through fantasy and adventure.

Memories floated up to the surface: A US Army helicopter taking out a Vietcong machine gun nest, by blowing a large hole into the middle of a 12-story apartment building; a plane dropping a bomb on a VC position on an island in plain view from our roof during the "Little Tet Offensive" that happened a few months after the infamous Tet Offensive of 1968. Me at six years old waking up in a US Army hospital to the blank stares of wounded Vietnamese civilians; me ignoring the pain of my tonsillectomy as I screamed at the top of my lungs for someone to get me out of there; and finally, my father killing the only thing I felt safe enough to open up to emotionally—my white pet rabbit.

The red, white and pink, swirling nightmare, had been made clear to me, as though a light had been turned on and before me was a tiger I had only heard and felt in the darkness of my remembrance: the white was the color of the fur of my rabbit; the red was the blood of my disemboweled friend as he was gutted by my father in preparation for that evening's meal. And, the pink swirl was my subconscious mixing the two together in a color similar to the color of blood on white fur.

I had been overweight throughout my teens, always eating to ease emotional distress. Now I was able to recall that night my mother roasted my closest friend in the oven. As the family sat down to dinner, my mother told me, "Eat it, it will make you feel better." And, the worst part was that it did. So, added to the horror of seeing a dear pet bludgeoned and gutted, was the guilt of actual pleasure from the taste of its flesh. But, there is a very important difference between a pet and a food source shot in the woods or harvested from the farm, which was the only value my father had given my pet. The killing of my dear pet, my closest emotional anchor to sanity, was the last memory I have of Saigon before we left in 1972. My father's reasoning was that the rabbit would end up on some Viet's table, and so being the pragmatic person that he was, better that his family be fed than another.

Within a week of regressing myself through all those moments of my childhood in Saigon, I had identified the reasons for my emotional disconnection and PTSD-filtered previous 15 years. I made peace with those memories and with my father, both his actions on that day, and for taking my brother, my mother and me to such a place during such a war!

Some say, considering I spent 11 months in that prison, I could have easily gone through the same healing by the fact that it is a long time to be afforded introspection. That may be the case for someone who was already on the path of introspection, but I had gone there not to think about myself and my history, but to make a little of my own history and record that to others. I was truly on an outward adventure in the beginning, much like Richard Knight, the British treasure hunter. When I think of him, I think of him as though we were both part of an experiment in a lab called a prison: he was the *control*, who did not use hypnosis in any form, and I was the *test*.

The difference in results was amazingly profound, aside from Richard being in his late-'40s, and me being in my late teens: he was always crabby and self-pitying, to the point that even the interrogators despised him, and his suicidal tendencies continued throughout the time he was there. He never made any attempts whatsoever to make a physical escape. After the first beating, I never pitied myself nor contemplated suicide, and every opportunity I saw to escape, I tried, even after the beatings; and the relationship between my interrogators and me softened to the point that they no longer looked at me in anger as the "American Imperialist": We became almost like friends.

And even after our release, Knight went on to continue hating his parents, and was last seen trading stories for booze in an Amsterdam bar, still trying to swindle people into following him back to Vietnam and getting what he felt was more of Captain Kidd's treasure. In contrast, I went on to become the combat photojournalist and writer I had dreamed of becoming, refining my skills in hypnosis and healing skills to help rehabilitate substance abusers in the American Indian community, continuing into book authoring, seminars and success coaching, and never again holding any anger toward my father and family for Vietnam or anything else.

There Is an old saying that like attracts like. Later, from my experiences in Central America war zones, and in the wilds of Alaska on the path of native healers, I have learned that to be very much the case: the negotiating and persuasion skills of interrogation, sales and politics are based on this premise. Initially, with Richard Knight, the similarity between him and me was a need to escape and a long-standing resentment towards our respective parents. But, Knight did not take care of his anger and ignored my suggestions of learning self-hypnosis, or at least some form of meditation.

When I was released a few months later, because the demanded ransom of $10,000 had been paid by family, friends and donations sent in by some very thoughtful and kind people from around the US. I had a chance to meet and become friends with a number of American Vietnam veterans. The question they almost always asked was whether I had a compulsion to return to Vietnam, something that many of them would end up doing once Vietnam opened up its borders during the later part of the 1980s. My answer to them was, "My being in that prison was my first step on the path to healing myself!"

Biographies and Contact Information

Special Kudos and Thanks to Our Esteemed Contributors

(In alphabetical order)

Dr. Al Krasner

A.M. Krasner Ph.D. is the founder and director of the American Institute of Hypnotherapy in Irvine, California. An innovator in the hypnotherapy profession, Dr. Krasner began his private clinical practice in Rhode Island over 20 years ago. He moved to Southern California in the late 1970s where he developed his highly effective hypnotherapeutic methods. Dr. Krasner founded the A.I.H. in 1981, to teach his methods to others. Since then, he has taught thousands of students from all over the world to help other people, using his unique hypnosis techniques. Email address: drkrazner@prodigy.net

Dr. Alfred Barrios

Alfred A. Barrios (B.S. Caltech 1955 in chemistry; Ph.D. UCLA 1969 in psychology) is Director of the Self-Programmed Control. He is the inventor of the Stress Control Biofeedback Card. In 1996, he was nominated for the Norman Cousins Award in Mind-Body Medicine and received the Cancer Federation Award in Psychoneuroimmunology. He is the author of *Towards Greater Freedom & Happiness*; *The Habit Buster* and *The Stress Test*. The latter, rose to number two on the Times best-seller list. His theory of hypnosis was recently published in *Contemporary Hypnosis*. Web site: www.stresscards.com. SPC Center,
11949 Jefferson Blvd. #104; Culver City, CA 90230

Anne H. Spencer, Ph.D.

Anne H. Spencer-Beacham, Ph.D. Founder: International Medical and Dental Hypnotherapy Association®, a referral service for hypnotherapists and Infinity Institute International, Inc. a state licensed Hypnosis Training School in MI; author of books, tapes, CDs, videos and DVDs; internationally known speaker whose vision is: *A hypnotherapist in every health care facility worldwide and staffed by IMDHA members*. Hosts *Annual Hypnosis* and *Holistic Living Conference*; editor of newsletter *Subconsciously Speaking;* free email *Hypnosis and Holistic Living Journal* and a complete web site with on-line store.
Web site: www.infinityinst.com. Telephone: 248-549-5594.

Dr. Baruch Elitzur

Baruch Elitzur, Ph.D. is a licensed psychologist in private practice in Long Island, NY. He worked for more than ten years as Chief Psychologist with the Nassau County (NY) Family Court Clinic and in his native Israel as Director of the Behavioral Medicine unit of Tel Aviv Medical Center. Dr. Elitzur has published three books (in Hebrew) and many professional articles, on applying hypnosis, mental imagery and relaxation techniques, while treating emotional and physical symptoms. Email: baruch@Elitzur.com

Bill O'Connell

Bill O'Connell teaches hypnosis to students all over the world through his powerful audio and video home study courses. Many students have written thanking Bill for making the learning process easy and fun. In addition to his private practice in St. Charles, IL, Bill is the founder and president of Hypnosis Secrets, Inc. Web site: www.HypnosisSecrets.com Hypnosis Secrets, Inc. P.O. Box 3544 St. Charles, IL 60174. Tel.:630-452-6986

Brian David Phillips, Ph.D.

Brian David Phillips, Ph.D., CH, is an Associate Professor at a national university in Taipei, Taiwan. An American expatriate, Dr. Phillips has lived overseas since 1989. He lives in Mucha with his wife, daughter, three cats, and two hamsters. Email: phillips@nccu.edu.tw
Web site: http://phillips.personal.nccu.edu.tw/hypnosis/index.html

Bryan M. Knight, MSW, Ph.D.

Bryan M. Knight holds a degree in psychology from Sir George Williams University, a Master's in social work from McGill University and a doctorate in counseling from Columbia Pacific University for his dissertation, *Professional Love: the Hypnotic Power of Psychotherapy*. Dr. Knight is the author of numerous articles and several books, including *the People Paradox*; *Enjoying Single Parenthood*; *Love, Sex & Hypnosis: Secrets of Psychotherapy*; *Health and Happiness with Hypnosis.* Dr. Knight created The International Registry of Professional Hypnotherapists and The Global Directory of Hypnosis Training.
Email: drknight@hypnosis.org, Address: 7306 Sherbrooke Street West, Montreal, QC, Canada, H4B 1R7; Phone (514) 332-7902. www.hypnosis.org

Calvin Banyan M.A.

Calvin D. Banyan, as a B.S. and M.A. (Psychology), has worked as a psychologist at the North Dakota State Hospital and as family therapist at Lutheran Social Services. He is the C.E.O. of the Banyan Hypnosis Center for Training & Services, a Minnesota State Licensed School where he teaches hypnotherapy. He is the author of two books, one with Gerald F. Kein, *Hypnosis and Hypnotherapy: Basic to Advanced Techniques for the Professional*, and is the sole author of *The Secret Language of Feelings*. He writes a regular column in the National Guild of Hypnotists (NGH), *Journal of Hypnotism*, as well as having published in scientific and popular publications. He is a Board Certified Hypnotherapist and Certified Instructor with the NGH. His awards include, Certified Instructor of the Year and Educator of the Year. Contact office at (763) 785-3390 or (800) 965-3390. Web site: www.HypnosisCenter.com

Chuck Mignosa

Chuck Mignosa is a Certified Hypnotherapist, NLP Master Practitioner, Time Line Therapy and Reiki Master Sensei. He has lectured and performs around the world. Since 1976, he has worked with Ormond McGill both performing and lecturing. In addition, he is a frequent lecturer at colleges and universities. He teaches both the art and science of "Hypnosis, Illusion vs. Reality," and the "Magic of the Mind." Chuck is a member of the National Guild of Hypnotists, the Psychic Entertainers Association and the Academy of Magical Arts. Address: 4136 Sunston Drive, San Jose, CA. 95136 Web site: www.reiki.com;
Email: chuck@reiki.com

Craig Eubanks

Craig is a dynamic individual who is highly motivated to see his clients reach their maximum potential. A certified hypnotherapist and Master Practitioner of NLP, he applies the understandings of how the subconscious works with his coaching clients to help them develop what he refers to as the "Success Mind." Craig is the Founder and President of San Francisco Bay Area Hypnosis & NLP practice group, Co-founder and Director of Act Now International L.L.C., Success Coach, author, trainer, and business consultant.
ceubanks@actnowllc.com, www.ActNowLLC.com

Dr. Daniel Araoz

Dr. Daniel Araoz, Professor of Mental Health Counseling at the C. W. Post Campus of Long Island University in Nassau County, NY, is a Fellow of the American Psychological Association and the Society for Clinical and Experimental Hypnosis. He is a Diplomat of ABPP in Counseling Psychology and in Family Psychology, of AASECT in Sex Therapy and of ABPH in Clinical Hypnosis. He has written many articles in professional journals and 11 books, some translated into French, German, Italian, Spanish, Japanese and Chinese.
Contact: daniel.araoz@liu.edu

Dennis K. Chong & Jennifer Smith Chong MD, MPNLP, CH, RN, PHN

Dennis and Jennifer have shared a conjoint practice in hypnotherapy and psychotherapy for 24 years. Their practice has also been the basis for their research into the fields of human Epistemology, Ontology, Semantics and Linguistics. They have co-shared their findings with the community of their peers in the scan of papers in journals published in Canada, United States, Britain and Australia. They have also co-shared their discoveries in professional forums that have seen them present in Spain, Belgium, Britain, Italy, Australia, Malaysia, United States, Canada and Malaysia. They have published five books to date of which the first, *do not Ask WHY?!* is also published in Germany.
Address: 441, Inglehart Street, Oakville, Ontario, Canada, L6J 3J5; Tel: 905 844 0864. Fax: 905 844 3212; email: cjade_2000@yahoo.com www.neuro-semanticprogramming.com ; www.dennisandjenniferchong.com

Don Mottin

Don Mottin first became interested in hypnosis while stationed in Japan, serving in the United States Marine Corps in 1972. In 1976, Mottin joined the police department and began refining his hypnotic techniques in the field of criminal investigations. Mottin chose to leave the police department and concentrate on hypnotherapy, and teaching others how to use hypnosis. Mottin has gained an international reputation as one of the foremost experts in hypnosis today. Every major hypnosis organization has presented Don with awards for his unique teaching abilities. These include "Educator of the Year," "Instructor of the Year," and the prestigious "Ormond McGill Award," just to name a few. Don Mottin is the only hypnotherapy instructor to ever be named "Educator of the Year" three times. Don has been featured on the cover of the Journal of Hypnotism. He is the author of the book, *Raising Your Children with Hypnosis*.
Contact: Tel. 636-585-2209,
Email: dmottin@hotmait.com, Web site: www.donmottin.com

Frederick "Cork" Graham

Frederick "Cork" Graham was born in Port of Spain, Trinidad. Cork has lived and traveled extensively throughout Asia, and Latin America, first as a Third Culture Kid (TCK), and then as an award-winning journalist. Cork was a guest speaker on NBC, CBS, ABC, PBS and Good Morning America. He lectures on many subjects including Vietnam, political prisons, guerrilla warfare, post-traumatic stress, hypnotherapy and environmental issues. Cork is also the second American trained by the US Navy Seals at the Salvadoran Naval Special Forces School. www.corkgraham.com; email: cork@corkgrahamc.om
Address: 951 Old County Rd., #231, Belmont, CA 94002. Tel. (650) 654-1448

Gerald Kein

A graduate of Rollins College, Winter Park, Florida, Jerry holds a degree in education. He serves as Executive Director of the Florida Society of Professional Hypnotherapists. He is Vice President of Chapter 104 of the National Federation of Hypnotists and is active in legislative protection and creation around the country. He is also a contributing author to *The Journal of Hypnotism*, serves on the Advisory Board of the National Guild of Hypnotists and on the Certification Board of the National Guild of Hypnotists.

Gerald F. Kein is the director of the Omni Hypnosis Training Center in DeLand, Florida, where he maintains a highly successful hypnosis practice and professional training center. Having trained thousands of hypnotherapists nationally and internationally in over 30 countries, he is widely recognized as one of this country's leading instructors of clinical hypnotism.

Jerry had produced many highly acclaimed training programs available on video and cassettes. Jerry is the coauthor of the successful book *Hypnosis and Hypnotherapy*. Gerald Kein is respected around the world for his valuable contributions to the field of hypnotherapy. He received numerous awards, which he was all too modest to mention. Address: 830 N. Woodland Blvd. Deland, FL 32720 Web site: www.omnihypnosis.com Tel.: 1-800 226-5346 or (386) 738-9188. Email: omni@omnihypnosis.com

Henry Leo Bolduc

Henry Leo Bolduc has a remarkable 40 years of experience in the field of hypnotherapy. He is the author of five books, numerous audio cassettes and also more than 200 published articles. Henry's focus is on healing the present through past-live experience. He is a board-certified past-life therapist of the International Board for Regression Therapy. Henry is the recipient of the professional award of Fellow in Clinical Hypnotherapy by the National Board of Hypnotherapists. Web sites: http://www.henrybolduc.com
http://www.creativespirit.net/henrybolduc/

Jerry Valley

Jerry Valley has appeared all over the world as one of the finest entertainers in show business today. He has been the featured hypnotist on the QE2, Princess, Countess, Sagafjord and Oceanic cruise ships, appearing with Hollywood stars such as Norm Crosby, Steve Allen, Jane Meadows, Barbi Benton, Jim Bailey, Jack Jones, Vic Damone, The Platters, Robert Klein, Phyllis Diller and Robert Vaughan. Jerry has also been the guest star on many television shows such as "Good Day," "People Are Talking" and on ABC'S "20/20."

Jerry has received numerous awards including the prestigious President's Award presented to him by the National Guild of Hypnotists. The International Hypnosis Hall of Fame presented Jerry with the first-ever award for Excellence in Stage Hypnosis. In 1999, the National Guild of Hypnotists presented Jerry with the highest achievement in hypnosis, the Rexford L. North award. Contact Valley Hypnosis, 236 Pleasant St., Methuen, MA 01844, Tel.:1-800-418-9664, email: avitale934@aol.com, www.valleyhypnosis.com

Jillian Lavelle

Jillian R. LaVelle is a certified stress management consultant and a clinical hypnotherapist. She holds a BA in psychology from the University of South Florida. She is the CEO of the International Association of Counselors and Therapists (IACT). The Citizens' Ambassador Committee in the field of hypnotherapy appointed Jillian special Ambassador to China. In 1999, she was the recipient of the Outstanding Clinical Contribution award by the National Association of Transpersonal Hypnotherapists. In 2001, she was selected to receive the Counseling and Therapy Award of the Year by the International Hypnosis Federation. Tel: (239) 498-9710 email: iactnow@aol.com.

Joann Abrahamsen

Joann Abrahamsen, a certified consultant in hypnosis, was named in 1992, "Person of the Year" by the "Association to Advance Ethical Hypnosis" and received the 2002 President's Award. Joann is a certified instructor for the AAEH and the National Guild of Hypnotists. In her private practice, she has helped many people achieve their goals by combining her award-winning hypnotic techniques with behavior modification. Joann was interviewed on cable TV for her Great American Smoke-Out program conducted at a local hospital. Abrahamsen has written and published hypnosis booklets and self help articles that have appeared in magazines and newsletters. Email: joann4@optonline.net
Web site: www.joannabrahamsen.com; Phone: (914) 476-8131 Address: 9 the Crossway, Yonkers, NY 10701

Dr. Joe Vitale

Dr. Joe Vitale is the world's first hypnotic writer. He is President of Hypnotic Marketing, Inc., and author many books, including the #1 best-selling book *Spiritual Marketing*, the #1 best-selling e-book *Hypnotic Writing*, and the best-selling Nightingale-Conant audio program, *The Power of Outrageous Marketing*. His latest books include *The Greatest Money-Making Secret in History*! *Adventures Within* and *The E-Code*. He and Calvin Chipman created a software program to help you write sales letters, ads, news releases, speeches and even entire books. It is called *Hypnotic Writing Wizard*. Joe is considered one of the pioneers of Internet marketing. He has made millionaires and helped create online empires. Web site: http://www.mrfire.com
Email: hypnotic@mrfire.com

Larry Garrett

Larry Garrett is a Certified Hypnotist with the N.G.H. He has been in practice since 1968, operating the largest and most sophisticated hypnosis center in Chicago. He received the 1991 Metzinger Award (which has only been presented six times). He received many awards from the N.G.H. for outstanding contributions in hypnosis. For 29 years, Larry instructed hypnosis at Morton College and Wright College. He has lectured and demonstrated hypnosis at over 400 colleges, universities and high schools in over 30 states. He has trained Chicago area police departments in forensic hypnosis. He worked with corporations like Baxter Travenal, R.R. Donnelley, ADP, General Motors, Kodak, etc. He appeared on over three hundred radio and TV talk shows. Larry began using electronic methods of hypnosis in 1973. That enabled him to hypnotize an estimated 60,000 individuals. Larry authored the book, *Healing the Enemy*, which involves his travels to Iraq to hypnotize an infamous leader. His philosophy is that all can benefit form the uses of hypnosis when applied correctly for each individual. Garrett Hypnosis and Wellness Center. 3020 N. Kimball Avenue, Chicago, IL 60618 Tel. (773) 395-6100, fax (773) 645-7081. Web site: www.garrettwellnesscenter.com ; Email: Mesmer1@aol.com

Marilyn Gordon

Marilyn Gordon is a hypnotherapist, teacher, healer and author from Oakland CA. She is the director of the Center for Hypnotherapy Certification and the author of the book *Extraordinary Healing: Transforming Your Consciousness, Your Energy System, and Your Life*. You can contact her at 800-836-0477. Web site: www.hypnotherapycenter.com.

Marx Howell

Inspector Marx Howell is a veteran of the *Texas Department of Public Safety*, a graduate of the *FBI National Academy*, holds a BS degree in *Criminal Justice* and served in the *United States Marine Corp*. He was a state trooper in the Traffic Law Enforcement Division and promoted through the ranks to Captain in the *Criminal Law Enforcement Division* and then to Inspector. Marx is a T.C.L.O.S.E. approved *Law Enforcement Instructor*. Marx served on the board of Directors of the *International Society of Investigative Hypnosis*. He lectures and trains over 2,200 people annually, had trained Texas Rangers in *Basic and Advanced Forensic Hypnosis interviewing techniques* as well as in *Criminal Personality Profiling*. Web site: www.marxhowell.com

Mike De Bruyn

Mr. De Bruyn has been working in hypnosis work since 1961. He lives and works in the Metropolitan Washington, D.C. area and focuses primarily in the area of personal growth using hypnosis and NLP. His operating philosophy is that human potential is unlimited. Any person can achieve what others have accomplished - and more. This can be done through the intelligent application of well-tested change techniques such as NLP modeling and hypnosis. There is no reason to settle for less, "If you can dream it, you can do it." He can be reached on the web at HypnosisNLP@Softhome.net.

Ormond McGill

Ormond McGill is known as the "Dean of American Hypnotists. He has an international reputation for his books on hypnotism, meditation and mysticism. Prominent in the field of hypnotism for over 50 years, he is author of *The Encyclopedia of Genuine Stage Hypnotism; A Better Life Through Conscious Self-Hypnosis; The Art of Stage Hypnotism; Hypnotism and Meditation; Power Hypnosis Hypnotherapy* and his autobiography *The Secrets of Dr. Zomb: The autobiography of Ormond McGill.*
P.O.BOX 1103; PALO ALTO, CA 94302

Chaplain Paul G. Durbin, Ph.D.

Paul is a United Methodist Minister serving as Director of Clinical Hypnotherapy at Pendleton Memorial Methodist Hospital in New Orleans, LA. Making PMMH the first hospital in the USA, to have a Department of Clinical Hypnotherapy. He has been practicing hypnotherapy there since 1982. Chaplain Durbin has been a Chaplain at Methodist Hospital since 1976. Mr. Durbin is a retired Military Chaplain who last served as Army National Guard Special Assistant to the Chief of Chaplain, Army with rant of Brigadier General. Chaplain has had two books published: *Human Trinity Hypnotherapy* 1993. Access Publishing. Ann Arbor, MI. *Kissing Frogs: Practical Uses of Hypnotherapy* 1996 (second edition) 1998. Kendall/Hunt. Dubuque, IA. Email: pgdurbin@cox.net Web site: www.durbinhypnosis.com

Richard A. Neves, Ph.D.

Richard Neves Ph.D. is a versatile and experienced expert in indirect induction methods, having been in the field of hypnotherapy for 25+ years. Dr. Neves is a Certified NLP Trainer and a Certified Spiritual Counselor, with a rich background in holistic healthcare. Combining elements from many disciplines and modalities enables Dr. Neves to present a multifaceted approach to hypnotherapy. He is known as a conscientious, intuitive teacher who brings out the best in students and clients alike. Dr. Neves is the President of the American Board of Hypnotherapy. Email: doc7raneves@sbcglobal.net

Robert Otto

Robert Otto has worked in the field of Mind Dynamics for over 20 years, having conducted in excess of 4,500 workshops and seminars in 29 states. Mr. Otto serves as convention faculty staff for The IMDHA, NGH, IACT, ABH, NBH, MAHC, NCHS, IHF and ACHE. He is the recipient of numerous awards including the prestigious "Ormond McGill Award" for "Outstanding Faculty Member" in 1997 from the NGH. The 2002 'Therapist of the Year' award from the MAHC, the 1996 Sealah Award from IHHF.

Robert presently sits on the board of directors for the International Medical and Dental Hypnotherapy Association. In October 2001, Robert was awarded the title of "Diplomat" and in October 2002 was honored to receive the prestigious 'Pebble in the Pond' award by the IMDHA. In May 2003, Robert was awarded the "Innovative Therapy" award for his contribution of the "Vertigo" induction by the IACT.

Robert was a guest on many TV and radio shows. He has been featured in numerous newspapers and magazines, is a regular contributor to professional hypnosis journals and is the producer of numerous programs on behavior modification and human potential. As a pioneer in the profession, he is the first hypnotist to receive a Certificate of Special Congressional Recognition listed in the Library of Congress. The Institute of Dynamic Hypnosis, RR #2 Box 2468, Laceyville, PA 18623 Ph: (570) 869-1021, Fax: (570) 869-1249, Email: rfotto@epix.net; Web site: www.RobertOttoHypnosis.com

Roy Hunter

Roy Hunter was certified by the late Charles Tebbetts. He was inducted into the International Hypnosis Hall of Fame in 2000 for his written contributions to the hypnotherapy profession, and was also the recipient of Charles Tebbetts Award from the National Guild of Hypnotists in 2001 for spreading the light of hypnosis. Roy's two texts (based on the client-centered teachings of Charles Tebbetts) are recommended highly by many hypnosis schools around the world. Recipient of numerous professional awards, he was granted a Fellowship by the A.P.H.P. Web site: www.royhunter.com.

Steve Andreas M.A.

Steve Andreas has been learning, training, researching and developing NLP patterns for the last 26 years. He is the author of the recent book, *Transforming Your Self: Becoming who you want to be, Virginia Satir: The Patterns of Her Magic,* and an anthology, *Is There Life Before Death.* Steve is also co-author (with his wife, Connirae) of *Heart of the Mind* and *Change Your Mind--and Keep the Change.* He lives with his wife and three teenage sons in the foothills of the Rocky Mountains near Boulder, Colorado. 1221 Left Hand Canyon Dr. Boulder CO 80302 Email: andreas@qwest.net; Web site: www.SteveAndreas.com

Steve Boyley

Steve Boyley is an experienced Licensed Trainer of Neuro-Linguistic Programming and Hypnotherapy. While he lives in BC, Canada, he trains people worldwide and is a successful Trainer, Hypnotherapist, Consultant, Salesman and Entrepreneur. Steve Boyley has a passion for teaching you what works and has been teaching communication skills in sales and business since 1984. His experiences as Trainer, Hypnotherapist, Consultant, Salesman, Entrepreneur and Family Man, are the insights he brings to his training. After training with Steven Boyley, seminar delegates are able to organize information and perceptions in ways that allow them to achieve results that were once inconceivable. The Performance Institute of NLP; Web Site: www.NLPmind.com; US/Can Toll Free: 888-657-6463; 250-964-8676; 3240 McGill Cr, Prince George, BC, Canada.

Susan Fox

Susan Fox is an internationally known, accomplished and highly respected hypnotherapist, trainer and writer. She is certified by the Hypnotism Training Institute of Los Angeles. Susan writes a column called Hypnotherapy Scripting for the National Guild of Hypnotists, the world's largest professional hypnosis organization. Susan received the 1998 international Hypnosis Hall of Fame's Woman of The Year award. She was nominated to receive the 1998 Sealah Award and Induction into the International Hypnosis Hall of Fame. Contact information: Tel. (740) 398-1221, Email: hypnoresearcher@yahoo.com
Web Site: www.sleepwhilesomeoneelsesnores.com

Wendi Friesen

Wendi Friesen is a Certified Clinical Hypnotherapist, NLP practitioner and Master Hypnotist since 1995. She is a popular, international speaker for trainings, conventions and shows. In 2002, she was chosen as a speaker at the NGH Solid Gold Convention, which honors the top six award winning NGH speakers in the country. Wendi has appeared on many local and national TV and radio shows. Some of her appearances include "The Man Show" on Comedy Central, "Queen Latifah Show," "Good Day Sacramento," *Washington Post*, *GQ* magazine, *Channels Magazine*, *Men's Health*, "Mike Gallagher Show," "Darian O'Toole Show," First for Women, Salon.com magazine, *Health and Fitness*, *Score Magazine*, Talk America and more. Wendi is the author of the book *Hypnotize Your Lover*. Her expertise was used by Market Makers on the Pacific Stock Exchange, Chancellor Media and by a Minister of Foreign Affairs to name just a few. Address: 1216 Suncast Lane #2, Eldorado Hill, California USA 95762, Tel: 916 933 0700, Web site: www.wendi.com

National Guild of Hypnotists

P.O. Box 308, Merrimack, NH 03054, USA www.ngh.net Tel. (603) 429-9438

CHAPTER 10:
APPENDICES, BIBLIOGRAPHY, GLOSSARY & INDEX

Appendices

Appendix 1:
Sample Client's Bill of Rights

Italicized sections are instructions to the writer to show where the document should be personalized.

Contact Information: My name is *(give the name.)* I can be contacted through my office *(list your address)* or by telephone at *(give your business telephone number).*

Education and Training: I was trained in hypnotism *(or "hypnotherapy")* at *(List the name of your school or training program; if the school was state-approved, say so.).* I am a Certified Member of the National Guild of Hypnotists and I do annual continuing education to maintain my training at a high level. The National Guild of Hypnotists is the oldest and largest hypnotism organization in the world and its certification is the most widely recognized credential for the professional practice of the hypnotic arts. Here you would list your degree if you mention a higher degree when offering services to the public. If your degree is accredited, say, "My highest degree is in [*state field of study]* and is accredited by an agency recognized by the United States Department of Education." If your degree is an alternative degree, say, "My degree in [*state the field of study]* is an alternative degree earned through intensive distance learning."

Notice: AS THE STATE OF *(State name)* HAS NOT ADOPTED EDUCATIONAL AND TRAINING STANDARDS FOR THE PRACTICE OF HYPNOTISM, THIS STATEMENT OF CREDENTIALS IS FOR INFORMATIONAL PURPOSES ONLY. Hypnotism is a self-regulating profession and its practitioners are not licensed by state governments. I am neither a physician nor a licensed health care provider and may not provide a medical diagnosis nor recommend discontinuance of medically prescribed treatments. If a client desires a diagnosis or any other type of treatment from a different practitioner, the client may seek such services at any time. In the event my services are terminated by a client, the client has a right to coordinated transfer of services to another practitioner. A client has a right to refuse hypnotism services at any time. A client has a right to be free of physical, verbal or sexual abuse. A client has a right to know the expected duration of sessions, and may assert any right without retaliation. *(This section should be in bold print with the first sentence in capitals, as shown.)*

Redress: I am a certified member of the National Guild of Hypnotists, and practice in accordance with its Code of Ethics and Standards. If you have a complaint about my services or behavior that I cannot resolve for you personally, you may contact the National Guild of Hypnotists at P.O. Box 308, Merrimack, NH 03054-0308, (603) 429-9438, to seek redress. Other services than my own may be available to you in the community. You may locate such providers in the telephone book.

Fees: The charge for my services are *(list fees).* You will be given *(state number)* days notice of any change in fees. *(You can also list here any other business policies you have that concern fees, such as a cancellation charge, whether you take insurance or credit cards, etc.)*

Date: *(enter current date).*

Confidentiality: I will not release any information to anyone without a written authorization from you, except as provided for by law. You have a right to be allowed access to my written record about you.

Insurance: I suggest you think of my services as something that you will pay for personally. That will both protect your privacy and help you value the work you are doing more. In general, insurance companies do not like to cover hypnotic services, and I caution you not to expect them to do so.

My Approach: *(Write a brief paragraph here that explains your theory of why hypnotism is effective and about how you use it. Be sure that what you actually do with a client is a good match for what you say here. However, keep this section broad and general. It should be more a statement of your overall philosophy than a list of specific techniques.)*

Client Signature: I have received and read this Client Bill of Rights and understand what I have read.

Client Name (print): ____

Client Signature: ____

Appendix 2:

BreakThrough Institute Inc.

(Your address, phone, email)

Assessment interview and consent form

Please complete this form as clearly and completely as possible. All information is strictly confidential.

Date____________

Name: ____ Age: ____ Sex: F M

Address: ____________________________________ City: ______________ ST____
Zip: ______

Phone: Home (_____) __________ Work (_____) _________ Email: ___________

Marital Status: Single, Married, Divorced, Separated.
Children - How many? ____ Living Parents? ______

Have you had previous experiences with therapy or consultation? (Describe)

____

Are you currently under Psychiatric or Medical treatment? Y N (Describe)

____

Have you had prolonged illnesses or major medical treatments? (Describe)

____

Informed Consent:

Zalman Segal BCH, CI is a personal coach and trainer of life mastery. Mr. Segal acts as a consultant and a guide to personal growth, behavior modification and self-fulfillment. Mr. Segal has extensive life experience and training in Hypnosis and Neuro Linguistic Programming (NLP). Mr. Segal does not provide mental health services.

I have read the above disclaimer. I am aware that Mr. Segal's consultation services are intended to be educational in nature and do not constitute Psychological treatment or Psychotherapy.

I also agree to maintain my scheduled meetings. If I make any changes or cancellations with less than 48 hours prior notice, I will pay one-half of the fees due for the amount of time scheduled.

What do you want to accomplish in this session?

____

____

____

How would you know that you have accomplished that? (Be specific)

____

____

____

Have you been hypnotized before? Y N Did you ever see a hypnosis demonstration? Y N

How did you hear about us? (Referred by): ______________________________

Address: ____

Comments:

____

____

____

____

____

____

____

____

Full name: ____

Signature: ________________________ Date: ______________

Fee: $ ________

Appendix 3:

BreakThrough Institute

Hypnosis@BreakThroughInstitute.com

Parental Consent form

Date: ___________________

This is to advise that I (Print Name) ______________________ am the parent and/or the legal guardian of the minor
(Print Name) ____
I, hereby, authorize The BreakThrough Institute to conduct Hypnotherapy sessions with said minor. I understand that Hypnotherapy is not an exact science and that the results attained from these sessions vary widely and depend on the individual.
Thus BreakThrough Institute does not guarantee the results of these sessions.

Name: ____

Address: ____

Phone: ____________________________

Appendix 4:

BreakThrough Institute

Hypnosis@BreakThroughInstitute.com

Medical Referral Form

Dear Mr. /Ms. ____

Your patient Mr. /Ms. ____________ wishes to undergo hypnotic conditioning and suggestions, for the purpose of helping him/her cope with issues that bother him/her, as well as improvement of his/her general well-being. In the interest of the welfare of Mr. /Ms ______________________________________

I require a referral from the current primary caretaker. I would appreciate your signature indicating your approval and your comments if any.

Please be advised that I shall keep you informed as to your patient's progress.

Sincerely,

Zalman Segal, Board Certified Clinical Hypnotherapist

Physician use only

Name: ____

Address: ____

Phone: ___________________

I see no indication that the use of hypnosis with Mr. /Ms. __________________ is counterproductive to his present course of treatment. I have these additional comments and suggestions:

____

____

____

Name: ________________________________ *Date:* ___________

Signature: ___________________

Please fax this form to me: (___) _____-_______ and have your patient deliver this copy.

Appendix 5:

Le Cron-Bordeaux Scoring System For Indicating Depth of Hypnosis

The Le Crone-Bordeaux scale is similar to the Davis-Husband scale. It is divided into six divisions rather than five. Two points are given for each symptom exhibited and the total score indicates the depth level. From 14 to 36 points indicates a light state of hypnosis; 38 to 54 a medium state; 56 or more a deep, somnambulistic state.

Depth	Score	Symptoms and Phenomena Exhibited
Insusceptible	0	Subject fails to react in any way
Hypniodal	1	Physical relaxation
	2	Drowsiness apparent
	3	Fluttering of eyelids
	4	Closing of eyes
	5	Mental relaxation, partial lethargy of mind
	6	Heaviness of limbs
	7	Catalepsy of eyes
	8	Partial limb catalepsy
	9	Inhibition of small muscle groups
	10	Slower and deeper breathing, slower pulse
	11	strong lassitude (disinclination to move, speak, think or act)
	12	Twitching of mouth or jaw during induction
	13	Rapport between subject and operator
	14	Simple posthypnotic suggestions heeded
	15	Involuntary start or eye twitch on awakening
	16	Personality changes
	17	Feeling of heaviness throughout entire body
	18	Partial feeling of detachment.
Medium Trance	19	Recognition of trance (difficult to describe but definitely felt)
	20	Complete muscular inhibitions (kinesthetic delusions)
	21	Partial amnesia
	22	Glove anesthesia
	23	Tactile illusions
	24	Gustatory illusions
	25	Olfactory illusions
	26	Hyperactivity to atmospheric conditions
	27	Complete catalepsy of limbs or body
Somnambulism	28	Ability to open eyes without affecting trance
	29	Fixed stare when eyes are open; pupilary dilation
	30	Somnambulism
	31	Complete amnesia

	32	Systematized posthypnotic amnesia
	33	Complete anesthesia
	34	Posthypnotic anesthesia
	35	Bizarre posthypnotic suggestions heeded
	36	Uncontrolled movements of eyeballs-eye coordination lost
	37	Sensation of lightness, floating, swinging, of being bloated or swollen, detached feeling
	38	Rigidity and lag in muscular movements and reactions
	39	Fading and increase in cycles of the sound of operator's voice (radio station fading in and out)
	40	Control of organic body functions, (Heartbeat, blood pressure, digestion, etc.)
	41	Recall of lost memories (Hypermnesia)
	42	Age regression
	43	Positive visual hallucinations; posthypnotic
	44	Negative visual hallucinations; posthypnotic
	45	Post auditory hallucinations; posthypnotic
	46	Negative auditory hallucinations; posthypnotic
	47	Stimulation of dreams (in trance or posthypnotic in natural sleep
	48	Hyperesthesia
	49	Color sensations experienced
Plenary Trance	50	Stuporous condition in which all spontaneous activity is inhibited. Somnambulism can be developed by suggestion to that effect.

Appendix 6:

Davis and Husband Susceptibility System

In 1931, L.W. Davis and R.W. Husband worked out a point scoring system, which is included here because it is still often referred to in hypnosis literature.

Depth	Score	Objective Symptoms
Unsusceptible	0	
Hypniodal	2	Relaxation
	3	Fluttering of lids
	4	Closing of eyes
	5	Complete physical relaxation
Light trance	6	Catalepsy of eyes
	7	Limb catalepsies
	10	Rigid catalepsy
	11	Anesthesia (glove)
Medium Trance	13	Partial Amnesia
	15	Posthypnotic anesthesia
	17	Personality changes
	18	Simple posthypnotic suggestions
	20	Kinesthetic delusions; complete amnesia
Somnambulism	21	Ability to open eyes without affecting trance
	23	Bizarre posthypnotic suggestions
	25	Complete somnambulism
	26	Positive visual hallucinations, post-hypnotic
	27	Positive auditory hallucinations, post-hypnotic
	28	Systematized posthypnotic amnesias
	29	Negative auditory hallucinations
	30	Negative visual hallucinations; hyperesthesias

The Code of Ethics and Standards of Practice

The National Guild of Hypnotists advocates a system of voluntary self-regulation that will protect your right to practice and help hypnotherapy become recognized as a separate and distinct profession.

Appendix 7: The Code of Ethics of the National Guild of Hypnotists

The National Guild of Hypnotists requires its members to conform to the following ethical principles, and shall hold members accountable for any departure from these principles.

A. Client Welfare: Members shall make the physical and mental well-being of each client a prime consideration.

B. Client Safety: Members shall not engage in verbal, physical or sexual abuse of any client.

C. Practice Limits: Members shall use hypnotism strictly within the limits of their training and competence and in conformity to the laws of their state.

D. Advertising: Members shall be truthful in their advertising.

E. Referred Practice: Members shall engage in hypnotic work with a client regarding a medical or mental disease only on written referral from an appropriately licensed medical or mental health professional, except when otherwise provided for by state law.

F. Reasonable Practice: Members shall withhold non-referred hypnotic services if a client's behavior, appearance or statements would lead a reasonable person to believe that the client should be evaluated by a licensed health care professional. Members shall provide services to such clients only after evaluation and with the approval of the licensed health care professional.

G. Colleagues: Members shall treat hypnotist colleagues without public defamation.

Appendix 8:

Recommended Standards for the Practice of Hypnotism

The National Guild of Hypnotists advocates the following standards for the professional practice of hypnotism. Except for members living in states where different practice standards are explicitly set by law, we urge our members to voluntarily conform to these standards.

Record Keeping: Members shall establish and maintain proper records necessary to a professional practice.

Scope of Practice: Members shall use hypnotism with clients to motivate them to eliminate negative or unwanted habits, facilitate the learning process, improve memory and concentration, develop self-confidence, eliminate stage fright, improve athletic abilities, and for other social, educational and cultural endeavors of a non-medical nature. Except where state law provides otherwise, members shall use hypnotism with clients regarding a medical or mental disease only on written referral from a licensed medical or mental health professional.

Titles of Practice: Members shall hold their hypnotism services out to the public using only those titles earned and approved by the National Guild of Hypnotists: Certified Hypnotist or Certified Hypnotherapist Certified Instructor, Board Certified Hypnotist or Board Certified Hypnotherapist, Fellow of the National Guild of Hypnotists, or Diplomat of the National Guild of Hypnotists, or titles protected by state law (State of NJ: HypnoCounselor).

Disclosure: Members shall truthfully disclose in writing to each client, using a Client Bill of Rights or similar written document, the nature and venue of the member's hypnotism training, the field of study of any higher degree used when holding services out to the public, the lawful limits of the member's practice of hypnotism, the practitioner's theoretical orientation or model, instructions for contacting the National Guild of Hypnotists should the client seek redress, and any business policies and practices maintained by the practitioner. Members holding advanced degrees from institutions that do not hold accreditation recognized by the United States Department of Education shall disclose to clients that the degree is alternative rather than academic. Members shall restrict the services described on this document to hypnotism.

Terminology: Unless qualified to do so by another credential, members shall avoid using the language of psychopathology or medicine when working with clients, except on referral from a licensed medical or mental health professional.

Public Hypnotism: Demonstrational hypnotism shall always be presented in a tasteful manner, which is considerate of the individuals who have volunteered to participate in a public demonstration. Individuals participating in such demonstrations shall be treated with courtesy and respect.

Age-regression and Forensic Hypnotism: Age-regression and forensic hypnotism shall be used only by those who have had additional training in these specific fields of study.

Imagery: Frightening, shocking, obscene, inappropriately sexually suggestive, degrading or humiliating imagery shall never be used with a hypnotized client.

Claims: Members shall not disseminate false or exaggerated claims regarding hypnotism, but shall attempt whenever possible to inform and educate the public with a true perspective of hypnotism. Members shall make only those specific claims for the effectiveness of hypnotism as can be justified by outcomes data. Members shall publicly maintain a professional demeanor toward other professions expressing divergent views on hypnotism.

Advertising: All advertising shall be factually presented in a professional and ethical way consistent with accepted standards. Members shall advertise services and capabilities as hypnotists in conjunction with other specialties, occupations, vocations, arts or professions only if duly trained, properly qualified and professionally recognized in those fields.

Education: Schools of instruction now existing and those to be established in the future shall provide a full curriculum consisting of the theory, practice and applications of hypnotism, instruction and supervised practice in hypnotic methodology, the possibilities and limitations of hypnotism, with thorough instruction on the Ethics and Standards of our profession as set forth herein. All curricula used at schools recognized by the National Guild of Hypnotists shall be approved by the National Guild of Hypnotists. Instructors at such schools are expected to be approved and certified by the National Guild of Hypnotists or to hold credentials judged by the Guild as equivalent.

Good Standing: Members, who maintain the required number of continuing-education hours, are of high moral character, conduct themselves and their practice of hypnotism in a professional and ethical manner and meet their financial dues obligation shall be considered as members in good standing of the National Guild of Hypnotists.

Recommendations: When a member recommends a client consult a colleague or health care professional, the member shall, whenever possible, provide the client with a list of more than one recommended name.

The Code of Ethics, the *Standards for the Practice of Hypnotism* and the *Client Bill of Rights* are reprinted courtesy of the National Guild of hypnotists.
For contact information log onto their web site www.NGH.net
Phone # (603) 429-9438 Address P.O. Box 308 Merrimack, NH 03054-0308

Select Bibliography

Many of the books listed here have gone through several editions. In each case, the date is that of the latest available edition. Some of the older ones are out of print, but well worth searching for. Try bookstores that specialize in older titles and in books related to hypnotism.

Al Krasner, A.M., *The Wizard Within.*

Anderson, S. and Rolhfs, A. *The Anderson Handbook for Hypnotherapists.*

Ansari, M., *Modern Hypnosis: Theory and Practice.*

Anthony Robbins: *Unlimited Power*.

Araoz, D.L., Edelstien, MG. and Zilbergeld, B., *Hypnosis Questions and Answers.*

Arons, H. (1961) *Master Course in Hypnotism*, So. Orange, NJ: Power Publishers.

Arons, H. (1977) *Hypnosis in Criminal Investigation*, So. Orange, NJ: Power Publishers.

Barnett, E.A., *Analytical Hypnotherapy*: Principles and Practice.

Bandler, R. and Grinder, 1. (1979) *Frogs Into Princes,* Moab, UT: Real People Press.

Barber, J and Adrian, C. (1982) *Psychological Approaches to the Management of Pain,* NY: Brunner/Mazel.

Beigel, H.G. (1980) *Hypnosis in Sex Therapy,* Springfield, IL: Charles C. Thomas.

Benson, H. (1976) *The Relaxation Response*, NY: Avon Books.

Bernheim, H. (1993) Hypnosis and Suggestion in Psychotherapy, 1886. Reprint. NY: Jason Aronson.

Bowers, K.S. (1976). *Hypnosis for the seriously curious.* Monterey, Ca. Brooks/Cole.

Braid, (1960) *Braid on Hypnotism-The beginnings of Modern Hypnosis*, NY: Julian Press.

Bramwell. J.M. (1956) *Hypnotism: Its History, Practice and Theory*, London: Grant Richards, 1903. Reissued, NY: Julian Press

Calvin Banyan & Gerald Kein (2003): *Hypnosis and Hypnotherapy.*

Calvin Banyan (2003): *The Secret Language of Feelings.*

Carol & Steve Lankton: *The Answer Within.*

Charles Baudouin*: Suggestion and auto Suggestion.*

Cheek, D.B. and LeCron, L.M. (1968) *Clinical Hypnotherapy,* NY: Grime & Stratton.

Cooper, L.M. and Erickson, M.H. (1954) *Time Distortion in Hypnosis*, Baltimore: Williams and Wilkins.

Covino, N., & Frankel, F.H. (1993). *Hypnosis and relaxation in the medically ill. Psychotherapy & Psychosomatics*, 60, 75-90.

Crasilneck, HOB. and Hall, L.A. (1985) *Clinical Hypnosis: Principles and Applications* NY: Grime & Stratton.

David L. Calof: *The Couple Who Became Each Other.*

David Gordon: *Therapeutic Metaphors.*

Dennis & Jennifer Chong (1994): The Knife Without Pain.

Edmonston, W.E., Jr. (1981*) Hypnosis and Relaxation: Modern Verification of an Old Equation,* NY: John Wiley

Elman, David. *Hypnotherapy.*

Ellenberger, H.F. (1970) *The Discovery of the Unconscious: The History and Evolution of Dynamic Psychiatry*, NY.
Erickson, M.H. and Rossi, E.L. (1977) *Experiencing Hypnosis: Therapeutic Approaches to Altered States*, NY: Irvington Publishers.
Erickson, M.H., Hershman, S. and Secter, 1.1. (1990) *The Practical Application of Medical and Dental Hypnosis*, NY: Brunner/Mazel.
Erickson: *The Phoenix.*
Erickson, Rossi: *Hypnosis Reality.*
Erickson: *Healing in Hypnosis.*
Erickson/ Rossi*: Hypnotic Realities.*
Erickson! Rossi*: Hypnotherapy.*
Estabrooks, G.H.: (1951*) Hypnotism,* NY: E.P. Dutton.
Francis, C. and Hughes, J.C.: *Hypnotherapy Scripts and Tips.*
Francis, C.: *Counseling Hypnotherapy: Synergism of Psychotherapy and Hypnotherapy.*
Fromm, E. and Kahn, S. (1990): *Self-Hypnosis:* The Chicago Paradigm, NY: Guilford.
Fromm, E., & Nash, M.R. (Eds.) (1992): *Contemporary hypnosis research.* New York: Guilford.
Gauld, A. (1992): *A history of hypnotism.* Cambridge, U.K.: Cambridge University Press.
Hadley, J. and Staudacher, C.: *Hypnosis for Change: A Practical Manual of Techniques.*
Hartland, J. (1984) *Medical & Dental Hypnosis & Its Clinical Applications*, London: Baillière Tindall.
Hilgard, E.R. (1965*): Hypnotic Susceptibilty*, NY: Harcourt, Brace and World
Hilgard, E.R. (1968): *The Experience of Hypnosis*, NY: Harcourt, Brace and World
Hilgard, E.R. and Hilgard, (1994): *Hypnosis in the Relief of Pain*, NY: Brunner/Mazel.
Hilgard, J. R.: (1979) *Personality and Hypnosis: A Study of Imaginative Involvement*, Chicago and London: The University of Chicago Press.
Hilgard, E.R. (1977). *Divided consciousness: Multiple controls in human thought and action.* New York: Wiley-Interscience.
Hughes, J.C.: *How to Do Breast Enlargement with Hypnosis (Includes Tape)*
Hughes, J.C.: *How to Present Like a Pro*
Hughes, J.C.: *Hypnosis: The Induction of Conviction*
Hull, C.L. (1968): *Hypnosis and Suggestibil4y: An Experimental Approach*, 1933 Reprint NY: Appleton-Century-Crofts.
Jacobson, E. (1962): *You Must Relax,* NY: McGraw-Hill.
Janet, P. (1925): *Psychological Healing, Volume 1.* NY: Macmillan.
Jay Haley: *Uncommon Therapies, The Collected Papers of Milton H. Erickson.*
Jerry Valley (1998): *Inside Secretes of Stage Hypnotism.*
John Kappas, J.G.: *Professional Hypnotism Manual.*
John J. Emerick, Jr.: *Be the Person You Want to Be;* 1997.
Kirsch, I., Montgomery, G., & Sapirstein, G. (1995): *Hypnosis as an adjunct to cognitive-behavioral psychotherapy*: A meta-analysis. *Journal of Consulting & Clinical Psychology*, 63, 214-220.
Kline, M.V: (1950*) Freud and Hypnosis*, NY: Julian Press

Kroger, W. S.: (1977) *Clinical and Experimental Hypnosis in Medicine and, Dentistry.*
Kroger, W. S. and Fezler, W.D. (1976): *Hypnosis and Behavior Modification: Imagery* J.B.
Laurence, J.R. and Perry, C.*: Hypnosis, Will and Memory: A Psycho-Legal History.*
LeCron, L.M. and Bordeaux, 1. (1949*): Hypnotism Today*, NY: Grime & Stratton.
Leslie Cameron-Bandler: Solutions.
Linden, W.: *Autogenic Training: A Clinical Guide.*
Lippincott Co.: *Conditioning*, Philadelphia:
Lynn, S.J., & Rhue, J.W. (Eds.) (1991): *Theories of hypnosis: Current models and perspectives.* New York: Guilford.
Marcuse, F.L. (1976*): Hypnosis—Fact and Fiction*, NY: Penguin Books.
Moll, A. (1958): *The Study of Hypnosis*, 1899 Reprint. NY: Julian Press.
Moss, A.A. (1952*): Hypnodontics: Hypnosis in Dentistry*, NY.
McGill, 0rmond: *Hypnotism and Mysticism in India.*
Mongan, M.F.: *HypnoBirthing: A Celebration of Life.*
O'Hanlon & Michael Martin: *Solution-Oriented Hypnosis.*
O'Hanlon & Hexum*: An Uncommon Casebook*.
O'Hanlon: Taproots.
Olness, K., & Gardner, G.G. (1988): Hypnosis and hypnotherapy with children.
Oppenheim, G.*: Who Were You Before You Were You? Past-Life Therapist Casebook.*
Pratt, G.J., Wood, D.P. and Alman, B.M. (1988): *A Clinical Hypnosis Primer*, NY: John Wiley & Sons.
Rhue, J.W., Lynn, S.J., & Kirsch, I. (Eds.) (1993): *Handbook of clinical hypnosis.* Washington, D.C.: American Psychological Association.
Richard Bandler: *Using Your Brain—for a CHANGE*, 1984.
Richard Bandler and John Grinder: *Frogs into Princes*, 1979.
Richard Bandler and John Grinder: *Patterns of the Hypnotic Techniques of Milton H. Erickson, Vol I.*
Richard Bandler and John Grinder: *TRANCE-formations*, 1980.
Ronald Havens & Catherine Walters: *Hypnotherapy Scripts.*
Rosen, S. (1982*): My Voice Will Go With You: The Teaching Tales of Milton H. Erickson*, NY: Norton.
Rossi, E.L. and Cheek, D.B. (1988): *Mind-Body Therapy: Methods of Ideodynamic Healing in Hypnosis*, NY: W.W. Norton & Co.
Rossi & Ryan: *Mind-Body Communication in Hypnosis*,
Salter, A. (1973): *What is Hypnosis?* NY: Farrar, Straus & Giroux.
Sanders, S. (1991) Clinical Self-Hypnosis: *The Power of Words and images*, NY: Guilford Press.
Scheflin, A.W. and Shapiro, J.L.: *Trance on Trial*
Simonton, O.C. and Matthews-Simonton, S. (1984): *Getting Well Again*, NY: Bantam Books.
Simpkins, C.A. and Simpkins, A.M. (1991): *Principles of Self-Hypnosis: Pathways to the Unconscious*, NY: Irvington Publishers.
Sheehan, P.W., & Perry, C.W. (1976): *Methodologies of hypnosis: A critical appraisal of contemporary paradigms of hypnosis.* Hillsdale, N.J.: Erlbaum.

Spiegel, H. and Spiegel, D: *Trance and Treatment: Clinical Uses of Hypnosis*, NY: Basic Books
Steven Heller: *Monsters and Magical Sticks*,
Stephen Gilligan: *Therapeutic Trances*,
Stephen Parkhill: *Answer Cancer.*
Stephen Wolinsky: *Trances People Live*,
Stephen Wolinsky: *The Dark Side of the Inner Child*
Tebbets, C.: *Self-Hypnosis and Other Mind-expanding Techniques*
Van Pelt, 5.1. Ambrose, G. and Newbold, G. (1957): *Medical Hypnosis Handbook*, Hollywood: Wilshire Book Co.
Weitzenhoffer, A.M. (1953) Hypnotism: An Objective Study in Suggestibility, NY: John Wiley
Weitzenhoffer, A.M. (1957): *General Techniques of Hypnotism*, NY: Grime & Stratton Weitzenhoffe, A.M. (1989): *The Practice of Hypnotism, Vol 1-2*,
Wolberg, L. M. (1948): *Medical Hypnosis, Volume 1*, The Principles of Hypnotherapy, NY: Grune & Stratton
Wright, M.E. and Wright, B. (1987): *Clinical Practice of Hypnotherapy*, NY: Guilford Press
Yapko, M.D. (1992): *Hypnosis and the Treatment of Depressions*, NY: Brunner/Mazel
Yapko, M.D. (1994): *Essentials of Hypnosis*, NY: Brunner/Mazel
Zahourek, R. (1990): *Clinical Hypnosis in Patient Care,* NY: Brunner/Mazel
Zeig, J.K. (Ed.) (1981) A Teaching Seminar with Milton Erickson, NY: Brunner/Mazel
Zeig: *Experiencing Erickson*

Glossary

ABREACTION: The act of reviving the memory of a repressed disagreeable experience and giving expression in speech and action to the emotions related to it, thereby relieving the individual of its influence.

AFFECT BRIDGE: A technique by which significant memories are recovered by inducing an intense emotional state in a client and asking him or her to remember a past instance when he or she felt the same way.

AGE PROGRESSION: Simulated time orientation. The hypnotic subject hallucinates living in the future while retaining his or her chronological age.

AGE REGRESSION: In age regression, the subject plays role acting out past events the framework of the present. A re-experiencing of earlier events in life, usually limited to a specific time or time period.

AMNESIA: Loss of memory; inability to recall. It may result from organic or functional causes and may be generalized or for a circumscribed period of time. Lu retrograde amnesia there is a loss of memory for events over a period of time prior to a trauma, as in the case of cerebral concussion. Hypnotic amnesia is always a reversible forgetting. It may occur spontaneously or be suggested, and may be partial or total.

ANALGESIA: The loss of reduction of pain sensation without the loss of consciousness. When analgesia is produced in hypnosis, it is called hypnoanalgesia. If used to decrease pain, hypnoanalgesia can be retained by posthypnotic suggestions.

ANESTHESIA: The loss of all sensory modalities. An agent that causes insensitivity to pain. In chemically induced anesthesia, there are two types: general, which produces unconsciousness; and local, which causes a specific area of the body to be insensitive to pain. In the context of hypnosis, this is called hypnoanesthesia, and is used in major surgical and dental procedures.

ANOREXIA NERVOSA: A life-threatening psychoneurotic symptom in which the client, usually a young woman, diets to the point of emaciation. As a rule, the anorexic has a loss of appetite with a loathing for food.

APPROACH: System of operation or way of working, characteristic modus operandi.

AUTHORITARIAN: The approach of hypnotic suggestion that is commanding and forceful in nature. A suggestion that conveys it is being imposed by the hypnotist.

AUTOHYPNOSIS: This term is synonymous with self-hypnosis.

AUTOSUGGESTION: Self-suggestions; refers to suggestions made by the subject to oneself.

BULIMIA: The bulimic has an insatiable appetite for food. Bulimia is a psychoneurotic disturbance resulting in a morbid increase of appetite whereby the individual wishes to eat constantly.

CATALEPSY: Temporary paralysis. A condition characterized by a rigidity of the skeletal muscles. May be accompanied by waxy flexibility in which the limbs of a cataleptic individual remain in almost any position they are placed, as though made of molded wax. The medical term for this phenomenon is Cerea Flexibilitas.

CLINICAL HYPNOSIS: Hypnosis used in a therapeutic context.

CONSCIOUS: Awareness; alertness; referring to the state of being subjectively aware. That which is known and experienced. The left hemispheric function, which maintains an interpretative contact of the individual with the environment.

DELUSION: An irrational belief tenaciously held in spite of all evidence to the contrary.

DISSOCIATION: The inherent ability of the hypnotized subject to become detached from the immediate environment. The subject can step out of himself, as it were, just as if her were viewing his body from another part of the room. Also, the dividing up of the psyche into two or more parts functioning independently at the same time (e.g., automatic writing).

ENDORPHINS: Any of several peptides secreted in the brain that have a pain-relieving effect like that of morphine. These analgesic chemicals are naturally produced by the body.

FORENSIC HYPNOSIS: Legal application of hypnosis.

FRACTIONATION: A procedure for deepening hypnosis by repeatedly hypnotizing and dehypnotizing a subject.

GLOVE ANESTHESIA: A hypnotically suggested anesthesia in the area of a hand normally covered by a glove. The hand is made insensitive to stimuli in a circumscribed area from the fingertips to the wrist. A condition that is Neuro-anatomically impossible.

HETEROHYPNOSIS: Hypnosis induced by a hypnotist.

HYPERMNESIA: Memory recall with retrieval of forgotten information. The brain stores everything, forgets nothing and most memories can be recovered when the proper association pathways are stimulated.

HYPERESTHESIA: Heightened sensibility to touch.

HYPER SUGGESTIBILITY: The capacity to respond to suggestions above a norm. The subject who is readily influenced and achieves a profound level of hypnosis is said to be hyper suggestible.

HYPNAGOGIC: The state intermediate between wakefulness and sleep.

HYPNOANALYSIS: The use of hypnosis in combination with psychoanalytic techniques.

HYPNOIDAL: Resembling hypnosis. When the term Hypniodal is used in the context of hypnotic susceptibility, it designates the lightest degree of hypnosis.

HYPNOSIS: An altered state of consciousness characterized by hyper suggestibility. It is a trance-like state psychically induced, usually by another person, in which the subject responds to the suggestions of the hypnotist.

HYPNOTHERAPY: Any therapy in which the use of hypnosis constitutes the core of the treatment.

HYPNOTIC: Pertaining to or associated with hypnotism.

HYPNOTISM: The study and use of suggestion. The science of hypnosis.

HYPNOTIZABILITY: Refers to suggestibility or individual susceptibility to hypnosis.

HYPNOTIC SUSCEPTIBILITY: A personality characteristic that determines a subject's ability to be hypnotized and to attain a given depth of hypnosis.

IDEOMOTOR ACTION: The involuntary capacity of muscles to respond instantaneously to thoughts, feelings and ideas.

IDEOSENSORY ACTION: The involuntary capacity of the brain to evoke sensory images; these may be kinesthetic, auditory, visual, olfactory, gustatory or tactile.

ILLUSION: A common misperception of some sensory stimulus. All sensory modalities are subject to illusions.

IMAGERY: The ability to perceive or mentally recreate ideas, pictures or feelings.

INDUCTION: The production of hypnosis by the use of specific procedures.

INDIRECT HYPNOSIS: The production of hypnosis without the subject's awareness.

MATCHING: Developed by the late Milton Erickson, and used by John Grinder and Richard Bandler in their system of neurolinguistic programming (NLP). The technique consists of adopting parts of another person's behavior, such as particular gestures, facial expressions, forms of speech, tone of voice and so on. Done skillfully, it helps create rapport.

NEGATIVE HALLUCINATION: A hallucination in which the subject fails to perceive something that is present.

OPERATOR: Synonymous with hypnotist or hypnotherapist.

PERMISSIVE: This approach to hypnotic induction is the opposite of authoritarian. A permissive suggestion is made in such a manner as to give the subject the option of responding. The subject, not the hypnotist, is made the perceived source of the response. Permissive suggestions never have an intonation of authority or command.

POSITIVE HALLUCINATION: A perception of a stimulus that does not exist in objective reality.

POSTHYPNOTIC RESPONSE: Acts carried out after the termination of hypnosis in response to specific suggestions are called posthypnotic. A suggestion given during hypnosis serves as the stimulus and the act becomes the response.

POSTHYPNOTIC SUGGESTION: A suggestion given during hypnosis that occurs in the subsequent waking state.

REVIVIFICATION: A reliving of a prior period of life. In revivification, the hypnotized person returns to a physiological state believed to have existed at the time to which the subject has returned. All memories following the age to which the subject has been regressed are removed.

SELF-HYPNOSIS: Hypnosis induced in oneself the ability to influence positive self-improvement through the inner processes of focused awareness.

SOMNAMBULISM: In everyday usage the term somnambulism is used for sleepwalking; however, in the lexicon of hypnotism somnambulism is used to designate the deepest stage of hypnosis.

SUBCONSCIOUS MIND: The psychic processes of which an individual is not conscious. They are often associated with the part of the mind involving imagination, memory, and creativity. The subconscious mind is particularly accessible through hypnotic suggestion.

SUBJECT: This term denotes an individual submitting to an induction of hypnosis. If hypnosis is, being used for hypnotherapy the term client should be used.

SUBJECTIVE TIME: Time as perceived by a subject (as opposed to real time).

SUGGESTIBILITY: The capacity to respond to suggestion. The propensity of a subject to accept and act on suggestions.

SUGGESTION: Hypnotic communication.

TIME DISTORTION: The ability of hypnotic suggestion to make subjective time seem to pass more rapidly or more slowly than real time.

TRANCE: A term widely used by Milton Erickson and his followers. The term trance is often used synonymously for hypnosis.

TRANCE LOGIC: The suspension of critical judgment on the part of a hypnotized subject and his or her ability to tolerate the coexistence of logically incompatible phenomena.

UNCONSCIOUS MIND: A term used in psychiatry to denote a postulated region of the psyche, the repository of repressed urges and wishes. The term subconscious is often used as a synonym for the term unconscious.

Index

To my dear readers who are seriously considering implementing hypnosis in their life but are still undecided. I would say: heed the words of this noble man and make the best of your life, one day at a time.

Our deepest fear is not that we are inadequate.
Our deepest fear is that we are powerful beyond
measure. It is our light, not our darkness, that
most frightens us. We ask ourselves, Who am I to
be brilliant, gorgeous, talented, fabulous?
Actually, who are you *not* to be?
You are a child of God.
Your playing small doesn't serve the world.
There's nothing enlightened about shrinking so
that other people won't feel insecure around you.
We are all meant to shine, as children do.
We were born to make manifest the
glory of God that is within us.
It's not just in some of us; it's in everyone.
And as we let our own light shine, we
unconsciously give other people permission to do
the same. As we're liberated from our own fear,
our presence automatically liberates others.

Nelson Mandela
1994 Inaugural Speech (excerpt)

Appendix 9:

Become a Certified Hypnotherapist!

Step One:

This book is the core curriculum of the *Hypnotherapy Certification Course*, conducted by Mr. Segal at Hunter College, Adult Education program in New York. This is your gateway to the world of hypnotherapy.

Upon completion of this self-study book you will be on your way toward a new career in hypnotherapy. Upon satisfactorily demonstrating your understanding of the material presented, you will be entitled to a certificate of completion in the theoretical studies of hypnotherapy principals and techniques. To download the test, logon to our website:

www.BreakthroughInstitute.com/Certification/Test-Hypnotize This

You may request that a test be sent to you via email or post office.
A small charge of $15 covers shipping and handling for your personalized certificate suitable for framing.

Step Two:

Get Certified as a Hypnotherapist.
First compete step one. Information on how to become a Certified Hypnotherapist will be mailed to you with your certificate.

The Faculty and Board of examiners of the

BreakThrough Institute Inc. New York City, NY

Awards Herewith This

Certificate of Accomplishment

To

Elizabeth Slatwinski

Upon having satisfactorily completed the required primary course of study and examination in

Hypnotherapy Theories & Techniques

and is hereby admitted the rights and privileges
belonging to that training and achievement
given under the Training Board seal.

In witness whereof *the signature of*
the adinistrator is affixed onto on this
22nd Day of January, 2004

Zalman Segal, President

Order Form

To order by mail send check, Money order or Cashiers check payable to:
BreakThrough Institute
20 Avenue A #4-i
New York NY 10009

Important note: Always check the address for changes at www.hypnotizethis.com or www.breakthroughinstitute.com

Order by phone: (212) 529-1028 (check web site for changes)

Order by email: order@hypnotizethis.com

Order on line: www.hypnotizethis.com

Fill in the blanks:
Please send (Quantity) ______ Books (Contact us for large quantity discount).
Circle your choice of the following formats:
Book- $111.00; CD-PDF format- $89.95; Downloadable- E-book- $74.95
Certificate of completion: $15.00

Your name: ____

Your address: Street ______________________ City: ____________

State: _____ Zip code: _________ Telephone #: ______________

Email Address: ____

New York State Sales Tax: add 8.75% for products shipped in NYS.
Shipping domestic: Book-$4.50; CD-$3.85; Download E-book - no charge.
Shipping International: Book-$9.00; CD-$6.

Note: Prices subject to change. Please check web site for changes in price.

Payment by credit card:
Name on card: ____

Card number: ________________________ Expiration Date: _________

Last three digits of security code on signature panel: _______________

Signature ________________

Guarantee: If not satisfied you may return the merchandise, in good condition, for full refund